Organizational Communication

THIRD EDITION

Alan Jay Zaremba

NORTHEASTERN UNIVERSITY

New York   Oxford
OXFORD UNIVERSITY PRESS
2010

Oxford University Press, Inc., publishes works that further Oxford University's
objective of excellence in research, scholarship, and education.

Oxford New York
Auckland   Cape Town   Dar es Salaam   Hong Kong   Karachi
Kuala Lumpur   Madrid   Melbourne   Mexico City   Nairobi
New Delhi   Shanghai   Taipei   Toronto

With offices in
Argentina   Austria   Brazil   Chile   Czech Republic   France   Greece
Guatemala   Hungary   Italy   Japan   Poland   Portugal   Singapore
South Korea   Switzerland   Thailand   Turkey   Ukraine   Vietnam

Copyright 2010 by Oxford University Press, Inc., 2005, 2002 by Southwestern College Publishing

Published by Oxford University Press, Inc.
198 Madison Avenue, New York, New York 10016
http://www.oup.com

Library of Congress Cataloging-in-Publication Data

Zaremba, Alan Jay.
  Organizational communication : foundations for business and
collaboration / Alan Jay Zaremba. — 3rd ed.
      p.   cm.
  Includes bibliographical references and index.
  ISBN 978-0-19-537904-4 (alk. paper)
  1. Communication in organizations.   2. Communication in management.   I. Title.
  HD30.3.Z3695 2010
  651.7—dc22

                                                                    2009016310

Printing number: 9 8 7 6 5 4 3 2 1

Printed in the United States of America
on acid-free paper

For Jack

BRIEF CONTENTS

CONTENTS

PREFACE

This text makes the case that communication is foundational to all organizational activity. In the same way that a foundation for a building supports and sustains the structure of an edifice, communication supports and sustains organizations.

Approach

The book describes the theory and principles of organizational communication. Care has been taken in each section to ensure that these foundations are presented thoroughly and accessibly. After completing the book, students will clearly understand why and how skills, culture, systems, ethics, new technology, and power are all relevant to organizational communication and organizational communicators. They will see, too, how communication practices not only serve as a foundation for the organization, but actually *create* and *define* the entity that we think of as the organization.

I believe that students best learn the nature of organizational communication when they see its importance in practice—in the organizations they know, in their future careers, and in a changing world of global communications and social networking. The theory of organizational communication can be brought most alive when presented in an engaging narrative, through case studies, and through the voices and perspectives of actual practitioners. I have been fortunate to have received prepublication reviews of the text that consistently point to its readability. These reviewers have described the book as both substantive and engaging. I hope you will similarly find the text to be valuable and applicable.

Organization of the Text

Even more than in past editions, this text examines communication in organizations from a full range of theoretical vantage points. It presents and describes each of these theories while explaining how applying them can have practical effects on the qualitative growth of organizations.

In Part 1 we put down the floorboards of the study:

- The pervasiveness and importance of organizational communication
- Principles and theories
- The ideas of systems, culture, and power
- Ethical issues in organizational communication

For this edition, coverage of the theoretical foundations has thus expanded to two chapters (Chapters 2 and 3). The discussion of ethical issues, too, has been brought up to date, with more attention to feminist perspectives.

In Part 2 we explain how organizational communication meets the needs of a systemic environment by examining:

- Information management
- Communication networks
- Communication culture
- Organizational teams

For this edition, Chapters 6 and 7 thus place more emphasis on gender, diversity, and power in defining communication networks and communication culture. At the same time, I have streamlined the coverage of written and oral communication, as best suited to introductory courses.

In Part 3 we examine four topics that have become particularly relevant at the beginning of the twenty-first century:

- Organizational communication in the global, intercultural village
- Crisis communication
- Communication auditing
- Emerging careers for organizational communication practitioners

Each of these again has its own full chapter. This part makes clear the great importance this text gives to the practice and relevance of organizational communication. For this edition, each has also been substantially updated, most particularly for the importance of intercultural communication.

New Technology and Social Networking

Each of the three parts contains other important changes as well for this edition to reflect the pervasive effects of new technologies. At the start of the twenty-first century few people would have known what a tweet was, been familiar with Facebook, or known what was meant by LinkedIn. Now, ten years later, it is unlikely that many readers will be unfamiliar with any of these terms.

In 2008, U.S. voters elected a president who employed social networks to communicate with the electorate. Web sites like YouTube allowed citizens to "campaign" for their candidates by singing their praises for either McCain/Palin or Obama/Biden. The new media democratized the election by engaging and involving in the conversation thousands who had previously been mere receivers on the sidelines.

New technology, of course, is not the only factor that affects organizational communication. Many other considerations are just as significant, and we discuss each of these in the text. Yet the changing nature of communications is undeniable, and it cannot fairly be confined to a single chapter or a boxed feature. For just a few among many examples, Chapter 5 on information management now takes into account Facebook and wikis, Chapter 6 now includes more on informal as well as formal communication networks, Chapter 7 asks how e-mails contribute to communication culture, Chapter 9 considers the implications of the loss of face-to-face communications in the global village, and Chapter 10 examines new means of crisis communication.

Everyday Examples

As part of this text's concern to connect theory to practice, I have introduced familiar examples throughout. Many come directly from the headlines. For example, the *Challenger* disaster illustrates working in teams and organizational culture at NASA, the investigation of Enron's corporate practices illustrates ethical issues in organizational communication, and JetBlue's response to long delays illustrates crisis communication. Many are given a human face. Students will see, for example, the real story behind the whistleblower played by Matt Damon in *The Informant*. As we shall see, many other cases and individuals are the basis of running pedagogical features.

However, many examples focus directly on a student's experience. All of us belong to several organizations. In addition to the college or university, students may belong to a social club, sports team, church or synagogue, community association, or political interest group. While studying, many also have a job, and most students are likely to have worked for some organizations prior to enrolling at school. Even families and extended families can be viewed from an organizational perspective. In each of these organizations, communication is an omnipresent phenomenon. In each of these organizations, communication has been a key to success and has shaped the formation and reformation of the organization.

Pedagogical Features

Four regular boxed features in the text similarly underscore the practice of organizational communication. They also add student interest and enhance readability through the voices of individuals. Many are new to this edition, and they include both women and men in many different roles within an organization—from CEOs to a lawyer for MasterCard and an NBA events planner.

- **Case Studies** open each chapter's main narrative.
- **Practitioner Perspectives** end each chapter. These present segments of interviews conducted with nonacademic employees and employers who offer their insights into the importance of communication for organizational success.
- **Ethical Probes** ask students to consider moral problems and respond to questions pertaining to organizational communication issues.
- **Apply the Principles** boxes challenge students to apply principles to a potentially pressing situation.

Each of these features begins or ends with questions to make students more active learners and to help them draw connections between the examples and theoretical foundations.

As additional reinforcement of the concepts, students will also find a chapter-opening **Chapter in a Nutshell**, a **Toolbox** summary at the conclusion to each chapter, and **Review Exercises**. The exercises vary in difficulty and include discussion questions, self-inventories, and group/role-play.

Supplements

An accompanying Instructor's Manual contains test questions as well as additional Case Studies and Practitioner Perspectives from past editions. An instructor's Web site at www.oup.com/us/zaremba offers the full Instructor's Manual and updated PowerPoint lecture slides by Doran Layne O'Donnell of Louisiana State University at Alexandria.

Acknowledgments

A number of people were very helpful with this project, and I want to gratefully and sincerely acknowledge them. I am indebted to the now close to fifty persons who gave up their time to be interviewed for the Practitioner Perspectives. I would also like to thank reviewers whose comments helped make this third edition stronger than ever: Kathryn Archard, Bridgewater State College; Melissa DeLucia, Albertus Magnus College; Paige Edley, Loyola Marymount University; William Kinsella, North Carolina State University; Michael Owen, Lewis-Clark State College; Michael Pagano, Fairfield University; Dora Saavedra, University of Texas–Pan American; Michael Stefanone, University of Buffalo, State University of New York; Robin Takacs, Virginia Wesleyan College; Dan Warren, Bellevue University; Edward Woods, Marshall University; and Jeff Youngquist, Oakland University.

This text continues to reflect the insights of reviewers of two past editions, including: Dawna I. Ballard, University of Texas at Austin; Cathy Boggs, University of California, Santa Barbara; Audra L. Colvert, Towson University; Barbara D. Davis, University of Memphis; Eric Embree, Brigham Young University, Idaho; Sandy H. Hanson, University of North Carolina at Charlotte; Zachary Hart,

Northern Kentucky University; Stephen J. Madden, Clemson University; Arah D. Martin, City University; Michael E. Mayer, Arizona State University; Trudy Milburn, Baruch College, City University of New York; Doran Layne O'Donnell, Louisiana State University at Alexandria; Michael K. Rabby, University of Central Florida; Karen D. Shearer, Queens University of Charlotte; and John D. Watt, University of Central Arkansas.

John Haber served as developmental editor for this book and was simply terrific in this capacity. Always prompt in responding to my inquiries, remarkably sensitive in his communications, and regularly suggesting ideas that made the book better, I am very fortunate that John was assigned to this project. Peter Labella first spoke with me about this third edition and was consistently supportive, considerate, and wise in his recommendations as we proceeded toward contracting for the book. It was John Challice at Oxford University Press who happened into my office one day and suggested I consider Oxford for the third edition. John introduced me to Peter, and I am very grateful for his recommendation and encouragement. Thank you also to Courtney Roy, who was prompt, responsible, and helpful in all matters from ensuring that contractual information got to me as well as reminding me diplomatically that certain sections still needed to be submitted.

Donna Glick, my dear companion for twenty-two years, endured the irascibility of an author with a deadline and was willing to read sections over and over again. Her insights and constructive criticism assisted in making this book as strong as it has turned out to be. I have had the good fortune to be blessed with loving and supportive parents, Meyer and Helen Zaremba, and with such a foundation it becomes easier to do anything. My father has penned his second book, *Thoughts of an Ordinary Man*. It is an extraordinary accomplishment, and its only weakness is that it is entitled inappropriately: no ordinary person could have compiled this work or provided such a solid foundation for his sons' accomplishments.

There are likely many more whom I have forgotten with these acknowledgments, and I apologize in advance for the omissions. To all of you who have helped me, I wish to communicate my thanks.

Alan Jay Zaremba
Northeastern University

ABOUT THE AUTHOR

Dr. Zaremba is a recipient of the *State University of New York Chancellor's Award for Excellence in Teaching* and has also received Northeastern University's *Excellence in Teaching Award* on two occasions, earning the honor in 1984 and then again in 2003. In June 2001, Zaremba was one of two Albany alums to received his alma mater's *Excellence in Education* award.

Alan Zaremba earned his doctorate from the University of Buffalo, and B.A. and M.S. from the University at Albany. He has been on the faculty at Northeastern University in Boston since 1981. In addition to his work in the Department of Communication Studies, Dr. Zaremba is the academic director for programs in corporate and organizational communication for Northeastern's College of Professional Studies. From 1976-1981 he taught at the State University of New York College at Fredonia.

Dr. Zaremba is the author of four other books:

Mass Communication and International Politics: A Case Study of Press Reactions in the 1973 Arab-Israeli War. (1988)

Management in a New Key: Communication in the Modern Organization. (1e 1989, 2e 1993)

Speaking Professionally: A Concise Guide. (2006)

The Madness of March: Bonding and Betting with the Boys in Las Vegas. (2009)

PART **1**

FOUNDATIONS

Chapter 1

Organizational Communication: An Introduction

Chapter in a Nutshell

Organizational communication is a relatively young field. The first college textbook in this area was published less than forty years ago. Many universities did not have a single foundational course in organizational communication until the 1980s or early 1990s. The growth in the last decade has been especially rapid. Now, scholars and business practitioners alike identify communication as (a) central to organizational activity, (b) multidimensional, and (c) problematic.

Most of us know, firsthand, that organizational communication can be difficult. We may attend poorly run meetings, hear long and rambling "briefings," observe the company grapevine overwhelm formally communicated messages, or interact with colleagues who seem to use communication as a tool to intimidate. Organizational communication deals with all of these areas and many others. This chapter introduces organizational communication to the reader.

When you have completed this chapter, you should be able to:

- Define organizational communication.
- Discuss why communication is central, pervasive, and multifaceted in organizations.
- Identify and debunk myths about organizational communication.
- Explain how communication can be studied as both a transmission and constitutive process.
- Explain why skills, networks, culture, and power are important to the study of organizational communication.
- Describe the range of topics and scope of this book.

CASE 1.1
Communicating with Chuck

Sam Ramirez supervises a group of fourteen engineers. The company he works for is a very large communications provider. Each engineer is considered the company's subject matter expert (SME) for her or his particular assigned technology. These engineers procure test equipment, provide technical support, and purchase spare circuit packs in support of front-line employees. The minimal experience required for an engineer's position is five years in operations and two years in engineering. Engineers typically experience a learning curve of one to two years and it is very difficult to recruit good people for the job.

Due to the results of several early retirement incentive programs, there are few individuals in the company qualified to work in the engineering group Sam supervises. Members of Sam's team are frequently offered jobs by other departments within the organization and also are lured away by competitors. The last time one of Sam's engineers chose to move to another job, Sam lost the vacancy as a result of downsizing.

Chuck, one of Sam's engineers, has been rated "outstanding" for the past five years. Chuck's technical expertise and knowledge are extraordinary. In recognition of Chuck's value to the company, he has received a large bonus in each of the past five years. Unfortunately Chuck's interpersonal and communication skills are minimal at best. Chuck is often perceived as condescending, dominating, demeaning, unrelenting, and self-serving. Nearly all of Chuck's peers avoid interacting with him and even avoid attending meetings in which he's involved. Chuck is not only verbally demeaning but also will make inappropriate facial expressions when dealing with others. Often, he'll pretend to be trying to suppress laughter when someone asks a serious question that Chuck considers foolish.

An internal customer phoned Sam one day to "express his condolences" for Sam having to be Chuck's manager. There is an even split among customers who call to praise Chuck's excellent work and those who refer to him as a prima donna and refuse to ask him for assistance.

Last year, Sam Ramirez's annual performance feedback session with Chuck took three hours, even though Chuck was to receive a significant bonus. Chuck vehemently disagreed with the "Needs Development" rating Sam gave him in the "Working with Others" skill category. Chuck even offered to trade his bonus in for an improved rating in this deficient skill category! Chuck argued that Ramirez had only heard from the people who did not like or appreciate Chuck. Chuck asked Sam to cite specific examples of poorly executed interpersonal exchanges. Sam decided to accommodate Chuck and began to list event after event. Ramirez stopped suddenly when he realized that Chuck was recording the names of the individuals involved in each example that Sam cited. To make the case that he had been unfairly criticized by the others, Chuck began to attack the character of each person involved in the cited examples.

> "Oh, you can't be serious believing Olga.
>   She is an idiot."
> "Pat is a loser, and you know that as well
>   as I do, Sam."
> "Harry? Please. Give me a break."
> Chuck's basic response was, "I'm okay. It's
>   the rest of the world that's crazy."

In order to improve his skill rating, Chuck worked diligently at improving his interpersonal interactions during the first half of last year. In response to the significant progress made, Sam rated Chuck's behavior as "Acceptable" during his midyear review. Unfortunately, immediately after that rating, Chuck stopped working on improving his behavior with others and quickly slid back into his old habits. On the basis of this regression, Sam wants to again rate Chuck as "Needs Development" during the current review period. Sam dreads the session and is considering giving Chuck an "Acceptable" rating just to avoid the tension.

- Are people like Chuck common?
- How should Sam Ramirez deal with Chuck during the current annual review?
- How might Chuck's communication patterns affect the culture of this organization?
- How might Sam's response affect the culture and perceptions of power relationships in this organization?
- Will someone like Chuck be able to change communication behaviors for extended periods of time?

Communication and Organizational Success

This book is based on the premise that communication is an integral and not peripheral dimension of organizational activity. The goal is to explain why communication is important for organizations and how individuals as well as an organization as a whole can become more efficient in terms of communication.

Organizational communication is a multifaceted area of study and involves issues that relate to skill sets, communication networks, culture, information management, and the potential abuse of authority. Daniel Webster said, "If all my possessions and powers were to be taken from me with one exception I would choose to keep the power of speech, for by it I could soon recover all the rest."[1] While Webster was referring to a particular type of communication, one could consider his comment more broadly. An understanding of the multifaceted principles of organizational communication can be genuinely empowering.

Each chapter in this book addresses an aspect of organizational communication and contains the research of scholars who have been writing and teaching in this area. As we will see, researchers have long argued that communication is vital for organizational success. In addition to the perspectives of scholars, each chapter also includes excerpts from conversations held with various organizational practitioners. Interviews were conducted with a former governor of Massachusetts, a corporate lawyer, a National Basketball Association executive, a prison warden, the CEO of an employee communication consulting firm, a corporate realtor, and several other individuals. The purpose of the practitioner interviews was to gather information that would complement the academic material.

The expectation was that the practitioner interviewees would comment that communication was an important part of their organizational activity. However, it was somewhat surprising to hear these individuals talk about communication so passionately and unconditionally as "critical," "essential," "crucial," and in one case, "the whole ball game." What each individual had to say varied of course. However, the theme was always the same. Every person suggested that weak organizational communication can undermine an operation—regardless of the inherent value of a particular product, the technical skills of individual employees, or even the work ethic of the women and men who form the organization. The message from both academics and practitioners is consistent: communication is vital to organizational success.

Chester Barnard was a practitioner who is now known as an early management theorist. In 1927 Barnard became the president of the New Jersey Bell Telephone Company when he was only forty-one. Subsequently he served as the president of the USO and later the Rockefeller Foundation. His often cited book, *The Functions of the Executive,* has been called a classic. In it, Barnard makes the following comment about the importance of communication: "[The] system of communication, or its maintenance, is a primary or essential continuing problem of a formal organization. Every other practical question of effectiveness of efficiency—that is, of the factors of survival—depends on it."[2]

Communication is vital because, as Barnard notes, the "factors of organizational survival depend on it." In organizations communication is a *central, pervasive,* and *multidimensional* phenomenon.

Sports executive, basketball coach, and management author Arnold Auerbach commented, "When it came to communications, my rule of thumb was simple. It's not what you tell them, it's what they hear."

Communication Is Central

Communication is necessary for nearly all forms of organizational activity and therefore necessary for organizational success. It shapes, limits, and defines perceptions of individuals and organizations alike.

Communication is not a frill that provides a "value-added" dimension to the organization or the individuals who comprise it. It is a central factor and as vital to an organization as your

> "Organizational communication is the vital link in the chain of events that is the process of managing a business. It is the single factor that makes an organization viable, successful, effective, enduring."
>
> — **ROY FOLTZ** in *Communication in Contemporary Organizations*[3]

heart is to your health. You might be able to function with a weak heart, but the weakness will put stress on parts of your otherwise sound body. Eventually there will be a malfunction, dysfunction, or a breakdown.

W. Charles Redding is often called the "father of organizational communication." Redding was a Purdue University professor whose 1972 book *Communication Within the Organization* is considered to be the first textbook in the field.[4] A prolific author, Redding is referred to as an academic "pioneer" and as one whose efforts principally "launch[ed] the field of organizational communication."[5] One of the last things he wrote before his death in 1998 was the preface to a book on organizational communication consulting. In it he made some comments about the centrality of organizational communication that are unequivocal.

> In every instance of organizational malaise that comes to mind, at some time and in some way, human communication behavior has been significantly involved. Indeed there are scholars who have persuasively made the case that a communication failure is at least one of the basic sources underlying *every* organizational failure.[6]

Phillip Tompkins was one of Redding's Purdue students and Tompkins became a prolific author in his own right. In his book *Organizational Communication Imperatives* and its 2005

Physicist Richard Feynman concluded that ineffective communication at NASA helped lead to the *Challenger* disaster.

sequel, Tompkins describes his involvement as a communication consultant for the Marshall Space Flight Center (MSFC).[7] He traces the history of the MSFC from its early days under the leadership of Dr. Wernher von Braun, through the disaster of the Space Shuttle *Challenger* explosion, and, in the sequel, through to the tragedy of the *Columbia*. It is Tompkins's contention—and he makes a very strong case—that the source of the *Challenger and Columbia* disasters was inefficient organizational communication.[8]

Tompkins uses his experience and the case of the MSFC to argue that organizations indeed have communication "imperatives." The message is that if organizations do not meet their communication "imperatives" the result will be some type of disaster. The disaster may not be as grand or grave as what happened to the *Challenger and Columbia*, but the results will be destructive nonetheless.

The centrality of organizational communication goes beyond the consequences of poor communication. Communication actually can be seen as an element of *the very fabric* that is the organization. Pace and Faules write, "Communication does not just service the organization; it *is* the organization. . . . Communication, then, is central to organizational existence and does more than simply carry out organizational plans"[9] (emphasis in original).

Consultant Paul Strassmann made the following claim.

> My view is that the principal job of the CEO is to be the information and communication architect for the firm. In the information age all that matters is information and communication. Just remember this, organization means communication, communication means connectivity, connectivity means knowledge, that's the mantra.[10]

Mantra or otherwise communication is central.

Communication Is a Pervasive Activity

Communication is an activity that nearly all organizational members are engaged in almost continuously. The responsibilities of persons in all units—executives, managers, and employees—regardless of rank or even job description—require regular communication. Researchers have attempted to quantify the amount of time managers, in particular, spend communicating, and the figure cited suggests that nearly 70 to 80 percent of a manager's total behavior involves some form of communication.[11]

At first glance, the statistic appears to be inflated. Do managers in organizations really spend 70 percent of their time communicating? If you consider the nature of organizational activity the statistic will not be surprising. Mintzberg identifies ten managerial roles in his book, *The Nature of Managerial Work*. They are:

- Liaison
- Monitor
- Disseminator

- Spokesperson
- Negotiator
- Figurehead
- Leader
- Entrepreneur
- Disturbance handler
- Resource allocator[12]

Penley, Alexander, Jernigan, and Henwood argue that the first five of these listed roles are *explicitly* communication related. Even the second five require managers to be skillful communicators.[13]

Mintzberg's book related to managers, but all employees' behavior involves a high percentage of communication-related activities. How many of your organizational activities do not involve communication? Waiters need to interact with diners, bar staff, kitchen help, and managers. Office administrators need to communicate with suppliers, colleagues, superiors, and clients. Lawyers interact with judges, juries, and assistants who do legal research. The postal worker at the counter has to communicate with the mail carriers, mail handlers, those who deliver parcels, neighboring offices, and central administration.

Let's examine three reasons why communication in organizations is such a pervasive activity and so essential for organizational success.

Organizations Function by Operating Interdependently

In order for a company to make a product or offer a service, the various units within the organization must interact. Even organizations with highly specialized divisions of labor and levels of expertise are inherently interdependent. Therefore, the quality of communication between units, and between employees within departments, is likely to affect the corporate product. Product quality directly affects corporate profit or whatever else marks the income for a particular organization. Poor internal communication, therefore, can quickly damage the corporate "bottom line."

Can your university be as efficient as it might be if the registrar is unaware of the policies of each academic department? How would students know which courses have prerequisites? How would the registrar know what students are eligible for classes? How would your college know if you have completed the requirements for graduation? How successful can a publishing company be if, for example, the sales representatives do not communicate with the people who edit and write the books? Can a professional theater survive if the set designers do not interact with the director and actors, or if marketing personnel are unaware of changes to the production schedule?

Organizations Must Relay Information about Expectations and Policy

If managers do not communicate effectively, how could employees be clear about responsibilities or organizational policies? How could employees gauge how well or how poorly management believes the individual employees are doing?

Similarly, if organizational men and women cannot make intelligent decisions about what types of communication channels to utilize (for example, e-mail or face-to-face communication), then other employees may receive information that is not clear, or too late, or irrelevant to them.

Communication is not a "one-shot" linear act. Those who send messages have to assume (and should desire) that receivers will have questions, comments, and reactions to the messages that they have communicated. If those who send messages are unprepared to receive, react, and respond to feedback, then information will not flow as efficiently as it needs to.

Poor Internal Communication Can Result in Bruised Interpersonal Relationships That May Undermine the Efficiency of an Organization

We know intuitively, for example, that it is essential for engineers who have designed a building to communicate with construction personnel who are actually putting the building together. If key figures in each area are at odds because of what are perceived as condescending snubs from the past, then the messages sent between these persons and units may be abridged or poorly relayed. To avoid speaking with an estranged other, an engineer may send an e-mail when face-to-face communication is really what is necessary. A construction worker may retrieve the message too late to utilize the essential information.

Organizational Communication Is Multidimensional

". . . Communication actually consists of a great deal more than what individual managers say or information that managements publish. Corporations frequently overlook *this obvious point* when they attempt to improve their communication systems."[14] (emphasis added)

— **SAUL GELLERMAN** in the *Management of Human Relations*

Organizational communication is multifaceted and complex. The range of communication issues affecting organizations is extensive, and the cause of any one communication problem is often more complicated than it appears to be.

A problem with organizational communication is that there are varied interpretations of what the word "communication" means in organizational contexts. To some communication refers to speaking, listening, and writing skills. To others communication is perceived as something related to the technologies that are employed to facilitate communication. Still others think of printed matter—newsletters, magazines, and internal memoranda—as what is meant by internal communication. Organizational communication issues include all of these areas and many more. For example, communication problems in organizations might involve:

- The inappropriate use of electronic mail: an overabundance of blasted e-mails that are indiscriminately sent to receivers who have no use for the information and are inundated with useless letters that they must wade through.
- A hyperactive grapevine: an unusually active "informal" communication network that contradicts "formal" communications.
- Informational briefings/presentations that are neither informational nor brief and are perceived as time wasters by subordinates.
- Administrative ignorance of new social media and how employees use social media to obtain information.
- A credibility problem within the organization that makes employees wonder about the ethical foundation of the organization and the truth of the messages they do receive.
- Poor intercultural communication reflecting an ignorance of, or insensitivity to, diverse needs and cultural differences.
- A defensive communication culture that discourages employees from utilizing their inherent communication skills.

- Poor updating of Web sites resulting in outdated information that is accepted as current by users.
- A heavy and inappropriate reliance on committees and meetings.
- An ineffective or unskilled method of interpersonally communicating to employees regarding how well or how poorly they are doing.

Overlooking the obvious point that organizational communication is multidimensional can create communication problems. If one is under the assumption, for example, that "business presentation skill" is a phrase that's synonymous with "organizational communication effectiveness," then administrators and consultants may design speaking skill programs under the assumption that these skill interventions will improve communication effectiveness. These programs, at best, will deal with a component of organizational communication and, at worst, deal with a meaningless component. Creating a program that provides the illusion of dealing with the core and/or breadth of organizational communication, while leaving the overall problems intact, creates a double negative. The real communication problems are not likely to be addressed, and yet the organization may believe that they have been meaningfully addressed.

Breadth of Topics

The Association for Business Communication (ABC) is an academic organization that publishes the *Journal of Business Communication* and *Business Communication Quarterly*. Annually the organization meets to discuss various issues germane to the field. The diversity of topics discussed at the ABC meetings is shown in Table 1.1, which reflects the focus of papers presented at recent conventions.

Sometimes people assume that academics are not in touch with the "real world." Yet the topics in Table 1.1 are very much real-world issues. This is supported by looking at the varied subjects discussed at recent meetings of the the International Association of Business Communicators (IABC). The IABC, unlike the ABC, is an association comprised predominantly of communication practitioners. The members are not those who study communication in the academy, but those who work in industry as communication professionals. Topics at these IABC practitioner meetings similarly reflect the diversity and breadth of organizational communication issues.[15]

Multifaceted Problems

Over the last twenty-five years I have collected statements from persons who were asked to describe communication problems they have had in their organizations. You will see cases throughout the book based on these self-reports. A review of them will reveal the diverse nature of communication problems in organizations. As you read through these statements, consider your own organizational history. Have you ever experienced communication problems related to these issues?

1. The problem I have is simply a matter of credibility and trust. I don't believe that my employers are being honest when they send me information. At the meetings the reps speak beautifully and do great PowerPoints. E-mails and the pieces in the electronic newsletter are written impeccably. However, when I read that "we did this because of whatever," I tend to question the legitimacy of the claim.

2. I come to work in the morning and am flooded with electronic mail messages. Many of these have been broadcast and are irrelevant to me. It takes me quite a while to weed through them, and, on occasion, I have missed some relevant communications because I have inadvertently deleted them.

Table 1.1 Topics Addressed at Recent Association of Business Communication Meetings

---

- Assessing abrasive interpersonal communication styles
- Communicating sympathy to employees who have suffered personal losses
- Communicating with employees who are handicapped
- Creating feedback loops for employees to communicate with employers
- Crisis communication planning
- Cultural effects of communicating in international business
- Development of non–English-speaking cliques in predominately English-speaking organizations
- Effects of corporate climate and culture on communication
- Effects of gender on communication in groups and dyads
- Effects of the organizational grapevine
- Ethical issues in business communication
- Interviewing techniques
- Intranet development and effective organizational communication
- Making quality presentations
- Nonverbal communication in organizations
- Same site electronic meetings
- Subordinate to superior communication issues
- Use and abuse of new electronic technology
- Using communication to create a team atmosphere
- Using visual support for presentations
- Writing reports collaboratively after team problem solving

---

3. When I attend briefing sessions from people in technical support I find myself lost. They use terminology that I do not understand. People ask questions that are beyond me, and I am frustrated both because of the time wasted and because I need this information. Yet no one appears willing to take the time to digest it for me.

4. Teleconferencing seems like a good idea on the surface, but, ironically, it doesn't work all that well in times of globalization. We have teleconferences with our American offices, and they want to set up a time that is very inconvenient to those of us in Europe, Asia, Australia, and Africa. In general, one region or culture doesn't seem to be very considerate of the needs of other regions and cultures.

5. The problem here is that the only messages I get are negative. It would be nice if every once in a while I heard something good about what I'm doing. But what happens is I get a sour face or a down e-mail, letting me know that such and such is in crisis or flawed. It's dispiriting and erodes my confidence.

6. Our meetings do not start on time and they are characterized by rambling orations. At no time does anyone in these meetings, including the department head, attempt to end these irrelevant discussions by speaking out. A meeting that should last only 30–45 minutes lasts an hour and a half.

7. I often get information too late for me to do anything about it. Last week I received a predated request for a lengthy report that was due the next day.

8. I'm a midlevel manager and need feedback on reports I send up the line. I need this feedback to make sure that the work I'm submitting is on target and what "they wanted." Despite repeated direct requests I get no direct response. My colleagues tell me that unless there's a problem I won't hear about it. Nevertheless, I'm not really comforted by the grapevine and need to know how I am doing. I sometimes wonder if the lack of feedback is an intentional ploy to keep me groping around, never knowing my status.

Managerial Perspectives

A study of 140 persons who were managers or who aspired to be managers revealed managerial perceptions that organizational communication problems are diverse. All participants in the study were part-time MBA students who worked during the day full time or who had very recently been employed full time (within one year of the time of the study). Each of the subjects was asked to describe a communication-related problem they had at work. They were encouraged to select incidents that were particularly difficult and ones for which they would like to have some solution should a similar problem surface again. Subsequently, a content analysis of the descriptions was conducted.[16]

The results support the conception of organizational communication as multifaceted. Forty percent of all problems dealt in some way with the absence of communication channels that permitted communication. For example, one manager commented that she needed to get information from a specific source but had little to no access to that source. Without the contact and resulting exchange of information, she could not clearly or accurately inform her own subordinates so that they could intelligently complete their tasks. Not only did this manager have little access to the source, she claimed to have few avenues available to communicate the need to have such access to anyone who might have prevailed upon the source to be accessible.

Thirty-two percent of the problems referred to issues with the quality of messages received in terms of timeliness, pertinence, credibility, and the manner used to disseminate the messages. For example, one manager claimed to be dunned with broadcasted voice mail that was irrelevant. Sometimes, she confessed, she would abort a message before listening to it in its entirety in order to get through her voice mail messages. On one occasion this habit created a big problem for her since a portion of the purged message was in fact pertinent, yet she was unaware of the relevance or the content of the message because in her haste she had deleted it prematurely.

Fifteen percent of the messages dealt with communication "culture" issues that tended to discourage managers and employees from exercising their inherent communication skills. One respondent wrote that the tensions within his department were so high that persons were reluctant to share information, fearing that any information shared might somehow be used against the person who had communicated it. In a particular instance information that had not been communicated created a crisis because incorrect assumptions regarding eventual product cost had been based on incomplete information.

Thirteen percent dealt with communication skill issues: for example, how to run a meeting or communicate during meetings; how to communicate sensitive personal information; how and when to use communication technology: how to communicate with members representing different ethnicities and nationalities; how to persuade others; how to use vocal inflection appropriately; and how to listen effectively. For example, several respondents commented about counterproductive

Applying the Principles—Test Yourself

What Is Essential for Organizational Communication?

As we discussed earlier in the chapter, Phillip Tompkins has made the argument that organizations must meet their communication imperatives or suffer some type of organizational disaster. The "explosions" will not typically be as dramatic, visible, or even as disastrous as that which befell NASA and the *Challenger* in 1986, but will have similarly corrosive consequences for the organization. Does this make sense to you? Can poor communication in organizations really cause "explosions"?

Following you will see a series of statements. For each statement indicate how important the item is for successful organizational communication. Use the following labels. Indicate whether the item is:

- Imperative (without it, there is likely to be a disaster)
- Somewhat important
- Neither important nor unimportant
- Somewhat unimportant
- Not important at all

(It might be helpful to consider a particular organization where you have been or are employed as you go through this exercise.)

1. All organizational personnel (managers, executives, employees) must be able to express ideas orally.
2. All organizational personnel must be able to use "new technology" for electronic communication.
3. All organizational personnel must be able to express ideas in writing.
4. All organizational personnel must be active and efficient listeners.
5. All organizational personnel must be able and willing to read distributed material.

6. All organizational personnel must be able to lead a meeting with three to fifteen members.
7. Information distributed throughout the organization must be perceived as credible.
8. Information distributed throughout the organization must be timely.
9. Information distributed must be accurate.
10. Information distributed must be sent only to those to whom the information pertains.
11. The method for communicating information must be appropriate. For example, one must know when to use e-mail, face-to-face communication, the phone, meetings, etc.
12. All personnel must be aware of organizational policies.
13. All personnel must be aware of their individual tasks.
14. All personnel must be aware of how well or how poorly they are doing in their job.
15. All personnel must feel as if other staff members are concerned about their personal needs. Therefore, it is essential for colleagues to ask, tactfully, about personal issues that may or may not be peripheral to work.
16. Networks must be established linking related departments.
17. Channels must be established allowing superiors to formally and regularly relay information to subordinates.
18. Channels must be established allowing subordinate staffers to communicate problems to superiors.
19. Channels must be established allowing subordinates to communicate ideas to superiors.

20. Networks must be established allowing communication to external audiences (for example, media, prospective students).
21. The informal network (grapevine) needs to be harnessed.
22. All personnel must feel supported and get supportive messages when they deserve them.
23. All personnel must get constructively critical messages when they deserve them.
24. All personnel must feel as if they participate in decision making that affects their jobs.
25. Messages from and by all staff members should reflect a commitment to organizational excellence.
26. Information that can be shared should be shared.
27. A proactive crisis communication plan must be in place so that the organization will be able to expeditiously communicate in times of such crises to internal and external audiences.
28. All communications should be concerned with ethical issues. Specifically, information communicated must be honest.
29. Sensitivity to the needs and concerns of a multicultural population must be the rule when communicating.
30. The organization must self-assess communication quality periodically.

tendencies during meetings, including "hogging" speaking time, unclear articulation of messages, contentious and gratuitous personal attacks, and time-wasting orations that were only tangentially related to the meeting topics.[17]

Clearly, organizational communication deals with multifaceted issues. As Gellerman asserts, communication in organizations does indeed consist "of a great deal more than what individual managers say or information that managements publish."

Misconceptions about Organizational Communication

There are several common myths or misunderstandings about what is meant by organizational communication.

Myth #1: Organizational communication pertains only to businesses and those who study business.

While organizational communication is certainly applicable to business, organizational communication is not a study confined just to businesses. We are all organizational women and men no matter where we work. We belong to athletic clubs, churches and synagogues, civic associations, and assorted other organizations. The head of your sorority/fraternity/club is a manager of sorts who must communicate information to the members of the organization and solicit communications from them. Your minister is in a similar position and must deliver homilies, use communication skills to counsel membership, and persuade the congregants that she or he is doing a good job. Your soccer teammates need to communicate with you while you are playing. The captain needs to relay the sentiments of your team to the coach. The coach has to convince the league coordinators to come up with the funds for new nets or uniforms. If you stop and consider it, you are probably now involved as a member or quasi-member of three or four organizations that are not businesses in the traditional sense of the word. Some have argued that the family unit itself can be considered an organization.[18]

Therefore, the notion that only those people who are going into business need be concerned about organizational communication is an inaccurate conception.

Myth #2: It is easy to train someone to be an effective communicator in organizations.

It is not easy to train someone to be a good communicator. Even if we were to simply (and incorrectly) define organizational communication as a speaking skill, it would be foolish to assume that it is easy to train someone to be an effective speaker. However, if we define communication correctly as a multifaceted phenomenon, the assumption that someone can be crash-course trained to be competent is not just incorrect, it is absurd. It would be as shortsighted as assuming that someone could become an accountant by cramming in math for a day or two.

"... You can't run [managers] through a charm school and have natural communicators."[19]

Myth #3: Organizational communication occurs within the domain of human resources or corporate communication departments. It does not apply to the average employee or manager.

Human resource and corporate communication departments certainly have communication-related responsibilities. However, this does not mean that the average employee does **not** have communication-related responsibilities. The average employee needs to be able to:

- Listen effectively
- Communicate during meetings
- Use new communication technology efficiently
- Write well
- Persuade colleagues
- Communicate interpersonally during performance review interviews
- Communicate cross culturally
- Make ethical decisions regarding how and what to communicate
- Know when, what, and how to communicate

When these responsibilities surface, employees do not and cannot call human resource representatives and have them complete the chore. Organizational communication is a responsibility of every employee.

Myth #4: People know how to communicate. We can all speak. We can all hear. Most of us can use the Internet and the new social media. Certainly intelligent people can communicate well.

Most of us can communicate to some extent. This does not mean we can communicate well. To assume that all people because of their *capabilities* have *abilities* is to make an incorrect assumption. In his autobiography, Lee Iacocca, the former Chrysler CEO, made the following observation: "I've known a lot of engineers with terrific ideas who had trouble explaining them to other people. It's always a shame when a guy with great talent can't tell the board or committee what's in his head."[20] We all know bright people who are weak communicators either because they do not understand what it means to communicate or because they cannot express what they need to write or say.

We have heard the expression, "It doesn't take a rocket scientist to figure out. . . ." Tompkins carefully documents that many NASA rocket scientists at the Marshall Space Flight Center in the 1980s were ineffective communicators.[21] The brilliant physicist, Richard Feynman, who was a member of the Rogers Commission that investigated the causes of the *Challenger* disaster, was startled when he came to the conclusion that, apparently, some of the rocket scientists were *deliberately* making it difficult for communication to take place.[22] More about Feynman's theory of organizational communication appears in Chapter 6. However, it is clear that intelligence does not guarantee communication competence.

Myth #5: Sharing a sophisticated vocabulary makes a group, and members of that group, effective organizational communicators.

A person is not necessarily an effective communicator because she or he knows a great many words. Being able to use words correctly for various audiences is an asset. Being able to understand a great many words is also an asset. However, extensive vocabularies do not, in and of themselves, guarantee effective communication.

Lawyers, doctors, technicians, even communication professionals have their own lexicon—a common language that they use among themselves and can understand. Having this shared language is helpful for those who are speaking to others within a similar group. However, knowledge of sophisticated pieces of information or language does not eliminate communication responsibilities. Lawyers may be able to speak "legalese" to their colleagues, and may even be able impress clients with jargon, but knowledge of terms doesn't preclude the need to inform associates about trial times, or to inform clients about what they need to do to prepare for court, or to select the best method for communicating any piece of information.

In short, language, while important, is not the lone criterion for organizational communication success.

Defining Terms

"All books end in definition" is the way one author began a monograph.[23] By this he meant that at the end of a book the reader ought to have a clearer, more defined understanding of the topic. In the same way as all *books* end in such definition, all good introductory chapters should also end in definition.

We have been defining organizational communication throughout the chapter. At this point we know that organizational communication is central to organizational success, is pervasive, and is multidimensional. We know that organizational communication is not solely about businesses, nor is it the lone responsibility of persons working in human resources. We know that organizational communication is not simply about speaking skill, intelligence, or even sophisticated vocabularies.

There are many definitions of organizational communication. Some, however accurate, are cumbersome and difficult to understand, rendering them less than valuable to a person studying organizational communication for the first time. Perhaps it is easier at this point in the chapter to examine these definitions now that you are more familiar with some organizational communication principles. Offered here is a sample of definitions.

Organizational communication is:

- The study of sending and receiving messages that create and maintain a system of con-sciously coordinated activities or forces of two or more people.[24]
- The process through which organizations are created and in turn create and shape events.[25]
- The coordination by communication of a number of people who are interdependently related.[26]
- The process of creating and exchanging messages within an organization in order to help that organization cope with the uncertainties of a changing environment.[27]
- The process of creating, exchanging, interpreting (correctly or incorrectly), and storing messages within a system of human interrelationships.[28]

These definitions all have valuable attributes. Organizational communication is a field of study.[29] It is a process that involves creating, sending, receiving, and interpreting information. Effective orga-nizational communication does help organizations cope with uncertainty and does exist within a complex system of interrelationships. Let's digest these definitions and create one that will be useful for this course:

> Organizational communication is the study of why, how, and with what effects organizations send and receive information in a systemic environment.

"Systemic environment" may be a confusing phrase in the definition. It will be explained more thoroughly in the next chapters. However, for now consider the organization as a combination of persons and departments that have a common goal and are, therefore—directly or indirectly—interdependent. This interdependence creates a system. What happens to one part of the organiza-tion has a direct or indirect effect on other parts. Organizational women and men need to acknowl-edge the systemic nature of their environment and the complex cultural and political dynamics that affect it.

The word communication itself requires some clarification. As S. S. Stevens remarked nearly fifty years ago, "Although no phenomenon is more familiar to us than communication the fact of the matter is that this magical word means many things to many people."[30] Half a century later, the same comment is true. The word communication summons up notions of Internet connectivity to some and public presentations to others. Having a clear understanding of what we mean by the word "communication" is central to any definition of organizational communication.

We will define communication as *a transmission and constitutive process that occurs when people intentionally or unintentionally send and receive verbal and nonverbal messages*. We will describe com-munication further as a *nonlinear* phenomenon that is *irreversible*. Communication does not mean the same thing as "understanding," nor is the act of "sending a message" synonymous with communicating.

Let's consider some key components of this description as they pertain to organizational communication.

- Communication is both a transmission and a constitutive process.
- Communication is a nonlinear phenomenon.
- Communication can be intentional or unintentional.
- Communication can be verbal or nonverbal.
- Communication is not synonymous with sending a message.
- Communication is irreversible.
- Communication is different from understanding.

Communication Is Both a Transmission and a Constitutive Process

When most people think of communicating, they consider it as an act of transmission. That is, they think that communication involves getting a message from point A to point B. The editor of the *Journal of Employee Communication* once told me that to him communication meant getting what is in his head into someone else's head. This is a standard notion of communication in organizations and an important one to consider. When managers present job descriptions to employees, for example, the desired outcome is for the employee to understand the job—in other words, get the information from the manager's head to the employee's.

The transmission perspective likens communication to an act of filling a bucket with water and transporting it from one place to another. Person A has a message to send to person B, fills her or his bucket with the message, and attempts to transport it so that B can receive it intact. This model recognizes that the bucket can be jostled en route to the destination, and analysts examine the variables that can impede the successful receipt of a filled unadulterated bucket. The transmission perspective can (or at least should) recognize that the transmission is nonlinear and that what "jostles" the bucket could be the nature of the feedback, prior and ongoing relationships, biases, selective perceptions, and a host of other variables. Nevertheless, the transmission perspective considers communication as something you do in an organization in order to accomplish goals.

However, let's consider complementing this notion with a constitutive perspective. This is an extraordinarily important viewpoint to consider. It is important if for no other reason than that a focus solely on the transmission perspective places the very real constitutive function on the periphery of practitioners' and even some scholars' radar screens.

The constitutive perspective assumes that the act of interacting is a process that also shapes and defines the relationships between people and, by extension, the nature of the evolving organization. As Robert Craig has posited, communication can be seen as a "process that symbolically forms and re-forms our personal identities, our social relations. . . ."[31] It is this notion that Pace and Faules describe when they write: "When the organization is conceived as people interacting and giving meaning to that interaction communication becomes an organizational-making function rather than just an organization maintaining one."[32] In this way the process of communicating can be said to have a *constitutional* function. Consider the following examples.

If a club is composed of verbose contentious participants who meet regularly to discuss the nature of the club, then—employing a constitutive perspective—communication at that meeting is not solely the act of transporting water/information from one person to the others. Communication at that meeting will serve to define and shape the organization itself so that this club will be a different entity than one that had shy participants. By the club engaging in verbose contentious discussions, the organization takes shape as an entity where disagreements and debates are valued. This will affect the evolving culture of the organization and also have implications for the identities of its members. Members who debate effectively will likely obtain and maintain a higher status than those who are less eloquent. People who are persuasive may be elevated to positions of authority, and candidates for club membership may need to prove their ability to survive during robust discussions. All this will be a factor in the formation and reformations of the club/organization.

Consider the family as an organization. Let's assume each family member is adept at transporting water/information from one member to another. However, how members of this family communicate—these are examples, and should not imply that these examples comprehensively determine how members communicate frequency of communication, tolerance for disparaging comments, implicit rules about who should talk when to whom and how to talk to various family members—all of this will serve to constitute what becomes the family.

Thus, when we consider communication in organizations we have to think about it both in terms of the transmission of messages inside an organization as well as the ongoing process that constitutes and creates the organization. This conceptualization allows us to recognize that an organization is not simply a container within which people communicate, but rather a protean entity that is formed and reformed by the very act of communicating. More about this constitutive notion in Chapter 7 as it relates to organizational culture.

Communication Is a Nonlinear Phenomenon

Theorist Harold Lasswell developed one model used to examine communication. Lasswell argued that communication could be analyzed by looking at "Who Says What to Whom (In Which Channel) With What Effect."[33]

If you were listening to a CEO deliver a "state of the organization address," the "Who" would be the CEO, the "What" the information contained in the address, the "Whom" that large diverse audience who listened to the presentation, and the "Effect" the reaction the various members of the audience had to the talk.

A problem with this model is that it appears to be linear.

Lasswell may not have intended it to be interpreted this way, but the model as is implies that communication goes one way and ceases when it reaches the receiver. Communication, in fact, is not linear; it is not a one-way phenomenon. Some scholars use the word "process" instead of "act" to describe communication because "act" seems as if communication reflects an isolated occurrence. Any one act of communication is unlikely to be a discrete event. It is likely to be a function of immediate and past history and should be understood implicitly as a process—the process that occurs when we communicate. As we have just discussed, this process must be viewed as a phenomenon that shapes relationships as well as transports information.

Consider this simple example, which illustrates the nonlinear nature of communication. Assume you are in a meeting listening to a technical presentation. The presentation, let's say, is a poor one. The trainer's wording is complex, the vocal qualities of the message monotonous, and the subject, in and of itself, dry. You become bored and steal a glance at your watch to see how much longer the session has to run. However, as you look down at the timepiece, you see from your peripheral vision that the trainer notices your time check. You feel a bit embarrassed, but subsequently notice that the instructor reframes the presentation, picks the pace up a bit, and has attempted to demonstrate an application of the material with an illustration to make it less dry. The next time this trainer speaks to your group she is prepared with more visual support, and now the people who create visual support become more important to those who make technical presentations.

"We cannot withdraw our cards from the game. Were we as silent and as mute as stones, our very passivity would be an act."

— JEAN PAUL SARTRE

The communication, in this instance, has not been linear. Any one "act" of communication was part of a process. You thought the presentation was boring, you looked at your watch, the trainer noticed you look at your watch, and she then changed the message. Obviously the persons who are initially the "Who" and the "Whom" can exchange roles and react to one another. Inherently, then, the communication process is nonlinear.

Communication Can Be Intentional or Unintentional

A message does not have to be intentionally sent to be communicated. For example, some colleagues may frequently be late to meetings. They may not intend to be communicating anything by their tardiness. However, other members of the group may feel that lateness reflects a lack of professionalism, or preoccupation, or disrespect. The fact that the latecomers may not have intended to relay any of these messages does not discount the reality that these messages could have been communicated. A manager who says to her group, "I want to really thank Janet in particular for her hard work on the project" may have communicated that, in general, she thinks more of Janet than anyone else when this may not, in fact, be the case.

The humorist Tom Lehrer introduced one of his topical songs in the following way:

> One problem that recurs more and more frequently these days in books and plays and movies is the inability of people to communicate with the people they love—husbands and wives who can't communicate, children who can't communicate with their parents and so on. And the characters in these books and plays—and in real life I may add—spend hours bemoaning the fact that they can't communicate. I feel that if people can't communicate the very least they can do is shut up.[34]

The remark may be amusing, but managers, employees, and executives have no choice but to disregard this advice. As we have discussed previously, organizational men and women must communicate to function. More significantly, people could not "not communicate"—even if they wished to "not communicate."

Imagine walking along your campus thinking about the various things you need to do. You have to do "in-person-drop/add" registration, call your supervisor at the restaurant where you work, check your e-mail, and read the first three chapters in a philosophy text. As you walk along, your thoughts are focused on how you will plan out the hours intelligently enough so that you can accomplish all of the tasks and still have time to work out in the gym.

While you are so engaged, an acquaintance from your philosophy class walks by in the other direction. The acquaintance raises a hand, gesturing hello to you while murmuring an almost inaudible "Hi." You don't see nor hear this person because, as he walks past, you are "in your own space" contemplating today's schedule—version four—which will permit your workout and "drop/add" registration when the lines will not be too long. You can recall, all too vividly, the last drop/add period when you had been stalled on an hour-long line standing next to some malodorous bore. He had groused for the entire time with nearly toxic breath about a course he had taken the previous semester.

Since as you walk you are preoccupied with your schedule and this unpleasant recollection, you don't even notice the philosophy class acquaintance. You walk right past him without acknowledging his presence. The acquaintance walks by and thinks to himself that you're a snob. You didn't respond to his gesture or his murmured greeting. He doesn't realize that you didn't see him despite the fact that you had appeared to be looking right at him.

Later in the term there is a project in your philosophy class that requires work in teams. You find yourself in a group with this other student. You cannot understand why, initially at least, he regards you with some disdain. It may irk you when he treats you this way. It is possible that after a period this tension could dissipate. Yet it is not impossible that the two of you will remain at odds and you will not know why.

This example illustrates both of the dimensions of communication we have already discussed. Communication need not be intentional, and communication is not a linear phenomenon. It also indicates the importance of nonverbal factors in the communication process.

Communication Can Be Verbal or Nonverbal

Communication can involve verbal and/or nonverbal messages. A verbal message is one that uses words to convey meaning. The sentences in this book are primarily verbal messages.

The word "verbal" is sometimes confused with the words "oral" and "vocal." Any message—whether spoken or read that uses words to relay meaning—contains verbal messages. A Web site contains verbal messages, as does a briefing session. Web sites and briefing sessions also are likely to include nonverbal messages. A nonverbal message is one that does not use words but nevertheless conveys meaning to receivers. The font and color used for branding on a Web site and the gestures a speaker makes during a briefing are examples of nonverbal factors that can convey messages to receivers. If a Web site is well formatted and esthetically engaging, we are likely to get a different impression than we would if the look of the site is primitive or the print so tiny as to make it difficult to read. If a speaker uses complementary hand gestures while addressing a group, we are likely to perceive a different message than if the speaker were to stand stiffly in front of the group.

In organizations other nonverbal factors are important to consider as well. Proxemics, or space, can affect perceptions of power; if an employee is removed from a cubicle and given an office with a door, she may have been elevated or perceived to be elevated by colleagues. Midlevel managers may become miffed if their offices are tiny compared to a newcomer's large space. Chronemics or time can relay information that suggests who is or is not powerful in an organization. Who is entitled to be late and who is not? Who commands meeting deadlines and who seems to be able to submit things late without consequence? Dress can indicate who has authority and who does not. At one organization a pin that read "Senior Employee" was a coveted item, and wearing this pin meant one had attained a status that was accompanied by implicit relaxation of rules. In organizations and elsewhere, much of what receivers perceive is based on nonverbal information. One researcher argued that 93 percent of what receivers perceive is based on nonverbal messages.[35]

Students of organizational communication need to remember that nonverbal messages do not actually mean anything until a receiver decodes them. Even verbal messages do not mean anything until receivers decode them. However, with nonverbal messages there is considerable room for misinterpretation, as Manusov and Billingsley suggest: ". . . when we view another's [nonverbal] behavior we may be inclined to judge that it is a direct reflection of some aspect of the other's character, mood, feeling, or belief. We may feel that we really have access to what is really going on in inside the other's mind or heart. But we are also likely to be wrong."[36] Committee members who never speak may be perceived as slackers when they may simply be extraordinarily shy. Candidates for job openings may wear poorly pressed garments to interviews, and one might assume that they are less than concerned about the positions. In fact, the candidates may appear disheveled for entirely different reasons.

Sending a Message Is Not Synonymous with Communicating

The act of *sending* messages, in and of itself, does not mean that communication has taken place. This is a foundational but often misunderstood aspect of communication, especially in contemporary times of new technology. If a senior administrator sends employees electronic reports, but employees do not read these reports, we cannot say that the manager has communicated the message despite the fact that a cogent message may have been sent. A posting on a Web site does not guarantee communication until the time when the appropriate audience visits the site and reads the message.

Hopper writes clearly, "Communication can be said to have taken place only when messages are received and interpreted."[37] Timm and DeTienne comment that communication occurs whenever someone attaches meaning to a message, and therefore that communication success is determined by the message receiver.[38] Hattersley and McJannet write, "Only what has actually been understood will have been communicated." A host of impediments, collectively referred to as *communication noise*, can thwart or distort messages that are sent such that these messages are received differently than intended if they are received at all.

In short, *message received is message communicated.* Or as Red Auerbach, the late general manager and president of the Boston Celtics, wrote, "When it came to communications, my rule of thumb was simple. It's not what you tell them, [it's] what they hear."[39]

Simply sending a message does not guarantee that an intended message has been communicated. The receiver may not actually receive it, understand it, or decode it in the way the sender expects.

Communication Is Irreversible

Once a message has been received it cannot be eradicated. Someone might say the words, "I take that back," but this does not erase the prior message. It can add on to the message, and the person hearing "I take that back" or "I didn't mean that" may consider the request. However, one cannot completely purge the message. Our computers may have delete buttons, but we humans cannot delete messages once someone else has attributed meaning to them. We can all recall messages we heard when we were children that our parents, siblings, and best pals wish they had never said and attempted to retract. We probably recall communications in organizations that have been bruising despite a colleague's effort to apologize. Communication is irreversible.

Let's assume that you have, repeatedly, informed all colleagues that a particular Tuesday is an important day at work. Let's assume further that an employee comes to you on Monday and requests to take that Tuesday off. Finally, assume that this is not the first time the employee has made a similar request for a day off when it promised to be a difficult one.

If you were to tell the employee that he could not have the day off, he might react by saying, "Okay, there's no harm in trying. No problem." If he were to do so, and even if he were to say, "I am really sorry to have asked; I know you told us this was a tough Tuesday coming up," the request will stay with you and may affect and re-form the relationship you have with the employee. The fact that he does not take the day off or that he expresses regret for making the request will not eradicate the initial message you received.

Communication Is Different from Understanding

Some people think of communication as being synonymous with understanding. Occasionally, exasperated colleagues will stop a discussion and say, "We're just not communicating." This seems

Applying the Principles—Test Yourself

What Meaning Do You Derive When?
- You meet your co-workers for the first time and they talk about how they attempt to deceive management?
- Co-workers annually remember your birthday and send congratulatory e-cards?
- Your boss shouts orders to the staff?
- An acquaintance takes out a cigarette shortly after you've met?

- A prospective employee comes to an interview in workout clothes?
- A customer where you work as a sales-person touches your hand during a sale?
- You meet someone at a dinner who is wearing strong perfume or cologne?
- A classmate is excessively fidgety during a group meeting?
- A friend takes you to her workplace and shows you her large office?

to imply, "We do not understand one another" or "We cannot seem to explain to each other what we'd like to explain." Even when two people who are conversing have trouble understanding each other, they are still communicating. They may not be communicating effectively, but they are communicating.

As significantly, an inability to come to agreement does not necessarily mean that two people are not communicating effectively. Two adversaries may be trying to reach agreement on a new contract. They may be unable to do so, but can very clearly understand the other's position. It is not a communication problem. They just disagree.

Defining Factors: Skill, Networks, Culture, and Power

Threaded throughout the book you will see references to communication skill, networks, culture, and power. Organizational communication and organizational communicators are affected by these interrelated factors.

Communication Skill

At the very least, organizational communicators need to have basic skill set competencies. We must be able to read, write, speak, listen, and use basic communication technology. A day is unlikely to go by when we do not have to read mail, speak coherently, listen effectively, and compose intelligible written messages. Unfortunately, communication skill competence is not universal. Assuming that it should be will not guarantee that it will be. Therefore, effective organizational communication requires understanding that basic skills are necessary and cannot be taken for granted.

"The [people] who think and do not know how to express what [they] think are at the same level of [those] who cannot think."

— PERICLES

Being a skilled communicator, however, involves more than just having skill competencies. Communication skill reflects the ability and willingness to apply capabilities intelligently. Knowing *how to* speak does not preclude barking gratuitously at employees when they deserve and expect a courteous thank you or even a civil good morning. Knowing *how to* write a clear e-mail does not preclude the indiscriminate mass mailing of that message. The ability to pass a test demonstrating listening competence does not preclude fussing with papers, taking phone calls, or looking continuously at a watch when employees come in for annual review sessions. The application of knowledge pertaining to communication and organizations reflects a very important communication skill.

In April of 2004, a CEO of an international firm based in Missouri sent an emissary to his head of human resources. The CEO desired to send what he thought was a simple message. He told the emissary to tell the HR chief to develop and distribute a policy for the company "exercise path."

One perk of this organization and a surprisingly alluring recruiting tool was a beautifully landscaped course for walkers or joggers located on company grounds. The path had been developed for the enjoyment of the employees and—as stressed in several company publications—to facilitate employee wellness.

The employees loved the exercise path. However, the CEO sensed that there were people who were abusing the privilege and therefore sent the emissary to the HR chief with the message asking her to create a policy for the path's use. The reason the CEO used the intermediary was because he sensed that the chief of human resources would not like to receive this message. His fears were well grounded. She refused to develop the policy and told the emissary that if the CEO wanted to discuss the matter, he could bring it up at their regular Wednesday "one-on-one." When the one-on-one took place, the CEO mentioned the need to develop a policy for the exercise path. The HR chief said that she would not do it. When the CEO asked why, she replied that she would not do it because of what she would be communicating to the employees if she were to develop and distribute such a policy. The CEO seemed perplexed and said that all she would be doing would be communicating the new policy.

The HR director disagreed. In fact, she said that the policy itself would not be the primary message that would be communicated. She even suggested that few would even "hear" the information about the new rules. She claimed that several other messages would be heard. She was prepared with a list of these other anticipated messages and described each one to her supervisor.

  a. Employees would think that senior management—faced with many *important* problems—had nothing better to do than create policies about the exercise path.
  b. Employees would think that top administrators were too cowardly to address the few miscreants who had abused the policy and therefore were sending out this new policy to the masses.
  c. Employees would wonder if senior management was making a statement affirming who was, and who was not, in power. The new policy could be perceived as a reminder that the path was available because of the largesse of executives and that such perks could be removed at the whim of management.
  d. Employees might think that senior management's claims reflecting concern for employee wellness were superficial if not fraudulent.
  e. Employees would begin to doubt the credibility of management and HR in particular. This erosion of credibility could affect and infect the organizational culture.

You may disagree with the HR director, but her behavior reflects her communication skill—more than any isolated assessment of eloquence might. The HR director knows, apparently, that unintended messages are often perceived as meaningful—even more meaningful than intended messages. She also knows that communication can affect the very fabric of the organization.

As significantly, she knows that this disagreement with the CEO would be best discussed face to face as opposed to being relayed through an emissary.

The understanding and application of organizational communication principles reflects desirable communication skill.

Networks

An organization requires networks to connect related units in its systemic environments. Establishing and cultivating these channels is a challenge. Departments within organizations may identify themselves as autonomous entities and resist creating or utilizing internal networks. In addition, organizations may not recognize the need to construct networks to external audiences and can realize the severe effects of this absence particularly during times of organizational crisis.

The word network is also used occasionally to refer to channel alternatives for communicating. The CEO in Missouri sent an emissary to relay a message. He could have sent an e-mail, made a phone call, stuck a note on the HR director's door, or sent her a formal letter copying all other members of the senior staff. The HR director also had options. She decided that she needed to talk to the CEO face to face. She was either fortunate that there was a network available for interaction or to be credited for having cultivated that network. Issues pertaining to organizational networks are examined in every chapter of this book.

Culture

As we will see in the next chapter and throughout the text, culture is important for organizational communicators in at least two ways. Organizations can be said to have their own cultures. Communication affects the evolution of these cultures, and, concurrently, organizational culture affects communication quality. A "my way or the highway" culture will exclude open respectful discussions of opinion between an HR director and a CEO. Conversely, regular disrespectful responses to employee suggestions can create a "my way or the highway" culture. In Chapter 5 you will read a CEO's perspective that a "Command and Control" culture can make effective communication more difficult.

Culture is significant in another sense of the word as well. The world is becoming much smaller than it has ever been. One can travel on a plane and be on another continent in a short period of time. Consequently, organizations are often multinational, and even those that are not tend to have a workforce that is ethnically diverse. In addition to ethnic diversity, a huge factor in contemporary organizations pertains to the distinctive cultures of younger and older workers. These disparate cultural perspectives compel students of organizational communication to examine how cultural factors can affect the nature of interpersonal, interdepartmental, and global interactions.

Power

Why is the word *power* relevant? There are two important reasons.

The first is that knowing how to communicate efficiently can be empowering. The HR director was empowered because she understood the communication process, knew how to communicate to her supervisor, had an avenue available to communicate with him, and was able to articulate her position. If she was not knowledgeable, perceptive, and capable, she may have reacted quite differently to the emissary who arrived with the request. She could have sat and stewed in her office for the afternoon, brooding about the CEO's request, not knowing quite why she objected to his

ETHICAL PROBE—PLEASE SIGN MY LETTER

An associate comes to you with a letter that he has written to protest an increase in parking fees at your organization. Your associate is upset since he drives in daily and has to pay what he considers to be an exorbitant amount to park his car near the office. Assume that you take the train to work or ride your bike. Also assume that you do not really think the boost in parking fees is that dramatic or inappropriate. Regardless, your associate comes to you and asks if you would be willing to co-sign the letter. He figures the letter will have more credibility with your signature on it since you do not drive and also because you have seniority in the company.

You read through the letter and notice the following line:

> You might think that the only people who are against the parking increases are motorists. In point of fact, as you can see below, one of us doesn't drive at all, but is still concerned with what amounts to an unfair tax on employees.

Finally, assume that you do not imagine that anything will occur positively or negatively to you if you sign the letter, but the truth is you do not agree with it.

- Would it be unethical to sign this letter?
- Would signing this letter be an irresponsible exercise of your power as a senior member of the organization?
- Would it be worth being unethical with this communication to preserve your relationship with your associate?
- What do you communicate to your associate if you tell him that you will not sign?
- What has your associate communicated to you by bringing you this letter?
- If the culture of the organization condoned such behavior, would that have an effect on your willingness to sign the letter?

request. She could have reluctantly sent out a new policy and incurred the loss of credibility she anticipated. She could have thought nothing of the CEO request, sent out the policy, and been startled to notice that the climate she had attempted to carefully cultivate was now damaged. Understanding the process and demonstrating understanding makes one feel and be empowered. Not getting it can be debilitating.

Power is important for organizational communicators for another reason. It is the contention of several contemporary scholars that people, either consciously or otherwise, use communication not as a tool for conveying information, but as a method for maintaining power. These writers, called critical theorists, argue that organizations can be seen as places where individuals are made to feel inferior by people who use communication to keep employees defenseless. By marginalizing the contributions of some and privileging the contributions of others, those in power can subjugate employees to the detriment of not only those who are abused, but to the detriment of the entire organization.

For example, what if the CEO listened to the HR director's comments and made the following response: "Very interesting comments. However, there are a few things you, apparently, do not quite understand. Number one, you may be in charge of human resources, but I am in charge of you. Number two, you seem to be concerned that employees may feel that by communicating this policy we are emphasizing our authority to limit their autonomy. **Well, that is precisely what I do want to convey.**"

PRACTITIONER PERSPECTIVE

Craig Ingraham: Vice President and Senior Counsel

Craig Ingraham served as the Vice President and Senior Counsel for MasterCard International Incorporated for ten years. He supervised a department of eight people in his St. Louis office and represented approximately 1,500 people in MasterCard's Midwest operation. He has also worked for the Talx Corporation in St. Louis as the Vice President and General Counsel for the Talx Corporation. His comments reflect his observations not specifically at Talx or at MasterCard but at other organizations where he has been employed as well.

As you read through this section, consider the following questions.

- Do you agree with Ingraham's comments regarding performance reviews?
- Are you surprised by his remarks pertaining to the centrality of communication to what he does?
- What are your comments regarding the bolded comments in his narrative?
- Do you agree with his position regarding ethical communication?

Candor and clarity of expression are the keys to effective communication in organizations. Subordinates at any level are uncannily adept at detecting deceptive, disingenuous communication no matter how cleverly disguised. To be viewed as having no credibility is the kiss of death in your role as manager.

It is not easy to train someone to be an effective communicator. However, even someone with rudimentary communication skills, with a lot of hard work and experience, can become at least marginally effective. If you're not naturally gifted, you better be prepared to work hard to get good at communicating. Still, subordinates appreciate candor and frankness over polish and facile presentations.

Communication is extremely important to what I do at work. On a weekly basis I am called upon to communicate tasks to employees, prepare written documents, occasionally deliver presentations to my superiors, run meetings when these are essential—and only when they are essential as meetings often needlessly consume valuable time—and listen to employees' suggestions, ideas, and complaints. The latter may be the single most important thing a manager has to do in terms of communication—listen attentively and give employees an opportunity to express themselves. **So many problems, I've found, are resolved somehow when I just give the employee quality time, listen carefully, ask questions.** Sometimes after I hear their comments I say, "Okay. I think I understand. What can I do to help alleviate this situation?" More often than not the subordinate says, "Nothing. I feel better after just talking about this and having the opportunity to do so."

It's also important to provide feedback to employees regarding performance. Fortunately, I am not required to prepare formal evaluations for employees more than once a year. A good manager gives constant feedback and should not need the artificial discipline of annual evaluations. These formal mechanisms are, sadly, a device designed in order to address the reality that there are so many noncommunicative managers who can't be counted on to give effective, insightful, reliable feedback on their own initiative. Good managers should be able to communicate consistently with their team on a regular basis.

I have little regard for people who are deceptive and deliberately ambiguous with their communications. If you look at the highest levels in this country, you will observe the political-speak of spin doctors, where no definitive statements are ever made for fear of alienating some constituency. The result is that instead of truth we are subjected to meaningless messages. This is a positive development? Bring back Harry Truman. A lack of integrity and consistency will cost you in the marketplace and with your own employees.

Many researchers cite examples like this one and argue that communication is employed in organizations to patronize, demoralize, and disable employees. Others argue that while communication should not be abusive, leaders have the obligation to use communication to articulate their authority. Issues pertaining to power and the ethical use of communication are addressed throughout the book, with particular attention in Chapters 3 and 4. Exercises related to these issues are found in each chapter.

Text Features

As you have seen in this initial chapter, explanatory exercises entitled "Applying the Principles—Test Yourself" have been placed throughout the book. Readers are encouraged to complete these exercises in order to, indeed, apply principles that have been discussed in the chapters. Readers will also find case studies in each chapter that require analysis and may be used by instructors to stimulate discussion in classes.

In addition, there are two other regular features in the text.

The first is called "Practitioner Perspectives." These sections will present segments of interviews conducted with executives who offer their insights into the importance of communication for organizational success. These inclusions will complement the research and perspectives of organizational communication scholars.

The second feature is called **"Ethical Probes."** These segments ask readers to consider moral questions pertaining to communication ethics and the appropriate use of power in the organization. Below is the first of these features.

SUMMARY: A TOOLBOX

- Communication is central to organizational activity
- Organizational communication is pervasive, multifaceted, and transcends the study of how to speak, write, and listen effectively.
- Effective organizational communication is not simple or a "given," even for highly intelligent people.
- We define organizational communication as the study of why and how organizations send and receive information within a complex systemic environment.
- Communication is
  - A nonlinear process that affects
    - The transmission of messages
    - The very constitution and fabric of an organization

- Either the result of intentionally sent or unintentionally sent messages that can be verbal or nonverbal
- Irreversible
- Not synonymous with understanding
- Organizational communication includes the examination and analysis of
  - Foundational organizational theory
  - Ethics and the effects of ethical decisions on communication in organizations
  - Information management: the exploration of what needs to be communicated and the best methods for communicating messages
  - Communication networks
  - Organizational culture and the interdependent relationship between communication and organizational culture
  - Communication skill set competencies in interpersonal, meeting, and professional presentation contexts
  - Intercultural and international communication affecting organizations
  - Crisis communication and image management
  - Communication assessment

REVIEW AND DISCUSSION QUESTIONS

1. How has communication at your university positively or negatively affected your experience at the school?
2. Have you been in a work situation where the quality of communication
   a. Enhanced the efficiency of the organization?
   b. Created problems for employees, management, or the organization as a whole?
3. Describe your typical day in terms of your communication contacts.
   - How much of your day is spent communicating using (a) electronic communication technology? (b) face-to-face communication?
4. Several myths are identified in this chapter.
   - Which myths are the most important to debunk to improve organizational efficiency?
   - Before reading the chapter, which myths did you believe were factual?
   - Which still seem more accurate than inaccurate?
5. Skills, culture, power, and networks have been identified as key factors in organizational communication. In your experience, which of these four have been most significant in determining organizational communication success?
6. Of the transmission and constitutive perspectives, which do you think is the more valuable perspective for those studying organizational communication?

SELF-INVENTORY

Below are several statements. Determine if you agree or disagree with each one. Then explain why you agree or disagree.
- Some people use communication as a tool for abuse.
- In today's global marketplace, company spokespersons **must be** multilingual.
- Intercultural communication will always be difficult regardless of how sophisticated an organization might be.

- There's nothing wrong with leaving a meeting if your cell phone rings and you need to take the call.
- Broadcasting e-mails is an efficient way to get information to organizational personnel. It's the individual receiver's responsibility to review the e-mails and react to those that are pertinent.
- Social media like Facebook are important networks even in formal organizations.
- The company manual should be put online instead of wasting paper printing a policy and procedures bulletin.
- Suggestion systems are necessary for healthy organizational communication.
- It's wise to be vague when conveying information if the truth will hurt you or your company.
- Informal coffee chats and lunches outside of the office are good places for getting a sense of what others are thinking.

GROUP/ROLE-PLAY

Below is a case related to organizational communication. At the end of the case are several questions.
a. Analyze the case in groups to gain consensus on the questions.
b. Have one group member assume the role of Annette and another the role of Ryan. Annette should attempt to explain her concerns to Ryan in this role-playing situation.

Annette is a financial analyst for a software company. She is supervised by a man, Ryan, who has difficulty communicating clearly and effectively with his employees. During the course of a conversation, Ryan constantly switches subjects without adequate transitions. He speaks almost in a stream of consciousness without organization to his ideas. Annette claims that Ryan does not use vocal inflection or any nonverbal cues to indicate that he has moved on to a new subject.

Employees have become frustrated by the difficulty and inefficiency of conversations with this manager. Often, different members of Annette's team derive varied meanings from Ryan's directions. As a result, team members are basing their work on inconsistent assumptions.

Annette and her colleagues are uncertain about how to deal with the situation. Because Ryan is a superior they feel awkward about confronting him. Annette also believes that there are gender issues that affect her ability to talk with Ryan about his problem. Furthermore any such confrontation—whether initiated by a male or female—would not mesh with the corporate culture at the company. Annette has said that it simply would not be "politically correct" to tell Ryan that he is difficult to understand. Some of Annette's colleagues have suggested that Ryan is deliberately confusing in order to keep employees in the dark, as if by keeping employees off balance and groping in the dark he would be able to manufacture power over them.

Annette has, while conversing with Ryan, asked him to stop and clarify what he is discussing. However, this can be done only so many times, and Annette doesn't want to appear to be ignorant or annoy Ryan by interrupting him too often.

- Have you ever worked with, or for, a person like Ryan?
- Does it make sense that an organization's culture can affect Annette's options?
- Do some people keep others in the dark in order to sustain and maintain power over those who are groping around in the dark?
- How should Annette communicate to Ryan about Ryan's communication problem?
- Assuming that Ryan wishes to be helped, what suggestions could Annette (or anyone else) make that would help Ryan improve his communication?

Chapter **2**

Management Theory and Organizational Communication

Chapter in a Nutshell

In this chapter and the next we discuss the theoretical underpinnings for organizational communication study. An understanding of these theories and how they relate to each other can explain why communication in organizations is essential and how to improve communication in organizations. A good theory is not an abstract conception that is valueless beyond a researcher's study. A good theory can provide a practical foundation for understanding and qualitative growth. In this chapter we explore contrasting perspectives on management. One perspective is called the classical approach, the other the human relations and human resources approach. These perspectives have features that apply directly to communication in the organization.

When you have completed this chapter, you should be able to:

• Explain what is meant by a theory.
• Discuss the practical relevance of examining theories.
• Identify the principles of classical theory.
• Describe the four stages of the Hawthorne Studies.
• Explain the distinctions between human relations and human resources theory.
• Identify the distinctions between Theory X and Theory Y.
• Explain the relevance of motivation-hygiene theory, contingency theory, and Maslow's hierarchy of needs to the evolution of organizational communication studies.

CASE 2.1
Communicating to a New Staff

Patricia Daniels was in her first week at the job. She knew she had to send a message to her subordinates but was unsure of what she should communicate to them and how she should communicate her messages.

Daniels had been hired from the outside to be a "change agent" and head of the technical support department at a software company. The department had twenty employees, including five part-time workers and two administrative assistants. One of the full timers was an associate director who had held the same position under the previous leader.

Daniels was told by the supervisor who had hired her that the former, now retired, director had been "laid back" about enforcing rules. The staff had been lax particularly about coming into work on time. Some employees were notorious for arriving as much as thirty minutes to an hour after the assigned opening time. These same persons would often take extra time before and after their lunch breaks. Lateness was just one issue. The staff wasn't professional in performance or appearance. One veteran took days off claiming they were "sick days" but, according to the supervisor, they were personal days. Part-time employees were similarly indifferent to their responsibilities. Also, despite being a technical support department, the group had a reputation of being gruff with employees who simply requested technical support. Even the workspace wasn't as clean as it could or should be. Meetings were haphazard informal sessions without any genuine agenda. These meetings were described by the supervisor as more of a social occasion than anything else.

Some employees enjoyed the laissez-faire approach of Daniels's predecessor. Others desired more professionalism, but did not want to carry the weight of that responsibility if others were not inclined to share the burdens. The supervisor warned Daniels before she took the job that there might be some angry employees because the associate director—a friend to many employees—had applied for the position but had been rejected. It wasn't that he wasn't qualified; however, he was tainted by his association with the former director. A hire from the outside seemed to be a good idea.

During her first week a few employees—three or four—had individually stopped into Daniels's office to wish her well. Privately they had said they were glad that she was there because the department had gotten out of hand under the former regime. Yet it was hard for Daniels to read the others as she passed them in the hall or when she met them briefly at a companywide session. When she first met the associate director, he had been cordial. He'd knocked on her door early in the first week apparently just to chat, but the meeting was very brief. He didn't seem abrasive, but Daniels was concerned that she hadn't come across assertive enough during their short conversation.

Patricia Daniels knew she had to somehow communicate her position to the staff. But what was her position? Were these people lazy delinquents seeking to maintain a sloppy status quo, or were they dedicated professionals seeking leadership that might be the catalyst for excellence? Did she need to lay down the law? If so, what was the law?

As significantly, Daniels wondered about the method and sequencing of her communication.

- Should she speak to the full-time and part-time employees separately?
- Should she write out a policy statement and distribute the document to employee mailboxes?
- Should she use the company intranet to send a "welcoming note from your new director"?
- Should she relay any messages at a social function outside the office environment instead of during work hours?
- Would she be wise to speak formally about her plans to the associate director before meeting with any other workers?
- Should she solicit input from all employees before crafting her message?

- Should she send out a formal agenda prior to any meeting, or would that send out the wrong signals—as if she was too "stuffy"?
- Should she wait a while to see how things unfolded before she communicated any message?

To complicate matters even further Daniels was the sole African American in the department. She'd been dealing with issues of race since she was a child, and she tried to block out the notion of potential prejudice when she entered into a new situation with others. It wasn't easy. It seemed as if her skin color was always there as a barrier or at least a factor. She remembered the time when, after a

preliminary phone conversation, she deplaned for an interview and was met by a host who seemed to be startled that Daniels was not white. He had fumbled for a moment and nearly blabbered something like, "You didn't sound black when we talked." Would race be something she'd have to overcome in this job as well?

The task of knowing what to communicate to her subordinates and how to say it was daunting and weighed on her.

- If you were Daniels, what would you assume about your audience?
- What messages would you want to convey?
- How would you convey these messages?

Demystifying Theories

The word "theory" is often misunderstood. It has the negative connotation of an abstract, impractical notion or assumption. One researcher documented this attitude by conducting a simple study. He asked students to complete a sentence that began with the six words, "That works fine in theory, but . . ." Typical responses were: "Not in real life"; "In practice it doesn't happen that way;" "Reality is a different story"; and "In reality things are a lot more complicated."[1]

Theories need not be impractical or confusing, although some poorly articulated theories do seem complex to students, business practitioners, and professors alike. A good theory can be clearly described and can provide a very practical foundation for understanding phenomena. One could make a strong case that a theory that does not provide a practical foundation for understanding how something works could not be a good theory. In much the same way as a building needs a foundation for it to be sturdy, what we know should "sit" on some assumptions that are themselves sturdy.

In *Building Communication Theory*, Infante, Rancer, and Womack define a theory as a "group of related propositions designed to explain why events take place in a certain way."[2] West and Turner write that a theory is "an abstract system of concepts with indications of the relationships among these concepts that help us to understand a phenomenon."[3] In essence, a theory is *an informed, explanatory or predictive conceptualization.* A good theory can help us think and act intelligently.

If you want to be an effective group leader and communicate efficiently in that role, you might study groups, observe how groups react to different leadership styles, "try out" the different styles yourself, and then formulate a theory that explains why groups behave as they do depending upon leadership. On the basis of your theory you may communicate in a particular way when you lead your group.

If you want to communicate efficiently in times of organizational crisis, you might study how some organizations successfully communicated when they were under duress. You might examine what they did that worked and what they or others did that was unsuccessful. You might read research reports on crisis communication and/or conduct some research of your own. On the basis of your exploration, you may develop a theory about the best way to communicate in a crisis. When your organization is faced with such a situation, you would want to apply the principles of your theory to the very real practical problems you face.

These are simplified examples of how theories are developed. However, the point is that theories need not be and should not be impractical. "There's nothing so practical as a good theory."[4]

Symbiotic Theory: What Is Symbiosis and Symbiotic Theory?

In 2000 Corman and Poole published a group of essays in a book entitled *Perspectives on Organizational Communication: Finding Common Ground*. Corman wrote the first chapter of the book, which serves as the introduction to the volume. He explains that the book evolved as a result of his sense that organizational communication studies needed to work to find a common ground.

> If the only tool you have is a hammer you tend to see every problem as a nail.
>
> — ABRAHAM MASLOW

Scholars, he claimed, spent much of their time "debating and defending . . . [their] paradigmatic containers" and that this seemed to be "more important [to them] than working together to discover things about organizational communication."[5] A review of many journals in organizational communication studies would suggest that Corman has an important point. (In fact, a review of the essays in the very volume designed to find common ground reveals a reluctance to relinquish the partitions.)

The purpose of this chapter and the next is to inform readers of the various theories that provide the foundation for organizational communication study. These theories should be seen as symbiotic.

Symbiosis refers to the intimate association of apparently dissimilar organisms. A symbiotic approach to organizational communication theory not only acknowledges that the theories we will be discussing are related, but moreover that they should be seen as part of an interdependent intimate mosaic—a composite of meaningfully related theories that only superficially appear to be distinct. One can view organizational communication from, for example, a systems theory perspective and still acknowledge and employ the contributions of critical, cultural, human resources, and classical theories to analyses of organizational communication.

As we begin the discussion of individual theories, keep in mind that these can and should be understood not as isolated perspectives, but as pieces of a composite that might seem dissimilar and may have contrasting principles, but when viewed as a whole advance the purposes of research and study in organizational communication.

Classical Theory of Management

The classical theory of management is associated with theorists Frederick Taylor, Henri Fayol, and Max Weber. Taylor is responsible for the ideas of scientific management, Fayol for administrative theory, and Weber for bureaucracy theory. These theories taken collectively provide the underpinnings for the broader label of classical management theory. While these writers published their theories more than half a century ago, many organizations—for worse or better—still operate using classical management principles.[6]

At the heart of classical theory is the assumption that an organization is akin to a machine. The best way to maximize organizational productivity, according to classical theorists, is to consider the most efficient ways to structure the machine and control the machine's operations. Bureaucracy theory described the best ways to structure the "machine" and administrative theory described the best ways to administer the structure or bureaucracy.

Classical theorists and human resource theorists have different perspectives regarding the importance of interpersonal relationships in organizations.

Classical theorists consider employees to be parts of the machine that is the organization. Just like a tire is part of an automobile and an efficient tire will maximize that automobile's performance, an employee was considered to be part of the organization and an efficient employee would maximize organizational performance. Therefore, management would need to consider how employees can do a job most productively. The communication responsibilities for classical managers involved explaining the tasks to these human parts of the machine and articulating the policies that governed the work of the machine.

Frederick Taylor and Scientific Management

In 1911 Frederick Taylor wrote a now famous book entitled *The Principles of Scientific Management.*[7] In it and in other writings, Taylor argued that "blundering, ill-directed, or inefficient" management resulted in "wastes of human effort."[8] There was a need, he argued, to eliminate such wastes and manage employees by developing a "true science, resting upon clearly defined laws, rules and principles."[9] His meticulously detailed book described this science.

Any job, according to Taylor, could be completed scientifically. It was simply a matter of studying the job, identifying the best way to do it, carefully selecting the right persons to do the job, compensating equitably, and training those persons to do the job effectively. If one managed scientifically there would be relatively fewer "wastes of human effort."

Taylor bemoaned the then current methods of apprenticeship training. In that system, an employee would be trained by another more experienced worker, who would model the task so that the newcomer would know what to do. Taylor argued that this process of training was inefficient because it resulted in workers performing the same tasks variously, more or less efficiently, depending on the quality of training they experienced. "Blundering, ill-directed management" did not understand that there was one best way to do a job, and therefore one best way to explain how to do the job. It should not be left up to individual mentors to communicate a task to an apprentice.

Soldiering and Systematic Soldiering

One plank in the foundation of Taylor's philosophy was that employees were essentially lazy and, left without precise direction, would underperform. "There is no question," he wrote, "that the tendency of the average [employee] is toward working at a slow easy gait."[10] He labeled this tendency *natural soldiering*. Natural soldiering was compounded by a phenomenon Taylor described as *systematic soldiering*. This occurred when workers slowed their pace after receiving implied or explicit communications from their peers.

Taylor considered systematic soldiering inevitable for two reasons. The first was that employees might observe a slower worker receiving the same compensation and decide not to exert effort because there was no monetary motivation to do so. "When a naturally energetic man works for a few days beside a lazy one, the logic of the situation is unanswerable. 'Why should I work hard when that lazy fellow gets the same pay that I do and does only half as much work?'"[11]

The second reason was a bit more complex. Taylor argued that hourly compensation was based on the assumption that it took a certain period of time to complete a particular task. If industrious employees could demonstrate that it could take less time to do the task, then employers might reduce the rate. Industrious employees therefore could be "rate busters." However, since "rate busting" would naturally be discouraged by peers, industrious workers would be told by their co-workers to slow down. "The natural laziness of men [sic] is serious," opined Taylor, "but by far the greatest evil from which both workmen and employers are suffering is the systematic soldiering which is almost universal under all ordinary schemes of management. . . .[12]

Taylor believed that the problems of apprenticeship training and systematic soldiering could be eliminated by utilizing scientific management. He conducted what have been called time and motion studies to determine exactly the best way to do a job and exactly how much time it could take to do that job well. Taylor described how he witnessed workers shoveling coal at the Bethlehem Steel Corporation machine shop. He noticed that certain types of shovels and shoveling techniques resulted in greater productivity. He studied how workers should shovel coal and on the basis of his research, workers were told what shovels should be used and what techniques to use when shoveling. Productivity went up dramatically. Tests could determine the most efficient way to complete a work-related task. On the basis of the tests you could prescribe an approach to make the organization as efficient as possible

Scientific Management and Communication

Taylor's idea of the role of communication was straightforward. Employees need to be aware of their tasks. Management needs to know the best way to do these tasks. Management has to articulate the best way to do the job and the rules that govern their work.

By his own admission, Taylor was not "noted for his tact."[13] His communication style is evidenced in one particular excerpt from his book. In it, Taylor describes how he selected a man named Schmidt to do a job and how he spoke to him about the job. This excerpt should be studied carefully by organizational communication students. It reveals very clearly the role of communication in classical theory and scientific management as envisioned by its pioneer, Frederick Taylor.

Is this "rather rough talk" appropriate?

In Chapter 1 we discussed the importance of conceptualizing communication from both a transmission perspective and a constitutive perspective. We also discussed the interdependent relationship between organizational communication and culture and the idea that communication in organizations can be a tool of abuse.

Was Taylor's communication effective?

What would be the residual effects on an organization if managers communicated the way Taylor suggests? Should organizational communicators be concerned with these residual effects?

Taylor included this excerpt as an example of how to deal with employees correctly. Are there any situations when such an approach should be used?

Henri Fayol—General Principles of Management

Communication for Taylor involved explaining how and what to do. Henri Fayol's work implied some additional communication responsibilities. In his book *General and Industrial Management*, Fayol lists fourteen principles and five elements of management (Table 2.1).[15]

A number of principles on Fayol's list clearly require effective communication. In order to

Taylorism inspired the efficiency of this Japanese bicycle factory—but also the image of a struggling industrial worker in Chaplin's *Modern Times*.

Our first step was the scientific selection of the workman. In dealing with workmen under this type of management, it is an inflexible rule to talk to and deal with only one man at a time, since each workman has his own special abilities and limitations, and since we are not dealing with men in masses, but are trying to develop each individual man to his highest state of efficiency and prosperity. Our first step was to find the proper workman to begin with. We therefore carefully watched and studied these 75 men for three or four days, at the end of which time we had picked out four men who appeared to be physically able to handle pig iron at the rate of 47 tons per day. A careful study was then made of each of these men. We had looked up their history as far back as practicable and thorough inquiries were made as to the character, habits, and the ambition of each of them. Finally we selected one from among the four as the most likely man to start with. He was a little Pennsylvania Dutchman who had been observed to trot back home for a mile or so after his work in the evening, about as fresh as he was when he came trotting down to work in the morning. We found that upon wages of $1.15 a day he had succeeded in buying a small plot of ground and that he was engaged in putting up the walls of a little house for himself in the morning before starting down to work and at night after leaving. He also had the reputation of being exceedingly "close," that is, of placing a very high value on a dollar. As one man whom we talked to about him said, "A penny looks about the size of a cart-wheel to him." This man we will call Schmidt.

The task before us, then, narrowed itself down to getting Schmidt to handle 47 tons of pig iron per day and making him glad to do it. This was done as follows. Schmidt was called out from among the gang of pig-iron handlers and talked to somewhat in this way:

"Schmidt, are you a high-priced man?"
"Vell, I don't know vat you mean."

"Oh yes, you do. What I want to know is whether you are a high-priced man or not."

"Vell, I don't know vat you mean."

"Oh, come now, you answer my questions. What I want to find out is whether you are a high-priced man or one of those cheap fellows here. What I want to find out is whether you want to earn $1.85 a day or whether you are satisfied with $1.15, just the same as all those cheap fellows are getting."

"Did I vant $1.85 a day? Vas dot a high-priced man? Vell, yes, I vas a high-priced man."

"Oh, you're aggravating me. Of course you want $1.85 a day—every one wants it! You know perfectly well that that has very little to do with your being a high-priced man. For goodness' sake answer my questions and don't waste any more of my time. Now come over here. You see that pile of pig iron?"

"Yes."

"You see that car?"

"Yes."

"Well, if you are a high-priced man, you will load that pig iron on that car to-morrow for $1.85. Now do wake up and answer my question. Tell me whether you are a high-priced man or not."

"Vell, did I got $1.85 for loading dot pig iron on dot car to-morrow?"

"Yes, of course you do, and you get $1.85 for loading a pile like that every day right through the year. That is what a high-priced man does, and you know it just as well as I do."

"Vell, dot's all right. I could load dot pig iron on the car to-morrow for $1.85, and I get it every day, don't I?"

"Certainly you do, certainly you do."

"Vell, den, I vas a high-priced man."

"Now hold on, hold on. You know just as well as I do that a high-priced man has to do exactly as he's told from morning till night. You have seen this man here before, haven't you?"

"No, I never saw him."

"Well, if you are a high-priced man, you will do exactly as this man tells you to-morrow, from morning till night. When he tells you to pick up a pig and walk, you pick it up and you walk, and when he tells you to sit down and rest, you sit down. You do that right straight through the day. And what's more, no back talk. Now a high-priced man does just what he's told to do, and no back talk. Do you understand that? When this man tells you to walk, you walk; when he tells you to sit down, you sit down, and you don't talk back to him. Now you come on to work here to-morrow morning, and I'll know before night whether you are really a high-priced man or not."

This seems to be rather rough talk. And indeed it would be if applied to an educated mechanic, or even an intelligent laborer. With a man of the mentally sluggish type of Schmidt it is appropriate and not unkind, since it is effective in fixing his attention on the high wages which he wants and away from what, if it were called to his attention, he probably would consider impossibly hard work.[14]

establish authority, maintain discipline, and create esprit de corps, management must effectively communicate with the workforce. One could argue that communication is important for each of the items that he identifies.

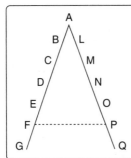

Henri Fayol believed in following the line of authority. However, he knew information would travel too slowly if messages had to move from person F to A, descend to P, ascend again to A, and then finally return to F. He suggested that the process be streamlined by establishing "a gangplank" linking F to P.

Figure 2.1 Henri Fayol's Bridge

Let's consider some other aspects of Fayol's theory that pertain to the study of organizational communication. Specifically, we will look at Fayol's conception of:

- Scalar Chain and the Gangplank
- Interdepartmental Communication
- Written vs. Oral Communication
- Nonverbal Communication
- Organizational Assessment

Scalar Chain and the Gangplank

Classical theorists believe in a hierarchical chain of command. The phrase *scalar chain* refers to this hierarchy. Fayol writes that "the line of authority is the route followed—via every link in the chain—by all communications which start from or go to the ultimate authority."[16] Fayol believed that in most instances the scalar chain principle for communication must be respected and observed. However, he acknowledged that the method of communicating via the chain can be slow. Fayol argues that a "gangplank" would be a remedy for this problem. A "gangplank," he argued, could connect departments in a way that would be "swift, simple, and pure"[17] (see Figure 2.1).

Classical theorists typically support centralized authority. When Fayol describes his gangplank notion (now commonly referred to as "Fayol's bridge") he comments that the

Table 2.1 Fayol's Principles and Elements of Management

General Principles of Management

- Division of Work
- Authority and Responsibility
- Discipline
- Unity of Command
- Unity of Direction
- Subordination of Individual Interest to General Interest
- Remuneration of Personnel
- Centralization
- Scalar Chain
- Order
- Equity
- Stability of Tenure and Personnel
- Initiative
- *Esprit de Corps*

Five Elements of Management

- Planning
- Organizing
- Command
- Coordination
- Control

ultimate authority should sanction such communication deviations and that it "is an error to depart needlessly from the line of authority." However, it is important to point out that in the absence of advice from a superior, Fayol comments that an employee should be courageous enough to initiate communicating across the gangplank.

Interdepartmental Communication

For classical theorists the primary direction of communication was downward along the scalar chain. However, Fayol knew that "each department [should work] in harmony with the rest" and "department divisions . . . [must be] precisely informed as to the share they must take in the communal task and the reciprocal aid they are to afford one another."[18] Fayol obviously knew that there was a value in linking departments with appropriate communication channels. He was also aware of the problems related to establishing such linkages.

> [Often] each department knows and wants to know nothing of the others. It operates as if it were its own aim and end, without bothering either about neighboring departments or the business as a whole. . . . Watertight compartments exist between the divisions and offices of the same department as they do also between different departments. Each one's prime concern is to take cover from personal responsibility behind a piece of paper, an order or a circular letter."[19]

Fayol's remedy for this problem was to have weekly conferences of department heads. He felt that weekly conferences would provide for "spontaneous collaboration" and that the "water tight compartment disappears when all department heads have to give an account of themselves, and be in agreement in the presence of a higher authority."[20]

Fayol's contention that these conferences would end problems related to interdepartmental communication was idealistic and shortsighted. As we will see in Chapter 8, departmental and interdepartmental meetings are often contentious, nonproductive sessions, which often surely do not result in "spontaneous collaboration." Also, "watertight compartments" often exist because of historical tension that meetings are not likely to eliminate. For example, in a May 2004 *New York Times* article, the lack of communication between police and fire departments in New York City was described as the result of long-standing enmity and cited as a cause of the inability to react as efficiently as possible to the 9/11 attack.[21] Fayol's conference remedy might not be sufficient, but his comments about the need for interdepartmental interaction reflect an awareness that is significant for people who study the roots of organizational communication.

Written vs. Oral Communication

Most researchers suggest that classical theorists favored written communication as opposed to oral face-to-face interactions. Written messages could serve as records and in this way, at least, could establish authority and facilitate organizational control. However, Fayol argued that there could be an abuse of the written communication channel. He claimed that orally transmitted messages were faster and could be made clearer than communication that was written. He even contended that animosities between departments could be fueled by written communications that would otherwise be harmonious if oral communication methods were employed.[22] This is a prescient comment in light of contemporary issues related to tensions provoked by e-mail flaming and the abuse of linear methods for communicating, which may avoid short-term confrontations but can increase long-term resentments. We will discuss the wisdom of alternative communication approaches in Chapter 5, but it is at least interesting to note that not all classical theorists defaulted toward written versus face-to-face communication.

Nonverbal Communication

One of Fayol's "elements of management" was command. An effective manager is obliged to get the most from all subordinates toward the objectives of the organization.

> It is taken for granted that every manager has authority to exact obedience, but a business would be ill served were obedience obtained only by fear of oppression . . . some leaders get obedience, energy, zeal and even loyalty without apparent effort. . . . One of the most effective methods of training is example.

When the manager sets an example of hard work no one dare arrives late, when he [sic] is active, courageous and loyal he is imitated. . . . But bad example too is contagious, and in coming from above it has
more serious repercussions on the unit as a whole."[23]

Fayol's comments pertain both to power relationships and to the relevancy of nonverbal communication. The spoken word can convey certain information. Providing a handbook can reinforce these messages and relay others. However, the nonverbally communicated messages present in
modeling behavior can complement or undermine these other verbalized messages.

Organizational Assessment

Chapter 11 will address the topic of communication auditing. As will be explained in detail later,
an audit is essentially an assessment that provides for a picture of the communication quality of
an organization. It is interesting to note that Fayol advocates "periodic audits of the organization."
He suggests that annually "a scrupulous study of the constitution of the organization is to be made
with the assistance of summarized charts." He goes on to suggest that these charts will provide a
photograph that will detect "faulty arrangements proceeding all too frequently out of hasty organic
modifications."[24] Similarly, audits attempt to identify problems with communication that may be
the result of "hasty organic modifications" as much as the result of faulty design.

Money and Motivation

A significant feature of classical theory is the assumption that employees were motivated strictly
by money. Classical theorists believe that people come to work primarily because they must.
Therefore should you desire that an employee work well, you would be wise to provide some
financial incentive for excellent performance. Sometimes referred to as the carrot-stick approach
to motivation, managers who adhere to classical theory would dangle some reward (a carrot) at
the end of a stick and entice employees to work harder in order to gain the reward of the carrot
or a piece of the carrot. Subsequently, the remains of the carrot or additional rewards would be
offered as enticements for excellence. Taylor advocated, for example, that employees be compensated not by the hour but on the basis of the work they had done. The more work accomplished,
the greater the pay.

It's important to *emphasize* that supporters of classical theory believed that employees were
NOT inherently motivated to work by factors other than financial incentives. Interestingly,
Taylor argues that management needs to offer employees what he calls a "plum" for coming
together with the "science." On the surface this motivation by reward is very consistent with
classical theory. Yet Taylor continues to argue that there "are many plums" and includes as
rewards "better treatment, more kindly treatment, more consideration for [employee] wishes,
and an opportunity to express their wants freely."[26] Nevertheless, those who implemented classical theory considered money and other financial remuneration the primary, if not lone, factor
that motivated employees to work.[27]

So, what are the lessons of classical theory as they pertain to communication? A basic tenet of
classical theory was that "management plans the work, and laborers follow through with the plan—
workers take orders from the foreman who is in charge of [a] particular task."[28] Therefore, management needed to inform employees about what they must do and how they must do it. Employees
needed to know about financial incentives so that they might work hard to obtain the remuneration. Nearly all communication in classical organizations was directed downward, from superior to
subordinate. Classical theorists would acknowledge few situations in which employees would need

Max Weber, Authority, and Communication

It is ironic that the word bureaucracy, first described by Max Weber as a positive and necessary concept for organizational management, should now be perceived as something negative. In his book, *Theory of Social and Economic Organization,*[25] Weber describes an efficient organization as one characterized by a clearly articulated hierarchy, governed by rules, and comprised of a stable order of authority.

Weber wrote about three types of authority: traditional, charismatic, and rational-legal. Traditional authority was authority attributed to persons because of long-standing convention. For example, the Queen of England would be an example of someone who has traditional authority. In the family context, mothers and fathers have traditional authority. Charismatic authority is a status that is derived from the personal qualities of a leader. Charles Manson and David Koresh had charismatic authority in that somehow they were able to attract followers to their abnormal sense of right and wrong because of their personal magnetism. A person in your cluster of friends may have charismatic authority and be looked up to as the leader of your group to the extent that you follow her or his suggestions when you make plans to study or travel.

Max Weber is more concerned with rational-legal authority. This authority is determined because of the rules that govern the organization. A chairperson is identified as the authority figure because the rules of the organization imbue her or him with this power. The sales manager has authority because of how the organization has defined the job and what powers the sales manager should have.

The articulation of the hierarchy, and particularly the specific rules that govern the organization, require communication. Like the other classical theorists, Weber saw communication as a process that followed the scalar chain of command and was directed primarily downward. Weber, like the other classical theorists, believed that the job was more significant than the person who was doing the job and that interpersonal relationships were relatively insignificant. Like the other classical theorists, Weber considered interpersonal relationships necessary only to the extent that these relationships were required in order to meet the goals of the organization.

In short, a bureaucracy required many rules. Those rules needed to be communicated to those affected by the rules. Leadership was established and maintained because individuals knew who had been granted authority and precisely what that authority allowed.

to send information to management. Nor would classical theorists believe there was any need to communicate in order to foster relationships.

Do you see any merit in classical theory?

The Hawthorne Studies

The Hawthorne Studies may be the most well-known studies ever conducted in the field of management. Almost any textbook in industrial or organizational behavior will have some reference to the studies, even if the treatment is superficial.

The Hawthorne Studies were so called because they were conducted in the Western Electric Hawthorne plant in Cicero, Illinois. The studies, which began in 1924, were conducted in order to examine and test certain principles of classical theory. The idea was to assess how workers would react to varied physical conditions in order to identify the optimal physical environment for productivity. Ironically, the findings of the studies compelled advocates of classical theory to reconsider their positions. In the final analysis, instead of serving to support and solidify classical principles, the Hawthorne Studies actually were a catalyst for the development of an alternate and contrary theory called human relations theory. (Later in this chapter we will discuss human relations theory in detail.) The studies were significant because they served to change, and change radically, attitudes about how/why people worked. Also, the Hawthorne Studies were noteworthy because they altered the perspective theorists had about the importance and nature of communication as an element of efficient management.

> "In all affairs it's a healthy thing to hang a question mark on the things you have long taken for granted."
>
> **—BERTRAND RUSSELL**

There were four parts, identified as segments, of the Hawthorne Studies.[29] The first is the most famous and the one that is likely to be familiar to readers who have studied organizational behavior previously. In this phase workers were observed while researchers varied lighting intensity. The assumption of the theorists was that increased lighting would increase productivity. If the lighting was better, people who did piece work would be better able to do their work and produce more.

As expected, when lighting was increased, performance increased. However, to the surprise of the researchers, as lighting was decreased, worker performance remained higher than normal, even when the lighting became very dim. Production only went down when the lighting became so low that the participants complained and said they could not see what they were doing.[30] In the control group where lighting remained constant, productivity also went up. The results were, well, illuminating, and the variable, apparently, was not illumination.

There had to be some other factor that compelled employees to be more productive. The researchers agreed that this motivator was related to observation, change, and implicit recognition.

The second phase of the Hawthorne Studies, referred to as the "relay assembly" studies, began in 1927. In this phase, work conditions such as hours, coffee breaks, pay incentives, and the quality of food provided was varied. The objective of this component was consistent with the first. The assumption was that if pay incentives went up, coffee breaks were increased in terms of frequency and duration, and working hours were more attractive, then productivity would increase accordingly. The idea, consistent with scientific management and classical theory, was to discover the optimal conditions.

As with the studies based on illumination, varying conditions did *not* have a direct effect on productivity. Regardless of hours, even if the hours were grueling, even if coffee breaks were eliminated, workers performed better than they had previously. *The Hawthorne Effect* is a phrase used to describe the results of these two parts of the study. In brief, the Hawthorne Effect refers to the fact that people tend to alter their behavior when they are observed. It may be startling to contemporary readers that the Hawthorne Effect surprised the scholars. Nevertheless, the notion that the motivational variable was the attention, as opposed to the altered conditions, compelled researchers to reconsider their attitudes about worker behavior.

It also made astute observers acknowledge that a certain type of communication was an important factor in managerial success. If observation and recognition were motivating factors for employees, then wouldn't managers need to be able to communicate more than just tasks, procedures, and organizational rules? Wouldn't managers have to acknowledge, either positively or negatively, the quality of employee performance in ways that transcended monetary acknowledgments?

The third component of the studies, which began in 1928, involved conducting interviews with employees at the plant. Some 21,000 employees were questioned about their attitudes toward work, co-workers, management, and the organization. The results of this phase of the study showed the researchers not only that the employees had gripes and would articulate their concerns, but also that employees enjoyed the opportunity to express themselves about the various issues. The employees seemed to be able to "vent" during these interviews in a way that made them seem happier. The findings from this third phase appear to contradict other beliefs of the classical theorists. The classical theorists were inclined to believe that communication in organizations need only go downward from management to subordinates. This third phase of the Hawthorne Studies seemed to indicate that there might be some value in allowing subordinates an opportunity to communicate upward and to initiate communication with management.

The last part of the Hawthorne Studies is called the bank wiring phase. Researchers observed employees and found that the employees established informal rules and norms that they abided by in order to complete their tasks. These norms were not necessarily consistent with the formal guidelines and procedures established by management. This again contradicted notions of the classical theory as the results suggested that informal networks were important. Classical theorists assumed employees received the only consequential messages from downwardly directed formal messages. Apparently the real rules might be established informally by social peer-related pressure and governance communicated horizontally from worker to worker.

Human Relations and Human Resources Theories

Human Relations Theory

The findings of the Hawthorne Studies provided the foundation for a new way to think about management, which has been called *human relations theory*. Some writers have questioned whether there was sufficient proof in the Hawthorne Studies to support its conclusions and warrant the jump to human relations theory.[31] However, there can be no doubt that the result of the Hawthorne Studies was a move toward a theory of human relations regardless of whether that move should have emerged from the studies.

The tenets of this new perspective were in contrast to those identified by classical theorists. Whereas classical theorists believed that employees were motivated by money, human relations theorists pointed to the Hawthorne Studies and argued that under the right conditions work could be enjoyable and that employees were motivated by observation and recognition. As opposed to the mechanistic assumptions of the classical theorists, human relations theorists believed that workers were, indeed, humans and had human needs that, if met, would enhance productivity. Therefore, in order to motivate employees, managers would need to communicate not only information about job tasks and policies but also information that recognized workers' accomplishments, respected their sensitivities, and, essentially, acknowledged that they were feeling animate entities.

The human relations theory emerged in the 1930s, but there is ample contemporary evidence to support the position of these theorists.

- An independent research company conducted a study for executive personnel consultants ("head hunters") who wanted to know why executives choose to leave jobs and seek other ones. The study revealed that 34 percent of the respondents cited **limited praise and recognition** as the primary reason for seeking other employment. Only 25 percent of the respondents cited compensation as the main reason.[32]
- A Harris Poll was conducted for an organization that wanted to get a better sense of what employees wanted. The organization assumed that employees thought that job security and money was of paramount importance. The poll discovered that there was a "perception gap" since "job security" ranked "far below" more human relations–related desires such as *"respect, a high standard of management ethics, increased recognition of employee contributions, and closer, more honest communications between employees and senior management."*[33] This finding is consistent with the comment made during an interview with a high-level engineer in a large South Carolina–based organization. "Many of our employee surveys," he said, *"indicate job recognition and positive feedback are as, or more important, than financial rewards and incentives."* [34]
- The Institute of Higher Education conducted a decade-long study and discovered that faculty morale at colleges was not related to salary as much as faculty opportunity to participate in the governance of their universities.[35]
- An advertising campaign for Southwest Airlines is intended to recruit potential candidates for work at Southwest. The focus of the promotion is the depiction of Southwest as an organization that views its employees as its greatest asset.[36]
- An eight-year study of organizations included the finding that *"effective communication relationships contributed most to job satisfaction."*[37]
- The transformation of the California Public Retirement System (CALPERS) may be the strongest current argument in support of human relations theory. In June 2001 James Burton, the head of CALPERS, accepted an International Association of Business Communicators award for excellence in organizational communication. Burton was hired to lead CALPERS at a time when performance levels were dismal. Burton hired a consultant to examine the source of the woeful morale and weak performance. The consultant found that the problem was related to employee perception of a lack of respect and recognition for job performance. As Burton documented in his acceptance presentation, CALPERS began an extensive campaign to communicate warranted recognition to employees. Within a short period of time, CALPERS improved from a dispirited underperforming organization to one that was and is highly successful. While Burton's program is recent, the success story of CALPERS could well have appeared under the headline of a 1982 *Wall Street Journal* article with a similar theme. The headline of that piece read, "To Raise Productivity, Try Saying Thank You."[38]

Opposition to the Human Relations Theory

The human relations theory encountered disapproval and criticism. Critics felt that human relations theorists put too much of an emphasis on the employee. Because of this, proponents were sometimes denigrated as "the happiness boys." Also, critics claimed that the managers who

Applying the Principles—Test Yourself

Communication and Motivation

What are your opinions on the following questions?

1. In your experience, what motivates people to work harder—communications that promise increased salary or communications that recognize performance?
2. In the absence of periodic salary increments, are employees likely to be motivated by managers who say things like, "I wish I could give you more money because you deserve it. You're a terrific worker and I really I appreciate you"?
3. Assume that two workers earn significantly more than they need to feed/

clothe/house themselves and their respective families. Assume they both perform their jobs well and both feel the other's work is adequate. Would it matter if one employee received a larger salary increment than the other when raises were distributed?
4. Assume a manager is upset because a few individuals have abused the flexible-hours policy at the organization. Specifically, out of ten employees, three keep coming in late and leaving early. If you were one of the diligent seven, how do you think the manager should communicate the message? If you were one of the other three, how would you want the manager to communicate the message?

employed human relations theory either misunderstood or misused human relations principles and attempted to manipulate employees by communicating bogus praise to entice productivity. Essentially, while principles of the human relations theory were sound, those who attempted to apply the principles diluted the theory's impact by establishing relationships and spewing praise in ways that were superficial, not credible, and ultimately counterproductive.[39] In Chapter 1 we referred to the concern researchers have for the abuse of communication and how people sometimes employ communication as a tool to maintain power. Critics of superficial applications to human relations theory argue that, ironically, the misuse of human relations theory can be a deliberate attempt to confuse employees and disempower them. This activity plants a seed that can eventually corrupt a healthy organizational culture.

Human Resources Theory

Human resources theory developed as a reaction to this criticism. In 1965 Raymond Miles published a transformational article in the *Harvard Business Review* entitled, "Human Relations or Human Resources." In the piece, Miles argues that human relations approaches were widely espoused but rarely meaningfully implemented. He suggested that a new conceptualization of the employee as a resource who could, should, and desired to be productive would be more valuable. Whereas a human relations theorist would argue that employees need to be acknowledged, a human resource theorist would extend that principle. Human resource theorists would argue that not only do employees need to be recognized for what they do, but management must recognize that employees can contribute in ways that are "untapped." Miles makes a number of important points in this groundbreaking article.

- Human relations theorists desire to make employees "feel useful and important" because this sense of participation will act as "a lubricant" that will get employees to do what management wants them to do.
- Human resource managers consider employees capable of making meaningful contributions. Management, therefore, has the responsibility to create communication channels and cultivate a climate that will facilitate employee participation.
- Most managers wish their own supervisors practiced human resource theory, but these same managers actually manage using human relations approaches. Most managers actually doubt that their employees can make meaningful contributions while considering themselves as capable as their own supervisors.
- Therefore, while the human resource model may have merit, it will not and cannot be satisfactorily implemented by those who do not acknowledge that their subordinates are as capable as the managers themselves consider themselves to be. "The benefits which the human resources approach predicts . . . will not accrue as long as managers cling to the human relations view."[40]

This last point is significant. While Miles endorses this new theory, he acknowledges that it cannot work—in much the same way that human relations approaches did not work—if management does not believe that employees can indeed be a resource.

A good way to explain Miles's distinction between human relations and human resources approaches is to consider the following classroom illustration.

If in classes your instructors communicate with you considerately *because they sense that this is the way to get your cooperation*, then they could be identified as human relations theorists. However, if in addition to treating you considerately, your instructors inherently and genuinely believe that your involvement in the class could enrich the class as well as increase your satisfaction as a student, they might be considered human resource theorists. Your perspectives on the text readings, your insights, and your out-of-class experiences, according to a human resource theorist, would render your involvement in the class more enjoyable to you AND improve the quality of the course.

In essence, a human resource theorist believes that management must attempt to communicate its respect for the potential contributions of employees and behave as if it believes what it has communicated.

It might seem as if the differences between human relations theory and human resources are only profound for those inclined to practice human relations superficially. Miles essentially makes this point in a footnote to his article.[41] Those inclined to accept the foundational principles of human relations theory would not need a new theory to know that human relations practices require involvement and not just establishing superficial relationships as a ruse to gain compliance. Kreps comments that "human resources theories developed in response to the cosmetic application of human

"... Routine work, that best of all anodynes which the twentieth century has tried its best to deprive itself of—this is what I most want. I would not trade the daily trip it gives me for all the mind expanders and mind deadeners the young are hooked on."

—**WALLACE STEGNER** in the novel, *Angle of Repose*

relations theory." One could argue that human resources theory does not contradict human relations theory but rather complements the theory by acknowledging the potential contributions of employers and encouraging management to utilize and respect that resource.[42]

Rensis Likert, Participative Management, and the Role of Communication

Rensis Likert has been identified as a human resource theorist. Likert wrote two books in the 1960s that were and still are very influential. Their titles reflect his belief that organizations needed to change their conception of employees as cogs in a machine. The books were called *New Patterns of Management and The Human Organization*.[43]

In *The Human Organization*, Likert describes four types of management systems, which he calls Systems 1, 2, 3, and 4. As indicated in Table 2.2, Likert described System 1 as a tyrannical nonparticipatory oligarchy. By contrast, System 4 reflects the human resource tenets of participation and involvement. It is, obviously, System 4 that Likert considers the most effective for management. A review of Table 2.2 and the description of System 4 reveals several communication implications of this human resources approach.

- Upward and horizontal communication, as well as downward communication, is important for organizations. An organization must develop a system of networks that will facilitate the flow of information in all directions.
- Employees should not simply be informed of organizational goals; they should actively and meaningfully participate in the discussions that determine these goals.
- Performance evaluations should involve lower as well as upper levels of management.
- The organizational climate should be characterized by mutual trust and respect. This environment allows employees to feel comfortable expressing their opinions and is the antithesis of the "don't think, we'll do the thinking" notions of classical theory.

Interpersonal communication is important because it provides the foundation for trusting interpersonal relationships that are vital for organizational success.[44]

Table 2.2 Table of Organizational and Performance Characteristics of Different Management Systems

Organizational variable	System 1	System 2	System 3	System 4
1. Leadership processes used Extent to which superiors have confidence and trust in *subordinates*	Have no confidence and trust in subordinates	Have condescending confidence and trust, such as master has to servant	Substantial but not complete confidence and trust; still wishes to keep control of decisions	Complete confidence and trust in all matters
Extent to which superiors behave so that subordinates feel free to discuss important things about their jobs with their immediate superior	Subordinates do not feel at all free to discuss things about the job with their superior	Subordinates do not feel very free to discuss things about the job with their superior	Subordinates feel rather free to discuss things about the job with their superior	Subordinates feel completely free to discuss things about the job with their superior

Table 2.2 *continued*

Organizational variable	System 1	System 2	System 3	System 4
Extent to which immediate superior in solving job problems generally tries to get subordinates' ideas and opinions and make constructive use of them	Seldom gets ideas and opinions of subordinates in solving job problems	Sometimes gets ideas and opinions of subordinates in solving job problems	Usually gets ideas and opinions and usually tries to make constructive use of them	Always gets ideas and opinions and always tries to make constructive use of them

```
|—+—+—+—|—+—+—+—|—+—+—+—|—+—+—+—|
```

Organizational variable	System 1	System 2	System 3	System 4
2. Character of motivational forces Manner in which motives are used	Fear, threats, punishment, and occasional rewards	Rewards and some actual or potential punishment	Rewards, occasional punishment, and some involvement	Economic rewards based on compensation system developed through participation; group participation and involvement in setting goals, improving methods, appraising progress toward goals, etc.

```
|—+—+—+—|—+—+—+—|—+—+—+—|—+—+—+—|
```

Organizational variable	System 1	System 2	System 3	System 4
Amount of responsibility felt by each member of organization for achieving organization's goals	High levels of management feel responsibility; lower levels feel less; rank and file feel little and often welcome opportunity to behave in ways to defeat organization's goals	Managerial personnel usually feel responsibility; rank and file usually feel relatively little responsibility for achieving organization's goals	Substantial proportion of personnel, especially at high levels, feel responsibility and generally behave in ways to achieve the organization's goals	Personnel at all levels feel real responsibility for organization's goals and behave in ways to implement them

```
|—+—+—+—|—+—+—+—|—+—+—+—|—+—+—+—|
```

Organizational variable	System 1	System 2	System 3	System 4
3. Character of communication process Amount of interaction and communication aimed at achieving organization's objectives	Very little	Little	Quite a bit	Much with both individuals and groups

```
|—+—+—+—|—+—+—+—|—+—+—+—|—+—+—+—|
```

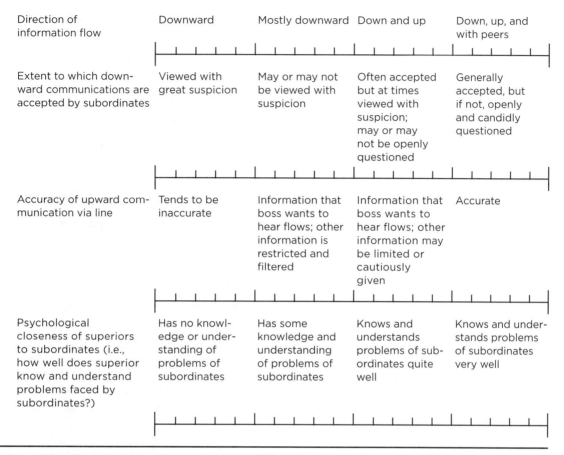

Direction of information flow	Downward	Mostly downward	Down and up	Down, up, and with peers
Extent to which downward communications are accepted by subordinates	Viewed with great suspicion	May or may not be viewed with suspicion	Often accepted but at times viewed with suspicion; may or may not be openly questioned	Generally accepted, but if not, openly and candidly questioned
Accuracy of upward communication via line	Tends to be inaccurate	Information that boss wants to hear flows; other information is restricted and filtered	Information that boss wants to hear flows; other information may be limited or cautiously given	Accurate
Psychological closeness of superiors to subordinates (i.e., how well does superior know and understand problems faced by subordinates?)	Has no knowledge or understanding of problems of subordinates	Has some knowledge and understanding of problems of subordinates	Knows and understands problems of subordinates quite well	Knows and understands problems of subordinates very well

Source: Likert, Rensis, *The Human Organization*, McGraw-Hill, 1967, pp. 4–6.

Theory X and Theory Y

A good way to contrast the classical and human relations/resources theory of management is by looking at Douglas McGregor's Theory X and Theory Y. McGregor, in *The Human Side of the Enterprise*, suggested that there were essentially two ways managers looked at employees. He called these discrete perspectives Theory X and Theory Y.[45]

Theory X tenets were similar to classical theory principles. Specifically, a Theory X manager would assume that employees did not want to work and only sought employment for the financial benefits that work provided. Given a choice between work and "play," an employee would quickly and eagerly choose to avoid work. A Theory X manager would assume that employees would certainly not naturally seek out responsibility. If you supported Theory X you would think that:

- Students who were not compelled to attend class would stay away.
- Construction workers who were not supervised would be less than diligent regarding meeting code specifications for safety.

- Office workers who were not threatened with financial punishment for coming in late would regularly be tardy.
- Salespeople who were not on commission would sell less aggressively and successfully than those who were on commission.

Advocates of Theory Y held beliefs similar to the human relations and human resource theorists. Specifically, a Theory Y theorist would argue that under the right circumstances work could be enjoyable and even desirable. Proponents of Theory Y assume that employees naturally seek out work and are motivated not only by money, but by recognition and job satisfaction. (See Table 2.3 for McGregor's Theory X and Theory Y.) If you supported Theory Y you would believe that:

- If a class was interesting and challenging, students would come to class even if they were not required to do so.
- Unsupervised construction workers would still be diligent because people take pride in doing work well.
- Office workers would be punctual regardless of penalties because they would want to be perceived as responsible and professional.
- Salespeople will work diligently regardless of whether they would be paid per sale because selling is what they do and they would want to excel at their work for personal fulfillment.

In order to further illustrate the distinctions between Theory X and Theory Y, assume that you had an office job that required you to answer the phones for a particular department. Assume further that the phones rang infrequently and that you had little or nothing to do.

An advocate for Theory X would think that you would be delighted with this job. You would go home and tell your friends, "What a deal! I sit in this office and I don't have to do anything and I get paid for that, can you believe it?"

An advocate for Theory Y would think that you would be miserable. You'd go home and tell your friends, "I'm going crazy at work. There's absolutely nothing to do. I ask my boss what to do and she says that I just have to answer the phone. But the phone doesn't ring. I'm going to look for another job."

Table 2.3 Douglas McGregor: Theory X and Theory Y

Theory X Assumptions	Theory Y Assumptions
1. People dislike work and avoid work when possible.	1. Under the right conditions people will view work as natural as play.
2. Workers are not ambitious and prefer direction.	2. Workers are ambitious and prefer self-direction.
3. Workers do not seek responsibility and are not concerned with overall organizational needs.	3. Workers seek responsibility and feel rewarded through their achievements.
4. Workers must be directed and threatened with punishment to achieve organizational productivity.	4. Workers are self-motivated and require little direct supervision.
	5. Workers are creative and capable of organizational creativity.

ETHICAL PROBE

Manipulative Human Relations?

Raymond Miles contrasted human relations theory with human resources theory by suggesting that the former was superficial and manipulative. Human resources theory and theorists assumed that employees desired to be, and could be, valuable resources for the organization.

Is there anything unethical about human relations theory as Miles portrayed it? That is, is there anything unethical about being kind to employees and pretending to be respectful of them so that you will be able to gain their compliance?

Assume you manage a group of five salespersons in a retail clothing store. Should you praise the employees, solicit their input on how to spur sales, and ask them to call you "Andy" even if you would prefer not to have them call you by your first name and have absolutely no sense that they could or will have any valuable ideas that could be implemented?

A proponent of Theory Y would think that while you were at work waiting for the phone to ring, you would look around the office for something to do—perhaps clean up the bulletin board or arrange materials in the supplies cabinet. A proponent of Theory X would think that you'd be unlikely to seek other tasks and would be content to count your lucky stars.

Which theory do you think is correct?

Maslow, Herzberg, and Woodward

Three researchers who worked in the 1940s, 1950s, and 1960s provided theories that support the principles of Theory Y and the human resource theorists. Abraham Maslow's work on the hierarchy of needs, Frederick Herzberg's identification of motivation-hygiene theory, and Joan Woodward's contingency theory are all foundational to understanding human resources theory and the value of communication in organizational contexts.

Maslow's Hierarchy of Needs

Abraham Maslow posited that people were motivated by five progressive layers of needs. These needs were sequential, i.e., once one layer was satisfied, the next became a motivating factor. The examination of this hierarchy suggests that managing using classical principles assuming Theory X tenets would be unlikely to yield a motivated workforce. Moreover, it will become clear to the reader that effective communication in the organization is essential to meet the upper-level needs in the hierarchy.

The first-level need Maslow identified was *physiological*. People were motivated to stay warm, well fed, and dry. Employees' first-level needs would be met if they were paid sufficiently to feed their families, had a comfortable place to work, and could purchase clothing for themselves and their families. The second level in Maslow's hierarchy was *safety*. For example, employees had to work with sufficient light to avoid injury, and they might require protective gear to reduce the chances of industrial accidents. These physiological and safety needs *are* consistent with classical theorists' perspectives. However, the next three levels in the hierarchy suggest that worker needs transcend physiological and safety ones.

Maslow argued that the third, fourth, and fifth layers related, respectively, to *affiliation, esteem,* and *self-actualization*. Each of these is consistent with human resources perspectives.

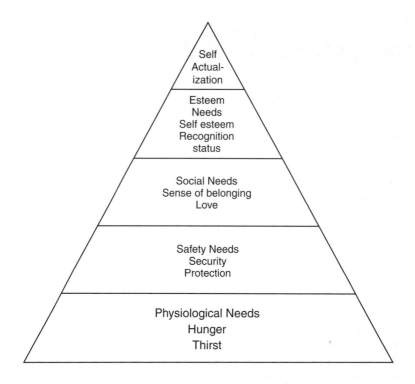

Figure 2.2 Abraham Maslow's Hierarchy of Needs

By *affiliation*, Maslow meant that employees would enjoy and could be motivated by social networks and the connections made with colleagues. *Affiliation* needs suggest that people have a desire to feel part of a unit. It is interesting to note that professional athletes in both football and baseball cited the importance of affiliation needs when they returned to work after they had been away from teammates as a result of labor-related strikes. Players like Carl Yastrzemski in baseball and Jim McMahon in football commented that what they missed most while they were away was the camaraderie of the clubhouse and interactions with the other players. You may have found in high school and even in college that when you returned to school after holiday breaks, you looked forward to seeing your classmates again even if you were not particularly yearning to address the academic challenges. Sometimes people will look forward to coming to work because of their relationships and communicative interactions with others at the job.

Level four in the hierarchy, *esteem*, refers to the desire people have to be respected and have their work acknowledged. In the absence of a warm place to work, safety requirements, and affiliation, esteem may not be especially significant. However, once the prior levels are met, esteem is important. The slang word "dissed" has crept into the lexicon over the last twenty years as colloquial shorthand for being disrespected. People have become enraged when they have felt so dissed by alleged friends, family members, rivals, and employers. If esteem was not a need, there would be no explanation for the bruising that occurs when individuals do not feel appropriately recognized and respected. Maslow suggested that people needed this respect and that without it they would be bereft of essential nourishment. Malnourished, they would indeed feel disrespected, and related behaviors would reflect the absence of the requisite nutrients. The fifth level, *self-actualization*, refers to realizing—actualizing—one's potential. Maslow suggested that once the other needs in the hierarchy were met, we would not be content at work unless we could exercise the creativity and capabilities that make us unique. People are motivated when they can work meaningfully and have an opportunity to excel.

If one agrees with Maslow's hierarchy, it becomes easy to see why so many people leave their jobs *less often* for Theory X–related reasons and *more often* for Theory Y–related reasons. That is, people leave their jobs because they don't feel connected—because of a lack of both communication of recognition and opportunities to excel. This hierarchical perspective is consistent with another relevant theory, called motivation-hygiene theory, attributed to Frederick Herzberg.

Herzberg's Motivation-Hygiene Theory

Frederick Herzberg's work is similar to Maslow's in that it suggests that employees have a tiered set of needs. His theory is a derivative of research he conducted by interviewing employees in the late 1950s. Herzberg wanted to discover what made people motivated to work and conducted what are called critical incident interviews. (These types of interviews, as we will see in Chapter 11, were used as part of the communication audit tool developed by the International Communication Association in the early 1970s.) Critical incident interviews essentially ask subjects to comment about specific situations that were particularly good or bad. In Herzberg's research about motivation, he asked employees to respond to the following: "Think of a time when you felt exceptionally good or exceptionally bad about your job, either your present job or any other job you have had. This can be either the long range or the short range kind of situation, as I have just described it. Tell me what happened."[46] On the basis of the responses Herzberg attempted to detect what motivates employees. It was Herzberg who wrote, rather colorfully, about motivation when he described "positive KITA" approaches.

> I have a year-old Schnauzer. When it was a small puppy and I wanted it to move, I kicked it in the rear and it moved. Now that I have finished its obedience training, I hold up a dog biscuit when I want the Schnauzer to move. . . . In this instance all I did was apply KITA frontally; I exerted a pull instead of a push. When industry wishes to use such positive KITAs, it has available an incredible number and variety of dog biscuits (jelly beans for humans) to wave in front of the employee to get him [sic] to jump.

This metaphor is uncomfortable because the association of dog with employee is what critical theorists, appropriately, attempt to address. Yet there is a salient point central to his study. He assumed that there are "an incredible number and variety" of motivators. It was his objective to discover what these motivators might be.

He concluded in fact that there were two tiers. The first factors were primary and he called them hygiene factors. Appropriate salary and benefits, understandable organizational policies, and efficient technical supervision were all in the category of hygiene needs in Herzberg's scheme. The hygiene metaphor suggests that this first tier is essential for health. On the basis of his research, Herzberg claimed that there was a second tier. Employees desire responsibility, challenging work, an opportunity to advance, a chance to achieve, and recognition for distinctive performance. These he called the motivation needs. Herzberg did *not* believe that satisfying the hygiene needs was inherently motivating. However, he felt that in the absence of these, employees could be demotivated. In the presence of met hygiene needs *and* second-tier motivational needs, employees could be motivated. Since the second tier relates to human resources principles, a conclusion from Herzberg's theory is that assumptions about motivation based solely on Theory X principles are incomplete.

You can probably relate to this theory by considering a job where your hygiene needs were met but where you were not particularly motivated. You were paid, it was not uncomfortable to be there, your supervisor efficiently managed and communicated organizational policies, but you were not especially enthusiastic about going to work. In the absence of the hygiene factors you would have been very dissatisfied, but in the presence of them you may have plodded along doing what you needed to do. However, add to the mix the possibility that you (a) were given a genuine chance to assume responsibility, (b) were told when you had done well and when you needed to improve, and (c) had been given a chance to advance within the company—you were likely to have been motivated to excel at work.

For both Maslow and Herzberg, classical theory principles alone would not get the schnauzer to move very much.

Contingency Theorists

Many theorists have worked on what have been called contingency theories. Joan Woodward is regularly identified as a key figure in the development of these theories. As opposed to scientific management, which argues that there is one best way to do a job, contingency theory suggests that given a host of organizational and personal variables, there could be several good ways to do a job. The best way to do anything may be contingent on relationships, rules that have developed formally and informally in the organization, personality styles, and varying needs of employees. In other words, Theory X and scientific management had failed because they were too parochially conceived and did not factor in other variables—other contingencies.

Schmidt, in the example used by Taylor, might be motivated by the $1.85 an hour he would receive for moving pig iron, but Jones might be motivated by the recognition that she was singled out for the task, or because of a respect that had developed between Jones and the manager, or because of a sense of identification with the organization. A Schmidt in one organization might be motivated by Taylor's ploy, but place Schmidt in another organization with different factors affecting the process, and Schmidt might not be motivated. Select someone other than Schmidt and the variables might change.

Essentially, contingency theorists argued that the notion of one best way is inconsistent with human realities. To take a Theory X perspective and assume that all people were lazy and motivated by money was to ignore the distinct permutations of variables that affect unique individuals and relationships. These contingencies reflected that a one-size-fits-all approach to organizational communication would be unlikely to be successful.

Concerns with Theory Y

As mentioned previously, the human relations theorists were disparaged. Similarly, the human resources theorists were criticized for being too prescriptive and myopic in their depictions of the average employee.[47] Rensis Likert's *The Human Organization*, published nearly forty years ago, identified the ideal management style, but as Miller has written, "an examination of the vast majority of present day organizations reveals the prevalence of classical management thought."[48] Let's consider some of the reasons why human relations, human resources, and Theory Y approaches might not work. There are three related reasons, one of which is essential to understand for persons studying organizational communication.

One problem with human relations and human resources theories is that they are too shortsighted to be sound. They make an assumption about workers that could not be universally true. The assumption that people under the right circumstances enjoy work as much as play might be true for the majority of us, but there are still many individuals who are delighted or would be delighted by a life of absolute leisure. How difficult would it be for you to think of a few people who would be thrilled to get an easy job where they were paid for very little effort? You probably thought of one such person instantly. Therefore, to build a theory on the notion of the inherent desire of people to work—as much as they like to play—is to have a plank in the foundation that is not nailed securely. Ironically, such a notion is as flawed as the classical theory that all people respond to financial remuneration as a primary motivator.

A second reason why the human resources theory is flawed is related to the first. It may be true that under the right conditions people will enjoy work as much as play. However, many of us are likely not to be working "under the right conditions." I enjoy what I do. I like to teach, write, and work with students. Yet I certainly have had some jobs—both blue collar and white collar—when I did not look forward to coming to work. I'd guess that most readers have had jobs that have been challenging and exciting and have had others that were either inherently unpleasant or were made unpleasant by some characteristic of the workplace. Therefore, the plank of human relations theory that posits that people can enjoy work as much as play is flawed. Superficially, it may seem true enough, but while

"*Pendleton, as of noon today your services will no longer be required. Meanwhile, keep up the good work.*"

people could be in a career or at a job that they like, they may also be working at jobs that are of no interest to them or have become uninteresting and stressful for them.

Most significantly for students of organizational communication, a principle of human resources theory is that employees are motivated by recognition and acknowledgment. In order for the theory to work, management would need to be effective at communicating recognition. A criticism of human relations and human resources theory is that managers are sloppy and insincere in their "people-oriented" messages of recognition. There may be more managers slapping backs, asking employees to "call me Pat," and effusively saying thank you, but if the messages are not perceived as credible by employees, if the employees consider the acknowledgment spurious, as if it is some grand ruse for motivation, then the foundation upon which human relations theory was built will disintegrate.

Consider some likely factors that could interfere with the successful communication of recognition.

Credibility

If all employees were to receive the same message of recognition, it is likely to assume that the message would lose credibility. It would violate principles of Maslow's, Herzberg's, and Woodward's theories. A note posted on a Web site that thanks all employees for their hard work will be meaningless if, when you receive it, you think that an employee who is considered a slacker has been sent the same congratulatory message. For example, one general manager signed all of her written notes to the staff with her name circumscribed by a red heart. After a while, the employees—instead of finding these messages touching—considered them absurd and ridiculed the director behind her back.

Skill Level

Some people have difficulty orally expressing praise and criticism. They may have problems maintaining eye contact, finding the right words to match their ideas, or using appropriate inflection when relaying information.

Choice of Channel

If an employer posts a bulletin thanking employees or sends out an e-mail, it may have less impact than a visit to that staff member's office and a face-to-face conversation. Selecting an inappropriate channel for communicating can affect the value of the message. (Chapter 5 deals in detail with the subject of selecting appropriate media for communicating.)

Applying the Principles—Test Yourself

The Congratulatory Memorandum

The woman who received this mailing was being notified that she had earned 30 minutes (annual) extra vacation time on the basis of her seven years of service and that she had already used 15 minutes. The recipient was incensed. She spent much of the day—far more than her annual allocation—deriding the source of the message.

TO: Jean Davidson, Theatre Arts

FROM: Roberta Gimpel, Account Clerk Personnel/ Affirmative Action Office

Employees who have completed their seventh year of service earn 20 days vacation each year until eligible to earn bonus days again. Administrative Unit is eligible again for a bonus after completion of their 15th year; Operational, Security, PEF and Institutional Units are again eligible for a bonus upon completion of their 20th year of service.

For the Administrative Unit, this equates to 5:45 hours, each payperiod with an additional 15 minutes twice a year. For the other units, this equates to 6 hours each payperiod with an additional hour four times a year. This extra time being added has become confusing in keeping your own leave accruals on the time sheets. To simplify matters, the Personnel/Affirmative

Action Office is going to add this extra time once a year for all eligible, *always on the day before your anniversary date.* (Ex., if your anniversary is on 5/2 each year, and you are entitled to 4 extra hours each year, add that four hours on your leave actual summary on 5/1 each year. If you earn 30 min. a year, add it the day before your anniversary in the same manner.)

This procedure will become effective 5/8/80. If you have already received part of those extra minutes or hours, the balance will be added on the day before your anniversary and no extra time will be added until then.

If you have any questions, please call me at 3434.

Your anniversary date is 10/19/70.
Your date to add extra vacation is 10/18.
The extra vacation you should add each
    year is 30 minutes.
You have already earned 15 minutes this
    year.

Assume you were the administrator who was responsible for distributing the notice. Assume also that it was company policy that such notices were to be distributed. Would you feel as if it was your obligation to send this information out in this manner? What might you have done differently?

In brief, the human relations theory, human resources theory, and Theory Y have meaningful components. It is, certainly, an uplifting set of theories. People *are* important and not inanimate equipment. To be successful, management has to understand that many individuals desire to do something meaningful with their hours at work.

It is easy to prescribe this, but a challenge to respond to the prescription. Two-day workshops in communication or human relations training will not guarantee competent or sensitive communicators. Managers coached to follow human relations principles may still harbor Theory X notions of the world and be unable or unwilling to credibly communicate recognition and support to employees. In a *Harvard Business Review* article entitled, "Asinine Attitudes towards Motivation," Levinson discusses what he calls a "jackass fallacy."[49] The "jackass fallacy" is the erroneous notion held by

PRACTITIONER PERSPECTIVE

Duane Vild: Complex Warden for the State of Arizona Department of Corrections; Bureau Administrator, Department of Corrections

In the Arizona State System, a Complex Warden is the chief administrative officer of a cluster of three to five prisons that are all located in the same region of the state. Mr. Vild served as Complex Warden in Douglas, Arizona, and also in Tucson, Arizona. These were both five-prison Complexes. At each location, Mr. Vild supervised 100–200 Complex staff employees, 500–900 Unit employees (Unit refers to one of the prisons in the Complex), and some 4,000 inmates. After his work as a Complex Warden, Mr. Vild became a Bureau Administrator for the Arizona Department of Corrections. In that role he was responsible for training persons who would work in Complex prisons.

As you read through this section please consider the following questions.

- What do you think about Vild's 33-33-33 rule?
- Is the bolded section consistent with your experience?
- If you were Vild, what would you consider your biggest challenge?
- Does critical theory apply to an organization like Vild's?

Communication wasn't simply *central* to what I did. It was imperative. It could make me or break me as warden. You want to talk about communicating with difficult people? I had to communicate with difficult people and I'm not referring primarily to the inmates who, relatively speaking, were not a problem in terms of communication.

The key to success as a communicator in my situation is being sensitive to your audiences, paying attention to them, knowing your audiences—*and knowing yourself*. Don't forget that last part. You have to know yourself and develop—if you don't have it—some humility.

When I first became warden I thought that the best way to communicate was to write memos. I wrote fifty memos a day. I thought I could write well and this way I would get my message across. I thought because of who I was and how well I could express myself I could communicate. But I needed to listen more, understand my audiences, and become a little more humble. We live in a fast-food society. I call it a Jack in the Box society. People need information presented concisely and quickly that is germane to their needs. **Sometimes managers get too impressed with themselves. Their egos get in the way and they think that the message they're relaying has clout and meaning because of how well they speak or write, and how much wisdom or power they have. Your writing skills and intelligence means little unless you know the people whom you're writing to and can get a concise understandable message to them.** In a world as diverse as a prison in terms of race, gender, educational background, and power, administrators must learn and listen, and not let their egos get in the way.

Prisons foster poor communication. There is a great deal of pressure on wardens to communicate effectively to all of the constituents: the media, your supervisors, your staff, and the inmates. You have a great many people who are entrenched in their positions or who want to retain power and their fiefdoms. You have people who do things that are inappropriate—and I'm not talking about inmates here—yet your staffers may stonewall you when you try to address a situation. If you want to get a

PRACTITIONER PERSPECTIVE *continued*

message through to those who are stonewalling you, you better not rely on your writing skills, but rely on your ability to discover what makes these people behave the way they do. And again, take a look at why you behave the way you do.

When I worked as the Bureau Administrator a supervisor came to me and said, "Vild, we have a problem with race and communication. I want you to run a half-day workshop and educate these people." Imagine that? Run a half-day workshop and deal with issues of race. Training regarding intercultural communication is doable, and we worked on a program for our staff, but it takes more than a half a day to conduct such training.

I think there's a 33-33-33 rule when it comes to coaching people about communicating

interculturally. One third of the people are going to be unwilling to acknowledge that there is a problem because they're stuck on their cultural orientation as being superior. One third of the population doesn't need the training because they communicate cross-culturally without the differences creating rifts, and one third of the people have problems but can be transformed.

The nature of my work at the complexes really tested my ability to communicate. Communication training should be part of any manager's background. People should be coached when they come into a managerial position and then annually discuss issues related to communication. You can be brilliant, personable, knowledgeable, but if you can't communicate to your internal audiences you can't function.

Theory X managers that employees are essentially stubborn fools or "jackasses." Levinson correctly contends, years after Miles made a similar claim, that if management views employees as jackasses, human resource type overtures will inevitably fail. He argues that employees will "automatically see management's messages as manipulative and they will resist them, no matter how clear the type or how pretty the pictures."[50] In a Winter 2002 piece in the *Sloan Management Review*, Bartlett and Ghoshal write that "in many companies, only marginal managerial attention—if that—is focused on the problems of employee capability and motivation. Somewhere between theory and practice, precious human capital is being misused, wasted, or lost."[51]

Managers and employers need to identify the skill sets necessary for effective communication, establish a culture that is conducive to employing these skill sets, create networks that facilitate the transmission of messages that Herzberg and Maslow identify as motivators, and identify abuses of power that demoralize the employee workforce.

The next chapter discusses three theories that examine the relationship of communication to networks, culture, power, and the development of communication skill.

SUMMARY: A TOOLBOX

• Theories need not be abstract and valueless. Good theories must actually be practical.
• Classical theories suggest that downward communication of information about tasks and procedures is essential.
• The Hawthorne Studies claimed to demonstrate that
    • communicating information about performance was important
    • upward networks were desired by employees
    • informal networks were inevitable

- The successful implementation of human relations and human resource approaches requires the credible communication of information about job performance and recognition.
- The work of Abraham Maslow, Frederick Herzberg, and Joan Woodward supports the idea that individuals may have needs that transcend monetary and physical considerations, and therefore organizations need to create an environment where these needs can be met.

REVIEW AND DISCUSSION QUESTIONS

1. Describe classical, human relations, and human resources theory.
2. What are the key distinctions between Theory X and Theory Y?
3. What are the organizational communication implications of the Hawthorne Studies?
4. Why would a classical theorist consider communicating recognition unimportant?
5. Have the managers where you have worked taken a Theory X or Theory Y orientation?
6. If you were a manager, would you be likely to follow classical or human relations principles? Why?

GROUP/ROLE-PLAY

- In a group of four to six, review the issues surrounding the Patricia Daniels case that begins this chapter. Attempt to gain consensus regarding the questions at the end of the chapter.
- For the role-play:
  - One member of the group assumes the role of Patricia Daniels.
  - Another assumes the role of the person who desired the job and did not get it.
  - The rest of the group assumes the role of the other members of Daniels's department.
- Role-play an initial meeting between Daniels and her team.

SELF-INVENTORY

Below are several statements. Determine if you agree or disagree with each one. Then explain why you agree or disagree.

1. Some organizations require Theory X and would be inefficient with Theory Y.
2. The third part of the Hawthorne Studies was an aberration. If the same study was conducted today, the results would be antithetical.
3. Systematic soldiering is a phenomenon that will never cease to exist, no matter how educated and sophisticated the workforce.
4. Social networks like Facebook render classical theories obsolete. Who cares about chain of command when you can tweet anyone you would like?
5. The distinction between human resources theory and human relations theory, as even Miles suggested, is simply a matter of implementation—not theoretical tenets.
6. Classical theorists are really not concerned with efficiency. They simply want to maintain power.
7. By behaving as they do, human resources theorists establish a culture that values comfort over productivity.

Chapter **3**

Theoretical Foundations: Systems, Culture, and Power

Chapter in a Nutshell

In Chapter 2 we looked at classical, human relations, and human resources theory and the applications to organizational communication. In this chapter we continue to examine theoretical foundations. Contemporary theorists consider organizations to be comprised of interdependent subsystems, which require effective communication in order for the organization as a whole to function efficiently. In the last thirty years scholars also have explored the relationship of communication to organizational culture and power. Are all departments in an organization inherently interdependent? Does internal and external communication seed an organization's culture? Can communication be used within an organization to create unhealthy power relationships that, inevitably, undermine the success of the organization? This chapter describes theories that are foundational to the examination of these questions.

When you have completed this chapter, you should be able to:

• Explain systems theory.
• Define key terms in the language of systems theory.
• Explain cultural theory.
• Explain the differences between functionalists and interpretivists.
• Describe the merit of using critical theory to study communication in organizations.
• Define key terms used by critical theorists.
• Apply the theories to analyze cases in organizational communication.

CASE 3.1

Sales Department, Service Department, and Customers

Background

The sales department of a small software company was a group that prided itself on being able to party all night and still close a deal at 8 A.M. the next day. This play hard but work hard attitude was fostered by the management of the department, who had never missed a quarter of achieving the quota and would do virtually anything to close a deal before the deadline of a quarter or fiscal year.

Recently, during the span of two years, the company was acquired twice. The 200-person software company that had enjoyed beers on Friday afternoons and concerts by the company band was quickly enveloped in a tornado of cultural changes and customs that seemed entirely too rigid and "corporate." The sales department suddenly realized that the days of special treatment for being the company breadwinners were behind them. The salespeople were now part of a national sales force, selling only a fraction of the products under the umbrella of a new parent company. Integration into the larger company was also accompanied by countless new political roadblocks that needed attention during each six- to nine-month sales cycle. One of the most frustrating new challenges for the salespeople was communicating with the new corporate services department.

Service Department Responsibilities

The new corporate services department implemented and properly configured the software for each new customer. As soon as a sale was complete, it was services' responsibility to step in and ensure that the product met each customer's exact specifications. It was not unusual for product configuration and customer training to last up to a year.

The services department was understaffed and overworked. Therefore, the services department felt that they had the authority to step in and stop or, more likely, postpone a sale because of a potentially complicated postsale implementation process. For a group of salespeople who were compensated based on the quantity and dollar value of their sales, this type of interference was unacceptable. As the services department became more stubborn, the sales force became more "creative" and resisted communicating with services in the sales process.

Results

The result of this was somewhat disastrous for customers. For the sake of closing deals, commitments were made to customers by the sales force, guaranteeing short and unobtrusive service implementation periods. When contracts were signed, the sales department often neglected to inform services. Therefore, services would discover a sale had taken place when an angry customer called asking why they had not received a phone call from services since signing their contract weeks prior.

This type of chaos was possible because the integration into the new parent company had been so haphazard that no formal governance had yet been established. The new parent had been communicating only through the HR department because they were so busy deciding how to run the division and determining which departments to eliminate. This resulted in a local management team that felt unsure of its tenure, resentful of this fact, and thus determined to reap as much in sales commissions and quota credit as possible before looking for new jobs.

- How might you have connected these two units of this organization?
- Would you say the sales group has a distinctive culture? If so, how would you describe that culture? Is the culture a factor that affects its communication? Will the culture change because of the communication or lack of communication under the new leadership?
- Have any of the units described in the case abused their power by how they communicated with other units?

Systems Theory

"Business and other human endeavors are also systems. They are bound by invisible fabrics of interrelated actions, which often take years to fully play out their effects on each other."[1]

According to systems theorists, an organization is a composite of interdependent units that must work cooperatively in order to effectively survive. The theory holds that organizations should be viewed as *open* systems. This means that an organization cannot live nor thrive without interacting with both its *internal* and its *external* environment.

Your university is an example of such an open system. The various units—the colleges, student affairs staff, maintenance and grounds, and senior administration—are all interdependent. What happens in one unit, either directly or indirectly, affects what happens in another. These interdependent units must communicate with each other in order for the organization to be efficient and thrive. In addition, in order for your university to succeed, it must interact effectively with external audiences: for example, high schools where prospective students are considering higher education; government agencies that may provide financial resources for the school; and academic associations, which may publish journals that keep faculty current and active in their areas of specialty.

Systems theory does not disregard principles of classical or human resources theory. In fact, it embraces components of each. In systems theory "questions of job duty, chain of command, span of control, and decision making [classical principles] are *equal* in importance to questions of attitude, morale, behavior, role and personality [human resources concerns]."[2] The conception of the organization as an entity that must link internal departments and be linked to its environment is what makes systems theory distinctive.

The relationship between systems theory and organizational communication is fairly obvious; if you believe in systems theory, interdepartmental communication becomes a prerequisite for survival. Let's examine a number of specific terms and concepts relevant to communication that are employed by systems researchers.

Open and Closed Systems

Organizational systems theory borrows heavily from the work of biologist Ludwig von Bertalanffy. Bertalanffy described an organism as an "open system . . . in which material continually enters from and leaves onto the outside environment." Likewise, an organization can be seen as an "open system" requiring material from the outside environment in order to survive. A closed organizational system—like an organism separated from the outside environment—would eventually be unable to sustain itself. Home Depot could not survive, for example, unless it viewed itself as an open system requiring resources from consumers, merchandise from vendors, equipment from suppliers, physical space from realtors, feedback from customers and competitors, and a host of other "materials" from outside its environment. If Home Depot ignored the reactions of customers, the trends in the economy that affected purchasing, the successes of competitors—it could not thrive in the vacuum it had created.

Hierarchical Ordering

Any organization can be considered a system that functions within a suprasystem and is dependent on the quality of its subsystems. This usage of the word system with all of its prefixes can understandably be confusing, but the following example may clarify the point. Let's assume you live in Smithville and you work in the Smithville high school. The high school includes English, math, language, science, physical education, and history departments. We can refer to the Smithville high school as a system. The high school is dependent on the quality of interaction within and between

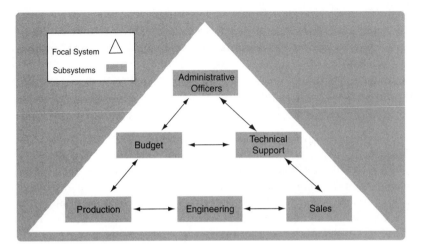

Figure 3.1   Hierarchical Ordering in Systems Theory

each of the subsystems that are the various departments. Let's assume that Smithville high school is one of ten schools in your community. If the focal system (the system you are focusing on) is the high school, then the suprasystem includes the central school system, which is composed of the administrative offices and the other schools in the district. The subsystems are the various departments within the high school. If the focal system is the physical education department, then the subsystems may be intramurals, team sports, adult recreation, facility scheduling and maintenance, and curricular development. If the focal system is team sports, then the subsystems would be the various teams the high school supports. Simply, the principle of hierarchical ordering highlights the interdependent nature of organizations and the importance of communication between and among the various units for the effective functioning of an organization. Each subsystem, like the focal system, must also be conceptualized as open as opposed to closed.

Relevant Environment

The relevant environment is that part of the external environment that is relevant to the system. One might make an argument that there is very little in our universe that is not relevant to a system's environment. However, some factors are more relevant than others. If Smithville high school is the focal system, the relevant environment involves the economic conditions that affect families moving to and from the community Smithfield serves, the quality and philosophy of the state education department, the birth rate, innovative educational technology, the idiosyncratic nature of politics in the central administrative offices, and the quality and number of teacher training institutions in the state. Even the world political arena can be part of Smithfield's relevant environment. A tragedy like the death of a recently graduated senior who was fighting in Iraq can create emotional trauma affecting the numbers of students in need of therapeutic counseling.

Permeability; Input/Output, and Throughput

In order for a system to operate efficiently, the boundaries of each system should be permeable, that is, information must be able to get from one subsystem to another and from the relevant environment to the focal system. The word permeable typically refers to a substance that can be penetrated.

Metaphorically, the boundaries of subsystems must be permeable to permit information to be transmitted. If unit leaders genuinely welcome news from related units and establish channels that allow receipt of information from these units, they are taking a step toward creating permeable boundaries. If leaders deliberately shut themselves off from other units, then the boundaries are, almost literally, not permeable. Systems theorists refer to the information that comes into the system as input. Information that is exported beyond the system is the output. The processing of information within the system is called the throughput.

Entropy and Negative Entropy

A closed system will eventually become disabled because of the disorder that results from not interacting with its relevant environment and its related subsystems. That state of disorder is referred to as entropy. Since systems theorists hold that organizations (as well as organisms) cannot function without permeable boundaries and input, the desired end for a healthy system is the negative entropy that results from interactions with the environment.

Requisite Variety

This principle of requisite variety is essential for systems theorists—as essential as the notion of open systems and permeability. Requisite variety means that a subsystem has to be sufficiently sophisticated internally to address the complexity of the potential inputs from its relative environment. In other words, a diverse and multiple set of inputs cannot be addressed by a very simple approach to dealing with that complexity. A Walmart franchise cannot respond appropriately to its myriad inputs if there is one person named Luke to whom all external information is funneled. If the walls of a subsystem are permeable, as they should be, the absence of requisite variety will preclude efficient communication with the relevant environment. A lone Luke will not have the resources or ability to meaningfully react to the multifaceted information coming into the system.

Homeostasis

An organization must achieve balance by responding to the communicated input that enters the system through its permeable boundaries. This balance—or state of homeostasis—is necessary in order for the organization to survive. For example, let us assume that your college admissions department informs the housing department that it has admitted 500 more students than they presently have room to house on campus. The system which is your university must react to this input by finding a place to house these 500 students. When and if it does so, it will have reached homeostasis, that is, it will have adapted to the information that made it wobble and will have returned to its desired state of balance. If a system does not have permeable boundaries, or the requisite variety for addressing the input that is as complex as the input itself, then achieving homeostasis will be difficult and the organization can continue to teeter unnecessarily and destructively. An example that is often given to explain homeostasis relates to your normal body temperature. If you become ill and your fever soars to 102 degrees, your body must react to the change and battle the bug in order to achieve the normalcy of 98.6 degrees. The system that is your body must be prepared to respond to the information that is indicating that there is a change. If your body cannot react, then you remain ill, out of balance, and not able to function normally. An organization that does not have the ability or inclination to respond to feedback from its relevant environment will remain as ill as you would be if your system did not respond to the feedback that was making you sick.

Equifinality

The principle of equifinality is in direct contrast to the classical theorists' argument that there is one best way to do a job. Equifinality suggests that multiple methods can result in the same outcome. In other words, the final result may be equal despite diverse methods having been used to arrive at the final results. If you run a 102-degree fever, there are likely a number of ways your body can respond to achieve homeostasis. Let's say that your university needs additional funds to meet its operating expenses. The system is out of balance because it has this deficit. It can respond to this deficit by admitting more students, increasing the tuition fees of students, charging a tax on all persons who use the campus gymnasium, asking faculty and staff to take a pay cut, or urging faculty to write grant proposals to obtain external funding. All of these responses to the information that indicates that there is a deficit may result in the same state of homeostasis and illustrate the principle of equifinality.

Learning Organizations

Peter Senge wrote, in *The Fifth Discipline*, of something he called learning organizations. He described a learning organization as one that was "continually expanding its capacity to create its future."[3]

The idea of a learning organization is consistent with the principles of systems theory because a learning organization does not suffocate by inhaling the air within its own unit, but rather gains knowledge by regularly soliciting and exchanging information from and with its relevant environment. Senge argued that an element necessary for a learning organization was what he called systems thinking. This means essentially that organizations and the individuals who comprise them had to realize that everything is interconnected, indeed, think like a system and think of the organization as systemic. In essence, Senge argues that in order to become a learning organization, the people who comprise the organization have to rethink their natural tendencies to see the organization as comprised of independent units and become more interactive and holistic. The result of becoming a learning organization is a natural orientation toward sharing information, which is conducive to qualitative growth.[4] More about learning organizations appears in Chapter 5 where we discuss knowledge and information management.

Shortly after the September 11, 2001, terrorist attack on New York's World Trade Center, it was discovered that certain divisions of the federal government had information that, if shared with other divisions, might have served to warn the United States of the possibility of attack. Government entities like the FBI, the Department of Defense, the INS, and the Department of the Treasury operate independently. Yet these independent units are inherently interdependent and need to share information. Melissa Bator, in her article, "Failures within the Intelligence Community," discusses problems with communication prior to 9/11. "Unfortunately" she writes, "there was never enough of a coordinated effort within the Intelligence Community to connect information across agencies dealing with counterterrorism."[5]

The office of Homeland Security was developed in part to address this problem. In a Fox News report on September 21, 2001, Fox correspondent Mike Emanuel commented that a goal of the new department was "to bring together a bunch of different government agencies that have a bunch of different information and may not have previously talked to one another about suspected terrorists." This issue of sharing information was discussed on many post-9/11 news reports. Congressman James Gibbons from Nevada made a similar statement.[6]

As we have seen, a systems theorist would argue that every department of an organization needs to be linked with every other one. There is no such thing as an autonomous independent department since the organization's product is a function of the interaction between departments. If we view the federal government as a focal system comprised of subsystems like the Department of Defense and the State Department, then the government is healthiest when relevant information is shared between these units, because the product—in this case the protection of U.S. citizens—is affected by this interdependent interaction. This very real-world example illustrates the practical value of theory and the importance of a systems approach to organizational communication.

Cultural Theory

Sharon Baxter had decided to change jobs. When she arrived for her first day of work at the new firm, she was startled to see that there was a banner strewn over the common area near her new office. The banner read "Welcome Sharon." She was delighted by the banner and even more taken by the reception "breakfast" that was set up apparently in honor of her arrival. As she thanked the colleagues who were gathered in the room, they jokingly thanked her because, they said, "there are usually just bagels out here." They told Sharon that it was normal to welcome new employees this way and that it was the vision of the CEO that the company be a friendly environment where "if you are not having fun, you are not working here" was the motto. In a whirlwind of conversation she was told that: (a) all employees were on a first name basis, (b) on Fridays they regularly wind down at a local bar, and (c) there was a company condo in Florida that was accessible to all who had worked for the company for at least two years.

This welcome and her new surroundings provided quite a contrast to her past job. There, interpersonal interaction was minimal and typically restricted to conversation that was required to complete a task. Her colleagues, even the ones she worked with frequently, called her Ms. Baxter and expected to be similarly addressed. There were no welcoming breakfasts or after-work happy hours. The motto that oozed out of her former employer was "be serious, be professional." Whereas the decor at the new job was contemporary and many people were dressed in jeans, the furnishings at her old job were austere and casual dress was discouraged. She did not know simple details regarding the personal lives of her former colleagues and, she mused now, had rarely had a desire to find out about them.

Things will be different here, she surmised.

- Is Sharon Baxter correct? If so, what "things" will be different?
- Will how she communicates with colleagues be affected by the atmosphere at the new job?
- Will the atmosphere at the new job be affected by how she communicates with her colleagues?

What Is Cultural Theory?

You may have heard the phrase "corporate culture" or "organizational culture" used where you have worked. Cultural theory as applied to organizations refers to the perspective that there is a phenomenon that can be called organizational culture and that this phenomenon is a factor affecting organizational life and success. Edgar Schein, a pioneer researcher in this area, has written that "there is now abundant evidence that corporate culture makes a difference to corporate performance."[7]

This perspective is relevant to organizational communication study because cultural theorists assert that communication is central to the evolution of organizational culture. Consequently, one reason to study organizational communication is to gauge how communication affects and determines this powerful phenomenon labeled organizational culture.

Functionalists and Interpretivists

Some theorists, identified as *functionalists*, consider organizational culture to be a function of communicative messages generated typically by management. These theorists suggest that diverse cultural products will be the result of variable messages that are communicated to members of an organization. Consequently, organizations that seek to engineer a desirable culture could do so by disseminating specific messages designed to create and sustain that culture. Consultants can be hired to explain to management how to engineer a culture by articulating specific messages that will eventually take root in the organization.

Other theorists, identified as *interpretivists*, disagree with this notion. These theorists suggest that what constitutes the organizational culture is the result of all communicative interaction and liken it to a "web."[8] As Pacanowsky and O'Donnell-Trujillo have put it, "the web of culture is the residue of the communication process."[9] Interpretivists assert that reality is based on how organizational women and men construct it, and how they construct it is based on how they communicate. Therefore, the culture is not dictated by managerial communication, it is formed by and emerges from the communications of all members of the organization: "For interpretivists, culture is not merely another variable that the organization has, rather culture is something that the organization is. . . . Interpretivists, more than functionalists, recognize that organizations are coalitions of participants with different aims and priorities, not monolithic, unified, entities."[10] It is the job of researchers to study and interpret these powerful, evolving organizational cultures by studying the communicative interactions of organizational members.[11]

These perspectives are not as disparate as one might think (or as some writers have suggested). Functionalists and interpretivists both agree that communication is central to the development of organizational culture, and both agree that organizational culture can affect organizational success.

Deal and Kennedy; Peters and Waterman

In 1982 Terrence Deal and Allan Kennedy published a book entitled *Corporate Culture: Rites and Rituals of Corporate Life*. The authors write that an organization's culture is a composite of its environment, espoused values, identified heroes, established rites, and customary rituals.[12] In addition, Deal and Kennedy make the point that the organization's culture develops and is perpetuated by what they refer to as the organization's "cultural network." This cultural network is the organization's informal and powerful communication system, which the authors claim is the "carrier" of the corporate values.[13]

There are a number of reasons why Deal and Kennedy's book and the positions contained therein are important for students of organizational communication. The first is that the authors are associated with the development and identification of the phenomenon called organizational culture. The second is that they identify elements of that culture. The third is that they acknowledge the importance of communication as a factor that constitutes and consequently creates the organizational culture.

Deal and Kennedy's work was followed by an extraordinarily best-selling book by Thomas Peters and Robert Waterman entitled *In Search of Excellence: Lessons from America's Best Run Companies*. In the book, Peters and Waterman identified the cultural trademarks of successful companies, including:

- A bias for action
- Close relations to the customer
- Autonomy and entrepreneurship

Applying the Principles—Test Yourself

Sexual Harassment and Whistleblowing

Assume that your new job involves work in the corporate communication department for a struggling local bank in a small community. Your work, in part, involves creating promotional material about the bank to be distributed throughout the community. You also make presentations to various groups about the bank and, on occasion, write speeches for administrators when they are required to deliver presentations.

Assume that after a few months you suspect that a manager—one of your new colleagues—is sexually harassing one of the female employees. Further assume that you approach the woman being harassed and she reluctantly acknowledges that your suspicions are, in fact, the case. However, she requests that you not say anything about the harassment because she intends to leave the organization shortly and does not want to get involved with what she believes would be a drawn-out battle of charges and countercharges.

You feel conflicted. You fear that while this woman might leave, your colleague may well begin to harass the employee who replaces the departed woman. Also, for all you know, this manager may have been harassing others at the bank for years.

On the other hand, one of the recurring messages in the promotional literature you write has to do with the character of the bank and how the bank and its officers are fine community citizens. The company's literature—which you compose—argues that "community integrity"—a phrase you yourself felt proud to coin—is a reason for local citizens to bank with your institution as opposed to going to a huge company with multiple branches where who knows what is permitted.

A huge factor creating internal conflict for you is that the job pays well and it is not easy to get similar positions. You need the steady income.

For several reasons, then, you are torn between keeping quiet and exposing the horrible behavior of a colleague. Eventually you decide to go to your superior and, without identifying the victim, describe the charges. Your superior listens to you and thanks you for your time. Subsequently, you are surprised to discover that no action is taken against the offending manager. Grapevine information, you discover, suggests that senior management is actually aware of the unconscionable behavior of the colleague, yet, apparently, is tolerating it.

The responsible action, you believe, would be to make public the sexual harassment and the fact that top management is ignoring it. To do this, however, would put your job in jeopardy. Even if you were to notify internal and external audiences anonymously, you would be jeopardizing the health of the struggling bank that pays your salary. To complicate matters, because of your specific organizational responsibilities, you have the tools and connections to reach a large number of people with your message.

- Can your decision in this matter affect the culture of your organization?
- How would you describe the culture of this organization?
- Is it your responsibility as a company representative and communicator to protect the organization?
- Is it your responsibility as a company representative to protect the people in the organization who might be victimized?
- How has the communication behavior of administrators affected power relationships in the organization?

- Productivity through people
- Hands-on, value driven
- Stick to the knitting
- Simple form, lean staff
- Simultaneous loose tight properties[14]

As with Deal and Kennedy, the authors argue that an organization would be wise to instill these cultural values, that is, it would be wise for a company to communicate that it, for example, (a) has a bias for action, (b) values close relationships to the customer, and (c) encourages employee independence and an entrepreneurial spirit.

As indicated previously, functionalists think of communication as a variable that will, depending on how it varies, determine the final cultural result. If a company wanted to instill the cultural value of "close relationships with the customer," it might produce a training video which has the CEO highlighting who it is in terms of how it establishes relationships, create a Web site that has a link to its "customer/client promise," or publish a slick internal magazine that regularly features (or establishes) company heroes who have maintained long-standing loyalty to generations of families.

Many scholars would argue that this approach is too prescriptive. Culture cannot be manufactured, and moreover the notion that there is a single cultural prescription for excellence is misguided. Culture is important, and culture is based on communication, but certain types of communications do not guarantee outcomes. One of Edgar Schein's books about corporate culture is entitled, *The Corporate Culture Survival Guide: Sense and Nonsense about Cultural Change*. In the forward to that book, Warren Bennis makes a very significant comment. "The subtext of this terrific book" he writes, "is that you just can't pop a culture in a microwave and out pops a McCulture."[15]

Chapter 7 is dedicated entirely to the relationships between organizational communication, organizational culture, and organizational climate.

Critical Theory

Have you ever observed or been affected by any of the following in organizational contexts? How many of these scenarios seem familiar to you?

1. Women and racial minorities are marginalized in that they are given infrequent meaningful opportunities to present their perspectives on issues. On those rare occasions when women and minorities are acknowledged, it seems as if those in power are not listening.
2. Some agenda items for meetings are placed in time slots that guarantee careful attention, while others are scheduled in periods that almost assure that they will be neglected.
3. While you can be easily accessed, it is difficult for you to gain access to others. Contacting certain individuals requires going through three or four levels of intermediaries.
4. Some persons retain information to maintain power over others. By retaining information about, for example, criteria for promotion, management can limit the advancement of some, facilitate the promotion of others, and protect its power to make unilateral decisions. Sophisticated communication technology is placed in the hands of powerful organizational members. Only some people, for example, have speedy Internet connections and state-of-the-art computers. During meetings, formal and informal rules are established that preclude contributions and/or voting privileges from certain members. These people are, nominally,

participants, but this is an illusion since they cannot meaningfully participate. This allows management to claim that these "participants" were involved in discussions, but limits these persons' influence.

5. Management uses belittling labels like "kids," "the boys," or "girls" to refer to those beneath them, but insists on being referred to by title.

6. Management explicitly or implicitly communicates that some tasks are suitable for women and some tasks are suitable for men.

7. The formally communicated rules absolutely forbid sexual harassment, but informal conversations suggest that management looks the other way.

8. The formally communicated rules forbid dishonesty and misrepresentation. However, these rules do not apply to those who have the power to enforce them.

9. Forms intended to document performance during evaluation periods seem to favor management and not allow employees a meaningful opportunity to express or record their self-assessments.

What Is Critical Theory?

Critical theory deals with the abuse of power. It derives its name because the theory advocates "relentless criticism"[16] of all those institutions that abuse power and consequently oppress others.

Critical theorists consider organizations as "sites of domination"[17] and consider communication within organizations "as ideological and power laden, not as a neutral medium for transmitting information."[18] They believe that an objective of organizational communication studies is to identify communication practices in the organization that are oppressive and to work toward eliminating these practices. For example, if male opinions are privileged in an organization and women and minority groups are regularly marginalized, critical theorists consider it essential to expose such practices and empower those whose voices have been silenced.

Critical theorists argue that management can:

*   Accept certain organizational players' input and ignore others.
*   Control access to technology; stipulate the rules that govern the use of Web sites and individual expression on the Web site.
*   Determine the communicative processes that are employed for decision making.
*   Prescribe the chain of command, thereby legislating who should talk to whom.
*   Use language as semantic kryptonite that debilitates employees.

The ultimate goal of critical theory is to "emancipate" those who are oppressed by such abuse. Essentially, the idea is that "relentless criticism" will free organizational women and men so that their thinking and behavior will not be encumbered by institutional and institutionalized manipulation.[19] Critical theorists seek to go beyond describing organizational communication practices and desire to change unjust practices.

Values of Critical Theory

Whenever a theory uses phrases and terms like "sites of domination" and "emancipation," it runs the risk of being categorized by some as a political doctrine of a discontented fringe group. However, regardless of your political orientation, it is valuable and responsible to consider the possibility that how people communicate in organizations can be oppressive to individuals and counterproductive to the organization. Such consideration may suggest why identifying and attempting to correct such communicative behavior has become a pervasive approach to studying communication in organizations.

In a *Communication Monographs* article, Lutgen-Sandvik describes managerial bullying behavior. She interviewed members of organizations who had stories of being abused by communication practices. Below are narratives about two *different* bullying managers.

(1) "The actual office environment was all glass, so he could see into all of the offices. Constant surveillance was deliberate and apparently part of his strategy of control. He could see through every office. . . . He'd scream and yell every day. Veins would pop out of his head; he'd spit, he'd point, he'd threaten daily, all day long to anyone in his way, every day that I was there. Every single day. Oh, yelling! . . . [From my office,] I could see his eyes bulging, his veins and everything, spitting, and pointing his finger. . . . That was daily, with many people, all the time. He would yell in the speakerphone at his general managers. He'd swear profusely, "You [expletive], you don't know anything. You [expletive] idiot! You couldn't run a [expletive] peanut stand. . . . "

(2) "He would call people to the fifth floor conference room . . . where he "held court." Summoning people to the conference room occurred every single day . . . with just a string of people. The intercom would be going off all the time, "So-and-so to the fifth floor conference room. So-and-so to the fifth floor conference room." I'd see people running, literally running, down the halls. . . . It's just bizarre! . . . He'd scream, oh yeah, screaming! You'd never know why he called you [to the conference room], so you couldn't prepare yourself, so you'd stand there with no answers to his questions, and that made him even madder. So his face would get beet-red, and he'd slam his hands down, stand up, and start shaking his finger at you, and screaming "Get out of here! Get out of my sight!" Everyone waiting outside heard all of it, and you'd go out, and the next person went in for the kill."[20]

Autocratic supervisors who keep employees uninformed in order to maintain their power may have no person's best interest at heart but their own. Such persons can make life miserable for employees and reduce organizational efficiency. Occasionally, as critical theorists argue, victims of oppressive communication are unaware of their victimization, as they have unwittingly bought into the legitimacy of the oppressive communication practices.

Ideology, Manufactured Consent, and Hegemony

Ideology is a term that is used by critical theorists to describe beliefs that employees consider normal and natural, but which may, in fact, not be normal or natural. However, these beliefs constitute an ideological framework that those in power wish employees to consider standard, foundational, and perhaps even sacred.

For example, it is taken for granted by most people that an organization should be arranged in a hierarchy. Typically, initial training sessions provide newcomers to a company with a handbook that includes an organizational chart that articulates the hierarchy. Critical theorists would consider this problematic. They would argue that the belief in the importance of organizational hierarchy reflects acceptance of an ideology that is inherently oppressive. In other words, accepting the concept of hierarchy as an indisputably valuable organizational construct will inevitably subjugate employees because they will have bought into the ideology that maintains that organizations must function by preserving positions of relative legitimacy and power.

The phrase *manufactured consent* is used by critical theorists to describe this phenomenon of buying into subjugating ideologies. It occurs when employees adopt and may enforce philosophies that could, in fact, be unhealthy for the organization and the individuals who comprise the organizations. What occurs is that communication patterns in the organization reinforce the ideologies. Consequently, the organization actually manufactures the buy-in from employees to insidious demeaning ideologies. A critical theorist might suggest that vituperations like those in the

Communication Monographs article might be perceived as necessary by some employees because the organization had manufactured the consent to the behavior. For example, athletes might argue that when a coach berates a player in front of the team, such public criticism is necessary for the team to function. In such a case, the athletes have bought into the ideology that it was a management function to excoriate underperforming players. Their consent to the behavior that might otherwise be considered reprehensible had been manufactured.

Hegemony is a term that has been in use since the 1500s. It essentially refers to domination and typically is used to suggest that one group of people has exerted its influence and customs over another. Western governments have often been accused of exerting hegemonic influence over the peoples of Africa and Asia. The word hegemony has also been used by critical theorists to mean what occurs when a dominant group—for example, management—has led another group to accept and even support domination by having them buy into the ideology of the group in power. As indicated previously, critical theorists see as their goal emancipation. They desire to "to lay bare hegemonic structures and processes" in order to free those who are oppressed.[21]

Multiple Stakeholder Theory, Workplace Democracy, Concertive Control

Many contemporary theorists have assumed the critical approach to organizational communication research. Stanley Deetz and George Cheney are among this group. Deetz has written about what has been called *multiple stakeholder theory*. He argues that an organization should reconfigure its perspectives of essential stakeholders to include both employees and shareholders as stakeholders. He argues that it is the objective of an organization to create a workplace democracy where all members of an organization think and act like an owner or at least an associate. Cheney has written that workplace democracy encourages "individual contributions to important organizational choices, and . . . allows for the ongoing modification of the organization's activities and polices by [members of] the group."[22] Workplace democracy requires that the role of supervisor not be confined to supervision and therefore managers both *do* and supervise others who are *doing what they do*.

It has become common to enter stores like Walmart and Target and see that employees are no longer called employees, but rather associates. A major university recently held a series of meetings with administrators where the agenda centered on "ownership"—individual units were encouraged to think of themselves as owners and assume responsibility like an owner as well as reap the benefits.

The key variable, of course, in workplace democracy and multiple stakeholder theory is credibility. That is, if an organization credibly reconfigures itself to render the organization to be a participatory democracy, then the idea of multiple stakeholder theory can take hold. It will, of course, have limited value if those declared owners discover that their labels were misleading and little more than a ruse.

The residual of the genuine application of multiple stakeholder theory can be what Tompkins and Cheney have referred to in their writings as concertive control. Concertive control assumes that members of organizations are not subjugated but work collectively toward the health of the organization like a team. The control is not hierarchical, but rather derives its power and influence from the collection of workers committed to the enterprise. More on concertive control is found in Chapter 7.

Critical theory is an important theory for organizational communication students to consider. Yet as with all theories, it has some problems. It assumes that a particular ideology—the critical theorist's—is a correct one. I tend to think that the egalitarian perspective that critical theorists endorse is desirable, but the theory presents nothing other than an ideology as all theories do. There is an inherent danger and irony that comes with criticizing the products of hegemonic ideology from the vantage point of the "correct" one regardless of how well intentioned you might be. Critical theory also appears to divide the organization into three discrete groups: the oppressors, the oppressed, and the enlightened. This is not an accurate depiction of humankind (although the bullying managers profiled in the *Communication Monographs* article do appear to be easily categorized as oppressors). Most people cannot be monolithically described as oppressors or oppressed. In fact, most of us, if we were willing to do some introspection, might see that we have often both been oppressed and oppressors, and there may be times when we have had certain roles that compelled us to behave in ways that others consider oppressive. Instructors who teach about critical theory probably impose restrictions on when papers can be submitted. Any such restriction is a derivative of the ideology that allows professors to determine rules for class work. However, this does not ineluctably render the instructor as an oppressor or the students as the oppressed. One could make the argument that were it not for articulated rules, and an ideology that provides the legitimacy for prescribing rules, then organizational women and men could not function and enjoy their work freely, because the absence of this ideology would yield a cumbersome, restricting, *and disabling* ambiguity. Finally, the objective of emancipation presents a daunting challenge. In order to realize that objective, critical theorists need to ensure that their message extends to the audiences who are in need of emancipation. This can be done, but many of the articles supporting critical theory are written for scholarly audiences and appear in journals that are typically read by sympathetic academic subscribers. In addition, some textbooks that endorse critical theory also advocate for managerial "strategic ambiguity," which has as a goal the "preservation of privileged positions." The mating of critical theory with strategic ambiguity will yield a confused and cynical progeny unlikely to be willing or able to advocate credibly for emancipation.

Nevertheless, it is wise to examine communication in organizations with an awareness of its power issues. In fact, *it could be argued that it would be irresponsible for students of organizational communication to avoid such analysis.* People do abuse power in organizations, and that abuse is facilitated by communication practices. The abuse of power can affect employee morale and organizational success. We will look at the abuse of power in the next chapter when we examine ethical issues in organizational communication.

Feminism and Critical Theory

Feminist perspectives on organizational communication have been utilized to examine power in organizations, especially those aspects of power that relate to gender. The word feminism has diverse meanings for various audiences. Some radio commentators and authors have derided feminists and obscured the objectives of male and female feminists.

Academics have defined feminism variously. Calas and Smircich have identified seven different approaches to feminist theory and inquiry:

- Liberal
- Radical cultural
- Psychoanalytical
- Marxist
- Socialist
- Poststructuralist
- Third World–postcolonial [23]

As those who explore the endnote will see, these variations reflect meaningful distinctions. However, the feminist perspective has been and can be generally described. Pamela Shockley-Zalabak has written that a feminist perspective "explores the marginalization and domination of women in the workplace and . . . attempts to move our society beyond patriarchal forms and social practices by critiquing power relationships that devalue women."[24]

Sanford Weill, CEO of Citicorp, meets with Sallie Krawcheck, CEO of Smith Barney. Do stereotypes cause people to view the performance of male and female executives differently?

Angela Trethewey's definition of feminism is somewhat more encompassing. She writes that feminism is "a political movement and a set of theories that attempt to account for women's and other marginalized groups' subjugated status and to find ways to overcome oppression and domination based on gender, race and other differences."[25]

In essence, feminist scholars believe that male voices have been privileged in organizations creating limits on women's and other minority group's capabilities to function and advance. Feminist scholars examine the effects of gender on communication behavior in organizations. In addition, feminist scholars argue that organizations favor certain perceptions of appropriate roles for women and men. These stereotypic assumptions affect and limit how women and men function in organizations and how the organization evolves. The stereotypes create planks in the organizational foundation that inevitably not only make footing for both men and women precarious, but limit the qualitative growth of the enterprise. In a *Management Communication Quarterly* article, Patricia Buzzanell writes that researchers have a "moral commitment to investigate the subordinated . . . and to explore the standpoints of women who have been rendered invisible by their absence in theory and research."[26]

Applying Symbiotic Theory

When we began our discussion of theory in Chapter 2, we discussed the benefits of assuming a symbiotic approach. This approach does not examine organizational communication phenomena from the perspective a single theory, but rather considers single theories, however dissimilar, as parts of a larger and valuable composite that are most valuable if they are applied together.

Let's return to the case that began Chapter 2. As you recall the case was about Patricia Daniels and her concerns regarding how to communicate with her new staff. How should Patricia Daniels approach her communication challenge? As a starting point, she might be wise to identify several realities that could be gleaned from looking at facets of various theories. The following are five such realities:

- If members of her group are like most people, under the right conditions they will wish to, and can, contribute meaningfully to decision-making processes.
- She will need to be clear when communicating any new department goals and expectations.
- Her department will have to interact effectively with other units of the organization in order to be successful.
- How she and other members of the group communicate will affect, if not constitute, the culture that evolves in her department. That culture will affect the nature and quality of work done in the department.

PRACTITIONER PERSPECTIVE

Robert Peterkin: Former School Superintendent

Robert Peterkin was the superintendent of schools for the city of Milwaukee for three years. Prior to that he had been the school superintendent for Cambridge, Massachusetts, and deputy superintendent for the city of Boston. He is both practitioner and academic. After leaving Milwaukee, Dr. Peterkin accepted a job at Harvard University, where he chairs a program for persons who aspire to be school superintendents. Peterkin has appeared on Good Morning America and other national media outlets. He has written on school choice, school governance, women in the superintendency, and the impact of school reform on the achievement of African American children.

As you read through this section, consider the following questions:

1. From your experience and perspective as a student, do you agree with Peterkin's highlighted comments?
2. Are retreats like the one Peterkin describes likely to have such positive effects? Can they backfire? What are the keys to successful retreats?
3. Peterkin notes the values of communication skill training. Think of managers with whom you have worked who had poor communication skills. Could these managers have improved if they participated in training sessions with communication professionals?

If I had to identify what typically gets in the way of effective communication, I'd say that people don't think through what they're trying to communicate. They don't think about their audiences and what's important to them. Also, most people don't listen actively, nor do they read and reflect on what they read. People possess the counterproductive dynamic that they have to win when they communicate. Instead of advancing the cause, they feel like communicating is a contest and in order to be successful they must win. Some messages and positions we take must be non-negotiable, but some issues are negotiable and communicating about them need not be a match to see who will be the victor.

Lack of internal communication is almost a cultural norm for public schools.

School systems are set up into divisions and that noun can be used in many ways, but what is created with these units *is* division, and the classic silo effect. Communication rarely flows between different organizational units because individual departments are typically not motivated to communicate interdependently. They are rewarded for doing a job in their own units. The lack of communication between levels and departments in school systems is legendary. There are many books written on superintendent and board dysfunction, and the biggest issue is lack of communication. In Texas there are mediators who go to Dallas and Houston and other urban areas to try to improve communication between the school board and superintendent. In our program here we spend so much time on communication-related issues because school systems rarely think about how to communicate within their organizations. I consider it such an important issue that we have on retainer a professional communication trainer who works with our students during their time on campus.

Communication problems are exacerbated in organizations because, typically, employees are not sufficiently trained. Look, when I first was a principal, I felt passionately about my mission. My wife has a videotape of a speech I delivered as a principal during that first year. When we watch this we can barely

PRACTITIONER PERSPECTIVE *continued*

make out what I am saying. I felt passionate, but I communicated little of my passion. One must practice to become a good communicator. And one would be wise to rely on the advice from professionals. We need feedback about how well we're doing. In Milwaukee, I had a cabinet of advisers. When we plan to disseminate a message that does not make sense, we need someone to say what one of my advisers said to me one day: "No clothes today, emperor."

We were able to create a positive atmosphere in Milwaukee, and we did this in large part because we worked at it. When I began there, I took the board on a retreat for a weekend with a professional facilitator. We did a day and a half workshop examining communication issues. Maybe we would have worked together well anyway, but some things came out from that retreat that set up a solid foundation for our subsequent communications. We worked with a common purpose and vision. I placed board members on our major committees, which is anathema for most school systems. I can't tell you how much good will and positive votes that brought us.

• She will need to be concerned with ethical decision making and participate in the creation of an egalitarian work setting. While accepting the responsibilities of leadership, she will have to be sensitive to persons' desires to be equitably empowered. If she is not so sensitive, the result might be the passive acceptance of a debilitating organizational structure.

These five realities reflect each of the theories we have discussed in Chapters 2 and 3: human resources, classical, systems, culture, and critical. Approaching Patricia Daniels's problem from any one theoretical perspective would ignore a dimension that must be addressed in order to remedy her situation. You may remember the Abraham Maslow quote from Chapter 2: "If the only tool you have is a hammer you tend to see every problem as a nail." A symbiotic approach helps researchers comprehensively assess organizational communication problems. Considering theories as symbiotic provides students with a toolbox, not just one tool.

In a May 2004 National Public Radio broadcast entitled "Jerks at Work," a professor from Wayne State University in Detroit and another from Stanford University entertained calls from persons throughout the United States who discussed problems pertaining to "jerks at work." One caller identified himself as the liaison between workers and a particular "jerk." Another person identified herself as a former "jerk" who was confronted by a "nonjerk" and realized the errors of her ways. The Stanford professor remarked that at his institution there was a saying about engineers that was often repeated: "Sometimes the best engineers come in bodies that can't talk." Stated somewhat differently, "Sometimes the best people come in bodies that do not understand the nuances of communication in organizations." The value of theory is that it can help us understand what those nuances might be. Perhaps the responsibilities of communicating tasks and rules as suggested by classical theorists are self-evident. However, ignorance of the subtleties of human resource, systems, cultural, and critical theories is likely to propagate "jerks at work."

In his novel *The Counterlife*, Philip Roth's character bemoans the complexity of his experience and wails, "Is an intelligent human being likely to be much more than a large-scale manufacturer of misunderstanding?" [27] Understanding theory can reduce the systematic "manufacturing of misunderstanding" in organizational contexts.

SUMMARY: A TOOLBOX

- Systems theories suggest that for organizations to thrive there must be:
    - Communication that links departments to one another
    - Communication that links the organization to its external environment
    - Effective communication of task and procedural messages
    - Effective communication of recognition and observation
- Cultural theorists argue that culture is an important dimension of organizational success and that communication plays a vital role in the evolution of that culture.
- Critical theorists argue that communication can be used abusively to maintain power and disable organizational women and men. These theorists believe it is in the best interests of the organization and the individuals who work within them to become aware of oppressive practices and become liberated from them.
- Multiple stakeholder theory, workplace democracy, and concertive control are all desired ends and methods to achieve desired ends for critical theorists.
- Feminist theories help students and researchers understand the perspective of marginalized populations and how communication practices have served to perpetuate such marginalization in organizations.
- Symbiotic applications of organizational theories can help persons understand the dimensions and applications of communication in organizations.

REVIEW AND DISCUSSION QUESTIONS

1. Why would a systems theorist consider interdepartmental communication important?
2. How does cultural theory relate to fundamental principles of critical theory?
3. In what ways can critical theorists improve the quality of life for people in organizations as well as the quality of the organization's product?
4. Are workplace democracy, concertive control, and multiple stakeholder theory realistic tenets? Can an organization create workplace democracy? Are attempts to engineer concertive control inevitably manipulative?
5. How can a symbiotic approach to theory be applied to help organizations with communication problems?

GROUP/ROLE-PLAY

- In a group of four to six, review the issues surrounding the case that begins this chapter. Attempt to gain consensus regarding the questions at the end of the chapter.
- For the role-play, one member of the group assumes a representative from sales. Another assumes the role of a representative from service. A third represents someone from the company that recently acquired the company.
- Role-play a face-to-face meeting among these three representatives that has been called and is led by a representative of the new owners.

Chapter 4

Ethics and Organizational Communication

Chapter in a Nutshell

In a March 2002 business publication, a photo of Enron CEO Kenneth Lay appears on the cover. The word "liar" is written in large yellow letters next to his image. The picture itself has been doctored so that the executive appears to have a Pinocchio nose. Beneath the elongated extremity is an excerpt from an e-mail that Lay had sent to all his employees on August 14, 2001. It read, "Our performance has never been stronger; our business model has never been more robust; our growth has never been more certain. . . ."[1] On July 10, 2004, two days after Kenneth Lay was indicted on charges that he failed to be fully truthful with accountants, investors, and employees, an article in the *New York Times* began with the following words: "If there is any message that has been delivered by the government in its almost three-year battle against corporate corruption, it is this: The truth will keep you free."[3] Kenneth Lay would not have spent much time being free. On May 25, 2006, he was found guilty of ten of the eleven counts against him. Each count carried a maximum five- to ten-year sentence. Less than two months later, prior to sentencing, 64-year-old Kenneth Lay suffered a fatal heart attack.

Researchers in the field of organizational communication have discussed the merit of honesty, credibility, and openness as imperatives for effective organizational communication. This chapter examines ethics as it pertains to communication within the organization.

When you have completed this chapter, you should be able to:

• Explain why ethical considerations are foundational for organizational communication study.
• List several ethical decisions that communicators must make in organizational contexts.
• Describe what is meant by the normalization of deviance.
• Explain what is meant by moral conflict.
• Explain the perspective of those who support, and those who reject, "strategic ambiguity."
• Identify methods that can be used to improve ethical decision making.

CASE 4.1
Lying to Rachel Adams

Rachel Adams was very marketable. Job opportunities were excellent for someone with her computer-related skills. During one week in October three headhunters had contacted her trying to woo her away from her present position at Ballinger Systems. However, Adams liked her job, was compensated well, and had just bought a new home with her husband that was within a fifteen-minute drive of her Ballinger office. Adams's husband was happily employed. With their two incomes, life was very comfortable. Adams was a computer design specialist, and part of her responsibilities involved managing other such specialists. She had an MBA, and when she was initially hired by Ballinger Systems she had four other job opportunities. Rachel Adams decided not to encourage the headhunters. Times were good; if they turned bad she figured she could still get another job easily.

Times did turn bad. The next November, just thirteen months later, Ballinger Systems' stock was plummeting. Not only was her company's stock plummeting, but so was the stock of several other similar organizations. Through the grapevine Adams heard that Ballinger was considering merging with a competitor. Adams set up a meeting with her superior, Janet, to ask if there were, in fact, merger talks. Her superior assured her that there were no such conversations. As far as she knew, claimed the boss, Ballinger would be independent forever. "I promise you, Rachel, we're not going anywhere."

This was reassuring to Rachel Adams. She was no longer as marketable as she had been. Nevertheless, one headhunter had very recently contacted her. The job he proposed was for a similar position in a nearby location. Rachel and her husband could stay in their home. The salary was a little less than what she was making with Ballinger, but the new company would, certainly, not be going anywhere. They were a major player and were not about to be merging. The headhunter reminded Rachel that times were not like they used to be. Adams, of course, knew this. The headhunter also commented about the possible merger of Ballinger that Adams herself had heard through the grapevine. "Consider this opportunity, Rachel. Listen to me. Times are not good and they will get worse. Anything could happen. I know you'll get this job I've lined up for you."

Adams weighed the idea of applying for the other job and decided against it. Janet had assured her that the merger talks were nothing but hyperactive grapevine rumors. She wanted to stay put and decided to do so.

Her subordinates, who had also heard of the possible merger, asked Rachel about it. "Look," she told them, "I was concerned, but I was assured by Janet that there will be no merger. Janet told me this point blank and I believe her."

In January all employees at Ballinger received a happy mailing announcing the successful merger with Wellburton Inc. Adams quickly set up a meeting with her superior. Janet apologized but said she had been under strict orders not to comment on any of the merger negotiations.

"I thought we had a good relationship. I trusted you."

"Look Rachel. I work for Ballinger. I have to be concerned for Ballinger. If I tell you about the merger, you might jump ship. If you jump ship, others might leave. This could jeopardize our day-to-day operations and also might make it difficult for us to close on this merger. You may think I had a moral obligation to tell you the truth, but I have a moral obligation to Ballinger to do my job. In this case doing my job means keeping you here. Keeping you here requires that I omit certain information."

"Omit certain information? You promised! You said, 'I promise you, Rachel, we're not going anywhere.' That's what you said."

"I didn't lie. We're not going anywhere. There will be some downsizing as obviously there will be duplication of responsibilities with the merger. However, Wellburton and their people are moving in here. We're not going anywhere. I didn't lie."

Adams was incredulous. She nearly screamed, "I cannot believe you would do this."

"Welcome to the real world."

"You know I told my subordinates that there would be no merger. I trusted you. I told them I trusted you. What should I tell them now?"

"Tell them what I just told you."

In February, one month later, Rachel Adams lost her position at Ballinger-Wellburton.

- Did Ballinger administrators have a responsibility to honestly inform all employees about the proposed merger?
- Does Adams have a legitimate reason to be upset?
- Is she responsible for her own predicament since she did not pursue the job that the headhunter had presented to her?
- Janet claimed that she did not lie when she made her promise. Did she lie?

Examining Ethics

"Outside [the heavenly city] are the dogs and sorcerers and fornicators and murderers and idolaters, and everyone who loves and practices falsehood."

—REVELATION 22:15

Years ago I wrote a controversial article about an issue related to college education.[3] Subsequently, I was invited to speak about the article on a local talk show magazine program. During the program both the host and phone callers would ask me questions about my positions.

There were to be three other guests on the hour-long program, and each of us would be interviewed independent of the other. Before the show began, we guests sat in the "green room" and introduced ourselves. On that day's program there would be a mayor of a local municipality, a female body builder, a psychic, and me.

The mayor was on first and discussed how his community had been wronged by a recently published book. Then I was brought in and talked about my article. Then the body builder entered and, dressed in appropriate garb, lifted astonishing amounts of weight to the beat of some bouncy music. Each of us handled a few softball questions from the host and took one or two calls from viewers.

Then the psychic entered. The psychic was, without doubt, the most popular of the four guests. She sat with the host and spewed predictions on every subject from foreign affairs to the stock market. While she was able to "see all," her specialty, she said, was predicting what would happen in individuals' romantic futures.

The phones rang nonstop. A caller wanted to know if he would ever meet the woman of his dreams. The psychic said that from "what she was feeling from what he was saying" there was a "positive surprise" in the future, but he "should be careful."

Another caller asked—frantically it sounded to me—if her husband would ever come back to her. This, the psychic said, was a tough one since "there were some clouds around it," but after she closed her eyes for a few seconds she began to nod her head. She said "yes, yes, this is not beyond the realm of possibility," but that the caller might want to consider whether the return of the spouse would indeed be a good idea.

The next caller said that she missed her cat, now deceased from a traffic accident. She wondered if she should replace her cat or if perhaps the death of the pet was a sign that she needed to seek some human companionship instead. The psychic responded that it "could very well be" that this was "a spiritual signal."

If the show did not have a time limit, the psychic might still be fielding questions. However, eventually the psychic returned to the green room with the mayor, the weightlifter, and me. After she settled down, she noticed me and said that she had enjoyed my segment. "Education is very important," she said. I concurred and mentioned that in the upcoming presidential election both candidates were making education a campaign issue.

"Oh yes," she said with interest—no longer the psychic but an interested citizen. "The election. It's going to be something. *Who do you think is going to win?*"

I couldn't avoid seeing the irony in her question. Who did *I* think was going to win? Here she was, a self-described contemporary soothsayer advising hungry, needy strangers about what she "sees" in their futures, and she had to ask me who was going to win the election?

"You're the psychic," I said. "You tell me who is going to win."

"Oh, oh," she stammered trying to recover, "Yes, well, uh, we in the psychic community think there will be Republican victories across the board, but there are still some clouds around the issue."

Ethical Decisions and Organizational Communication

All persons make ethical decisions when they communicate. Those decisions may be conscious ones or passively subconscious decisions. It struck me when I met the psychic that she had made some poor decisions.

Perhaps there are those who are psychically gifted, but this person did not appear to be so blessed. Her career as a romantic seer was a lucrative one. Yet her musings on others' emotional predicaments could have consequences, and, it seemed to me, there were some moral responsibilities that she neglected as she plied her trade. Certainly the callers were responsible for their willingness to participate, but by posturing as omniscient—occasional "clouds" notwithstanding—the psychic was violating a very basic ethical principle. She was being disingenuous.

Does it matter if she could get away with it? Does it matter if such psychic advice is often dispensed or that there are willing and eager receivers waiting for the message?

Organizational communicators are not sleight-of-hand psychics. Yet organizational communication requires making ethical choices. While the repercussions may be less dramatic, the effects of unethical communication can be both dramatic and significant, or at least be perceived as such by employees. Whether one works in an office of corporate communication, is a manager who must relay information to subordinates, or is a nonmanagerial employee who regularly needs to communicate intra- or interdepartmentally, one makes ethical choices that can affect interpersonal relationships and organizational quality.

Actor Matt Damon in the 2009 movie *The Informant* plays the real-life character Mark Whitacre, an employee of the Archer Daniels Midland company. Readers of the Kurt Eichenwald book on which the movie is based can come to no other conclusion than that Whitacre is an incorrigible liar. Nevertheless, Whitacre is employed by law enforcement officials to expose price-fixing activity at his company. In essence, Whitacre—a liar—becomes a whistleblower who conspires with police to expose other liars. In the course of his cooperation with investigators, it becomes clear that not only is Whitacre a liar and that his entire company had been rife with liars, but his company conspired with competitors to lie and fix prices on products.

How typical is Mark Whitacre? How typical is it for organizations to be filled with people who think nothing of lying if, they claim, it is in the best interests of an organization? Throughout the text we discuss organizational communication in terms of culture, power, networks, and skills. To what extent does duplicity, regardless of the rationale, corrupt the culture of an organization? To

Mark Whitacre exposed price fixing at Archer Daniels Midland. He served as the model for the whistleblower played by Matt Damon in *The Informant*.

what extent can deceptive communication subjugate the victims of the deceit? Will dishonest communications infect the credibility of formal and informal networks? Will pervasive disingenuous communication foster, organically, a workforce of skilled liars?

It seems apparent that ethical attitudes are foundational to the study of organizational communication. To illustrate this point, please take a few moments to complete the reader survey on the following page.

As you probably discovered as you completed this exercise, many communication-related activities can be affected by ethical decisions.

In the fall of 2008, the world was rocked by a financial crisis that made middle-class citizens fearful that their life savings might be lost. The stock market plummeted nearly daily. In the United States bleary-eyed citizens checked their computers in the middle of the night, fearful that they might read that a downturn in Far East or European markets would portend another drop in their net worth once the stock market opened in New York. Reconsider item 15 from the survey in light of this recent news. To what extent is presenting misleading information about an organization's health harmful?

Antidepressant medication prescribed to thousands of patients in need of therapy seemed to satisfy an immediate need. Subsequently some of these products, it appeared, had created physical problems for those people who had consumed the product. Reconsider item 17. Is a misleading description of a product an innocuous ploy that is fair game in the world of capitalism?

In March 2008 the state of New York, was shocked, and soon afterwards so was the nation and then the world. It became clear that Eliot Spitzer, the governor of New York, who had successfully run for office on a morality platform, had spent thousands of dollars visiting a brothel while governor of the state. Reconsider item 2 from the survey. Is a bogus mission statement by a leader—a misleading claim of values and platform for governance—harmless?

Applying the Principles—Test Yourself

Below you will see a numbered list of communication-related activities. For each item:

- Explain how ethical decisions can affect these activities.
- Identify the repercussions, if any, of communicators not being concerned with ethical factors that pertain to the item.

1. Creating job descriptions
2. Constructing mission statements
3. Evaluating employee performance
4. Describing organizational achievements
5. Describing departmental achievements
6. Orienting incoming employees
7. Conducting informational interviews
8. Expressing concern for individual employees' welfare
9. Articulating personal achievements
10. Responding to personal performance evaluations
11. Persuading colleagues to agree to policy changes
12. Phoning in "sick"
13. Persuading customers
14. Constructing advertising copy
15. Accurately communicating the financial health of your company to stockholders and government.
16. Updating project status
17. Identifying product virtues
18. Discussing changes to health and retirement benefits
19. Claiming responsibility for successes
20. Accepting responsibility for problems

Is Honesty Overrated?

Recently an MBA student made the following comment during a discussion of ethics and organizational communication: "What's so wrong about lying in certain situations?" she asked. "Isn't honesty overrated?"

> Trust and integrity are precious resources, easily squandered hard to regain.
>
> **—SISSELA BOK** IN *LYING*

Organizational communicators should respond negatively to the student's second question for practical reasons alone. W. Charles Redding, the research pioneer in organizational communication, made it clear that the communication climate of an organization was far more critical than individual communication skills in determining the overall communication quality in an organization.[4] As we will see in more detail in Chapter 7, Redding identified five criteria for what he called the ideal communication climate. One criterion was organizational *credibility*. Another was *openness*.

Remove credibility and openness as organizational trademarks and you have eliminated important planks from the foundation of your enterprise. Individual communication skills are relatively insignificant in an environment where organizational communication is distrusted by default. If honesty is devalued by those who disseminate information, organizational credibility and communication will inevitably be damaged and difficult to repair or restore. Honesty is not overrated if only for the practical reason that dishonesty can be insidiously corrosive.

The Normalization of Deviance

The phrase the normalization of deviance has been attributed to sociologist Diane Vaughan. She writes, ". . . repetition, seemingly small choices, and the banality of daily decisions in organizational life,—indeed in most social life—can camouflage from the participants a cumulative directionality that too often is discernible only in hindsight."[5]

Similarly, in the 2008 memoir *Extraordinary Circumstances: The Journey of a Corporate Whistle-blower,* former WorldCom vice president Cynthia Cooper comments on the subtle acceptance of unacceptable behavior. In 2002 WorldCom, a telephone giant, imploded ignominiously because of scandal and unethical activity. Almost overnight, WorldCom earned the derisive sobriquet, World-Con for its duplicitous behavior. In her book, Cooper writes, "People don't wake up and say, 'I think I'll become a criminal today.' Instead it's often a slippery slope and we lose our footing one step at a time."[6]

Camouflaging "Cumulative Directionality"

The insidious problems related to the normalization of deviance can be illustrated by the following example.

Let's assume that a group meets periodically to examine the status of an ongoing activity or a project. Let's assume further that the way it is supposed to look is like what appears in the first panel of Figure 4.1, a blank rectangle. Now assume that the next month, the screen looks like the second panel in Figure 4.1, a rectangle with an asterisk in it. A likely response from a participant in this group would be: "There appears to be something wrong here. There is an asterisk in our rectangle. That is not right."

If the asterisk is still there the following month, the group might say, "We continue to have a problem. The asterisk is in the rectangle again." If in each meeting for three months that asterisk— that deviant phenomenon—remains, and there has been no calamity, there may be an acceptance of the deviance even if all are aware that the presence is not what it should be. This acceptance becomes apparent if during a subsequent meeting there are two asterisks as indicated in the fifth panel in Figure 4.1. Then participants might be unnerved again.

We can appreciate the insidious consequences of the normalization of deviance by looking at the sixth panel. If at a following meeting the participants look at the rectangle and see that it has reverted back to one asterisk, there will be a relief: *"Good. Back to normal, only one asterisk in our rectangle."* Enron, WorldCom, Archer Daniels Midland, Lehman Brothers, and other cases of corporate duplicity seem to suggest that unethical communication in organizations has become normalized. The anomaly of duplicity is no longer anomalous. There has been one asterisk in the rectangle for so long that it has ceased to be a problematic aberration. Vaughan's comment is worth repeating, "Daily decisions in organizational life [have] camouflage[d] a cumulative directionality that too often is discernible only in hindsight." This is put more simply in a *USA Today* piece. *"Lying* has become such an integral part of society that no one seems outraged by it anymore, even when that lie has extraordinary and painful consequences."[7] Deceit can have "extraordinary and painful consequences." As Cooper wrote about WorldCom/n, "[w]hatever rationalization was applied to the deceit, it brought nothing but ruin, the consequences of which are still felt today, and will continue to be felt for years to come."[8]

David Callahan, in *The Cheating Culture,* discusses interviews he conducted with septuagenarian graduates of the Harvard Business School. Callahan reports that these seniors were disgusted at the behaviors of the Enrons and WorldComs. Their sentiment was that "today's business values normalize felonious behaviors."[9]

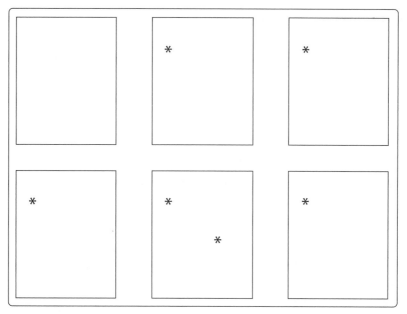

Figure 4.1 Cumulative Directionality

Do they? Has deception and duplicity become normalized?

Organizational culture is not an entity that can be instantly manufactured. It does not evolve simply because of declarations from a CEO, by signage asserting cultural values, or by publishing a code of ethics. It develops due to "repetition, seemingly small choices, and the banality of daily decisions in organizational life." What becomes an organization's culture is the residual of all organizational communication. Communications, formal or informal, that reflect openness and honesty are seedlings for a culture that values transparency. And conversely, communications, formal or informal, that condone duplicity will also be seedlings for cultural values that implicitly assert that pecuniary or other gains trump candor. The normalization of deceptive communication, regardless of how it is labeled, can intoxicate organizational cultures. As with any intoxicant, the effects are insidious because the disoriented organizations operate under a dangerous illusion: the illusion that deceptive communication is necessary and innocuous. Lying for professional benefit, organizational benefit, or personal benefit has been normalized and rationalized with curious if not spurious theories and logic.

Ginger Graham was a CEO of a 300 million dollar subsidiary of Eli Lilly. In an April 2002 *Harvard Business Review* article entitled "If You Want Honesty, Break Some Rules" she writes, "Openness and honesty need to be ingrained into a company's culture. . . . In many organizations, despite repeated calls for open and honest communication, several dynamics work together to create cultures of misinformation and unproductive speculation."[10]

Phillip Tompkins's books about the *Challenger and Columbia* disasters clearly make the case that transparent communication is imperative in order to avoid organizational calamity. The *Columbia* resulted in loss of lives, and deceptions in religious, financial, and political institutions created spiritual, economic, and international disasters in the first decade of the twenty-first century alone.

Moral Conflict

Pearce and Littlejohn use the phrase "moral conflict" in their book about ethical issues. Moral conflict may mean something other than what readers initially think when they first see the phrase. It does not refer specifically to internal conflicts about whether one should assume a moral course. When WorldCom employees were first confronted with requests to misrepresent data, they were faced with a moral decision: should they keep their job and do what they had been asked to do, or should they quit over principle?

Pearce and Littlejohn's important book uses "moral conflict" in another—related—way. Moral conflict "happen[s] when people deeply enmeshed in incommensurate social worlds come to clash. . . . The intensity of moral conflicts is fueled when such actions [taken by the opposition] are treated as malicious or stupid by the other side."[11] In other words, moral conflicts arise when people in an organization or elsewhere disagree about fundamental moral issues and become entrenched in positions that, inevitably, characterize opponents as villains. Examples of moral conflicts on your campus may involve whether ROTC programs should be permitted at the university; whether companies that subjugate third world nations should be allowed to recruit graduating students, or whether the university should purchase vehicles for their motor pool from foreign automakers. The ethical decisions germane to moral conflicts are very difficult to address. The authors write that these issues are "self sustaining. The original issue becomes irrelevant, and new causes for conflict are generated by the actions within the conflict itself. . . . [I]ronically perpetuating the conflict is seen as virtuous by those involved."[12] For example, a pro-life/choice supporter may consider it virtuous to block a doorway, prohibiting students who wish to listen to a speaker from the other side deliver a lecture on campus.

In for-profit organizations, moral conflicts can exist between people who feel that it is unwise to partner with another company that is involved with controversial activities. As another example, if a company donates moneys to needy agencies, should the company be concerned with the mission statements of these agencies?

In the nonprofit world a moral conflict could exist if a theater company hires an outstanding actor for a part despite the performer's expressed admiration for Nazis. Should a play written by a misogynist be produced regardless of the inherent content of the play?

A moral conflict could even conceivably exist between parties who believe in ethical organizational behavior and those who consider it moral to make shareholders' concerns paramount in decision making.

Barnett and Pearce's recommendations for addressing moral conflicts are on target but not easy to implement. Essentially they argue that persons on opposing sides commit to transcending "evaluation" and "obstructionism" and engage in "transformative conversations."[13] The key to this success is a willingness to transcend the conflict and, at least, agree to respect the perspective of those who feel as strongly as you do in the opposite direction.

Strategic Ambiguity

There are those who have written in support of what is referred to as "strategic ambiguity" in organizational contexts. In this section we will discuss:

• What is meant by strategic ambiguity

Applying the Principles—Test Yourself

Assume that a famous photographer wishes to display her works at the museum you head. However, some of her photographs are controversial. While brilliant in many ways, they depict intimate behaviors that are offensive to many people. Even if the offended people have the opportunity to avoid the museum or the exhibit, there is outrage within your workforce that you would even consider displaying these photos given how offensive it will be to patrons AND to some people who work for you. On the other hand, some workers will be outraged if you decide not to show the exhibit—not simply because they like the photos, but because of the principle of free expression that such a decision would repudiate.

Do you show the exhibit?
How do you communicate with the people in your office about this matter?
How do you communicate with your community about this matter?

- The purported value of strategic ambiguity
- Problems with strategic ambiguity

What Is Strategic Ambiguity?

In 1984 Eric Eisenberg published an article in *Communication Monographs* entitled "Ambiguity as Strategy in Organizational Communication."[14] In essence, strategic ambiguity refers to purposefully being vague in order to derive personal and/or organizational benefit. Eisenberg's article gained "an appreciative audience."[15] He questioned the notion that open communication is inherently desirable in organizations and argued that "at all levels, members of an organization stand to gain by the strategic use of ambiguity."[16]

There is evidence of the acceptance and application of "strategic ambiguity." Paul and Strbiak, in a special *Journal of Business Communication* issue devoted to ethics, published "The Ethics of Strategic Ambiguity," which discussed under what circumstances strategic ambiguity could or would be ethical.[17] Organizational communication anthologies include Eisenberg's article or related articles, and textbooks describe the advantages of strategically ambiguous communication.[18] One such text contains an exercise that requires students to alter a series of explicit messages to statements that are strategically ambiguous.[19]

A master's thesis entitled "Strategic Ambiguity in Sales Communication" refers to the "new competitive economy [that] may encourage the use of strategic ambiguity within organizations and filter down to the customer level during the persuasive process of personal selling." The thesis examines a specific marketing campaign by the author's former employer, a major drug manufacturer. The employer intended to increase sales for an antidepressant drug that the author of the thesis referred to as "No Blues." A passage from the thesis reads as follows:

> [The drug company] chose to utilize an aggressive product strategy toward those physicians who treat depression in women of childbearing years. At that time, the FDA had categorized all other antidepressants in the US market as "not approved for use in pregnancy." My product was labeled for "use at the doctor/patient discretion" but was not cleared by the FDA for use in pregnancy. Our sales message was

to convince the medical community that no other antidepressant was safe to use in depressed women of childbearing age because of the possible negative effects on the reproductive system. The marketing message was as follows:

"Doctor Smith, while other antidepressants are categorized by the FDA as 'do not use in pregnancy' No Blues is the only antidepressant in the US market that does not fall into this category. No Blues has been available in the US for 10 years and is the most studied and safest antidepressant in the world. Since drug safety is a major concern for all physicians and their patients, No Blues makes for a great choice in the management of your depressed female patients. Isn't this the type of drug that you would want your depressed female patients to have?"

When in late 1997 the FDA added *No Blues* to the "do not use in pregnancy category" the sales force responded by reminding doctors that the use of *No Blues* in pregnancy was never advocated, thus allowing the salesperson to "save face" if in fact the doctor had prescribed the drug to a depressed, pregnant patient. . . . Eisenberg points out that a strategically ambiguous message like this allows the source to reveal or to conceal should it become necessary to save face."[20]

Purported Values of Strategic Ambiguity

Eisenberg and Goodall Jr. digest the concept of strategic ambiguity and list its advantages. The authors write that strategic ambiguity:

- Promotes "unified diversity"
- Facilitates organizational change and creativity
- Preserves privileged positions
- Is deniable[21]

Unified Diversity

"Unified diversity" appears to be an oxymoron. If an organization is unified, how can it be concurrently diverse? Eisenberg and Goodall Jr. argue that "strategic ambiguity takes advantage of the diverse meanings that different people can give to the same message."[22] They argue that strategically ambiguous messages can result in employees "giving diverse meanings to the same message" while, concurrently, the organization is creating a sense of unity.

Consider Avis's long-standing slogan, "We Try Harder." The slogan will mean different things to different members of the organization. "We Try Harder" applies to the people who clean the cars as well as those who rent the cars. If the slogan was "We are the car-renting specialists," it would be less inclusive. Thus, if an organization generates an ambiguous message, receivers may interpret the message variously, yet the message may result in receiver perception of organizational unity.

Eisenberg uses the specific example of "academic freedom" as an ambiguous phrase that promotes unity. Professors and students may have divergent and even contrary conceptions of what is meant by "academic freedom." Nevertheless, the ambiguity of the phrase "academic freedom" can create a sense of unity within colleges and universities. Such unity would disappear if the phrase "academic freedom" was to be defined specifically.

This ability to create the illusion of unity when, in fact, there is—or may be—diversity is considered by proponents to be an advantage of strategic ambiguity.[23]

Facilitation of Organizational Change and Creativity

The advocates for strategic ambiguity claim that by being vague, organizational communicators can facilitate change and creativity. For example, if a manager tells an engineer to design a chair but is ambiguous regarding what type of chair, the resulting design may be for an innovative product that would never have been created had the directive not been ambiguously communicated. If you tell employees precisely what to do, they may do precisely that, and only that which is prescribed. If you are strategically vague, you might receive work that reflects creativity and innovation.

The cruise ship industry is cited by proponents as an example of how strategic ambiguity facilitated organizational change. At one time ships were used primarily for transportation. When the airplane became the dominant means for international travel, the shipping industry had to make some changes. They did so by defining themselves ambiguously. Instead of thinking of ships in terms of transportation, the industry survivors defined themselves ambiguously as "entertainment or hospitality" vehicles. This ambiguity allowed for the evolution of cruise lines that became floating hotels, casinos, and restaurants.[24]

Preserving Privileged Positions and Deniability

Eisenberg and Witten in "Reconsidering Openness in Organizational Communication" comment that by using strategic ambiguity "organizational participants can express their feelings and can deny specific interpretations, should they arise."[25] In essence, supporters of strategic ambiguity argue that persons in authority can use ambiguity to "plausibly deny" blame and maintain their privileged positions. This, as we will see shortly, is a controversial advantage. Yet it is identified as something positive by those who support the notion of "strategic ambiguity."

> "Labor to keep alive in your breast that little spark of celestial fire called conscience."
>
> **—GEORGE WASHINGTON**

Problems with Strategic Ambiguity

One of the advantages of a free society is that it allows disparate ideas to surface. People can express their opinions, and others can assess the merit of these positions. As you might imagine, the idea of strategic ambiguity has been debated and criticized. I have and will continue to be one of the critics. It is difficult to reconcile the purported advantages of strategic ambiguity with its ethical problems and the practical consequences of advocating for ambiguity.

The identification of "strategic ambiguity" as an academic theory is discomforting. Journal article titles like "Reconsidering Openness" or "The Ethics of Strategic Ambiguity" create a membrane of legitimacy for behavior that is morally indefensible, individually (as opposed to organizationally) self-serving, and incontrovertibly dangerous. Arguments articulated in support of strategic ambiguity seem to be contrary to ethical principles. The following are examples:

- "The use of strategic ambiguity complicates the task of interpretation for the receiver."[26]
- "By complicating the sense-making responsibilities of the receiver, strategically ambiguous communication allows the source to both reveal and conceal, to express and protect, should it be necessary to save face."[27]
- "Ambiguity can be used to allow specific interpretations of policy which do more harm than good, to be denied, should they arise."[28]
- "Strategic ambiguity preserves privileged positions by shielding persons with power from close scrutiny by others."[29]
- ". . . strategic ambiguity is said to be deniable; that is the words seem to mean one thing, but under pressure they can seem to mean something else."[30]

Eisenberg and Goodall Jr. do acknowledge the ethical problems with strategic ambiguity.[31] However, the theory has been advanced despite these acknowledgments. According to a February 2003

Applying the Principles—Test Yourself

The human resources department within a large college of business feels as if other units are not giving them the respect that they are due. They suspect that other departments—finance, marketing, and accounting, to be specific—believe that the human resources unit has a weak faculty, weaker students, and unsuccessful alums. For years the human resources department has been getting less financial support from the college in terms of additional faculty, computers, and research equipment. Also, faculty members feel that their chances for promotion and raises are diminished because of the collective departmental reputation. In brief, the faculty feels disrespected by their colleagues and college administrators.

Each year the college publishes a bulletin that presents information on the units within the college. The bulletin includes the following information on each department:

- Faculty and staff profiles
- Mission statement
- General student descriptions in terms of academic qualifications (average test scores, for example)
- Alumni success (the alums are profiled in terms of their salary levels)
- Criteria for maintaining active student status

For the last three years, in addition to the bulletin, all of the information found in the bulletin is also available on the Web. An interested visitor could go to the college Web site, click on a particular department and then, by navigating that unit's pages, find out about the program. While the publication is sent out primarily to people within the university and, on occasion, to prospective students and faculty who visit the campus for interviews, the Web site is accessible without any kind of password by anyone so inclined to visit the site. *The departments themselves create the information that will be placed in the publication and on the Web site.*

An agenda item at a spring meeting of the human resources department was to update material for the following year's bulletin and Web site. At the meeting several faculty members suggested that revising the bulletin/Web site was an excellent way to boost the sagging perception of the unit to external audiences. These persons suggested that the department *inflate* the SAT score statistics and grade point averages of current students and the *income level* of the graduates. The specific arguments in support of falsifying the data were as follows:

- Every other unit does essentially the same thing. It's time that the human resources department stops getting kicked around. They need to play by the real rules. And the real rules, euphemistically, are "to put your best foot forward."
- The department can "put its best foot forward" by being strategically ambiguous and can avoid overtly "lying."
- For example, when describing the salaries of alums, they could write, "The average salary of our alums *in human resources is. . . .*"

Using this phrasing they could justifiably calculate the average salary by *excluding* any alumnus who had been unable to land a job in human resources. The proposed language could be seen as meaning either that the students *were working* in human resources or that they had *studied in* human resources. By using figures pertaining to the former interpretation, the department could easily inflate the salary figures without "really lying" by excluding any low-salaried alums who either were not working in HR or had taken menial jobs. Also, by defining positions *in human resources* narrowly, they could exclude even some HR jobs that were low-paying ones.

Playing with the language similarly would allow the department to inflate the statistics about student SAT scores. Some students were admitted to the department on a pro-bationary basis because their high school test scores were low. If they achieved in classes they could remain in the department. The pro-bationary students took all the same classes as the other students, so, in essence they were part of the department's student popula-tion. However, by excluding the probationary student's SAT scores, they could elevate the "average SAT score" published in the bulletin and on the Web. This would elevate the per-ceptions that other units would have about the HR department.

- The end result of gaining greater respect justifies the deception. Once they become better respected, then they can go back to what they'd done before.

The opponents to this proposal made the following counterarguments:

- If we're caught, our image could be even worse than it is now.
- It might not affect our image positively anyway.
- It's lying no matter how you finesse the language.
- It doesn't matter how many other departments are doing it.
- Given the Web, the information could go to many external audiences now as well as internal audiences.

Despite the opposing arguments the depart-ment decided to make the adjustments to the language in the publication and on the Web site.

- Did the HR department do anything wrong?
- Did the HR department lie, or were they just being strategically ambiguous?
- Are the three arguments they used to justify the behavior valid arguments?
- What are the merits of the five counterarguments?

article in the *Journal of Applied Communication Research*, "virtually all deception scholars" define a lie "as a deliberate attempt to mislead." Some writers elaborate on this definition by adding the words "without the prior consent of the target."[32] Using even the latter, more restrictive, definition, is there any meaningful distinction between strategic ambiguity that attempts to "complicate the sense making apparatus of the receiver" and a lie that is a "deliberate attempt to mislead"?

Consequences of Strategic Ambiguity

Tompkins refers to the dangers of strategic ambiguity in *Organizational Communication Imperatives*. Writing about the space shuttle *Challenger* disaster, he remarks: "Those who find the concept of 'strategic ambiguity' appealing should read the addendum to Chapter V of the Rogers Commission Report. They will be sobered by the possible consequences of ambiguity, strategic or not. Ambiguity was a factor in the *Challenger* accident"[33]

The problem with fostering the idea of strategic ambiguity is that the theory provides a license for people to be misleading. Strategic ambiguity promotes the notion that deception is defensible. Deception, simply, is dangerous. Deceit is corrosive to the organization and to the people who comprise the organization. This is the consistent message of all those who argue for organiza-tional transparency. The advantages of strategic ambiguity are not organizational advantages but individual advantages—and even these are short term. In Chapter 10 we will see that most experts in crisis communication argue for transparency and openness when dealing with organizational crises. Deliberate ambiguity militates against transparency and openness.

Bok argues that those who are deceived become "resentful, disappointed and suspicious. . . . They see that they have been manipulated, that the deceit made them unable to make choices for themselves according to the most adequate information available."[34] She comments that even those who are inclined to deceive others desire to be treated without deceit.[35] Further, she argues that the damage of deceit transcends the effects on the deceived and includes the erosion of societal trust.[36] Stephen Covey's heralded 2006 book *The Speed of Trust* is subtitled appropriately—trust is *"The One Thing That Changes Everything."*[37]

In organizational communication terms, deliberate dishonesty is likely to result in bruised interpersonal relationships that will affect the organization's climate and culture. The affected relationships and damaged climate can undermine organizational communication and efficiency. Dalla Costa, in *The Ethical Imperative: Why Moral Leadership Is Good Business*, comments that the reason for developing an ethical orientation in organizations comes "not just [from] what we gain from being ethical, but in realizing what we lose—in economic, social, natural, and personal terms—by succumbing to irresponsibility."[38]

Assessing Attitudes toward Ethical Communication

Individual attitudes toward honesty in communication are important to assess. Merrill points out that "the only valid ethics is that which is within each person."[39] This seems self-evident. Individual ethics, as a practical matter, transcend institutional codes of ethics in that personal convictions, more than company policy, fuel what becomes the amalgam of corporate philosophy. Of course, the reverse can occur. Individuals can adopt behaviors that are the attitudes of the organization. In either case it is valuable to examine how those with whom we work feel about ethical issues. If organizational communicators are compelled to make ethical decisions, and if those decisions can affect the performance of an organization, it is wise to explore the range of attitudes employees have that pertain to ethical considerations and organizational communication.

In an issue of the *Journal of Employee Communication Management*, I reported the results of a study I conducted on attitudes toward ethical organizational communication.[40] Fifty-six participants, all of whom were part-time MBA students (and concurrently full-time employees), were asked to rate eighteen communication actions, policies, or tendencies in terms of the ethical nature of each of the behaviors.[41]

Before reading further, please take a few moments and respond to the questions in the survey on the next page.

What Constitutes Ethical Communication?

Three groups of respondents participated in the study. After the individuals within each group had completed the survey, the members of that group discussed their positions on the items. The discussions were revealing for a number of reasons.

Different Value Systems
Attitudes on what constituted ethical communication varied dramatically. What some persons considered inappropriate or amoral was deemed perfectly legitimate by others. These differences led to several bouts of incredulous staring, head shaking, and less than dispassionate arguments. Both the polarity and the disbelief are worth noting. The respondents seemed stunned to discover that others with whom they could be working would have such disparate values and might behave according to their principles.

Applying the Principles—Self-Inventory

The following statements refer to various communication behaviors. Please assess the ethical nature of these behaviors by placing a number, 1–5, next to each item using the following scale.

1 = Highly unethical
2 = Somewhat unethical
3 = Neither ethical nor unethical
4 = Ethical, for the most part
5 = There is nothing unethical about this at all

Statements

1. Articulating a department or organizational policy that cannot and will not be enforced in order to make the department or organization look good to outsiders.

2. Responding to a crisis by denying allegations that you know to be true when you know you can get away with the fabrications.

3. Not overtly lying, but omitting key facts when communicating to the media about a crisis within your organization.

4. Deliberately lying to employees about layoffs because the truth will demotivate them.

5. Telling employees that they are empowered in order to boost their willingness to work when you have no intention of so empowering them.

6. Deliberately using vague wording on job descriptions to allow management more flexibility in assigning tasks.

7. Deliberately communicating a high evaluation for employees when lower evaluations are more appropriate in order not to create tension among employees.

8. Deliberately communicating a low evaluation to employees who deserve higher evaluations in order to get more out of them.

9. Using e-mail to communicate bad news to employees when you know the employee never uses e-mail so you can have a record of the message and never have to face an angry employee.

10. Not answering your phone and allowing the voice mail to pick up when you know who is calling and don't want to speak with them.

11. Deliberately calling someone when you know they are not in so that you can speak to a machine and avoid the person.

12. Placing the names of all members of a committee on a report supposedly generated by the committee when only one or two persons had anything to do with the document—either the actual writing of it or the ideas therein.

13. Requiring employees to sign an "I have read the policy manual" statement when you know they are unlikely to have read it, but you can later hold them responsible for having read it.

14. Deliberately telling two employees to do the same task without informing the employees that they are both doing it independently with the goal being to get the best product.

15. Excessive use of e-mail for personal use as opposed to business use. (Excessive here means you use e-mail more for personal use than for business use.)

16. Having a suggestion box and not reading the suggestions.

17. Having a better external network for customers with complaints than an internal network for employees with complaints.

18. Using the informal grapevine to spread inaccurate information that will tarnish the integrity of a rival within the organization.

One person commented that "[u]nless I preface what I say with, 'This is the truth,' then it is the receivers' obligation to discover whether what is being said is the truth. It is not the source's responsibility to be truthful. Therefore there's nothing unethical about deception unless a falsehood is prefaced with 'this is the truth.'"

While several participants visibly shuddered when hearing this person's perspective on honesty, there were others who nodded their heads in agreement. The reality is this: there is a great range in attitudes on what constitutes ethical or unethical communicative behavior.

Ethical Behavior Is Justified on the Basis of Personal Experience

Participants often defended communication activity as ethical not on the basis of the action's inherent integrity, but because they themselves had communicated similarly or because such "things are done." This indicates that what prevails becomes ethical to some by virtue of the fact that it prevails. It was remarkable how often respondents, without hesitation, would say, "That's perfectly fine. I do that all the time."

On occasion there would be some contextual justification, but often the fact that it had been done, in and of itself, served as evidence of the legitimacy of the activity.

Victimization as Criteria for Ethical Communication

Items were often considered unethical when the respondents had been victims, or perceived themselves to be victims, of the particular act. This became apparent in discussion about item 4:

> Deliberately lying to employees about layoffs because the truth will demotivate them.

Those who had been victims during layoffs considered "deliberately lying to employees about layoffs" unethical communication. Those who had experience communicating to subordinates during layoffs felt differently.

Organizational Responsibility as Justification for Ethical Behavior

Ethical legitimacy was often assessed in terms of organizational pragmatics. Some persons defended what others called unethical behavior on the basis that questionable behavior is not unethical if it, in fact, could be considered good management. In other words, these respondents claimed that if an act was considered to be in the best interests of the company, then the act was ethical because it is right to do what is good for the company. Similarly, if an act was perceived to be a waste of company resources, then it was considered unethical. The communication act was considered unethical because it would reflect poor management, and, it was reasoned, it is unethical to manage poorly when one's job is to manage well. Other discussants found this crucible to be meaningless when examining ethical issues.

Highs and Lows

Table 4.1 provides a breakdown of the results from the study. As indicated previously, there were great differences in terms of attitudes about ethical communication. However, the items considered most unethical were those that involved deliberate malice, overt lying (as opposed to deception by omission), and promulgation of spurious policies and evaluations.

The specific items were:

- Lying about potential layoffs (item 4)
- Using the grapevine to unofficially damage others (item 18)

- Denying accurate allegations during crises (item 2)
- Disseminating bogus messages about empowerment (item 5)

Items considered relatively benign included those that involved ambiguity, omissions (as opposed to overt lying), and avoidance.

The specific items were:

- Deliberately writing job descriptions vaguely to allow subsequent "flexibility" (item 6)
- Exacting unrealistic pledges of familiarity with company policy (item 13)
- Deliberately phoning others when the caller is aware of the absence of the receiver (item 11)

How did your individual responses to the survey questions correspond to the survey responses reflected in Table 4.1?

Table 4.1 Average Scores for Each Item

1= highly unethical   5 =nothing unethical about the behavior.

Ten of the items were considered more *unethical* than *ethical*. In rank order they are presented below.

Item	
18. Using the grapevine to spread damaging information	Avg. = (1.33)
8. Evaluating negatively to motivate employees	(1.53)
4. Deliberate lying about layoffs	(1.6)
2. Denying allegations during crises despite charge authenticity	(1.63)
5. Disseminating spurious messages promising empowerment	(1.82)
9. Communicating bad news via e-mail to persons who don't use e-mail in order to have a record of the act and avoid confrontation	(1.96)
16. Operating spurious suggestion programs	(2.14)
1. Articulating spurious policies for window dressing	(2.15)
7. Evaluating positively in order to decrease tension	(2.45)
12. Crediting nominal participants in project submissions	(2.71)

Eight of the items were considered more ethical than unethical.
In rank order they are presented below.

Item	
10. Screening out undesired phone callers	Avg. = (4.41)
11. Calling when you're aware that the receiver is not present	(3.75)
6. Wording job descriptions vaguely for subsequent flexibility	(3.64)
13. Requiring unrealistic pledges of familiarity with policy	(3.46)
14. Telling two persons to perform same task to get better result	(3.35)
17. Having better external than internal network for complaints	(3.14)
3. Omitting key facts when speaking to the media after crises	(3.1)
15. Using e-mail for personal use more than business use	(3.07)

Making Ethical Decisions

Honesty in organizational communication is not overrated, nor is it an ethereal concept only suitable for after work musings. It is central to the job of communicating with and to employees and clients. We all are offended when we have been misled, and it is difficult to justify misleading others. Even for those who have little patience with "golden rule" logic, the practical consequences of dishonesty can be significant.

Resolving Ethical Issues in Organizational Communication

Not everyone cares about ethical considerations. For some, ethics is an academic enterprise with no place in a practical world. In your class discussions you may have already discovered this. However, as we have seen, ethical factors can affect what is communicated in your organizations. This section is intended to suggest some guidelines for making the difficult decisions regarding ethics in organizational communication.

Establish Codes of Ethics

Individual, unit, or industry codes of ethics can, but do not always, set a meaningful guideline for ethical organizational communication (see sample in Table 4.2). These codes will work only if the individual, unit, or industry is serious about making them work. Four requirements are essential:

- There needs to be a well-thought-out list of guidelines. This includes a clear definition of any gray terms. A good way to hammer out a code of ethics is to try to respond to ethical cases using the code. In short, the code must be functional.
- The guidelines need to be published or otherwise disseminated in a manner that makes access to them easy. The guidelines must be familiar to all who work in the organization. Sometimes an organization has published a code of ethics, but some members of the organization are not even aware that such a code exists.
- There needs to be a commitment from top management to enforce the code. If the code is merely window dressing, then the charade should be eliminated.
- A meaningful method for enforcing the guidelines has to be a component of the code. If there are no punishments for violations, then the code becomes valueless.

Employ Ethical Yardsticks

Philosophers have long discussed ethical issues. Some of their approaches to resolving these matters are presented below.

The Categorical Imperative: Often associated with Immanuel Kant, this approach assumes that there are universal absolutes regarding what is ethical and what is not. In assessing any particular act, what one needs to do is use the absolute as a guideline. This philosophy is actually clarified by defining the utilitarian approach, with which the categorical imperative is often contrasted.

Utilitarianism: John Stuart Mill wrote of "The Greatest Happiness Principle." Essentially Mill's argument was that what made an act moral was whether the action benefited the greatest numbers of those affected by it. Obviously, the categorical imperative is at variance with utilitarianism. The former argues that receivers' collective happiness is no yardstick. The yardstick is hard and fast. The latter argues that collective benefit is the primary yardstick.

Table 4.2 Sample Code of Ethics: International Association of Business Communicators

Professional communicators:

1. Uphold the credibility and dignity of their profession by practicing honest, candid, and timely communication and by fostering the free flow of essential information in accord with the public interest.

2. Disseminate accurate information and promptly correct any erroneous communication for which they may be responsible.

3. Understand and support the principles of free speech, freedom of assembly, and access to an open marketplace of ideas, and act accordingly.

4. Are sensitive to cultural values and beliefs and engage in fair, balanced communication activities that foster and encourage mutual understanding.

5. Refrain from taking part in any undertaking "which" the communicator considers to be unethical.

6. Obey laws and public policies governing their professional activities and are sensitive to the spirit of all laws and regulations and, should any law or public policy be violated, for whatever reason, act promptly to correct the situation.

7. Give credit for unique expressions borrowed from others and identify the sources and purposes of all information disseminated to the public.

8. Protect confidential information and, at the same time, comply with all legal requirements for the disclosure of information affecting the welfare of others.

9. Do not use confidential information gained as a result of professional activities for personal benefit and do not represent conflicting or competing interests without written consent of those involved.

10. Do not accept undisclosed gifts or payments for professional services from anyone other than a client or employer.

11. Do not guarantee results that are beyond the power of the practitioner to deliver.

12. Are honest not only with others but also, and most importantly, with themselves as individuals; for a professional communicator seeks the truth and speaks that truth first to the self.

http://www.iabc.com/about/code.htm August 9, 2009

Veil of Ignorance: Philosopher John Rawls argues that justice should be blind, and this approach suggests that ethical arbiters go behind a veil to make decisions that do not take into consideration role, financial influence, or political power. The veil of ignorance, if people legitimately accept the challenge of standing behind it, guarantees dispassionate assessments and is likely to increase the chances of quality decision making.

Aristotle's Golden Mean: This refers to Aristotle's approach that between two poles in decision making there is a golden mean that would make for an optimal decision. The mean, a statistical term referring to the arithmetic average of any sum, would be that decision that falls between the extremes. Such a mean, according to this approach, is a golden resolution to ethical dilemmas.

Would These Yardsticks Help Janet in the "Rachel Adams" Case?

Obviously, these approaches are only useful if the individuals, units, or industries care to employ them. Even so, the applications of any of the principles are a complex matter. To see how difficult it is, I suggest that you attempt to apply any one of the yardsticks or methods to either the Ballinger case (Case 4.1) or the Ethical Probe about the human resources department.

It is relatively easy to contemplate morality. It's more difficult to be moral and ethical. The dollars and cents issues that surround organizations are catalysts for instrumental rationality. If an employee believes that she or he can get a raise, or credit, or perhaps a promotion by being unethical, then perhaps at that point to that employee, ethics will take a back seat to the financial considerations. People are quite capable of justifying borderline behavior when unethical behavior provides some political, economic, or personal reward.

We have discussed the reality of disparate value systems. One of the problems with Kant's categorical imperative (or other ethical guidelines) is that few can agree on terms. What ethics means to me may have no meaning to you. Also, many of the absolutes that have been agreed upon have been codified into law. Therefore many of the issues not so codified become areas of disagreement without any real procedures for enforcement.

It's difficult to apply ethical yardsticks when people disagree on the number of inches to a yard or whether a situation needs to be measured at all. What's racist to some is egalitarian to another. What's obscene to some is benign to another. Defining and controlling ethical behavior is like trying to add two numbers when the parties involved cannot agree on numeric values and give lip service to the rules of arithmetic.

Ethics is part of the fabric of organizational communication. Individuals, departments, and the collective that is the organization are affected by ethical decisions pertaining to how and what is communicated in organizations. The question becomes to what extent an organization and those within it are willing to work to ensure that communications are characterized by honesty and integrity.

Working to ensure that communication is ethical is worth the effort. The bottom line is that ethical communication affects the bottom line. The residual of open, honest, transparent communication is an environment that is characterized by trust. Ciancutti and Steding, in *Built on Trust: Gaining Competitive Advantage in Any Organization*, write that we are a society in search of trust. An organization in which people earn one another 's trust . . . has a competitive advantage.[42]

Dalla Costa lists several tangible benefits of what he refers to as an ethical corporate character:

- A trusted company attracts and holds on to good people.
- A trusting work environment creates the support that fuels creativity.
- A trusting company is motivated to produce excellence in both revenues and social results.[43]

The challenge for organizational men and women is to realize these benefits by communicating ethically. The challenge for organizations is to seek out those employees who are willing to accept the responsibility to communicate ethically.

In December 2001 the University of Notre Dame, in essence, fired football coach George O'Leary. O'Leary had been named head coach only weeks before. The university accepted his resignation because it was discovered that O'Leary had included inaccurate information in prior biographical releases. The coach's bios had stated that he'd earned letters for playing college football when, in fact, he had not. He'd also indicated in these bios that he had earned a master's degree, and he had not. O'Leary had been a successful football coach at other institutions. Neither the letters nor the graduate credential had been prerequisites for the Notre Dame job. What had, apparently, been a prerequisite was honesty.

On the basis of the university's decision, would you be more or less inclined to work or study at Notre Dame University?

Victoria Kohlasch: Managing Director of Marketing

Victoria Kohlasch is the Managing Director of Marketing for CRIC Capital. CRIC Capital purchases real estate from, and leases it back to, companies through a variety of customized net leases. These leases allow the organizations to free up capital for their core businesses. Ms. Kohlasch is responsible for CRIC 's marketing and advertising programs. She has more than 12 years of experience in brand development and strategic marketing and has worked with several organizations to improve both their internal and external communications.

As you read through this section, consider the following questions:

- How would a critical theorist react to Kohlasch 's perspective regarding the short-term benefits of deceptive communication and new truths ?
- What is your feeling about her position on sharing information?
- Does her position about the attractiveness of Footprints make sense?
- How would a cultural theorist react to the bolded comments?

The benefits of deceptive communication are, at best, short term. In the final analysis dishonest, misleading communication has a corrosive effect on the organization. When you lie you are not creating a new truth. You may think you are, but what you are creating is a foundation for pervasive deception in your organization. You're not convincing people that x is y, you're convincing people that it is okay in your organization to say that x is y, even though x may not be y.

Now, the people who run a business have a responsibility to know their internal audiences. Being honest does not mean flooding audiences with irrelevant information. There are some people who do not need nor want to be swamped with details about a particular transaction. To give people all information about some matters is likely to make communication more, not less, difficult. There are some things to share with employees and other things to not share—not because you want to deny people information, but because some people can't or don't want to process that information, or because releasing such information could jeopardize the company from a legal standpoint.

You have the responsibility not to intentionally mislead your audiences. And this responsibility is practical as well as moral. Here at CRIC Capital, for example, Adam King developed a wonderful internal newsletter called *Footprints*. *Footprints* has been a very valuable communication tool. People, even people who provided information to Adam for *Footprints*—who know what's in a particular edition—look forward to getting the newsletter. How eager will people be to read information about a company if the organization has a reputation for being deceptive with its communication? Do you want to read about a company's financial status if it's common knowledge that the top brass tacitly approves of misrepresentation? *Footprints* is valuable here not only because it is handsomely and intelligently put together, but because people trust the information that's in it.

If a company lies about what its product can do, the employees say to themselves, "Can our product really do this?" and when they say, "No, it really can't," you lose their passion and their commitment. You lose work productivity. You lose a lot of things that are not easy to measure. You would have high turnover and would have a hard time maintaining consistency because with high turnover it's difficult to maintain your institutional history.

PRACTITIONER PERSPECTIVE *continued*

All of these things affect bottom line profit.

There's no place for lying in business. However, there are many places where business-people routinely lie. This is, unfortunately, life. If you were to go to every office in this building complex and ask the people if they thought lying is wrong, 70 percent would tell you that lying is wrong. However, I'd estimate that only 10 percent of those offices would be telling you the truth. That's the irony. Ninety percent of the people who tell you that they value truth either are lying or are kidding themselves because—as their behavior demonstrates—they are at times deceptive or purposefully vague to cause confusion. That's life. But, just because it's life doesn't make it right or bright. Codes of ethics are valuable if, and only if, they are adhered to and enforced. Otherwise the codes become another type of deceptive communication.

SUMMARY: A TOOLBOX

- Researchers such as Redding and Tompkins have argued that credibility, honesty, and openness are essential for effective organizational communication.
- Most organizational communication activities are affected by ethical decisions.
- What has been called the normalization of deviance has affected ethical decision making, organizational behaviors, and organizational success.
- While strategic ambiguity has been advanced by some writers, the value of deliberately being vague is suspect.
- Perspectives on ethical behavior are wide ranging. Criteria used for determining ethical communications vary.
- Techniques can be used as guidelines for ethical communication, but they require dedication and work.

REVIEW AND DISCUSSION QUESTIONS

1. Identify five communication activities in which you engage that require making ethical decisions. What are the criteria you employ when making these decisions?
2. In your opinion, is honesty overrated?
3. What are the advantages and disadvantages of strategic ambiguity?
4. Which of the ethical yardsticks identified in this chapter is most valuable for the ethical decisions you need to make when you communicate?
5. What does the phrase "put your best foot forward" mean to you?
6. Does deviance ever truly become normalized?
7. Assume that an instructor announced that she or he would be administering an exam on the following Friday. Assume that you asked what would be on the exam. Would it make sense for the instructor to be vague about the nature of the test so that you would be encouraged to study comprehensively and not just focus on identified question topics?

GROUP/ROLE-PLAY

In a group of four to six, review the issues surrounding the case that begins this chapter. Attempt to gain consensus regarding the questions at the end of the chapter.

For the role-play, one member of the group assumes the role of Rachel and another assumes the role of Janet. The remaining members assume the role of people who are on Rachel's team.

- Role-play a meeting of Rachel, Janet, and Rachel's team members held immediately after Rachel realizes there has been a merger and before Rachel has been laid off. Assume Rachel has asked Janet for a meeting to explain (a) Janet's rationale for being ambiguous and (b) Janet's prediction about the future.

PART **2**

COMMUNICATION IN A COMPLEX SYSTEM

Chapter **5**

Managing Information

Chapter in a Nutshell

People in organizations have more alternatives now than ever before when they select media for communication. As opposed to even just fifteen years ago, the revolution in communication technology is staggering. Now nearly everyone has access to e-mail, the company intranet site, and a mobile phone with multiple features. As before, managing information requires the intelligent use of the various communication alternatives available. But now the number of alternatives available has mushroomed. Should a Web site be the main place for posting organizational information? Should e-mail be used in lieu of face-to-face interaction? Should a company utilize the new social media, like blogs or wikis? Information management also involves understanding what types of messages need to be communicated in organizations. Most people would agree that employees require information about safety, benefits, job tasks, and organizational policies. However, do employees need to know about the activities and successes of other workers? Do they need to know what the marketing director has accomplished or the changes implemented by the new coordinator of community outreach or that Tuesday is Joan's thirty-fifth birthday? This chapter examines what needs to be communicated in organizations and what methods can be used to communicate these messages effectively.

When you have completed this chapter, you should be able to:

- Define *task, maintenance,* and *human messages.*
- Identify five characteristics of effectively communicated information.
- Define media richness.
- Describe the distinction between first- and second-level effects of technology.
- Explain what is meant by new social media.
- Define the phrase "knowledge management."
- Discuss the implications of knowledge management for the development of organizational culture.
- Explain the perspective of those who support the need for *human moments.*

CASE 5.1

Communicating Tasks, Policy, Recognition, and Culture

Rayna Smith worked in a hospital and was familiar with a piece of hospital equipment used for conducting diagnostic tests on patients. She'd worked with it and knew how to use it, and management thought she could teach others to use it. Smith was not a trainer, but she was called into her superior's office and asked to train twelve other individuals to use the equipment. Her superior was very supportive. She smiled and said, "I know you can do this and we really need your help."

Smith was unsure, but decided to accept the responsibility. In a way, she was excited by the challenge. She had never had to explain how to use the equipment before and thought it might be enjoyable in the way that work can sometimes be fun. Smith carefully planned a training program that included an assessment mechanism.

Rayna Smith implemented the program. She followed her plan and orally explained how to use the equipment. She demonstrated some techniques and asked the others to watch and follow her. Afterwards she took any questions the trainees had. Finally, after a digestion period, she observed each of the twelve as they successfully completed the test.

Smith was elated. She had gotten the message through to all of them.

She phoned her superior to relay the news of the trainees' success and was disappointed when the boss was not in. She left a voice mail message indicating that all twelve had completed the training. Smith didn't hear back from her boss that day and that bothered her a bit, but a day later she coincidentally ran into her superior as they both passed in the hallway. The boss seemed to be in a hurry, but as they came close the boss winked at her and gave her a "thumbs-up." Smith gave her the thumbs-up sign in return and went on her way. The boss's thumbs-up was the only acknowledgment Smith ever received from her superior about her training effort.

Weeks later, a thirteenth person needed to be trained, and management came again to Rayna Smith and asked her to explain the operation to the thirteenth employee. This time the request was unwelcome, which was made clear by the way Smith sighed and then nearly gasped when she was asked, face to face, to take on the responsibility. While she had enjoyed the work, she had other tasks to do. What's more, it would have been nice to receive some type of acknowledgment for her initial effort. After a moment, Smith agreed reluctantly and indicated her agreement by tersely saying, "Fine, get me his e-mail address and I'll do it."

The thirteenth person, Tom, couldn't get it. No matter how hard or how many times Smith attempted to explain how to use the equipment, he simply could not get it. She told him to do one thing and he would do another. She told him to watch her and do what she did. Tom watched and then didn't follow Smith's lead. Exasperated this time, and not exhilarated, Rayna Smith left a voice mail message for her superior explaining that the trainee seemed to be unable to understand the information. She didn't want to talk to her boss, so Smith made the call at a time when she knew her boss would not be around. After leaving the voice mail message, Smith figured that was the end of it.

The hospital, however, needed another person to perform the operation. Without Smith being aware of it, her manager approached Tom and asked him if he could operate the equipment. Tom, the unsuccessful trainee, commented that he, in fact, could work the equipment. Rayna Smith was not consulted.

When she discovered that Tom was operating the equipment, Rayna Smith was livid. She approached her superior and literally shouted her objection. Her boss said that Rayna's tone of voice was inappropriate. The boss also commented that Smith was now "out of the decision-making loop. I thought Tom could handle it and I made the call."

"On what basis?" shouted Smith. "Tom is an idiot!!!"

"Why are you so upset?"

"You know exactly why I'm upset."

The boss tried to placate Smith. "Maybe you did a better job than you think you did." Smith was implacable and repeated, "He was incompetent!!" Then, very sarcastically, she added, "It's nice to know that what I communicate to you is valued and respected, thanks a lot."

Subsequently, communication and relationships between Rayna Smith and her superiors were strained. Conversations were typically short and solely focused on business issues. When her superiors attempted to lighten the mood, Smith frowned, got back to the point, and then moved away. Smith eventually left the hospital.

In her exit interview she said, among other things, that it was never communicated to her that she was a valued employee despite her extra efforts. The only message of appreciation she received was the nonverbal thumbs-up. She said that the absence of communication when hiring the thirteenth person to operate the equipment was one of the worst things that had ever happened to her while working in an organization. She implied that if she were

a man and the thirteenth trainee were a woman, this never would have happened. "I wonder if I would have been consulted if my name was Tom and the trainee's name was Rayna," she said.

Did Smith communicate effectively with her boss when she:

• Described the success of the initial training?
• Informed the boss of Tom's failure?
• Expressed her outrage at Tom's hiring?
• Intimated that there had been gender discimination?

Did Smith's boss communicate effectively when she:

• Expressed appreciation for Smith's work?
• Hired Tom to do the work that Smith attempted to train him to do?

Did the communications:

• Reflect the organizational culture?
• Help create the organizational culture?

How would a critical theorist respond to this case?

July 8, 2008, shortly before 7 A.M., ESPN 2 "Mike and Mike in the Morning"

Mike Golic: How was your vacation?

Mike Greenberg: Terrible. We land and I have no access with my Blackberry. I panic. No e-mail. My wife talks to the kids as we leave the airport. We drive into the city and she points out the sites and scenery. Not me. I panic. No Blackberry? What am I going to do?

Mike Golic: Maybe talk to somebody. You know people have just forgotten how to talk.

Mike Greenberg: I don't want to make light of it because I have never been addicted to anything, but apparently now I am addicted to the Internet.[1]

Information and Organizations

Daft and Lengel begin and end a *Management Science* article with a simple question: "Why do organizations process information?"[2] The answer, they conclude, is to "effectively manage uncertainty and equivocality."[3]

Uncertainty refers to the absence of information in organizations. *Equivocality* refers to the existence of conflicting or ambiguous information. Organizational women and men need to receive messages so that they will be able to function as the valuable organizational resources that they can be. In the absence of knowledge, or the presence of ambiguity, not only will employees be frustrated, but the organization as a whole will be frustrated. For example:

- Without information about a product's specifications, a salesperson can not effectively sell the product.
- When two messages about organizational policy seem to conflict, an employee may select the wrong information and follow a counterproductive course.

Information and Organizational Health

An organization can *survive* with uncertainty and equivocality, but the absence of important information can reduce organizational efficiency. Consider the following metaphor. Think of information as oxygen in our respiratory systems—that is, imagine information to be that which facilitates the physical operation of the organizational system. Organizations that communicate poorly can "live," but like the ingestion of unclean and perhaps toxic air, equivocality and uncertainty will result in a system that does not function as well as it might. At some point, the system might even "get sick," malfunction, and become significantly less productive. Uncertainty and equivocality can affect the fiber of the organizational foundation.[4]

Not all managers acknowledge the merit of this fundamental principle. Tompkins writes about a perspective some administrators hold about managing information. This perspective assumes that the organization is better off when employees do not receive information pertaining to the organization. Tompkins reports that "too often" managers keep employees in the dark and periodically shower them with valueless information in order to keep them uninformed while concurrently creating the illusion that information is being relayed.[5] The notion that good management is facilitated when useless memos, bulk e-mailings, and thick but meaningless reports are sporadically dumped on employees is inconsistent with any credible management theory. Uncertainty and equivocality are deleterious to organizational health. Therefore the twofold question becomes: What types of messages need to be communicated in organizations, and how should these messages be relayed?

Types of Messages

In order to be efficient, organizations must be adept at communicating three types of messages to their internal audiences. These types of messages have been labeled task, maintenance, and human messages.[6]

Task Messages

Task messages refer to those communications that explain employee jobs or responsibilities. For example:

- If you need to write a draft of a speech for your CEO by Wednesday at 4 P.M. then you need to be informed that that is, in fact, a job task.
- If you are a manager in a convenience store and you inform an employee to move the soup from aisle A to aisle B, you are relaying a task message.
- When your instructor announces a reading that will be due for the next session, she or he is communicating a task message.

Task messages are important regardless of whether you are a classical, human resources, systems, cultural, or critical theorist. Task messages, at first glance, may seem to be simple to communicate and not to present a great challenge. However, because of inattention to detail or unwise choice of communication media, even task messages can result in communication distortion. Consider the following examples:

(1) I manage thirty-five full-time and fifteen part-time staff members. Each of my subordinates is responsible for specific tasks, which require accessing accounts via a PC. The users have varying levels of computing knowledge, and therefore the degree of assistance they need from the systems people varies. A while back my office received forty new computers to run Windows NT. Each staff member attended a short training session on the basic operations of NT.

The communication problem occurred three weeks after the computers were installed. Due to the nature of the system, any errors that occur on the network server would now be observed by all end users. There was a problem with a product called Chameleon, and therefore all of my people were unable to access accounts. This halted work in the office. I was notified of the problem and was told how users could fix the problem.

As I mentioned, there are fifty people who work for me. I broadcast an e-mail explaining **precisely** what they had to do in order to rid the computer of the Chameleon problem. Only an idiot wouldn't have been able to complete the task. Some users followed my directions and fixed the problem. A large number, however, didn't read my e-mail. One by one an army of these people paid a personal visit to my office. When I told them that I'd sent them comprehensive step-by-step instructions, I heard a host of incredible responses that included:

- I deleted it.
- I didn't know it pertained to me.
- I didn't have time to read it.

I'm busy. I don't have time for this kind of thing. After the fourth or fifth visitor approached me, I lost patience. The sixth or seventh met a very unhappy camper. Believe me, I couldn't have explained what they had to do more clearly.

(2) I'm a salesperson and our store recently changed managers. The replacement manager came from a different branch of the same nationwide chain. He was well experienced in management, but not in communication. For instance, I think he was intimidated by the salespeople. He is a relatively shy and quiet person who doesn't say much—even in conversations that are not job related.

When he came to us he noticed that our store wasn't as tidy as his other unit had been. He wanted to tell us about his dissatisfaction. He wanted to tell us to clean up more, but he just couldn't do it.

Instead he wrote a small note addressing the problem and placed it on a tiny bulletin board in an obscure spot in the back office area where no one spends any time at all. Of course, the tidiness of the store stayed the same. I really lost a lot of respect for the new manager and I believe he turned the situation into a larger problem than it had been originally.

(3) I'm a manager. About ten people work under me. On a Monday I assigned a worker to a project that absolutely had to be taken care of within a week. I explained this in detail—face to face. I asked on a number of occasions if he understood the assignment, and I was explicit about the need for the work to be completed after the following weekend.

On Friday, this particular worker came to the office with a bad cold. He was sneezing and coughing and looked under the weather. I knew that he'd been working hard on the project, so I figured if I let him go home a bit early, he could rest up and bang it out at home over the weekend when he felt better. People work at home all the time in this business. I told him to take the rest of the day off, but to make sure that he got the work done when he felt better. He told me "no problem" and left. On Monday, after he got settled,

I asked for the completed work. He looked at me like I was crazy and said that I'd told him that I could complete it on Monday. I nearly went berserk. He saw me getting angry and said almost indignantly that I had told him that he could take the day off on Friday, so he assumed that that meant he could work on it for an extra day. I was very upset at the irresponsibility because now I had to either go to my superior and explain why the work was late or complete the whole thing myself within an hour.

These examples illustrate that communicating task messages may be more difficult than we think. Each instance reflects a different problem. In case (1) the choice of media and receiver responses to e-mail affected the communication of information. In case (2) the interpersonal skills of the manager and media choice affected the process. In case (3) the manager did not recognize the phenomenon known as *selective perception*, i.e., the tendency for people to choose what they want to receive from a message. In each instance, the result of the poor communication transcended inaccurate receipt of information and resulted in negative attitudes. These attitudes lingered and affected the evolving climate of the organization or department.

Maintenance Messages

Maintenance messages explain guidelines, rules, policies, regulations, objectives, and any related procedural information. The word "maintenance" is used to describe this category of message because these communications help *maintain* the operation of the organization.

The list of courses for your next semester, whether presented in a brochure or posted on your university's Web site, is an example of a compilation of maintenance messages. An e-mail that lets you know when the computers will be down, or who the new vice president will be, or what the procedure is for requesting a salary increment—all of these are examples of maintenance messages. Sometimes maintenance messages can be used in conjunction with task messages. If a task message informs employees to record all incoming client calls, the maintenance messages would include the procedures for recording client calls.

Maintenance messages may also seem simple to communicate, but as was the case with the task examples, there are instances when poorly conceived approaches are used to relay this information. The following are two examples:

(1) Three weeks ago I joined a small biotech firm where I oversee all financial activity for two of the company's five manufacturing facilities. Since I started working at this new company, my boss has spent little time with me. He is extremely busy and under a lot of pressure. He has given me assignments and quickly rushed through instructions about how to do them. I ask as many questions as I can about the procedures for an assignment before he gets called to a meeting or receives an urgent phone call and I am left to fend for myself.

While I do have experience in financial matters and can sometimes figure out the procedures that govern a particular task, I frequently need information that only my boss possesses. Different organizations have varied policies on how to process financial information. When my boss vanishes, I'm forced to wait "in limbo" until I can again speak with him and clarify questions so that I can obtain the information I need.

While I am "in limbo," I have attempted to ask my boss's other subordinate for the information. While this sometimes remedies the problem, it frequently complicates it. Often the information I receive from this subordinate contradicts what my boss has told me. This is because my boss and this subordinate do not communicate either because of their busy schedules and, moreover, are apparently following different procedures when doing the same tasks! The bottom line is this: I know what I'm supposed to do but need information to understand the guidelines. I can't get it.

(2) I work as a cocktail waitress. Right in the middle of a shift on a Saturday night, my manager approached me with the new updated employee handbook of rules and regulations. He also had

with him a clipboard with signatures on it. The following words were written at the top of the sheet on the clipboard: "I have received and read my copy of the employee handbook, and am fully aware of the regulations and penalties therein."

I had a whole section of people waiting for drinks and absolutely no time to read the handbook, which was about thirty pages long. I thought that since he approached me with the handbook at such a hectic time, it didn't matter that much to management whether I read the handbook or didn't read the handbook. I signed the clipboard and tossed the handbook behind the bar where it is probably still sitting. I don't know of any waitress who read it. For the most part, people just laughed when they saw it. I think that the reason for the whole thing was to make it easier for the management to fire us if we screwed up.

In the first example we have an instance where there is both uncertainty and equivocality. What is the problem in the second instance? Media choice? Source credibility? Audience analysis? Ethical factors? Which of these factors (or others) create the noise in the second instance?

Human Messages

Human messages, as the name suggests, are concerned with the human needs of employees. Messages pertaining to performance evaluation, employee morale, attitudes, gripes, and relationships would all fall into the category of human messages. All of the following would be considered human messages: inquiring about a colleague's baseball-playing child; commiserating with someone who'd lost a loved one in the Iraq war; congratulating a subordinate on an excellent submission; contributing during a "good of the order" session at a department meeting.

Human messages are every bit as vital as task and maintenance messages. Some people might even argue that human messages are more important than task and maintenance messages since human messages help create an environment that makes it easier for receivers to be interested in task and maintenance messages.[7] For example:

- The head of a department may be quite clear about what you need to do and what regulations govern your work, but if you never hear a word from this person about how you're doing, you may begin to wonder about whether your work is meeting expectations and may be reluctant to listen to task assignments.
- If you've never had an opportunity to voice your opinions regarding certain policies, you might be reluctant to follow them as religiously as you would if you had participated in the decisions that resulted in the policies.
- If after you've lost a loved one a manager does not extend an expression of sympathy, you may balk at responding to task messages that are just marginally beyond your job description.
- You could become displeased if, after submitting an assignment that you labored over, your instructor decides to congratulate all students similarly—regardless of effort or quality of submission. Perhaps you'll work less diligently on the next task.

As we saw in Chapter 2 in the discussion of human relations and human resources theory, it is not uncommon for employees to remark that messages of appreciation mean a great deal. A cleaning woman once told me that a stuffed animal she received from a grateful administrator meant "the world to me." A colleague recently yanked me into his office and retrieved an e-mail, placing it on his computer screen. A former student that we both knew had written some very complimentary words. My colleague said that this was almost as valuable as the raises we were to receive. His remark was quite consistent with Herzberg's motivation-hygiene theory discussed in Chapter 2. An

Applying the Principles—Test Yourself

Select any one of the organizations in your life, for example, your school, a club, your most recent job, or a fraternity or sorority. Then complete this exercise by following the following steps:

(a) Review the bulleted questions listed in the following and write a 1, 2, 3, 4, or 5 next to each item. A "1" indicates that you do not receive enough information on the subject. A "5" indicates that your manager or organization is very efficient at disseminating this information to you.

(b) Return to each question and write a second number. In this case a "1" would indicate that it is *very important* that you receive this information. A "5" would indicate it's not at all important.

(c) Determine whether each item refers to task, maintenance, or human messages.

(d) What types of messages does your organization most effectively communicate?

(e) What types of messages are most important to you?

How satisfied are you with information you receive about:

• What you have to do each day?
• Organizational policies?
• Changes in personnel or policies?
• Other related departments?
• External audiences, e.g., clients, potential members?
• Competing organizations?
• Organizational sponsored activities, e.g., lunchtime speakers, sponsored outings?
• Organizational plans for the future?
• How well or how poorly you are doing?
• Whether you are appreciated for what you accomplish?
• Whether people are concerned for your personal needs?

arts administrator who had decided to step down from her position told me over lunch that she was overwhelmed by the e-mails and calls that had poured in for her indicating how much she would be missed. Everyone likes to have their work acknowledged, regardless of income bracket.

One could argue that there are times when employees' needs in this area are excessive. One cannot argue, however, with the general premise that managers need to communicate these messages when situations warrant it or the premise that the organization's evolving culture reflects the existence and sincerity of these human messages.

Five Criteria

As we have seen, task, maintenance, and human messages have to be communicated in organizations. Those who send this information should be concerned with meeting five communication-related criteria. Specifically, the messages that are communicated should be:

• Timely
• Clear
• Accurate
• Pertinent
• Credible

Applying the Principles—Test Yourself

Was United at Fault?

After booking a flight to Chicago on United's Web site and getting an electronic confirmation for that flight, John was stunned to arrive at the airport and be told that he did not have a ticket. There was a lengthy heated discussion with the agent, who despite seeing the printed version of the confirmation maintained that John had no ticket. Rather than pay over four times the cost of his discounted fare to buy a new ticket, John was forced to travel to a different airport and fly on Southwest, a carrier for which he had a free "Rapid Rewards" coupon. When he returned home, John checked his e-mail correspondence to see if he had received any notification from United indicating that his ticket had been canceled. He noticed that in his electronic in-box there was a message from "Technical Support." The subject line was "Message from UN." Technical Support was the subject line for all messages John received internally at work from the computer staff. Typically, information about computer downtimes would be listed in messages from Technical Support. Often, as was the case in this instance, John would not open Technical Support messages since they rarely pertained to him.

He clicked on the "Technical Support" message with the subject line "Message from UN" and saw that "Message from UN" was an abbreviated version of "Message from United," which informed John that there had been some problem with his credit card electronic purchase and that if he did not respond by a date (which had come and gone weeks before) his e-ticket and reservation would be canceled.

John investigated and found out that the problem with his credit card was that he'd provided a new zip code number with his payment. His credit card company, however, still had the old zip code address on file. The disparity caused the computer to spit out his reservation and generate the "Message from UN."

John was furious with United and wrote an angry letter. They responded by saying that they'd communicated the message and could not be held responsible because John had not checked his e-mail.

- Was John responsible?
- Was United at fault?
- If you worked for United, would you have communicated differently?
- What is the source of this communication problem?

The first criterion relates to *timeliness*. Receivers must get messages at a time when the information is meaningful. The message is meaningless if it arrives too late for the receiver to do anything about it. If you receive an urgent e-mail with an exclamation point adjacent to it about a report due on Wednesday late on Tuesday afternoon, the notice that you receive may reduce uncertainty but will not allow you the opportunity to complete the assigned task. As significantly, you might be angered by the short notice, and this anger may affect how you perceive subsequent messages from that same source. This note, especially if it is not abnormal, can add to an infection that corrupts the organizational culture. It may add to a perception that superiors are abusing the power they have and contribute to the perception that abuse is normalized in organizations. Therefore, one must choose a method that will ensure that messages will reach the receiver in a timely fashion.

A second criterion is *clarity*. Whatever method used must be one that will likely result in the message being received clearly. Face-to-face methods allow for immediate feedback and include nonverbal cues, which improve the chances for a clearly received message. A problem with face-to-face methods is that the sender may be unable to articulate orally as clearly as he or she might be able to in writing. When we post Web content or even send an e-mail, we have the opportunity to write it and rewrite it before sending to make sure we express what we'd like.

It's a good idea (but not always possible) to complement a written message with an oral communication to ensure clarity. Often, businesspersons will distribute a written document to employees, who will later meet and discuss the documents. After reading the materials the employees can ask questions for clarification.

The third criterion is *accuracy*. Accuracy and clarity are closely related, but there is a difference. Assume that you receive a very clearly written e-mail about an upcoming assembly. The message includes the following information. You are invited to attend a meeting. It is to begin at 5:15. The meeting is to be held in Blackman Auditorium. The agenda will include four speakers. The session will end at 6.

The written message could not have been more clear. Assume, however, that the information is inaccurate. Assume that the meeting will actually be held at 4:45 and convene in Richards Hall. Even if everyone who received the mailing subsequently receives a follow-up e-mail that corrects the error, a good portion of the attendees will go to the wrong place at the wrong time. If this happens habitually the inaccuracy will have a corrosive effect on the organizational culture. Conversely, if an organization has a reputation as sensitive to the needs of employees to receive precise accurate information, this might have a positive effect on the culture.

A fourth factor relates to *pertinence*. The receiver of a message should view the message as relevant to him or her. Otherwise messages that are irrelevant may begin to taint the value of those that are relevant. Sometimes managers must blast messages for reasons of timeliness. However, if, as a matter of course, all messages are broadcast to all receivers, eventually the value of any one of these messages will be reduced. It has been argued that receivers in organizations have the responsibility of reading all their messages—that such activity is part of the job. This may be a legitimate claim. A reality, however, is that organization members will not consume all messages sent their way. People selectively receive information and this selection is sometimes based on how inundated they may be with information. Marking messages URGENT will only work if the URGENT indicator turns out to be credible.

This leads us to the fifth criterion, which is *credibility*. Messages received must be believed or they will be disregarded. Will a posting on a Web site, accessible to all, thanking all for hard work, make sense? To a large extent the credibility of the message is dependent on the source as opposed to the method used for dissemination. However, the method can play a part in how a message will be received, and, therefore, one should consider whether a particular method will increase or decrease the credibility of the message.

Selecting Media Options

Disseminating task, maintenance, and human messages to reduce uncertainty and equivocality is an important aspect of organizational communication. It's necessary then to consider how to send information to meet these three message needs and to ensure the timeliness, accuracy, credibility, pertinence, and clarity of receipt. Various options are available. Managers can send e-mails, post information on a Web site, blog, hold meetings, employ "corporate video," meet with employees interpersonally, or employ a host of what is now being referred to as social media, for example, wikis or Facebook sites. Since how you send information may affect the nature of receipt, there's reason to intelligently identify criteria for using one method over another.

William Hamilton © 1988 Chronicle Features

"Not only have I been left on hold, it's been 'Moon River' the whole miserable time."

Effective communication in organizations involves more than just having communication equipment or technology. New technology, when used inappropriately, can be more of a burden than an asset.

Media "Richness"

Daft and Lengel define media richness as a medium's capacity to change understanding.[8] If a medium is rich, then it has a better chance of reducing equivocality and uncertainty and therefore may "change understanding." Daft and Huber, as well as Sullivan, identify three criteria for determining richness. A medium's richness is dependent upon the:

• Opportunities for immediate feedback.
• Presence of multiple communication cues.
• Capacity of the medium to tailor a message to personal circumstances.[9]

Opportunity for Immediate Feedback
A medium becomes richer if, in order to decrease equivocality, a receiver can respond immediately to gain a clearer understanding of any message sent. The absence of immediate feedback reduces the chances for decreasing equivocality. E-mail, as it relates to this criterion, would be less rich than face-to-face communication, but richer than a conventional memorandum.

The term "asynchronicity" is sometimes used to describe a medium that does not require that the source/receiver be present at the time of communication. E-mail is asynchronous, and that is both advantageous, in that messages can be transmitted for subsequent receipt, and disadvantageous, because feedback that could reduce equivocality is not instantaneous.

The Presence of Multiple Communication Cues
This criterion for richness refers to the perspective that the more communication cues there are when a person communicates with another, the greater the chances of reducing equivocality and uncertainty. A message can be communicated verbally (with only words), nonverbally, or both verbally and nonverbally.[10] If you see me when I speak to you, you can observe my facial expressions, hear the tone of my voice, and notice any complementary gesturing. If you read a brochure you may have words and visual components, but you will not have any vocalic cues. If you participate in video conferencing, you have some visual and some vocal cues, but you will not have any haptic (touching—e.g., handshaking, pats on the back) cues, and the range of your visual cues will be reduced by camera angles and directors' or camerapersons' decisions.

Students take courses in organizational communication on ground, online, and sometimes in a hybrid format. There are advantages to each approach, but one major reason for including on-ground contexts for learning is that communication in these contexts allows for immediate feedback and can provide multiple communication cues.

The Ability to Tailor a Message to Personal Circumstances
A broadcasted e-mailing is, of course, less likely to address personal circumstances than a one-on-one face-to-face meeting. Print, in general, is less "able" to be tailored to particular circumstances unless it is a personal memorandum or letter. Messages in company brochures and manuals cannot be easily tailored to literacy levels of large diverse populations.

Ranking Media in Terms of Richness

Huber and Daft ranked six media options using the criteria for media richness. The following list reflects their rankings, with the richest media appearing at the top of the list:

1. Face to face
2. Videophone and video teleconferencing
3. Telephone
4. Electronic mail
5. Personally addressed documents (memos and letters)
6. Formal unaddressed documents (brochures, pamphlets)[11]

Can you understand the rankings given the criteria?
Where would you place Web postings on a company's intranet?
Where would you rank messages sent via social media like Facebook?

An interesting finding in research conducted on media richness is that often users do not employ the richest medium possible. Utz, in a 2007 *Information, Communication, and Society* article, cites a series of studies that indicate that users not only do not select the richest medium possible, but moreover often think they are selecting the richest medium possible. "Studies in media choice have revealed that people are not rational actors that choose media according to their appropriateness. . . . [P]erceived media richness is a better predictor of actual media use than objective media richness."[12]

In your daily decision making, how significant is the richness of the medium when you make choices about how to send messages? What determines how you make your decisions?[13]

Additional Criteria When Evaluating Media

Side Effects—Information Overload

When evaluating media choices it is important to consider the derivative effects of the use of that medium. This factor is addressed in the following section, which describes the first- and second-level effects of new technology. However, as we discuss media options here, the issue of overload is important to consider.

In organizations, communication is not an isolated event that happens once or twice a day. Organizational men and women are bombarded with messages. The use of particular approaches to communicating may result in the receipt of so many messages that any one message becomes less likely to reduce uncertainty. The accrual of many messages may render electronic mail, for example, less rich because while it *could* change understanding, it may never do so, because recipients may not, in actuality, ever get the message.

In a *Fortune* article entitled, "Surviving Information Overload," Mark Rosenkar, a vice president of Public Affairs for the Electronic Industries Association, was quoted as follows:

> Let me put it this way. E-mail is an incredibly valuable service, but when you become inundated, it gets to be just like junk mail. I wonder if we're not getting e-mail trashed. It's reaching the point where I'm spending an hour a day going through junk, or using a key board to respond to junk, or thinking about junk, or reading junk."[14]

When considering a medium's potential for reducing uncertainty, a consideration has to be whether the receivers will have accrued so many messages from this medium that they will not likely attend to any individual message.

Permanence

Permanence refers to the enduring qualities of a message. Electronically communicated information can be permanent. A person has the opportunity to keep, get, or review a copy of the communication after the initial receipt. There are two valuable advantages of permanence. The first is that you have a record of communications. The second is that you can return to the message subsequently when convenient. Complex procedural manuals can be reviewed by the receiver when necessary. A compendium of all organizational rules is not intended to be read cover to cover, but can be used as a resource when a user needs to access particular information.

Speed

Speed refers to how quickly a message can get to and is received by the receiver. In order to deal with issues of timeliness when reducing uncertainty or ambiguity, speed of transmission has to be considered a factor.

Cost

Cost is a consideration in nearly all organizational contexts. It does *not*, however, directly affect media richness. A medium isn't rich or effective *because* it's inexpensive. For example, it may be cheaper to train hundreds of employees at once using videotape than having trainers conduct several orientation sessions. Using the videotape may be cost effective but reduce the value of the communication. One doesn't reduce a whole lot of uncertainty if receivers who watch poorly made videotapes snooze through the mandatory viewing.

Social Media

When electronic typewriters replaced standard typewriters, there were administrative assistants who made the transition only very reluctantly. When word processing replaced the electronic typewriter, some people retired rather than learn how to use the new equipment. The advent of voice mail was greeted with disdain by technophobes, and it took time for some workers to become comfortable with electronic mail. Teenagers now startle their parents with the dizzying speed at which they can "text" their friends. And teens serve as trainers for their elders as they explain the nuances and multiple applications of cell phones. The revolution in communication technology moves on and at such a rapid pace that whatever one can purchase now will be available in a more sophisticated version in months. The director of education at a large nonprofit organization once told me half in jest: "Look, I'll buy the equipment. I'll use it. Under one condition. Promise me that they'll stop inventing the next iteration."

What has been collectively called social media is the newest phenomenon. While newer versions will undoubtedly be developed, the general concept behind social media is here to stay. At the 2008 International Association of Business Communicators (IABC) meetings in New York, more than ten programs dealt either specifically or indirectly with this topic. Men and women in organizations—whether they wish it were the case or not—have to become familiar with this new phenomenon that complements traditional approaches to disseminating information.

What Is Social Media?

Social media is an umbrella phrase that describes a number of activities that integrate new technology with social interaction within organizations, outside organizations, and from business to business. Marketwire defines social media as technology that uses the "wisdom of crowds" to connect

During the 2008 presidential campaign, political parties effectively employed social media. Now President Obama maintains a Facebook profile.

information in a collaborative manner.[15] Social media has the effect of democratizing organizational communication since access and participation is extended to persons who might otherwise not be involved in the collective conversation.

Types of Social Media

There are several categories of social media. Social networking is enabled with applications like Facebook, MySpace, and LinkedIn. Blogs and podcasts facilitate ongoing conversations with parties who have common interests. Blogs are also becoming popular with CEOs. J. W. Marriott, CEO of the Marriott hotel chain, was a keynote speaker at the aforementioned IABC meetings and discussed the value of his blogs, not only as a method for disseminating information but also to humanize the leadership and improve organizational culture.[16] Diggs, wikis, and bulletin boards are repositories for information that people can share. Almost all readers of these pages will have used Wikipedia, an online encyclopedia, that is different from its conventional predecessors because individuals with information can add to the entries, supplementing what appears for each one. Social media includes sites where you can share personal or organizational content—for example Flickr for photographs and YouTube for video content. There are virtual network platforms like Second Life and There, where people can "congregate" in a virtual three-dimensional universe, and—with There, for example, "meet friends, chat using text or voice, play games, create your own line of virtual products, build a dream home, and explore cool new places."[17]

The reality of social media and its enormous popularity means that organizations must realize that conventional methods for communicating might not be the most efficient. The innovative reality of social media suggests that managers are less likely to be as familiar with the media as younger associates. (In fact, student readers of this section are likely to be more familiar with social media than some instructors, who might be otherwise experts in organizational communication.) In traditional business contexts, the result of relative managerial ignorance means that administrators may miss out on information and opportunities to communicate effectively until they become aware of popular methods for interaction. The 2008 presidential election provides an excellent example of how the Democratic Party was aware of the value of social media and employed it to its advantage. Not only were, for example, Facebook and MySpace used by candidates, but supporters themselves used YouTube and other social media to convey their sentiments. The use of social media became a tool for the citizens to stump for their favorite candidate.

Impact of Social Media

On March 30, 2009, *The Boston Globe* reported that the National Basketball Association fined Dallas Mavericks owner Mark Cuban $25,000. Cuban had criticized basketball officials on Twitter, the online social network. Twitter may have been on the periphery of some radar screens, but not the National Basketball Association's. Quipped Cuban, you "can't say no one makes money from Twitter now. The NBA does."[18]

Social media and its descendents are here to stay. It would be as foolish for administrators to dismiss the impact of social media as it was for managers twenty years ago to refuse to use e-mail. Acknowledging that social media is a reality compels realists to understand it completely and measure its impact. Those who assess the social media are concerned with (1) "traffic," or how many people visit sites, (2) "velocity," or the relative change in daily attention to a site, (3) "conversation ratio," or how many comments are generated for each original posting, and (4) "participation ratio," or the percentage of account holders that actually participate with the social media, as opposed to just read and "lurk."[19]

Because many use search engines to research companies, organizations are concerned with something called search engine optimization (SEO). A company would like to create a site that will attract cyber explorers. Therefore, a company will study the algorithms that particular search engines employ. In this way a site can be created to optimize traffic and users will be steered toward your site when exploring.

New Technology: Examining First- and Second-Level Effects

Two professors, Lee Sproull and Sara Kiesler, make a distinction between first- and second-level effects of communication technology.[20]

First-level effects of technology refer to the "efficiency effects," in other words what the technology was designed to accomplish. The first-level effects of the telephone enable us to speak to persons regardless of our receivers' locations as long as those persons have access to a phone and are present at the time when we make the call. The first-level effects of wikis include the ability to collaboratively share knowledge with members of an organization by posting messages electronically.

Second-level effects of technology refer to the derivative effects of using the technology. Some may argue, for example, that increased telephone use resulted in a decrease in literacy. As more people stopped writing and began using the phone for conversation, fewer people became adept at writing and reading.

A second-level effect of the intranet and other forms of electronic communication has been that face-to-face encounters have become relatively infrequent. It's possible to stay in your cubicle all day and "talk" to colleagues. Organizational "friends" may be people that you have never seen. Relationships develop without face-to-face interaction, and a new informal network develops among those who use the intranet. Typing proficiency has increased among the average worker. Whereas twenty-five years ago most businesspeople gave their hand-written notes to assistants for typing, now nearly everyone is capable of using a keyboard for a first draft of a document.

Flaming and Self-Disclosure

Other second-level effects of electronic communication relate to the relative anonymity associated with the technology. E-mail allows for communication without complete source attribution. You may know that a message came from ajones@aol.com, but you may not know what ajones looks like, where ajones is located, or even if ajones is a male or female. Sproull and Kiesler claim that a second-level effect of this relative anonymity is flaming—the tendency for employees to write bruising comments via e-mail that they probably would not express in face-to-face situations.[21] Similarly, in an article published in the *International Journal of Technology Management*, I reported results that suggest that the relative anonymity of e-mail can increase the number of messages sent and the self-disclosing nature of these messages.[22]

The issue of flaming and the potential for cowardly, mean-spirited communication is evident on Web sites where individuals can disparage others with impunity. Individuals who are maligned may never be aware of the often repulsive characterizations. Daily, it seems, one or another site will appear that allows anonymous critics to log in and ridicule a classmate, co-worker, or manager.

"Throwing Automation at Them"

In a piece entitled "Planning for Information Effectiveness," Valdis Krebs, a project leader for Toyota's computer systems, writes that organizations often deal with communication needs by "throwing automation at them. . . . This often results in doing the wrong things faster."[23] The perspectives of Sproull and Kiesler explain to some extent why Krebs's declaration is very true. If organizational men and women focus on the first-level effects of any method for communicating and ignore the likely second-level effects, then inaccurate and/or unintended messages may be communicated—rapidly or otherwise. Sproull and Kiesler argue that second-level effects of electronic communication include reduction of authority and perceptions of "who is important, what is legitimate, what is prestigious."[24]

The ramifications of second-level effects are significant and relate to our choice of message-sending alternatives when we communicate. The idea that we can have a meeting spanning time zones using video teleconferencing equipment is undeniable. We can share information and see the other participants who may be residing in other countries. However, if teleconferencing results in the reduction of after-hour informal social relationships that typically develop during conventional meetings, and if those social relationships have an effect on the success of our persuasion during our formal meetings, then while we may have eliminated the time barrier and costs, we may have also eliminated a catalyst for successful interaction. If some persons are camera shy and participate infrequently in teleconferences, whereas they might have participated regularly during a conventional meeting held in the office conference room, then the first-level benefits of video teleconferencing are undermined by the second-level effects.

It is interesting to note that Verizon conducted a study of its own employees' perception of internal communication and discovered that the three major issues with communication were information overload, the lack of a single place for messages, and trust and confidence in the message source. Employees identified face-to-face communication as their most preferred communication approach in a context that was unscripted, informal, candid, and ongoing.[25]

Knowledge Management

Over the last ten years the phrase "knowledge management" (KM) has been used more and more frequently by academics and organizational practitioners. Several books have been written on the subject, and academic conferences devote sessions to discussing it. Some organizations actually will employ individuals who serve in positions called director of knowledge, director of intellectual capital, or intellectual assets manager.[26]

What Is Knowledge Management?

KM has been defined variously. The definitions include:

- The industry buzzword used to describe a set of tools for capturing and reuse of knowledge.[27]
- Capturing, storing, transforming, and disseminating information within an organization with the goal of promoting efficiency at the least, and innovation and competitive advantage at the most. [28]
- The use of computer technology to organize, manage, and distribute electronically all types of information, customized to meet the needs of a wide variety of users.[29]
- A business process that seeks to gather, manage, and disseminate information, data, and experience throughout an organization. The goal is to be sure all in the organization know what they need to know and are able to leverage what they know.[30]

As you can see, there are similarities in these definitions. Essentially, knowledge management refers to *the finding, organizing, and dissemination* of organizational knowledge. The objective of KM is to provide organizational women and men with access to information that can be valuable to their individual and collective activities.[31]

It is no coincidence that interest in KM evolved concurrently with the proliferation and availability of sophisticated electronic communication. Knowledge management is not synonymous with accruing technology, nor is it dependent entirely on the existence of available technology. However, the value of knowledge management has become apparent, in part, because of communication technology. With so many people having easy access to so much knowledge, it has become obvious that identifying, cataloguing, and disseminating knowledge effectively is a best practice that can provide a competitive advantage to organizations.

The idea that knowledge is important or that knowledge is power is hardly revolutionary. It makes sense that any organization will become more efficient when it and those persons who work within it are able to access all of its "intellectual capital." If you take a moment to consider the effects of knowledge management on your own ability to work *independently*, you may more fully understand and appreciate the value of knowledge management for *interdependent* organizational activity.

Assume that you have to complete a take-home exam for a course. Your ability to do well on that exam will be based in part on how well you can identify, access, and apply: your notes from the course; relevant portions of your textbook; any reading you did related to the assignment that was not required by the course; anything you might know from your own experience about the topic; what you know about the instructor; what you know about the instructor's tendencies to grade; which Internet and conventional library sources are available to help research the topic; who you know who might be an expert in the area; what newspaper article you read once that was pertinent; where you can locate that newspaper article; and how much your Aunt Joan who works in the field knows about the subject. If you were able to find, organize, and then consider all this, you would be leveraging what you know in order to maximize the quality of the product—in this case your take-home exam. The less knowledge you are able to gather, or the less you know about how to gather it, the less likely you are to submit the best answers to the exam questions.

Organizations are in similar situations. However, the problems of managing knowledge in organizations are compounded by the numbers of persons within them and the factors that affect organizational interaction. When you work independently, it is your job to discover what you know, catalogue that information, and then use it. When an organization works cooperatively and interdependently, the task of discovery, cataloguing, and application is far more complex. Each step in the process of knowledge management—identification, acquisition, dissemination, utilization, preservation, and measurement—involves significant challenges.

For example, it might seem simple to identify who in an organization has knowledge and not particularly difficult to acquire it. However, these basic steps are more complicated than they appear to be. Some people are not even aware that they have the knowledge they possess. Others may be reluctant to share what they know for fear that, once it is shared, they will lose their value to the organization. How does a so-called knowledge manager identify and acquire knowledge from persons who do not or will not acknowledge their knowledge?

In addition, valuable knowledge, very worthy of management, may not be considered important by decision makers. Is a trainer's strategy regarding how to work with reluctant trainees a tangible intellectual asset? Is a librarian's idiosyncratic method for searching the Web valuable knowledge? Is a supervisor's awareness and application of nonverbal communication principles during performance reviews an intellectual asset? While all of these should be considered important, there is no guarantee that this knowledge will be recognized as such.

The Learning Organization and Knowledge Management

In Chapter 3 we discussed learning organizations in terms of systems theory. A systems orientation that fosters subsystems with permeable walls is structured to be a learning organization. The phrase "learning organization" has also been used in conjunction with knowledge management. A learning organization, as the name suggests, is one that is dedicated to collective discovery and the application of this discovery.

Pegasus Communications, a consulting company based in Waltham, Massachusetts, publishes a series of what appear to be children's books, which are actually fables written to explain principles related to organizational activity. One such fable is entitled

> "For [a learning organization], it is not enough merely to survive. 'Survival learning' or what is more often termed 'adaptive learning' is important—indeed it is necessary. But for a learning organization, 'adaptive learning' must be joined by 'generative learning' that enhances our capacity to create."[32]

Outlearning the Wolves: Surviving and Thriving in a Learning Organization.[33] In the story a group of sheep are regularly terrorized by wolves, and the sheep, sheepishly, assume that it is their plight to be so demonized and accept the condition. However, a leader among the sheep encourages the others to think together in order to outfox the wolves. The sheep become a learning organization. They work cooperatively to identify what they know. They apply their collective knowledge. And eventually they outfox the wolves. This is the essence of a learning organization and a foundational plank in knowledge management. Other foundational planks pertain to the application of theoretical principles. (Unfortunately for the sheep, at the end of the tale the wolves appear to have united to become a learning organization as well.)

Knowledge Management and the Application of Theory

Knowledge management requires a commitment to learning. In addition, knowledge management requires understanding and applying a number of the theories that we discussed in Chapters 2 and 3.

Human Resources Theory
Human resource theorists argue that individuals can make valuable contributions to the organization and under the right conditions will desire to participate. In order to manage knowledge effectively,

managers have to respect employees' innate desires to contribute to the knowledge base of the organization and also meaningfully acknowledge these contributions. Managers who assume that employees are classically lazy are unlikely to seek and identify the knowledge that employees possess.

Systems Theory

Systems theorists argue that organizations are comprised of interdependent departments. These units must be linked to each other and be conceived of as open. As mentioned above, knowledge management requires open channels for communication to allow information to be accessed by and disseminated to those who must utilize the relevant knowledge. (We discuss in detail the types of organizational networks in the next chapter.)

Cultural Theory

Cultural theorists argue that communication within organizations is affected by and affects the culture of that organization. A culture that values sharing, collective activity, and participatory decision making facilitates the management of individual and collective knowledge. Communication that reflects a willingness to work cooperatively can foster a culture conducive to knowledge management. (Culture and the interdependent effects of culture and communication are discussed in detail in Chapter 7.)

Critical Theory

Critical theory challenges the abuse of power. As it relates to communication, critical theorists argue that communication can be a tool for abuse. Some people do not want to share information precisely because to relinquish a hold on information is to reduce the power that comes with having knowledge. This is not only counterproductive but dispiriting to individuals within organizations. The notion that the way it is how it should be is an example of what we discussed in Chapter 3 as manufactured consent. In the cases of manufactured consent, employees buy into the notion that administrative retention of knowledge and deliberately keeping employees in the dark represents how things are supposed to be. Critical theorists would also be interested in knowledge management when examining how disinformation can be disseminated for the purposes of subjugating employees.

Human Needs: The Human Moment

Edward Hallowell, a practicing psychiatrist, published an article in the *Harvard Business Review* entitled, "The Human Moment at Work."[34] Hallowell's argument in the piece is that essential face-to-face communication is being reduced by the proliferation of communication technology. Moreover, he suggests that there are serious negative consequences of not having human contact.[35]

> "Not until a machine can write a sonnet or compose a concerto because of thoughts and emotions felt— and not by chance fall of symbol—could we argue that machine equals brain. No mechanism could feel pleasure at its successes, grief when its values fuse, be warmed by flattery, be made miserable by mistakes, be charmed by sex, be angry or miserable when it cannot get what it wants."
>
> —**SIR GEOFFREY JEFFERSON**, June 9, 1949

"Human moments" are defined as communications requiring (a) the physical presence of the two communicating parties and (b) emotional and intellectual attention. Hallowell states that organizational men and women need these moments to "maintain their mental acuity and their emotional well-being." He does not suggest the elimination of technology, but rather complementing electronic interaction with communications that include these human moments. As an unidentified executive quoted in the article comments, "You cannot have high tech without high touch."[36]

In a special issue of *Human Resource Management,* Argenti expresses related sentiments when he writes: "With all the sophisticated technology available to communicate with employees today such as electronic mail, newsgroups, desktop publishing, and satellite meetings to far-flung places, the most important [managerial] responsibility . . . is to listen to what [employees] have to say and get to know who they really are as human beings."[37]

What do you think of Hallowell's position? Are there tangible consequences of not having "human moments?" Is an inherent weakness in online education related to an absence of "human moments?" Is Argenti's perspective accurate?

Shoveling Coal and Human Moments

In the context of human moments, it might be appropriate to recall the observations of classical theorist Frederick Taylor and the results of the Hawthorne Studies. If you remember from Chapter 2, Taylor was the originator of "scientific management"—the idea that job tasks could be measured and examined in order to ascertain what was the best possible way to complete a job. Taylor observed employees shoveling coal and noticed the best way for employees to shovel coal. He advocated that all organizations test to see the most effective way for employees to complete tasks and then prescribe these methods as policy. As we discovered in Chapter 2, the Hawthorne Studies results were at odds with the mechanistic notions of the classical theorists. People are unlike machines. Managers might be able to discover the most efficient way for a machine to shovel coal, but unless they factored in human needs and desires they couldn't compute the best way for humans to shovel coal—at least in the long run. (As we discussed, Taylor's proposals for coal shoveling were successful initially.)

When considering media options, it's important to remember the lessons of the Hawthorne Studies. When we identify the factors that affect "media richness," we need to consider not only the richness of a particular medium, but the residual effects of communicating information using that medium. In the human organization we may need "human moments" now and again to make us effective organizational players and to facilitate receipt of future messages, however they may be sent.

In an article entitled, "The Guru's Guru," management expert Peter Drucker comments that the "computer is a moron."[38] Maybe so. Computers cannot think and feel like humans can, so perhaps machines should be excused for being moronic. Humans, on the other hand, who have the capacity to acknowledge what separates the animate from the inanimate, have no such excuse. We cannot use machines intelligently without acknowledging what distinguishes us from the machines we use.

Information Needs and Selecting Media: A Recap

Let's summarize our discussion. Following is a list of ten principles related to information management and selecting media. The principles are based on the previous sections and what we've learned about communication in prior chapters.

1. The objective when communicating is to get information to receiver(s), not simply to send information. Therefore, a method for communicating should not be selected primarily because of the sender's comfort level with the medium or how easy it is to generate information using the medium.

Gordon Rudow: CEO

Gordon Rudow is the CEO of Bonfire Communications, an organizational communication agency specializing in employee engagement and strategy implementation, located in San Francisco. Bonfire earned a "Best Places to Work in the Bay Area" award every year from 2006 to 2008.

As you read through this section, consider the following questions:

1. In the first paragraph, Rudow explains what Bonfire does. Can an external company like Bonfire affect another organization's internal communication? In what ways? Rudow mentions that Bonfire can and does sometimes "equip management with the tools and training" to do the work itself. Which do you think is the better method?
2. In the highlighted excerpt, Rudow describes Bonfire's three-tiered system. Which of these tiers is most essential to Bonfire's approach?
3. Rudow also discusses the "democratizing effect" of new media and the value of employing them. Do you agree that this factor is likely to result in higher employee retention and satisfaction?
4. Would you like to work for a company like Bonfire?

Most of Bonfire's clients hire us because of a significant shift in direction or vision at their company that needs to be supported by new communications strategies and vehicles. For example, there may be a change in leadership, a merger or acquisition, a repositioning of the company's products or services, or some external news that is affecting it. Our goal is to ensure that employees understand and

embrace the change by engaging their hearts and minds via strategic communications. Bonfire is often hired to drive the entirety of these communications efforts, or equip management with the tools and training it needs to propagate behavioral change on its own.

We use a three-tiered approach we call "awareness, understanding, and action." Specifically, we create awareness of changes, promote understanding of the meaning of the changes, and articulate the actions necessary to respond to these changes. In addition, being audience-centric is critical to the success of Bonfire's internal communications. We thoroughly study and respect the audiences that will consume the information. How we craft and communicate messages directly relates to the nature of the audience. Specifically, the tone, complexity, and detail of the messages, as well as the way they are delivered, must be tailored to those receiving it. You may have the most wonderful information and intent, but a lack of understanding of your audience's mindset will impede your ability to accomplish your mission.

New media, including multimedia content and social networking, can be highly effective in internal communication. However, Bonfire is sensitive about where and how these tools are used. It all comes back to "audience-centricity." Is the intended audience open to these vehicles? Do they possess the technical savvy? Do they have the time to deal with them? Does the company have the infrastructure and policy framework to implement them? Those are a few of the questions we ask.

Another consideration of new media is the democratizing effect it can have. Typically, these outlets offer the potential of interactivity and community as they break down the hierarchical walls that separate management and staff. Some companies are ready to take this step, and others, more focused on traditional "command-and-control" structures, are not. In Bonfire's experience, companies willing to take this step enjoy higher employee satisfaction and retention. It is important to note that new media is also key for attracting millennial talent to ensure that companies are fueled by next-generation talent.

One major issue our clients face relates to creating a common understanding between different age groups. Often, different age groups have varying perceptions and interpretations of change messages. People who have been at a company for thirty years have diverging perspectives compared to twenty-year-old newcomers to a firm. Messages one staffer finds appealing may seem perplexing, alien, or even threatening to another. Therefore, communications must often be tested and validated to ensure that they are appropriate for and resonate with multiple audiences.

Much of Bonfire's work deals with establishing and evolving change within organizational cultures. Instead of performing a "cultural lobotomy"—attempting to sever connections to the old culture and implanting the new—our approach to cultural change promotes a "collective conversation" so new attitudes can organically take root and grow. This often involves replacing silo-based communication, as well as recognition and reward systems, with more collectively focused, broad-scale efforts that create a sense of a shared mission and values.

The field of internal communications is expanding dramatically. The unique and exciting opportunities available for your students at firms specializing in this work are immense. Some PR firms are trying to get into this field, but too often they use old techniques that lack an audience-centric focus. Addressing the unique needs of internal audiences is a very different art form from going after broad-based consumer segments. Internal communications is not about selling products to people. Rather, it's about making people feel like they are part of a larger purpose and providing the critical context and understanding they need to perform, while ensuring they know they play a special role in realizing it.

Bonfire practices what it preaches. We are proud to have been named a *Best Place to Work* three years running. Part of that can be attributed to the fact that we have monthly training sessions, have weekly company-wide huddles, and employ new media through internal blogs and a company Wiki that serves as a learning center. We coach both our clients and our employees, to empower them to do great work that matters to them and their clients. Bonfire is all about propelling success throughout the entire ecosystem we represent.

2. Three types of messages need to be communicated to employees: task, maintenance, and human messages.

3. Receipt of information must be timely. Information must be perceived as credible and pertinent. Information received must be clear and accurate.

4. The method used for communicating can affect the quality of communication. There are different strengths and weaknesses for each media choice.

5. The "richest" media are those that provide multiple cues and opportunities for instantaneous feedback and that can be used to personalize messages.

6. When selecting media, communicators need to consider the possibility of information overload, speed of transmission, and whether the message communicated needs to be "permanent."

7. New technology is not a panacea and must be viewed in terms of both first- and second-level effects.

8. It is wise to use complementary media when communicating.

9. There is a need for human moments, regardless of the sophistication of the communication technology that might permit the exchange of information without human moments.

10. When considering information management, consider both the transmission and constitutive definitions of communication. A goal is indeed to make sure that information is received. However, the organization's culture will be affected by how sensitively and efficiently information is managed. Negligent practices will create a structure for subsequent communication that can be insidiously corrosive.

SUMMARY: A TOOLBOX

• Information is communicated in organizations to reduce uncertainty and equivocality.
• Employees require information pertaining to job responsibilities, organizational policies, and individual performance.
• The various options that are available for communication (for example, e-mail, oral communication, print) have distinct characteristics.
• New social media, for example, blogs, wikis, and social networks like Facebook, need to be acknowledged as effective methods for managing information and knowledge.
• Selecting the best media option for communicating any particular message is an organizational communication responsibility that should be taken seriously.
• When evaluating methods for disseminating information, it is wise to consider both first- and second-level effects of the method for communicating.
• Technology in and of itself is not a panacea for organizational communication problems.
• Effective knowledge management requires communication networks, a human resources orientation, and a culture that will support a learning organization.

REVIEW AND DISCUSSION QUESTIONS

1. Describe the distinction between *task, maintenance,* and *human messages.*
2. What does it mean to say that a medium is "rich"?
3. What is meant by knowledge management?
3. What is the difference between *uncertainty* and *equivocality?*
4. What is a first-level effect of fax machines?
5. What is a second-level effect of teleconferencing?
6. Please respond to the following questions. Answer by indicating whether you *Strongly Agree, Agree, Neither Agree nor Disagree, Disagree,* or *Strongly Disagree* with the statement. In addition, indicate the rationale for your reasoning in each case.
   a. Social media like Facebook should be incorporated into the formal networks of an organization.
   b. Instead of convening in Chicago or some other major city, executives can accomplish the same work by having a video conference—a meeting via video where the executives see and talk to one another on television.
   c. How one manages information affects the organizational culture.
   d. E-mail should be restricted to use for business purposes only. Employees should not use e-mail to discuss social activities, book clubs, or just to "talk" as one might on the telephone.
   e. Training by having employees watch DVDs that describe protocol is a good way to get these messages to employees.
   f. Typically operation manuals that explain how equipment works or how to assemble equipment are easy for the layperson to understand.

g. When you place a call to a business, you would prefer to hear an automated receptionist that gives you options than to speak with a human being who would subsequently forward your call to the correct party.

h. Blackberries are essential for organizational communication. If you don't have one you are out of the loop.

GROUP/ROLE-PLAY

In a group of four to six, review the issues surrounding the case that begins this chapter. Attempt to gain consensus regarding the questions at the end of the case.

• For the role-play, one member of the group assumes the role of Rayna. Another assumes the role of Tom. A third represents Rayna's superior, who gave the thumbs-up signal.

• Role-play a face-to-face meeting of these three persons that has been called by Rayna's boss to try and restore positive relationships among all three. Assume this takes place shortly after Rayna's outburst.

Chapter 6

Communication Networks

Chapter in a Nutshell

Organizations are open systems composed of interdependent units. Systems theorists contend that organizations must create, cultivate, and nourish communication networks in order to survive. In the same way that motorists require highways to get from one place to another, individuals within organizations need communication highways. Department heads cannot share knowledge with each other if there are no navigable channels for interaction or if the existing channels are poorly engineered and rarely utilized. In addition to formal networks, organizations must be concerned with resilient informal networks that inevitably evolve. These networks reflect and affect the organization's culture, power structure, and communication quality. A group of supervisors, for example, may have an informal network that trumps formally designed ones and, in effect, leaves certain supervisors out of the information loop. This chapter discusses the types of networks organizations need to have, the advantages of using these networks, and characteristics of particular communication networks.

When you have completed this chapter, you should be able to:

- Explain the distinction between messages and networks.
- Define internal and external networks; upward, downward, and horizontal networks; and formal and informal networks.
- Describe the importance of each type of network.
- Explain the problems related to using each type of network.
- Evaluate the quality of communication networks that exist in an organization with which you are familiar.

CASE 6.1:

Internet Development, CCS, and Customers

Trent McGuire works for a large mutual fund company. One division of the company is focused on improving the Internet services for shareholders. Within that division there are several departments. One department is called Internet Development. Another department is called Communications/Customer Service (CCS).

The Internet Development department works on enhancements and new applications for the company Web site. Currently, shareowners have the ability to view various products and offerings on the site and can access information about their accounts online. In the near future shareholders will be able to perform very sophisticated transactions online. Over the past twelve to eighteen months, the Web site has gone from offering basic product information to allowing customers the opportunity to perform all types of financial transactions. In this time frame there have been a great many cosmetic changes as well as application changes to the site.

Trent McGuire does not work in the Internet development department. Trent works as a manager in the CCS side of the division. CCS is in constant contact with the shareholders. CCS has the sole responsibility of setting up new shareholders so that they will have the ability to access their specific accounts. If there are any problems or questions concerning account access or any information regarding the Web site, then CCS is usually the first to hear about the problems from external customers. CCS representatives are expected to answer customer questions and resolve any problems.

Interdepartmental Communication and Customer Service

In order to best service the customers it is vital for CCS to be updated with any problems or changes in the site by the Internet development team. However, communication regarding this updating has not always taken place. For example, there are times when the account access features are not functional and CCS will find out about the problems not from the Internet development team, but from annoyed customers. On numerous occasions, new product or marketing text has been updated on the public site, yet CCS was not notified. Calls would come in referencing specific information on the site and CCS representatives would have no idea of the changes. Finally, with the rollout of new account access features to the customers, CCS was not consulted to test the application or provide any feedback prior to the application's availability for public use.

Numerous issues arose from this which caused the company to be reactive to customer response rather than proactive. In short, interdepartmental communication between the Internet development team and CCS is lacking and customer satisfaction with the Internet services has been negatively affected.

In addition, the grumblings between departments have seeped out to the organization as a whole. The grapevine is carrying information that the two units are at odds. Sometimes people outside of Internet development and CCS share humorous stories and shake their collective heads at what seems like childish tensions between the two groups. Spoofing on Trent's last name, behind their backs these two groups are called the "Hatfields and the McGuires." Somehow this problem has not yet wafted up into the highest levels of the organization, so while the tension exists at the customer level and infuriates the likes of Trent McGuire, top management is outside the loop.

- What can Trent McGuire do to facilitate effective communication between his department and the Internet development team?
- Is it important that top management be involved?
- Does it matter if the grapevine is making fun of these two departments within Internet services?
- How does this case relate to systems theory? Cultural theory? Critical theory?

What Are Communication Networks?

"Just remember this, organization means communication, communication means connectivity, connectivity means knowledge, that's the mantra."[1]

—BUSINESS CONSULTANT, PAUL STRASSMANN

In order to drive from one place to another, motorists need highways. Without Interstate 70 or other alternate routes, it would be difficult to drive from Kansas City to St. Louis. It does not matter whether motorists drive beat-up pick-ups or state-of-the-art luxury cars, they still would have trouble getting to St. Louis by automobile if there were no viable routes. Similarly, organizations require routes to facilitate the transportation of information. Managers must create, cultivate, and nourish these networks in order to permit the flow of information.

Networks do not refer to specific messages such as an interoffice memo or a broadcast e-mail. These examples are analogous to the vehicles that use the highways. The networks refer to the communication channels themselves. An interoffice memo or broadcast electronic message travels on communication networks.

To some, the distinction between networks and messages may seem to be minor and not particularly meaningful. Indeed, some new technologies like the social media discussed in Chapter 5 blur the distinction. Nevertheless, there is a fundamental difference between messages and communication networks that is not insignificant. To illustrate this, analyze the following two examples. The examples point out that the root of the communication problems in both cases is not the method of sending information, but the absence of any way for important messages to get from one place to another within the organizations.

Example 1: Buckley, Marshall, and Keyes

John Buckley, a newly hired middle manager, noticed that his department was wasting a great deal of money. Since he had worked in a similar capacity previously, he was aware of a cost-saving method for production that would reduce expenditures by 30 percent.

Buckley was excited by the prospect of contributing to the department so early in his tenure and was also eager to improve his own personal stock with his superiors. He approached his immediate supervisor with the suggestion and was informed that such changes were out of her hands. It seemed as if the only person who could authorize that type of move was a vice president named Marshall.

Buckley attempted to make an appointment to see Marshall and was told by Marshall's assistant, Keyes, that as a general rule Marshall did not meet with middle managers. Buckley tried to impress upon Keyes the importance of a meeting with Marshall, but Keyes insisted that no interviews would be granted and became annoyed at Buckley's tenacity.

Buckley did not give up. He wrote a three-page explanation of the cost-saving measure and sent it to Marshall through e-mail with a hard copy sent through interoffice mail. Two weeks later, after hearing nothing, he phoned Marshall and was intercepted by the assistant, Keyes. Buckley inquired about the proposal and was told, peremptorily, that Marshall was a very busy person and it was unlikely that the proposal would be reviewed in the near future.

Buckley discovered afterward that Marshall's mail—electronic and hard copy— was always screened by the protective Keyes and that it was unlikely that Marshall had ever received the proposal. At this point Buckley decided to forget the matter. His enthusiasm faded to indifference. "Let the company continue to lose money," he thought. "It doesn't matter to me."

Example 2: The Patel CDs

A retail CD company sold CDs and audio accessories out of a retail outlet as well as through electronic mail order. The mail order division consisted of a sales department, a billing department, and a credit department that pursued customers with debts.

A Mr. Patel purchased two CDs via mail order and received the merchandise and billing simultaneously. He played the CDs upon receipt and discovered that one was damaged. He proceeded to send a package by mail to the company. In the package he placed the damaged CD, the original order form, a check for the good CD, and a simple note requesting a replacement copy for the defective product. On the note, Patel indicated that he would pay for the defective CD when he received the replacement.

Two weeks later, Patel received a second bill from the company with "Second Notice" stamped on the form. The bill contained a placating message that read, "If you've already paid your bill, please disregard this message." Patel assumed that the sales office would soon be in contact with the billing department and did nothing. This assumption proved to be incorrect. Three days went by and Patel received a package from the CD company. In the package Patel found another copy of the good CD he had previously received, two copies of the defective CD he had returned for replacement, and a bill for the three CDs.

Patel rifled a letter to the company indicating that he had not wanted to order two copies of the damaged CD and that he had no use for another copy of the CD that had arrived in good condition. The letter was caustic, and Patel demanded that the matter be cleared up immediately. He went to the Web site and wrote a shorter note to the "contact us" address, similarly demanding resolution. There was an immediate response to the electronic note that was not reassuring. It contained a standard message: *"Thank you for contacting us. Your comments are very important and we will take them into consideration. We appreciate your interest and concern."* Patel hoped for a more personal reply in the U.S. mail.

He didn't get one. Ten days later Patel returned from work to find a Third Notice billing from the company for the original order, and a Second Notice billing (complete with placating message) for the second package he had received.

With the Third Notice in his angry fists, Patel drove to the nearest retail outlet of the CD company. He approached the manager and demanded immediate intervention. The manager told Patel that the retail outlets had absolutely nothing to do with the mail order division and that there was no way the manager could or would communicate with the mail order people. If Patel wanted to resolve the matter, he was told, he would have to write to the mail order division directly. It was suggested that he use the Web site—a recommendation that irritated Patel further because he had already, without success, pursued that route.

Patel asked for and received a phone number. He called and went through a foot-tapping and mind-numbing set of menu options. He opted to speak to an associate, but that choice yielded only elevator music interrupted periodically by what seemed like a demon saccharinely maintaining that "your call is very important to us." When he finally got through, he felt as if he was speaking to someone who had been robotically programmed to utter meaningless remarks regardless of the query. "There is nothing we can do for you at this time;" "Sorry for any inconvenience;" and then, incredibly, at the end of the frustrating call: "Is there anything else I can do for you?"

One more time Patel wrote to the mail order division explaining the situation, sending a similar letter to the "contact us" address on the Web site. The electronic contact resulted in the same immediate, now maddening, response: *"Thank you for contacting us. Your comments are very important and we will take them into consideration. We appreciate your interest and concern."* He did not receive any more CDs. He did receive a letter from the credit department, however, indicating that his "case" had been brought to the attention of that department for appropriate action. The letter was admonishing and sternly warned of repercussions if the matter was not addressed immediately.

It took Patel three months to straighten out the situation. During the course of Patel's investigation, he discovered that there was very little interaction between the sales, billing, and credit divisions. They perceived themselves as autonomous units within the larger organization, and there were no systematic channels available to facilitate the movement of information on matters like his problem. Simply, the left hand did not pay much attention to what the right hand was doing.

The Patel and Buckley cases are, unfortunately, not uncommon situations. Organizations must be concerned with developing channels that facilitate the flow of information. The Patel case, especially, is so typical that it is doubtful that many readers have not experienced a similar situation as consumers. Patel's situation in fact, was easy. It can take more than three months to sort out similar confusion.

Because we are aware of the frustrations that Patel experienced, it makes sense as organizational communicators to recognize the problem and take proactive measures to eliminate the chance that we will alienate our own external audiences in the same way that Patel was alienated. The Patel matter could have been easily remedied if the organization had a system of networks connecting the different units of the organization.

Types of Communication Networks

There are three basic network systems that operate within an organization. These systems depend on location, formality, and direction.

Location: External and Internal Networks

External Networks
In organizations external networks refer to those channels that carry information from within the organization to outside the organization, or those networks that carry information from outside the organization to inside the organization. Typically, external networks carry advertising messages, messages related to public relations, and messages relaying information about consumer complaints, concerns, and recommendations. The phone numbers and Web site addresses you find on many products are examples of external networks.

Herb-Ox Beef Bouillon has a message on its container that reads "Questions. Comments? Or Recipes? Please Call" and provides the relevant contact information. Contadina's Recipe Ready Crushed Tomato label includes the words, "We'd like to hear from you! Please write to Contadina Consumer Services at . . ." The label on Near East Curry Rice lets consumers know that "If you have questions, comments, or would like recipes, call us at 1-800- . . . , weekdays 10 a.m.–5 p.m. Eastern Time."

As we discussed in Chapter 5, most people who seek information about companies no longer look at labels but use search engines like Google or Yahoo! to connect them to a Web site. All companies that are not mired in the past have such a site, which can be navigated to locate a Contact Us link. Type "Near East Curry Rice" into a Web browser, click on a link provided by the search engine, and you are transported to QuakerOats.com, where "Near East Curry Rice" is listed as an item within its portfolio and a Contact Us link is provided.

These companies are establishing external communication networks with their customers. If your university schedules regular informational meetings with area high schools to explain the merits of your institution to prospective students, those question-and-answer sessions are external networks for communication.

External networks do not function independently. In order to communicate to external audiences, internal agents must be connected to other internal populations. As is the case with most organizational interaction, there is an interdependent relationship between the external and internal communication networks. The importance of this relationship is indicated in the Trent McGuire case that begins this chapter. Consider another example. The incident that follows illustrates how poor internal management can affect the functioning of the external network.

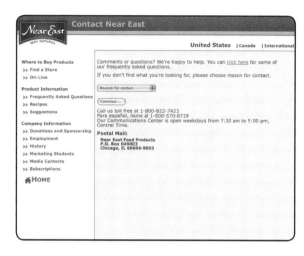

External networks are channels that link the organization to its outside audiences. This company clearly displays contact information on its home page.

A student intern, Stuart Markwardt, was working in the public relations department of a large high-tech company. Interns were favored by this company because high-tech magazines would frequently call the company in need of information for articles regarding new products. The public relations department was understaffed and swamped with these inquiries. Since most of the time these callers asked simple questions that any employee with some information about the organization could answer, the student interns satisfied a real need for the department.

On a particularly busy day a writer for a nationally known financial periodical phoned because she wanted to write a story about a word-processing package that had recently been introduced. The full-time employee she reached was swamped with work and passed the writer along to Markwardt.

Markwardt took the call and answered the journalist's questions. At the end of the interview the journalist asked for, and was given, Markwardt's name.

Three months later, the magazine came out with a positive review of the new product. The review concluded with the information that Stuart Markwardt was the product manager for the new software and the contact person for questions regarding the product.

This, of course, was not true, but to the more than 250,000 readers of the magazine it certainly seemed like Markwardt was the person to call with questions. By the time the article was published, Stuart Markwardt was back in school and no longer working for the corporation. Nevertheless, the company received hundreds of phone calls from persistent customers who insisted on speaking to Stuart Markwardt and to no one else. Some people will not settle for second fiddle, and many callers would not be put off in their quest and clamoring for Markwardt.

The company president was flabbergasted. After he read the article he allegedly shouted, "Who is this guy, Markwardt? What's a Markwardt anyway? I don't remember us hiring any Stuart Markwardt."

One year later, the company was still receiving phone calls and letters addressed to the intern. Over 2,000 calls have come in asking for Stuart Markwardt.

Internal Networks

Any channels *within* the organization that carry information are called *internal networks*. This can refer to *intra*departmental routes and *inter*departmental routes. The systems theory of organizations described in Chapter 3 suggests the necessity for organizations to establish channels for interdepartmental interaction. If an organization is a system with interdependent parts, the organization must have a way to link the interdependent parts. As was the case with Mr. Patel and the CD company, the lack of such conduits can result in customer frustration.

Often the internal channels exist but are myopically constructed and therefore impede traffic, as was the situation with Buckley. The presence of innovative technology does not, in and of itself, make for efficient internal networks. A sophisticated e-mail system, intranet, electronic bulletin board, and teleconferencing capabilities do not guarantee that people who desire to connect will do so. A posting on a Web page does not guarantee that persons who should access the page will visit it. As was discussed in the section on second-level effects of new technology, it is not inconceivable that new technology will actually reduce the chances of effective networking. A wiki could be established as a communal place for sharing information in lieu of periodic meetings. However, if important members of a group prefer face-to-face contact or are not inclined to use technology, then employing the wiki is actually counterproductive, at least initially, if it is used as a substitute and not a complementary network. Technology may facilitate efficient networking, but its existence cannot be considered the cure. In the case of Trent McGuire, for example, the combatants were, by job description, technologically savvy, and yet interdepartmental networks were not employed.

Formality: Formal and Informal Networks

Formal networks are those that are prescribed by the organization. These are the official, appropriate channels for people to follow when relaying information. Often these official channels have not been described as "communication networks." They have come to be the appropriate channels because they conform to the corporate organizational chart. These charts indicate who is to report to whom and what the appropriate chain of command is in an organization. The fact that a network is a formal network does not guarantee that communication "traffic" can utilize the particular channel. In the Buckley case, for example, Buckley was supposed to see Marshall, but he had to go through Keyes to do so. Keyes proved to be an unyielding roadblock.

To continue the highway metaphor, there are roads that appear to exist on a highway map, but for sometimes curious reasons, these roads are closed to motorists. Similarly, there are networks that appear to exist on the organizational chart, but these networks are in actuality closed to subordinates or organizational peers. Of course, there are times when "roads" might need to be closed. Vice presidents cannot be at everyone's beck and call. However, if the formal policy implies that a network is open, it can be frustrating not to be able to use that network. If the conduit is simply superficial and, as a practical matter, is not available, the company runs the risk of not receiving valuable information and of alienating its workers. Managers need to make sure that the formal networks are indeed available for the sending and receiving of organizational messages.

Informal networks are those channels that carry information on routes that are not prescribed by the organization. Typically, these informal routes are referred to as the grapevine, and for a number of reasons the grapevine is an important network. Keith Davis is the researcher most associated with the grapevine. Davis wrote a groundbreaking article, published in the *Harvard Business Review*, that described characteristics and types of organizational grapevines. Almost sixty years later the perspectives presented in this article are still relevant and frequently cited by those who conduct research and write about organizational networks.[2]

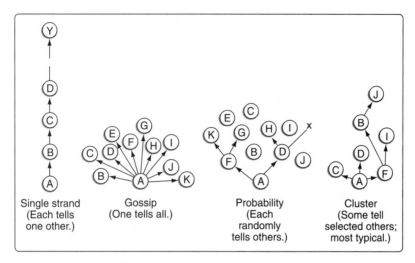

Figure 6.1 Types of Grapevine Chains
Source: Davis, Keith, and John W. Newstrom, Human Behavior at Work: Organizational
Behavior, 8th ed., McGraw-Hill, 1989: p. 373.

Davis identifies several types of grapevine patterns. They are:

- **Single Strand**: One person tells another, who then informs a third in a single linear format.
- **Gossip**: One person tells a host of others.
- **Probability**: Individuals randomly inform others.
- **Cluster:** Of those individuals informed, one tells others. Of those others informed, one tells others, etc.

Development of Informal Networks

By definition, the grapevine is not prescribed. While managers might attempt to engineer its development, the informal networks usually generate on the basis of factors that are only peripherally related to corporate policy.

The nature of the grapevine will be affected, for example, by the physical layout of the buildings and offices within the buildings. If production and advertising share a common lounge area and restroom facility, it is likely that an informal network will develop among those people who populate the departments of production and advertising.

Common hobbies and activities play a large part in the development of the grapevine. If seven employees from different departments jog together at lunch, information is likely to be passed along in the course of the run. The friendships that develop because of the common activity will result in social gatherings outside of the organization, during which information about the organization will be passed along as well. If Liu in Production wants to find out about a policy in Engineering, Liu may not call the Engineering manager as prescribed on the formal network, but contact Resnick, her jogging buddy.

It is not difficult to list the factors that contribute to the growth of this important network. Lunch schedules, family ties, social relationships, and common home towns can affect the growth of the network. Even the formal network can affect the growth of the informal network. If you participate on a committee and in the course of your conference sessions become friendly with a person who previously had been a stranger, that budding friendship creates a part of the informal network. The explosion of social media like Facebook, MySpace, and LinkedIn contribute to and expand the informal network. The proliferation of Web sites also expands the informal network. As Spangler, Kreulen, and Newswanger write in their article, "Machines in the Conversation," "Developments in the Internet and associated applications have made it possible for the scale of a single conversation to grow to one involving the simultaneous input of thousands of people."[3] Want to find out who is the best teacher for Introduction to Marketing? You could go to your assigned academic adviser and ask her or his opinion. You could read the descriptions of the instructors' backgrounds on the department Web site. You may be more likely, however, to go to RateMyProfessor.com or ask a friend if she or he had gone to a similar site to obtain the information.

On the basis of grapevine development individuals assume certain characteristics. Hellweg and others refer to these as "roles" we "play as a function of our positioning and the structure of the network."[4] These roles include:

- **Isolates:** Individuals who are essentially "out of the loop" of grapevine communication.
- **Bridges:** People who are members of a department and serve as links between their department and others.
- **Liaisons:** Persons who link one department with another, but who are not members of either department.

Think about the various organizations of which you are a member. Are you in the grapevine loop? Are you a bridge? Isolate? Liaison?

Traffic, Speed, and Accuracy

Many messages travel along the grapevine and do so relatively quickly, that is, information moves more rapidly on the grapevine than it moves on the formal network. The existence of the grapevine and its innate speed can pose some serious organizational problems. Rumors spread speedily, and inaccurate incendiary news can move throughout a large organization in hours. Incorrect information is difficult to stall once it begins to travel on the informal networks. As the British politician James Gallagher once said, "A lie can be halfway around the world before the truth has its boots on" (http://www.brainyquote.com/quotes/quotes/j/jamescalla141485.html July 21, 2009).

Although the grapevine can and does distort information, the grapevine can be, and often is, a rapid conveyor of accurate information as well. Often this accurate grapevine information reaches its destination before the chugging formal network can relay the message. The obvious result is employee anger and organizational embarrassment. Organizational communicators are occasionally placed in positions where they have to deny the accuracy of information employees have received via the grapevine until such time as the formal networks, dawdling along at a glacier-like pace, can officially inform the receiver of the information. Because of the swiftness of the informal network, the relatively slow formal network, and the occasional denials issued until the formal network catches up with the grapevine, the credibility of the formal network and those who operate it can be damaged.

Resilience

It is important to remember that the grapevine is not only fast and often accurate, but that it exists whether we like it or not. No number of directives from senior executives or threats will stop the informal network from operating. As long as there are cocktail parties, gyms, lunchroom cafeterias, water coolers, bathrooms, coffee machines, two chairs in an office, sexual energy—and technologies that allow for like texting and instant messaging, there will be informal networks. Therefore, managers must try to manage the informal network rather than attempt to eliminate it.

Credibility and Power

An indication of the accuracy of the informal network is that people often use the grapevine to check on the accuracy of messages they receive on the formal network. A formal e-mail may be broadcast to the entire organization announcing that an administrator has decided to step down from a position of authority. This formal message may include a list of achievements and effusive appreciation

"Trust me Mort—no electronic-communications superhighway, no matter how vast and sophisticated, will ever replace the art of the schmooze."

for the erstwhile administrator. However, when people receive such a message, they often employ their internal connections to discover what the e-mail really meant. Did Erika really step down? Was she forced out? Did she do something egregious? Does this mean others will be similarly displaced? Since the grapevine is often accurate, and the formal network sometimes suspect, people in organizations tend to check their sources to verify information that is formally communicated.

The power of the informal network is considerable. An indication of that power is the enormous growth of studies on *buzz* and the impact on *buzz*. The explosion of the Word of Mouth Marketing Association (WOMMA) and companies like ChatThreads is an indication of both the power and the influence of informal communication.

> **The Conversation Value Model.** Walter Carl is professor of communication studies at Northeastern University. He is also the Chief Research Officer of an organization called ChatThreads, a company that examines the value of everyday conversations to organizations. Carl notes that society has several expressions that discount the value of talk (e.g., "all talk and no action," "just small talk," and "talk is cheap"). Yet talk, he says, is in fact anything but cheap. It is actually quite important. In this and other chapters we have discussed communication as a constitutive process. Carl similarly posits that what may seem to be trivial conversations "are actually the building blocks of social life and are quite consequential to how we order and make sense of our worlds."
>
> Everyday talk also affects commerce. Informal conversation includes many "word-of-mouth" episodes about companies, brands, products, and services. A study Carl conducted found that over 15 percent of informal conversations make reference to a company, brand, product, or service. The Word of Mouth Marketing Association (WOMMA) has evolved because of an increasing awareness of the effects of these everyday conversations in advancing sales of products.
>
> Carl's organization ChatThreads was founded to commercialize a research methodology developed to assess how brand-related conversations spread from person to person. His trademarked methodology, which he calls the Conversation Value Model, is used to quantify the value of word of mouth. Like WOMMA, ChatThreads defines word of mouth to mean interactions among consumers about organizations, brands, products, and services. These conversations can take place in online or offline venues and can be synchronous or asynchronous.

Carl believes that attention to word of mouth is a strategic imperative for a company and its brands, because word of mouth is a leading factor in driving attitudes and purchasing decisions. Tracking and measuring conversations over time and assessing their value are also ways for companies to effectively examine the quality of their conventional marketing and media initiatives. You can visit the Web sites of WOMMA (http://womma.com/) and Chat-Threads (http://www.chatthreads.com/) to learn more.

Management

Managing the informal network is difficult. The tendency is to try to eliminate the grapevine because the grapevine is so troublesome. Its very existence makes it hard for employers to manage information. Management will occasionally issue directives in order to curtail or eliminate the informal network. Such attempts are likely to be futile. They either will not work or will not work for long. Grapevine communication is a reflection of natural human behavior.

Consider one case. The memorandum that follows was distributed throughout a major international corporation headquartered in New York State. The objective of the memorandum was to attempt to curb the grapevine.

TO: Personnel Relations Directors
FROM: [a corporate vice president]
SUBJECT: Employee Networks

*There have been questions about how we feel about **employee networks** and how management should react to them. The attached statement describes our corporate position on employee networks. Please share this with managements and staffs.*

Employee Networks
A network is made up of individuals who interact in a formal or informal structure for the purpose of self-improvement, and the exchange of ideas and information intended to enhance their ability to successfully pursue their careers. The company realizes that networking and employee networks exist within [the company]. It is the company's desire to encourage self-improvement and the exchange of ideas, and hence, there is an expectation that any such networking activities will make a positive contribution and not be negative. Of course, company management cannot overlook activities that violate company policies or are contrary to our business purposes or employ company resources or property for purposes other than [the company] business. . . .

This memo contains a veiled threat. It suggests that some networking "activities" that "violate company policies or are contrary to businesses purposes" would not be "overlooked."

In some quarters this memorandum might have had the desired effect. In others, the memorandum may have had the opposite effect and may have fueled the proliferation of "employee networks" and the grapevine. I have this memorandum, in fact, because of the grapevine. A manager whom we'll call Doris received this "Employee Networks" memo. She read it and sent it to a high-ranking company official with a note attached. The note read:

"Anne:
What is this about?
Doris"

Anne received Doris's note and then sent the memorandum along to a colleague of hers, who is an acquaintance of mine and knows of my interest in organizational communication. Anne also attached a note. It read:

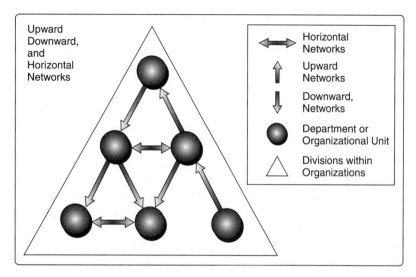

Figure 6.2 Types of Networks

"Richard,

Do you believe this? Send this to Alan.

Anne"

Richard, my acquaintance, then mailed the memorandum to me: the grapevine at work. Instead of stifling the employee networks, the attempt to curb the interactions was a catalyst to use the informal networks.

Although the grapevine, and the problems endemic to the grapevine, are realities, there are ways to deal with them.

Get Information Out; Use the Formal Network

Rowan reports that it's essential to "[g]et the facts and get them out fast."[5] Hellweg argues that management "needs to provide important information to employees openly, honestly, and quickly to reduce speculation."[6] Kreps writes that employees "have an insatiable appetite for meaning" and naturally will seek out information.[7] Pace and Faules make three specific recommendations for grapevine management:[8]

- Keep downward, horizontal, and upward networks open.
- Maintain supportive supervisor–subordinate relationships.
- Communicate awareness and acceptance of grapevine information.

Use the Informal Network

As it pertains to the second and third bulleted items above, remember that the informal network is natural and inevitable.[9] One can, as indicated, curb its proliferation by using the formal network. However, some of the grapevine will, and even should, remain. Davis writes that the grapevine ". . . cannot be abolished, rubbed out, hidden under a basket, chopped down, tied up, or stopped. If [it is] suppressed in one place, it will pop up in another. . . . It is as hard to kill as the mythical glass snake which, when struck, broke itself into fragments and grew a new snake out of each piece."[10] He argues that management should acknowledge that it "accepts and understands the informal organization."[11]

The informal networks will exist and do work. Use them. Complement the usage of the formal networks with the informal network. Concede that the grapevine exists, attempt to find out how it operates, and, when appropriate, use the grapevine to communicate information.

Direction: Upward, Downward, and Horizontal Networks

Messages in organizations, whether they are formal or informal, travel in one of three directions: upward from subordinate to superior, *downward* from superior to subordinate, or horizontally between employees on the same level.

Upward Networks

Without question, the formal channels that are used the least are those that carry messages from subordinate to superior. Even when these networks exist, they often are spurious.[12] Often the upward communication routes appear to be an existing channel for subordinate-to-superior communication, but in reality the routes are not extant or are used infrequently.

Consider the following example. It took place within a federal agency and is a prime example of bogus upward networks:

> One day, all the employees of a federal agency received the same letter. It was hand-delivered by their immediate supervisors. The letter indicated that a $50 reward would be offered to any employee who could present an idea to management that subsequently would be implemented by the organization.
>
> A new employee received the letter and immediately began to contemplate a series of $50 checks being made out in his name. The employee could think of dozens of organizational problems and saw this as an opportunity to make some reward money and also to impress management. Almost immediately, he began scrawling down ideas that he intended to refine and later submit as recommendations for his reward.
>
> A veteran of the agency watched this scenario unfold, and while the newcomer feverishly scrawled, the old-timer issued the following advice: "Make sure you put that idea on a soft piece of paper."
>
> The newcomer was surprised, but continued writing. Again came the warning, "Make sure you put it on a soft piece of paper."
>
> Again, the new employee paused only momentarily from the lists. Finally there was a third, "Make sure you put it on a soft piece of paper."
>
> "Okay." said the rookie, "Why should I put it on a soft piece of paper?"
>
> "Cause that way." said the old timer, "it won't leave a scar when they throw it back in your face."
>
> The beginner was momentarily stunned by this cynical advice. He began to ask around and discovered that the organization issued similar "calls for suggestions" on an annual basis. However, no one could identify a single employee who had ever received any monetary reward for any idea submitted. The grapevine information was that no one even read the suggestions. Requests for suggestions were issued to create an illusion of participatory decision making, but it was nothing short of a ruse.

Any such disingenuous attempt will not only retard the flow of information in the subordinate-to-superior network, it will also help demoralize the workforce.

An examination of upward networks requires an understanding of the:

- Specific values of upward networks
- Problems related to creating genuine upward networks
- Ways to manage and implement the upward network

Values of Upward Networks

The upward networks are very important to the organization. If administered effectively, these channels carry valuable information from subordinates to superiors. People on lower levels of the organization are often aware of problems that people on the top levels of the organization could not possibly be privy to. If a machine is malfunctioning on a certain level, it might take an unnecessarily long time for that malfunction to come to the attention of the appropriate manager, if not for a subordinate-to-superior network.

In addition, subordinate-to-superior networks provide a vehicle for obtaining feedback for messages that have been sent downward. When a superior sends a message to subordinates, that superior should want to get some reaction. Subordinate-to-superior communication networks facilitate the acquisition of this feedback.

"*Mr. Smith's office doesn't have a door. You have to batter your way through the wall.*"

Upward networks allow the employees to feel like they are valuable resources—as if they have "a piece of the rock" and their opinions matter. This opportunity, all other things being equal, is likely to improve morale.[13]

Employees may have suggestions that can be valuable for the organization. For example, McDonald's Egg McMuffin, Filet-O-Fish sandwich, and Big Mac were all ideas that came from McDonald's franchisees.[14] It's almost difficult to imagine the fast-food giant without these offerings, yet had top management been resistant to accepting recommendations from subordinate levels, these sandwiches (and their clones) might never have been part of fast-food menus.

Finally, subordinate-to-superior networks can be valuable because employees on different levels of the organization have specialized knowledge and expertise. It is in the best interest of the organization to allow this esoteric knowledge to be ventilated to upper management. Even the brightest manager is unlikely to know as much about a particular operation as the person who performs the operation daily. It is wise to solicit and tap the knowledge that is available from experienced and knowledgeable employees.

Problems with Upward Networks

Despite the value of upward communication networks, a common and valid complaint among employees is that there are not appropriate vehicles available to carry messages from subordinate to superior. Once again, upward communication networks are rarities and are often not authentic when they do exist. This is due more to human nature than to ignorance of the value of these networks or the sophistication of them.

People, no matter who they are and no matter how confident they might be, are reluctant to solicit rejection. When managers use the upward network, they invite criticism. Occasionally, that criticism will not be constructive. Sophomoric and destructive criticisms may surface only once in a great while, but they will still be painful regardless of their relative infrequency.

For example, department heads in many organizations are required to solicit evaluations from their subordinates. After reading many positive comments, these managers are still bothered when they read caustic negative comments. They would be less than human to react differently. After reading a particularly caustic evaluation, it is unlikely that a manager will say philosophically, "Well this troubled employee represents a mere .05 percent of the subordinate population. I shall not concern myself with this silly and apparently bitter comment."

Likewise, if top management solicits feedback and encourages suggestions from subordinates, these managers will run into similar problems. Imagine a manager reviewing a number of subordinate suggestions sent on an anonymous electronic bulletin board:

Suggestion (1): There are not enough work cubicles or desks for us over in Development. It is, it would seem, a minor investment to address this need and it would improve not only productivity, but morale as well.

The manager might react to this message by thinking, "I didn't realize there was a problem with inadequate work space. How come I wasn't aware of this? I'll check on the cost of getting more equipment and contact LaFlamme to see if this could be done. This idea of encouraging subordinate input is a good one."

The manager continues to review the postings:

Suggestion (2): We would appreciate more meaningful and frequent evaluative sessions. As it is, and I think I speak for many, we often don't know how top management is reacting to our work until it is too late. Also, the evaluations we do have seem to be meaningless formalities. Thank you.

Again the manager might think that the suggestion process is a good idea. The manager may decide not to do anything about the particular evaluation issue but may discuss the matter with others. At the very least, the manager has learned something that could, at some point, be important for the health of the organization. The manager reads a third post:

Suggestion (3): Your management style is suffocating. I feel imprisoned here and it seems as if you enjoy the role of warden. I want you to know that I resent your condescending manner, your clearly phony reference to the company as "one big family," and my daily ordeal of working here. Thanks for making my life miserable.

Even though this comment might be the only one of its kind, it may be difficult for the manager to continue to think of soliciting subordinate recommendations as a good idea. In fact, the manager may want to know who posted the "suggestion" and attempt some type of retribution. The manager might disregard the legitimacy of the other suggestions because of this caustic one, or may try to purge the negative comment card from the others, fearing that it could besmirch the manager's status if someone else were to come across it. [15]

A simple reason for the underutilization of upward communication networks is that few people like to hear bad things. There is a basic self-defense mechanism that operates, and there is the concomitant feeling of, "If they knew what I know, they'd be where I am."

Earthquake Prediction Business

Another problem with upward networks relates to what Dr. Wernher von Braun referred to as the "earthquake prediction business." [16] When von Braun was the director of NASA's Marshall Space Flight Center, he commented that senior people at the center were in the "earthquake prediction

Applying the Principles—Test Yourself

Clogging Networks

Assume that you are a mid level manager who has to fight annually in order to get money for your department. When you make your case to the persons in charge of budget allotments, you are competing in a zero-sum game with other mid level managers who are doing precisely the same thing.

What you have found works best is to claim that your department intends to diversify and will accept additional responsibilities. This argument is effective because it implies that there will be a consequential increase in revenues because of the diversification and increased workload.

You suspect that your subordinates would be aghast were they to hear what you typically tell the budget director because they would claim that such goals are impossible to meet with current staffing. You suspect that the budget directors have "heard it all" before, so you do not mind implying to them that additional revenues will be the result of actions that are unlikely to be accomplished.

Is there anything unethical with intentionally:

- Not informing your employees about the claims that you will be making in order to get the financial resources?
- Actively or passively discouraging any information that might come from subordinates that would preclude you from "honestly" telling the budget director that your anticipated activities could be completed? Does nonverbally suppressing information constitute an abuse of power?
- Implying that the result of your work will be increased organizational revenue?

business" in that they needed to "put out sensors" to detect tremors that would reflect upcoming "earthquakes" (i.e., potential disasters). The problem, von Braun suggested, is that when one is in the earthquake prediction business, one is likely to hear of many potential "earthquakes." Some people "are too sensitive; they overreact. Someone else might underestimate. . . . Others make a lot of noise just to get the mule's attention."[17]

A problem with upward networks is that a great deal of information can travel on a well-cultivated and receptive upward network. Managers have to address all these messages in a timely manner. Sometimes the information will be valuable. Administrators do need, and should want, to hear about impending earthquakes. But the challenge of knowing which messages are important to consider can be daunting—so daunting and exhausting that a manager might not attend to the messages that come up from the upward network.

Feynman's Theory and Upward Networks

The late physicist Richard Feynman was a member of the Rogers Commission that studied the 1986 Space Shuttle *Challenger* disaster. Feynman is most famous for his work as a Harvard physics professor. He also wrote some best-selling nonacademic books, including *Surely You're Joking, Mr. Feynman!* and *What Do You Care What Other People Think?*[18]

In a *Physics Today* article Feynman recounted his experience working on the Rogers Commission and discussed some perspectives he had regarding upward communication. Feynman observed that subordinates often had valuable information that had not been communicated to managers. In one

Types of Upward Networks

- Opinion surveys
- Question-and-answer sessions
- Suggestion programs
- Electronic or telephone systems (see sample below)
- Advisory boards

- Ombudsman—the organization has a representative whose job it is to seek out employee attitudes and convey it to management
- Skip-level interviews—senior management meets with employees who are levels below them[24]

instance he attributed this lack of upward communication to the fact that workers had poor written communication skills.

> They had a lot of information, but no way to communicate it. The workmen knew a lot. They had noticed all kinds of problems and had all kinds of ideas on how to fix them, but no one had paid much attention to them. The reason was: Any observations had to be reported in writing, and a lot of these guys didn't know how to write good memos.[19]

In another instance Feynman documented that the engineers at the Marshall Space Flight Center and the managers at the center were not "on the same page." He asked three engineers to write down the chances of flight failure on the basis of engine failure. He also asked a manager to approximate the chances of failure. The engineers all predicted a rate of about 1 in 200. The manager predicted 1 in 100,000![20]

This glaring inconsistency flabbergasted Feynman and the engineers.[21] Feynman advanced a theory of organizational communication in an attempt to explain how it was possible that the managers could be so out of touch with the engineers.

Deliberate Suppression of Information

Feynman conjectured that what happens in organizations is that, at times, managers feel compelled to exaggerate the capabilities of the units they manage. He argued that in order to ensure that resources continue to flow into a department, managers feel as if they must highlight the accomplishments of the department and downplay the problems. Managers might, therefore, claim that their units can do various things that they may not be able to do in order to guarantee that the unit will continue to be funded.

What happens in these instances—according to his theory—is that upward communication gets "clogged." Employees who are aware of information that would refute the exaggerated claims of managers are discouraged from communicating this information. If managers were to receive this information, they would be unable to continue to exaggerate the accomplishments of the department. In other words, Feynman contends that managers don't want to know certain types of information and actually discourage it from coming up the line.

> I believe that what happened was . . . that although the engineers down in the works knew NASA's claims were impossible, and the guys at the top knew that somehow they had exaggerated, the guys at the top didn't want to *hear* that they had exaggerated. . . . It's better if they don't hear it, so they can be much more "honest" when they're trying to get Congress to Okay their projects.[22]

Sample of an Upward Network

A major healthcare provider uses the following voice mail system to facilitate the generation of upwardly directed communications:

Step 1: Employees call a specific number in the voice mail system. This number is advertised in the internal newsletter and can be found inside most formal publications disseminated by the organization.

Step 2: Employees who make the call hear a recorded message from the president of the company. "This is Gwen Osterbrook, chairman of . . . . Thank you for your call. Your call is very important to us. Please leave us a message with your name and phone number if you wish to receive a return call. We will address your concerns and return your call within 48 hours. Thank you again."

Step 3: At the end of each day an assigned employee retrieves each of these messages. In order to do this, he or she follows a specific accessing procedure, which requires the use of a confidential, and regularly changed, password.

Step 4: The assigned employee, listens to, saves, and forwards the messages. The employee completes a form to record each and every suggestion. Then, depending on the nature of the suggestion, he or she forwards the suggestion to the relevant department. In addition, all messages are concurrently sent to the CEO Osterbrook. The messages are sent out with an introduction. For example: "Hello, this is Ann Williams forwarding a message to you that we received today, November 6, 2001, on the employee communication hotline. This message concerns Jim Rogers, who did not receive a paycheck last week. This message is also being forwarded to Marty Peters, in HR, and Wendell O'Malley, Rogers's immediate supervisor. As you know, the company policy is to respond to our employees who use the hotline within 48 hours. Thank you very much. If you have any questions, please call me, Ann Williams, at. . . ."

Step 5. The relevant department responds to the employee and concurrently contacts Ann Williams, explaining the nature of the follow-up.

Step 6. All hotline calls and responses are recorded on an Excel spreadsheet including:

• Name of the caller
• Location within company
• Contact information of caller
• Nature of the problem
• Person to whom the problem was forwarded
• Problem resolution

What do you think of Feynman's theory? Have you ever been in a leadership position when you "didn't want to know" certain information?

Suggestion Systems

Despite the problems, subordinate-to-superior networks are extremely important for organizational health. However difficult, they must be dealt with to improve the functioning of the organization. Edmondson in a *Journal of Applied Communication Research* article argued that three criteria had to be in place when soliciting information from employees through surveys: (1) trust in the organization's survey process, the researcher(s), and the organization, (2) elimination of adversarial relationships that often exist between management and employees who speak up, and (3) evidence that the organization does more than purport to value the things that it says it values.[23] Meeting these criteria is challenging but foundational to the success of surveys and formal upward networks in general. The thread that runs through each of the three recommendations is trust in the legitimacy of the communication channels.

If the upward networks are suggestion systems of any sort, the network should meet four specific criteria. The program should have:

- Support from top management.
- A program administrator who has this responsibility as a primary or sole job responsibility.
- Efficiently communicated instructions regarding the procedures, rules, and rewards.
- Timely and meaningful feedback for all those who participate in the program.

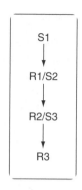

Figure 6.3

Downward Networks

The downward networks are the channels that are most likely to be formalized. They carry a great deal of the official superior-to-subordinate information. Formal downward networks travel relatively slowly.

It is important to emphasize that downward networks should not be "one-way streets." Messages sent along the downward networks are only valuable if they reach their destinations. If conceived and perceived as "one-way streets," downward networks are not likely to encourage feedback. Without some form of feedback, senders will not know if information they sent was received or how it was received. Certainly, information has to travel downward for all the reasons we identified in Chapter 5, but what is the value of the voyage if the information winds up in a cul-de-sac and the source is unaware? Therefore, downward networks should be utilized in conjunction with upward networks.

In addition, the effective utilization of downward networks requires an understanding of the organizational communication phenomenon known as serial distortion.

Serial Transmissions and Serial Distortion

I work for a large paint company. At one point the organization advertised an incentive plan for employees. The plan called for monetary rewards to those who sold the most paint and paint accessories. In addition to salary increments, prizes like television sets and stereos would be distributed to employees who were successful at selling.

Although this promotion had the potential to be a big success, it was not due to the fact that the information never reached the employees. My manager had received a newsletter explaining the incentive program but had failed to relay the information to the salespeople or post the newsletter in a public area where it could be read by employees.

Messages traveling on downward networks in organizations are frequently transmitted serially. That is, often there are intermediary stopping points between the original source of the message and the desired receiver of the message. Serial transmissions can and do occur on other networks as well.

Consider the diagram in Figure 6.3. A message might emanate from a CEO (S1) intended for all employees (R3). The message might be orally diffused at a meeting of the CEO and all organizational vice presidents (R1/S2). A vice president might phone her department heads (R2/S3) and ask

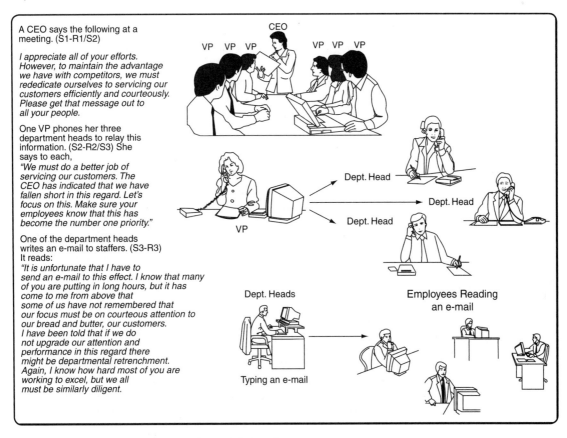

A CEO says the following at a meeting. (S1-R1/S2)

I appreciate all of your efforts. However, to maintain the advantage we have with competitors, we must rededicate ourselves to servicing our customers efficiently and courteously. Please get that message out to all your people.

One VP phones her three department heads to relay this information. (S2-R2/S3) She says to each,
"We must do a better job of servicing our customers. The CEO has indicated that we have fallen short in this regard. Let's focus on this. Make sure your employees know that this has become the number one priority."

One of the department heads writes an e-mail to staffers. (S3-R3) It reads:
"It is unfortunate that I have to send an e-mail to this effect. I know that many of you are putting in long hours, but it has come to me from above that some of us have not remembered that our focus must be on courteous attention to our bread and butter, our customers. I have been told that if we do not upgrade our attention and performance in this regard there might be departmental retrenchment. Again, I know how hard most of you are working to excel, but we all must be similarly diligent.

Figure 6.4 Serial Transmissions Can Lead to Aerial Distortions

them to relay the information to the employees (R3). A department head might send an e-mail to be distributed to all employees (see Figure 6.4).

Such serial transmission can result in serial distortions that go beyond those that occur when children engage in the game "telephone." Some distortions may, as is the case in the telephone game, be caused simply because of the frequency of encoding and decoding. However, some distortions occur for reasons that are related to organizations and the relationships that develop within organizations.

There are four categories of serial distortion:

- Adding
- Leveling
- Sharpening
- Assimilating

Adding takes place when an intermediary adds onto the original information. Some people are more verbose than others and speak or write more elaborately than others. This may seem relatively harmless, but the result of adding can be serial distortion. "Tell Angela we appreciate her efforts" changes meaning when an intermediary writes a lengthy message congratulating Angela on work well done and intimates in the mailing that there might be a monetary reward forthcoming.

Leveling is the opposite of adding. In leveling, the intermediary abridges the message. Just as some intermediaries are verbose, others are reserved and therefore shorten messages because it is not their style to speak or write a great deal. Sometimes messages are leveled not because of speaking tendencies, but because there are strained relationships between the intermediary and a receiver.

Sharpening refers to distortions that occur when intermediaries make information they are relaying more sensational than the news needs to be. For illustration assume that Richard Duncan, a middle manager, receives a phone call from his supervisor, Jane McCoy. McCoy tells Duncan that two workers will have to be temporarily laid off due to some budget cuts. McCoy gives Duncan the names of the two employees who will be laid off and asks that Duncan take care of the matter immediately. Duncan calls a meeting of his employees and somberly informs the group that two people will have to be temporarily laid off. Duncan concludes his speech with the following: "Right now it's only two. Who knows what's going to be? Times are tough. This could be the start of something major. I get that feeling." In this illustration, the message has been sharpened.

Messages are *assimilated* when the intermediary alters the message to make it more palatable to the recipient of the message. This is a very common kind of serial distortion. Few people like to convey devastating news to individuals. Some may want to startle groups, but it's not enjoyable to have to tell a friend or even an acquaintance that a superior is furious with performance or that one's employment is terminated. If one is told to relay such negative messages to individuals, it's not unlikely that the intermediary will attempt to make the message more palatable to the receiver. For example, consider the following message traveling on a downward network:

> Tell Schober that in a service industry we cannot tolerate mistakes like the one he made last week. Our customer base must remain strong and that kind of error, however unintentional, can dilute that strength. Frankly, I would be inclined to terminate him immediately given the magnitude of the transgression. However, I am willing to give him another opportunity to prove his worth to our organization. Make sure you impress upon him how close he is to termination. Are we clear?

If assimilated, the message may be conveyed in this way:

> The boss was unhappy about last week. She was upset, but you know how they all are upstairs. She'll get over it, trust me. I know your worth. However, I wanted you to know that she registered some concern when we last met. Let's just be more careful next time

Any interaction between a single source and a single receiver is subject to communication noise and message distortion. The serial nature of communication on downward networks creates additional noise and the chance for serial distortion. It is not possible to eliminate all intermediaries when communicating information downward in organizations. However, it is the responsibility of organizational men and women to be aware of the potential for serial distortion and be careful and vigilant as they relay information.

Horizontal Networks

Horizontal networks transport information along the same strata in an organization. Katz and Kahn, in the *Social Psychology of Organizations*, comment that "[o]rganizations face one of their most difficult problems in procedures and practices concerning lateral communication."[25] Formal horizontal networks are rarities, particularly at the lower levels of the hierarchy. Top managers may meet periodically to discuss the nature of each manager's division. At the lower levels, however, employees are unlikely to have many formal horizontal contacts. There tends to be what is referred to as a "silo mentality" in organizations. This means that units within organizations perceive themselves as discrete entities that perform independently. As we discovered when we discussed systems

Figure 6.5 A Silo Mentality Is Counterproductive Since Departments in Organizations Are Inherently Interdependent and Not Independent

theory, such a silo mentality is counterproductive since departments in organizations are inherently *interdependent* and not independent.

Organizational Penetration and Horizontal Networks

Tompkins discusses the value of "consciously created redundancy of communication channels."[26] He strongly supports the idea that a systems orientation requires horizontal networks linking departments to ensure that relevant messages get from one unit of an organization to another. He extends horizontal networking to include what he refers to as "organizational penetration." Tompkins contends that if an organization hires external contractors, it is the responsibility of the organization to "penetrate" the contractors so that the external unit becomes, temporarily, like a unit of the organization. As a temporary unit of the organization, horizontal networks need to be created to facilitate interdepartmental communication and reduce the deleterious effects of silo mentalities.

Richard Feynman conducted an experiment while on the Rogers Commission that reflects problems that can occur when penetration and horizontal networks are both lacking. Feynman dipped a "model of the [Space Shuttle *Challenger*] field joint complete with the inserted O-ring" into some ice water and demonstrated conclusively that the O-rings on the *Challenger* were not resilient enough to withstand freezing temperatures.[27] The contractor, Morton Thiokol, was aware that the O-rings were not resilient below certain temperatures. However, when Thiokol recommended delaying the *Challenger* launch, the Marshall representatives were unwilling to accept the recommendations from Thiokol. Eventually, Thiokol relented. Had the Marshall Space Flight Center established horizontal networks and, in fact, penetrated Thiokol, they would have known to the same extent as the Thiokol representatives knew—just as Feynman demonstrated that any casual observer would have known—that the O-rings were not resilient under the launch conditions. Yet effective horizontal networks had not been established, penetration had not occurred, and a disaster was a result.

Similarly, if units within the same organization do not establish horizontal linkages, important information that must be shared will not be shared. It's unlikely that there will be an explosion as spectacular as that which shattered the *Challenger* and NASA, but an organization could be devastated nonetheless.

The importance of communication networks for organizational effectiveness cannot be overstated. The problems associated with inadequate networks are exacerbated because management often views communication parochially and as a back-burner issue. What may be the most powerful argument in support for the conscious development and nurturing of communication networks

PRACTITIONER PERSPECTIVE

Mike Armani: Vice President for Marketing and Communication

Mike Armani is the Vice President for Marketing and Communication at Northeastern University. Before coming to Northeastern, he had been in a similar position at Harvard University for ten years. We spoke in his office on April 1, 2009. He was calm and relaxed during our meeting. However, for the entire time he held a cell phone in his hand.

As you read through this section, consider the following questions:

1. Can slogans like "Together We Can" create unity within an organization? Do you agree with the highlighted sentences in the excerpt?
2. Is it inevitable that someone in this position will have to compromise her or his ethics?
3. Would you enjoy a job like the one Armani has?

My work involves transmitting the university's messages to internal and external audiences. My ability to communicate accurately to external audiences is, to a large extent, a function of my ability to communicate with internal audiences. I have been doing this job either here or elsewhere for many years, and it really comes down to basic blocking and tackling—that is, understanding your audiences, knowing the organization's mission, and clearly communicating relevant content to these audiences.

I would agree that clarity, accuracy, timeliness, pertinence, and credibility are keys to effective communication. I will add a sixth item to that list, brevity, and also emphasize the importance of credibility. In this business what you have is your credibility. You earn it by being credible. Lose it and your ability to function is undermined.

I see no role for deliberate ambiguity in this position. When some organizations employ slogans that are meaningless, like a recent "Together We Can" campaign slogan, it is too vacuous to be effective as a unifying message.

My feeling about branding is that the idea has gained more traction than it deserves. Before anything is branded, we have to develop what we intend to brand. Once that is done, and once we have earned respect for what we have developed, then the branding can provide a complement to the action. But it is shortsighted to assume that branding in and of itself will communicate change. **Effective communication takes time and repetition and cannot be accomplished solely by hanging a banner and sloganeering.**

I am involved with crafting the president's messages and often reviewing communications that are going to go out in the name of the organization. Our group has a weekly meeting on Monday morning when we discuss how we will attack the week. I also meet periodically with a group called the Communication Council that comprises anyone who works for the university in a capacity related to marketing and public relations.

The effects of new technology on what I do, and what I have done, are huge. The ability to post a message on the Web and have that message be accessed by many audiences has been an asset that I did not enjoy when I first started working as a director of communication.

[A moment before the interview was to end, Armani had a phone call. He excused himself, took the call in my presence, and asked the caller if he could phone back momentarily. He could not. Whatever the issue was, we had to stop the conversation. Mr. Armani was very calm about it but said "This happens regularly. There is some issue I need to address. I will get back to you."]

is this: fourteen years after the Rogers Commission and Richard Feynman described the communication problem at NASA, seven years after Tompkins wrote about the significance of horizontal and upward networks specifically at the Marshall Space Flight Center, two panels concluded that NASA's 1999 Mars Polar Lander failure was a function of poor interdepartmental communication. As the *New York Times* reported: "The reports issued today found failures in communication between project officials and managers at the jet propulsion laboratory, which oversees interplanetary missions, as well as between these managers and Lockheed Martin."[28]

Thomas Young, who chaired the team reviewing the agency, commented, "People were trying to do too much with too little and not adequately conveying their concerns to others, particularly upper management. . . . No one had a sense of how much trouble they were actually in."[29]

Remarkably, causes of the February 1, 2003, *Columbia* tragedy were also related to inadequate internal communication networks.[30]

SUMMARY: A TOOLBOX

- Communication networks are the channels that provide "highways" for information travel.
- Organizations must create, cultivate, and nourish these networks.
- The following networks are necessary for effective organizational communication:
    - Upward, downward, and horizontal networks
    - Formal and informal networks
    - Internal and external networks
- Vigilance in terms of maintaining these networks is as essential as vigilance in terms of maintaining the quality of motor highways. Without navigable routes, messages can not be communicated inter- or intradepartmentally. The result of poor networking can be organizational chaos and disaster.

REVIEW AND DISCUSSION QUESTIONS

1. How can communication networks affect an organization's culture?
2. What is the distinction between formal and informal networks?
3. Does Feynman's theory of organizational communication apply to any organization with which you are familiar?
4. Identify three problems with establishing genuine upward networks in an organization.
5. How does serial transmission affect the quality of messages that travel along downward networks?
6. Why would systems theorists consider horizontal networks essential?
7. Why would human resources theorists consider upward networks essential and informal networks inevitable?

GROUP/ROLE-PLAY

In a group of four to six, review the issues surrounding the case that begins this chapter. Attempt to gain consensus regarding the questions at the end of the case.

- For the role-play, one member of the group plays Trent McGuire. Another assumes the role of a representative from the Internet development team service. A third represents someone from upper management.
- Role-play a face-to-face meeting of these three persons that has been called by McGuire. Assume McGuire is taking these steps to improve communication and establish formal networks linking each unit to each other, to the customers, and to upper management.

Chapter 7

Culture, Climate, and Organizational Communication

Chapter in a Nutshell

An organization's culture affects the quality of that organization's communication. At the same time, routine daily communication behavior establishes, nourishes, supports, and sustains the nature of the evolving organizational culture. A phenomenon related to culture is organizational climate, "the surface representation of organizational culture."[2] It is true that employee reading, writing, speaking, and listening skills are imperatives for effective organizational communication. But will employees exercise the skills they have if they are led by tyrannical supervisors? It is true that horizontal networks are essential for interdepartmental interaction. But will employees use these networks if there is tension and distrust between departments? Ethical decisions are indeed crucial for effective organizational communication. But will ethical factors be considered in a corporate culture that supports the credo: "Just close the sale; just get it done"?

This chapter explores the interdependent relationships between culture, climate, and organizational communication.

When you have completed this chapter, you should be able to:

- Define and describe the phrase "organizational culture."
- Define and describe the phrase "organizational climate."
- Explain the relationship between climate and culture.
- Describe the interdependent relationship between organizational culture and organizational communication.
- Describe and discuss the characteristics of supportive communication environments.
- Explain what is meant by organizational assimilation, socialization, and identification.
- Identify key factors that affect the evolution of organizational culture.

CASE 7.1:

The Elan Corporation

Background

An economic recession was looming over the international manufacturing community. The Elan Corporation was not immune to the effects of the recession. Elan was faced with the prospects of downsizing and restructuring in order to cut costs and maintain its position as a globally competitive organization. Elan's communications regarding the restructuring affected (a) the credibility of management, (b) subsequent communication of information, (c) the quality of upward and horizontal communication networks within Elan, and even (d) employees' willingness to exercise their communication skill sets during meetings. What had been an atmosphere characterized by shared values and open communication eroded into an atmosphere characterized by distrust, adversarial relationships, and poor organizational communication.[3]

The VSP and QBS

The initial step in Elan's downsizing involved implementing a Voluntary Separation Program (VSP). The program, announced in August, allowed employees to voluntarily leave the company in exchange for an attractive severance package. Management's (unannounced) goal was to eliminate 200 positions before December 3.

On October 20, nearly two months after the announcement of the VSP, the Elan Corporation announced that there would be a second downsizing plan. This one would not be voluntary. It was called the Quality Based Selection program or QBS for short (QBS). The QBS program essentially required all employees to reapply for their own jobs or lower-level jobs. On the basis of the quality of their candidacies, the employees would either be retained or let go.

An important piece of information was not communicated to employees when the QBS program was announced. Employees were NOT informed that any QBS-related cuts would only take effect if by December 3 the VSP program had not yielded the desired 200 resignations. The employees assumed that the QBS cuts would be in addition to any downsizing that resulted from VSP.

It was the hope of management that the QBS announcement would serve as a stimulus for VSP participation. Each supervisor provided employees with information about the QBS in one-on-one face-to-face discussions. Each employee had to decide whether to participate in the QBS or opt for the VSP.

Management's hopes were realized. The QBS turned out to be a powerful means for encouraging employees to retire voluntarily before they might be required to leave involuntarily. Employees, apparently, did not relish the idea of being reevaluated for their current or subordinate positions. The QBS was so successful that on November 16 the Elan Corporation happily announced in a mass e-mailing that the QBS program would be put on "hold." Two hundred persons had already opted for the VSP.

However, many of those persons had opted for VSP because they had assumed that QBS was inevitable. Many of those who had not opted for VSP had already gone through the time-consuming and the emotionally wrenching activity of completing forms and applying for their own or subordinate jobs because of the QBS. Employees were angry that managers had not explained during their one-on-one sessions that the QBS would only be implemented if the VSP failed. Many managers claimed that they were not aware that QBS could be canceled. Employees, by and large, found this defense not to be credible.

Ramifications

While the desired downsizing had been accomplished, the QBS and VSP programs had dramatic effects on the climate and culture at Elan.

- The credibility of upper management was questioned.

- The shared values such as mutual trust and respect that had been characteristic at Elan were no longer part of the fabric of the organization.
- Production activities were paralyzed from the time QBS was announced until the time QBS was put on hold. Afterwards, production activities did not resume to their pre-VSP and -QBS levels because of employee resentment.
- Most employees who had been with the company more than ten years expressed feelings of abandonment, betrayal, and rejection even after the downsizing was completed and their jobs had been saved.
- Discussions between employees and supervisors led management to believe that QBS was actually a failure since the program had persuaded some of the better performers to opt for the VSP program.
- The absence of trust made subsequent communications between management and employees very strained and resulted in noncooperative and even adversarial relationships.

- Overall, VSP and QBS resulted in a loss in respect for top management, poor morale, loss of productivity, and negative behaviors of employees.
1. Should Elan have communicated that the QBS program would only be implemented if the VSP program failed?
2. Did the communications regarding the VSP and QBS create a poor working atmosphere, or would that atmosphere have been negative no matter how these programs were communicated?
3. Can the post QBS climate at Elan affect:
    - Quality of upward and horizontal networks?
    - The desire of employees to exercise their communication skills sets at meetings, during interpersonal exchanges, or when composing written documents?
4. How might the Elan organization recreate a positive communication culture in the wake of VSP and QBS?
5. How would a critical theorist analyze this case?

Climate and Culture

In Chapter 3 we discussed cultural theory and the importance of examining organizational communication as it relates to organizational culture. In Chapter 1 you were introduced to W. Charles Redding, the late Purdue professor who was a pioneer in the field of organizational communication. In

"Culture is the sea we swim in—so pervasive, so all consuming, that we fail to notice its existence until we step out of it. It matters more than we think."[1]

one of his books, *Communication Within the Organization*, Redding made the following comment about organizations, communication, culture, and something he referred to as the organizational climate: "The 'climate' of the organization is more crucial than are communication skills or techniques (taken by themselves) in creating an effective organization."[4]

Redding's point is important to consider. He argued that the environment within which individuals interact was more important than individual employees' communication skills. If an organization employs 500 people and all of these employees have excellent communication skills—that is, they can speak, write, and listen well—it will matter little if, for example, the workplace has and generates an unpleasant atmosphere that discourages interaction.

All but the charmed reader can recall jobs where a negative atmosphere damaged internal communication. Perhaps it was some ornery supervisor, belligerent co-worker, or defiant subordinate that contributed to the problem. Perhaps it was simply a system or culture that cultivated defensiveness. Whatever it was, your eloquence or willingness to listen meant very little. The defensive atmosphere undermined your potential and the organization's potential.

Attempting to cultivate and maintain a culture that is conducive to a supportive climate is an essential responsibility of all members of an organization—especially those who have leadership roles. No expensive seminar on reducing interpersonal conflict, no workshop on conference dynamics, and no external training consultant hired to improve subordinate-to-superior communication will be of enduring value unless the organization maintains a supportive culture and climate. As significantly, no workshop devoted to improving the communication culture and climate will be meaningful unless the organization's actual routine communication behavior serves to foster a supportive culture and climate.

> "Information and communication [in organizations] . . . are surface manifestations of complex configurations of deeply felt beliefs, values, and attitudes."[3]

What Is Organizational Climate?

Taguiri defines climate as the "relatively enduring quality of the internal environment of [the] organization that (a) is experienced by its members, (b) influences their [the members'] behavior, and (c) can be described in terms of the values of a particular set of characteristics (or attributes) of the environment."[5] Kreps writes that the climate "is the internal emotional tone of the organization based on how comfortable organizational members feel with one another and with the organization."[6] Weinzimmer et al. write that climate is the "surface representation of organizational culture."[7]

Many authors use, appropriately, a weather metaphor when describing the organizational climate. They argue that "nasty," "cold" conditions retard organizational communication and "warm," "sunny" conditions are conducive to interaction.[8] The weather metaphor was used illustratively by Guion when he compared the organizational climate to the "wind chill index." Just as the wind chill index is a function of two objective conditions—temperature and wind velocity—the organizational climate is a function of two objective conditions: the actual conditions in the organization and the perceptions employees have of these conditions.[9]

In essence, the climate is the atmosphere in the organization that either encourages or discourages communication. A supportive climate is likely to encourage interaction and the flow of information. A defensive climate is likely to retard the flow of information.

Gibb identified dimensions of supportive and defensive climates. He characterized defensive climates as:

- Evaluative (e.g., blaming, destructively criticizing)
- Manipulative
- Indifferent to personal needs of others
- Superior (condescending—leaders, for example, who consider employees to be beneath them)
- Certain (Gibb used "certainty" in the sense of intransigence and dogmatism. "Those who seem to know the answers, to require no additional data, and to regard themselves as teachers as opposed to co-workers put others on guard." The *certain* individual needs to be right and wants to win more than to solve a problem correctly.)

Supportive climates were characterized as:

- Nonjudgmental
- Spontaneous (in the sense of being devoid of deception and manipulation)

- Egalitarian (in the sense of considering others as equals and respecting others, thereby not being condescending)
- Concerned and empathic
- Provisional (in the sense of not being dogmatic or *certain*) [10]

How would you describe the organizations to which you belong? Are they characterized by defensive or supportive climates?

In an attempt to describe the conditions necessary for effective organizational communication, Redding constructed a list of elements that he deemed necessary for what he called "the ideal supportive climate."[11] The following section describes these five elements.

Supportiveness: Condescension, destructive criticism, and inconsideration of others are deleterious to the climate of an organization. Therefore, the ideal supportive climate is characterized by respect and constructive evaluation. We've previously discussed human messages and the theoretical foundations for relaying human messages. Redding's point is that human messages are essential for the ideal supportive climate. This does not mean that administrators should march around distributing candies while disingenuously stroking employees. It means that managers must acknowledge the human needs of employees and, without artifice, communicate messages that reflect this awareness.

Credibility, Confidence, and Trust: Employees need to have confidence and trust in their superiors so that they may approach these managers in order to explain problems, concerns, or make suggestions. Credibility—as we will discuss in more detail later—is a significant feature of the supportive climate.

Openness: Openness in this context means both relaying information openly and being open to approach from employees.

Participatory Decision Making: Redding argued that when employees are able to meaningfully contribute to the decision-making process, the climate tends to be more supportive. This does not mean that executives must relinquish decision-making powers. The idea is to, legitimately, include employees and genuinely consider their contributions. As we discussed in the previous chapter, employee involvement has several benefits related to organizational efficiency and organizational communication. One benefit is that such involvement tends to improve the organizational climate.

Emphasis on High-Performance Goals: Some may believe that a relaxed environment is conducive to a supportive climate. Relaxed environments may be conducive to productivity, but an organization must emphasize that the company exists in order to achieve and excel. Otherwise the climate will not be as supportive as it can be. Employees might initially be pleased if a manager were to say, "Look, I don't care what you do, as long as you don't make waves and I don't get in trouble." However, as suggested by the Hawthorne Studies and human resources theory, given the right conditions most people actually want to accomplish something meaningful with their work hours. Therefore, an attitude of "we will accept nothing but excellence" will resonate with workers assuming all other factors for a supportive climate are in place.

An easy acronym can be used to help remember the ingredients of Redding's ideal supportive climate. By taking the first letter of each of the elements, the word SCOPE is formed:

Supportivenees
Credibility
Openness

Participatory decision making

Emphasis on high-performance goals

When you think of ideal supportive climates, it is important to remember how rare it is for organizations to be so characterized. Therefore, it is like a breath of fresh air when we work in, or observe, an organization that has such features. SCOPE provides the elements for a breath of fresh air.

Additional Factors and Features

Pace and Faules elaborate on Redding's list in their summary of the literature. They conclude that six additional factors affect employee perceptions of the organizational climate:

A genuinely supportive climate can facilitate effective communication in organizations.

- The way employers attempt to motivate employees.
- The quality of decision making (i.e., to what extent workers feel as if what they have to do is a function of good or bad decisions made by management).
- The sense that human beings are perceived by the organization as important.
- The quality of resources (e.g., computers, furniture, and furnishings).
- The opportunities for upward communication.
- Overall quality of organizational communication.[12]

What Is Organizational Culture?

Organizational culture is an elusive concept. One reason for this is that the phrase has been defined in various, and sometimes incompatible, ways. However, there is a basic theme to most attempts at describing organizational culture. Below you will see a series of definitions that reflect this theme.

Organizational culture refers to:

- The set of key values, norms, and assumptions, that is shared by members of an organization and taught to new members as correct.[13]
- A pattern of shared basic assumptions learned by a group as it solved its problems of external adaptation and internal integration that has worked well enough to be considered valid and therefore to be taught to new members as the correct way to perceive, think, and feel in relation to those problems.[14]
- The values, heroes, myths, and symbols that have been in the organization forever, the attitudes that say:
  - Challenge administrators
  - Be entrepreneurial
  - Challenge yourself
  - Take risks
- Pervasive, deep, largely subconscious, and tacit code that gives the "feel" of an organization and determines what is considered right or wrong, important or unimportant, workable or unworkable in it, and how it responds to the unexpected crises, jolts, and sudden change.[15]

Applying the Principles—Test Yourself

The Informal Orientation

Assume that it is your first day of work at a well-respected, very successful restaurant. Further assume that your manager takes you aside and gives you an "off-the-record" orientation speech before you begin serving your tables. Below are two versions of that talk. As a new employee at this restaurant, which would you prefer to hear?

• "Look, this restaurant will make money no matter what. All I ask is that you get here on time, treat the customers with respect, get the meals out promptly, and clean up afterwards. When your shift is over you can disappear as far as I'm concerned. Bottom line: I don't want to hear about you. You don't want to hear from me. Got it?"

• "Listen. We have been here for fifty years and we have been here for fifty years because we make real sure that we are the best. Our food is the best, our kitchen staff is the best, and our waitstaff—where you come in—is the best. Every single person in this dining hall is striving to make this establishment the finest restaurant in the county if not the whole state. If you can be like all the other employees here, well, welcome aboard. If you don't feel so motivated, then there are plenty of other restaurants that need waitstaff. Do you understand?"

Now that you have selected the better of the two choices, construct a message you would prefer to either of the above options. What are the key points you wish to convey with your message?

Let's distill these definitions. We can say that, in essence, the culture of an organization is concerned with the belief and value system of that organization. This value system is passed along to the employees when they begin work and as they continue to be socialized at work. Employees learn the culture by becoming acquainted with organizational heroes, rites, rituals, and slogans. The culture is reinforced when employees interact with company storytellers who promulgate the mythology of the organization. The mythology depicts the attitudes, mores, goals, and credos that are, symbolically, foundational planks supporting how and why a company operates as it does.

Consider some of the examples below. They illustrate how storytellers explain organizational culture in terms of heroes, rites, rituals, and slogans.

• "Twenty years ago Milton Weiss worked eighteen-hour days for twenty-nine days straight—Saturdays and Sundays included—in order to close a deal. Our stock rocketed after that. Now we have a name for working weekends on something major. We call it a 'Milton.' Last year I only pulled one Milton, but after 9/11 we were all pulling Miltons. In a way you don't want to do too many Miltons. But there was something special about the energy when we were all doing those Miltons together."

• "After your first mega sale you're taken to Alfie's by Sharon. When Sharon takes you to Alfie's, you know you've reached a new level. Making Alfie's is a big deal around here."

• "Once a month on Tuesday evenings we meet after hours for a 'good of the order' session. There's beer and sandwiches, and we sit around and bring up anything that's bothering us. It's great. Clears the air."

- "We are a 'play hard, work hard' environment. 'Second place is no place' around here. Our motto is simple: 'Get it done.'"

Think about your current or a former employer. How would you describe that organization in terms of its:

- Heroes?
- Rites?
- Rituals?
- Slogans?

Relationship between Climate and Culture

There is a relationship between the concepts of corporate climate and culture. Denison, in an exhaustive article entitled "What IS the Difference between Organizational Climate and Culture?" comments that some research that claims to be involved in examining organizational culture is indistinguishable from climate-related research.[16] He makes the case that climate and culture may, in fact, be the same phenomenon examined from different vantage points. However, the article does point out what readers by now may have deduced is the distinction between the two concepts.

In essence, the organizational culture contains the root value systems that create the organizational climate. Denison comments that culture relates to "underlying values and assumptions," whereas the climate reflects the "manifestations" of those underlying values and assumptions.[17] Therefore, the culture affects the climate. If a cultural slogan is "Don't test or question your boss," it is unlikely that "participatory decision making" will be an organizational trademark. Since participatory decision making is a criterion for ideal supportive climates, the cultural credo that "the boss is always right" is likely to destabilize climate conditions. If an organizational hero is a manager who "went to the mat" for employees and whose word "you could take to the bank," then the climate would reflect that cultural value in that it would be characterized as "supportive and credible." Using the weather metaphor that was introduced earlier, one might think of the culture as the weather factors that, when taken collectively, generate the weather conditions, i.e., the climate.

Culture, Communication, and Assimilation

If culture provides the roots for the climate, and both culture and climate affect the organization, obvious questions come to mind:

- Can a desired culture be consciously seeded?
- If so, how can this be accomplished?
- If not, how does the culture become the culture?
- What is the role of communication in the evolution of culture and climate?

We began to address these questions in Chapter 3 when we examined cultural theory and organizational communication. You may remember the contributions of Deal and Kennedy, the perspectives of the interpretivists versus the "functionalists," and comments made by and about Edgar Schein—a pioneer in organizational culture research. In this section of this chapter we continue to explore and address these questions pertaining to climate, culture, and communication.

Assimilation, Socialization, and Identification

"The trouble with these guys is that after you've been with them for a couple of weeks you start to play like them."

—BASEBALL PLAYER SID GORDON AFTER HAVING BEEN TRADED TO THE HAPLESS 1951 PITTSBURGH PIRATES

Organizational assimilation theory is associated with the late Frederic Jablin, a scholar who wrote extensively about organizational communication. Jablin's meticulous and comprehensive research addressed several subjects, including subordinate-to-superior communication as well as organizational assimilation. The thorough nature of Jablin's work is evidenced by the 86-page article he wrote for the *New Handbook of Organizational Communication*, which explains organizational assimilation theory.[18]

Jablin describes organizational assimilation as "the processes by which individuals join, become integrated into, and exit organizations."[19] The terms assimilation, socialization, and identification all relate to organizational culture and communication. The terms are all *interre-*lated. Organizational assimilation requires socialization and will affect levels of organizational identification.

Organizational Socialization

You may be familiar with the term *socialization*. It was developed by sociologists to describe the various processes by which individuals learn about society and culture. As children, adolescents, and even adults mature, they observe and are taught about values, rituals, and appropriate/inappropriate behaviors.

Organizational socialization is a very similar concept. It has been defined as the processes by which "people learn the values, norms, and required behaviors of an organization's culture."[20] If an organization can be viewed as a minisociety, then organizational socialization refers to the processes by which members of that organization learn about the culture of that society.

Stages in the Organizational Socialization Process: Anticipatory Socialization

Prior to working for any organization, individuals become familiar with the notion of work, the nature of a particular industry, and some specific characteristics of the organization in which they subsequently may be hired. Anticipatory socialization refers to this process of learning about a culture that you expect to enter. In middle, high, or maybe elementary school, students begin thinking about careers and what the work world is like. For young children, working is an alien experience quite different from their own routines. Part of the organizational socialization process begins when young people begin to consider what this other life is like.

At some point, individuals typically contemplate a specific type of work they may wish to go into. For example, high school students may decide that they desire to work in public relations. They may have read about public relations, have heard about such careers, or know of someone who enjoyed public relations work. When it comes time to seek employment, these persons will explore various public relations work opportunities. Three specific job openings in PR may be available, and the prospective workers may learn all they can about these organizations.

Encounter

This type of socialization refers to the socialization processes for an entering employee. Persons begin to be socialized when they are interviewed and contract for a position. Subsequently, they

Factor 1: Management Connection				
My colleagues and I frequently criticize management*				
Upper management has a different idea about the organization than I do*				
My ideas are ignored*				
I don't feel respected by the organization*				
I get good advice from my boss				
Factor 2: Invested Self Concept				
I'd experience a sense of loss if I left the organization				
If the organization failed, I'd feel like I failed				
It would be hard to leave this organization even for a better job				
How I feel about myself is influenced by the organization's image				
I'd experience a sense of loss if another company took over this organization				
I feel defensive when others criticize the organization				
Factor 3: Integrated Goals and Values				
I share the organization's goals				
I act upon messages from the organization's leaders				
I share the organization's values				
I have a lot of pride in the organization's product/ service				
I feel like I influence things at work				
Factor 4: Coworker Connection				
My coworkers help me make sense of what's happening at work				
The people I work with are a lot like me				

Figure 7.1 Organizational Identification Scale
Source: Parker, R. E. & Haridakis, P. (2009). Development of an Organizational Identification Scale: Integrating Cognitive and Communicative Conceptualizations. *Journal of Communication Studies*.

typically go through an orientation period where they are told about policies and meet with representatives of various departments. In the first few weeks of employment, the newcomers develop relationships that will form the basis of their informal network in the organization. Newly made acquaintances explain the nuances of the organization and "how they really do things here." Entering employees continue to enlarge their sphere of contacts and exposure to the organization. They may eagerly or reluctantly adapt to the values of this organization or reject these values.

Metamorphosis

Franz Kafka's famous story "The Metamorphosis" is—on the surface at least—about a man, Gregor Samsa, who wakes up in the morning to discover that he has changed into a cockroach. The word metamorphosis is, in general, a neutral term. It is a noun and refers to a transformation. As it applies to organizational socialization, at some point in the evolving and continuous socialization process, newcomers cease to be newcomers and have become "one of them." They have morphed from fledgling to bona fide members of an organization who now participate in the socialization process of other newcomers. Often a result of metamorphosis is called "organizational identification."

Organizational Identification and Concertive Control

Organizational identification refers to the extent to which individuals identify with the organization in terms of its goals and values. If you work for McDonald's and you feel as if the values of the organization, the quality of the food product, and the way they train and treat their associates are all exemplary, then you likely will begin to identify with McDonald's. Your allegiance to the company will be entwined with your sense of yourself.

   If, on the other hand, you reject the culture that surrounds you and wonder if you belong in such an organization, you will not, obviously, identify with the culture of the organization. It makes sense that persons who have low levels of organizational identification would seek to work in another organization or at least work less passionately than those who respond positively to the organization's culture and identify with it. In essence, identification occurs when a person has been socialized to the extent that they consider that "the way they are is the way I am." Our McDonald's worker would not say "*they* brought out a new sandwich line," but rather "*we* brought out a new sandwich line." As Modaff, DeWine, and Butler have written, organizational identification "involves an individual's sense of membership with an organization."[21] Bullis and Tompkins have said that it occurs when "the organization becomes as much a part of the member as the member is a part of the organization."[22]

   In one of his books, Tompkins writes about how he began to think about organizational identification after a period of working at the Marshall Space Flight Center in Huntsville, Alabama:

> . . . as I began my long drive home from Huntsville to Detroit, I realized that I had entered a state of identification with the organization. I felt a part of it, a sense of belonging, and had persuaded myself that we had common interests: What was good for the space program was good for me. There was an inherent emotional component, positive in nature, a symbolic satisfaction in my relationship with the organization. . . . The organization became part of me. . . .[23]

Have you ever experienced a similar sense of identification with an organization? Would identification make you desire to work more industriously and cooperatively for the organization?

   Tompkins and Cheney have written extensively about organizational identification and a concept they call concertive control. Concertive control occurs, as the label suggests, when employees work "flexibly and in concert to get the work done."[24] When high levels of concertive control exist, employees do not work simply to comply with a manager's directive; employees work because they have bought into the goals of the organization, identify with the organization, have themselves established rules and norms to guide their own activities, and make decisions consistent with the organization's cultural values. They do this because the organization's cultural values have, in fact, become their own. As Gossett put it in a 2006 *Management Communication Quarterly* piece, employees come to recognize that "their personal identities are joined with [the] organization and thus make organizationally apparent decisions without the need for direct managerial oversight."[25]

The presence of concertive control in an organization is not insignificant. As opposed to bureaucratic control or administrative control, with concertive control workers have assimilated to the extent that they are self-motivated, self-directed, and desire to perform in the best interest of the organization with which they identify. Concertive control should not be considered as a desired end that management should plot to manufacture. There is always the potential for controlling and disingenuous ploys used to create illusions of identification. Critical theorists, as they should, are vigilant about citing attempts to manufacture concertive control. We will discuss this further in a few pages when we discuss illusory cultures and teams.

Organizational Assimilation: An Illustration

The experience of traditional undergraduate students who attend college after completing high school may serve as a clarifying illustration of the basic principles of organizational assimilation.

At some point in middle or high school, students begin to think about the idea of college and what college life might be like. Subsequently, they consider particular types of schools and then some individual institutions that are attractive to them. They begin to read about these colleges and universities. This phase of the assimilation process would be categorized as anticipatory socialization.

In their junior or senior year of high school, the students likely visit some schools, have interviews with representatives, and decide to attend particular universities. During their first week at the school or perhaps in the summer before school, they attend an orientation program where they are compelled to listen to what seems like dozens of voices, all explaining the importance of procedures pertaining to academics and student life. Various offices provide them with pounds of literature intended to explain best practices for getting tasks accomplished. Students who move into dormitories became acquainted with residence directors and/or upperclassmen, who explain the nuances of the organization. Commuters meet other commuters, who discuss the commonalities of their experience. Within a few days the new students meet instructors, student service providers, and other more experienced students. On the basis of these contacts, they begin to get a better sense of how things really work. The students may ask questions, attempt to test the official rules, observe how the Romans do what they do, and learn the ropes. All this is part of the encounter phase of assimilation.

Subsequently, these students are the persons a bewildered transfer student approaches looking for the place to get a parking sticker. They are the persons that a newcomer seeks in order to discover if Professor Jones "is any good" or if it is worth it to pay the extra ninety dollars to join the Ski Club. At some point there is a metamorphosis, and the students are "one of them."

There is no guarantee that the students will all identify with the culture of the organization. Students may learn the culture, reject it, and say to themselves, "I don't belong here and I need to find a better fit. This culture is inconsistent with who I am. These people are all cockroaches. If I stay here longer I will become a cockroach." On the other hand, the students may enjoy the metamorphosis,

Applying the Principles—Test Yourself

Jamie at the Wayfarer

How does Jamie's experience in the case below relate to *culture, organizational assimilation, organizational identification*, and *concertive control?*

Background

Jamie Levesque worked at the front desk of Longfellow's Wayfarer Inn for one year. At the time of Levesque's service, many of the Wayfarer's over one hundred employees had been working at the inn for more than a decade. The 130-acre inn has ten rooms for lodging as well as a chapel and restaurant. There's also a gristmill on the premises. Because of its historic status, the inn is a nonprofit organization.

After her first six months of employment, Levesque heard through the grapevine that Mr. Osias, the innkeeper, was planning to retire. The rumor was not taken seriously by most of the Wayfarer's employees. Osias had contemplated retirement on several occasions in the past and had always decided to stay on at the inn. However, this time Osias did follow through and retire.

Before and After Osias

Mr. Julius Osias had inspired a strong loyalty toward the inn among his employees. He worked hard to ensure a family environment and offered many perks to employees that had endeared him to the staff. Some examples of these perks were:

- The free daily lunch and dinner, eaten with Mr. Osias, provided to all employees.
- The opportunity to always hire a relative in need of employment.
- The annual certificate given to every employee entitling him or her to a free dinner, as a patron, in the restaurant.

Mr. Osias was highly regarded by both the employees *and* the patrons. He was always visible, twelve hours a day, six days a week, either helping the employees during busy times or chatting with the customers. Osias had taken charge of the failing inn during the mid-1950s and reestablished its classic reputation solely by word-of-mouth advertising. According to Levesque, Osias's leadership created an environment that made employees desire to maintain the excellent reputation the inn enjoyed.

Osias operated more like an innkeeper than a businessperson. His motto was "if it isn't broke, don't fix it." This would apply to the inn operation as well as to equipment. He would rather spend his time repairing the broken tractor in the field or the dishwasher than replace it with new technology developed for the twenty-first century.

This is how Levesque characterized communication channels at the inn under Osias:

Formal Channel: none

Informal Channels: (a) impromptu meetings held in the employee break room for those eating lunch or dinner prior to their shift; (b) grapevine

The New Innkeeper

After Osias retired, Brendan Gagnon replaced him as the new innkeeper. Brendan was thirty-eight years younger than Osias and full of energy and new ideas. He had big plans for implementing the inn's first computer system. He also intended to increase the restaurant sales volume through both an advertising program and a reduction in meal prices. Mr. Gagnon ran the inn as a business. He worked from 9 A.M. to 5 P.M. and spent the majority of his time in his office planning the inn's future.

Gagnon was not well received by most employees. Two weeks after his arrival, all employees received a memo with their paychecks informing them of a scheduled morning meeting. At the meeting, Gagnon introduced himself and informed people that the "fun and games"—as he put it—were over. His first two decisions were to lay off all of the part-time employees and discontinue the employees' free lunch and dinners. In addition, he expressed the importance of speaking with one's immediate supervisor if there was a problem. Mr. Gagnon wanted to communicate only with the supervisors.

This is how Levesque characterized communication channels under Gagnon:

Formal Channels: (a) scheduled meetings by the innkeeper for all employees during nonoperating hours; (b) other specified channels described to employees in an encyclopedic, first-time-ever employee handbook

Informal Channel: wild, angry grapevine

Reactions from the Employees

The employees were devastated and angry regarding their friends' layoffs. They also felt that the full-timers should be compensated monetarily for lost benefits. Many employees expressed their anger by spending much of their spare time breaking the equipment or stealing food from the kitchen. Most did not volunteer to help with extra work as they had in the past.

The employees were upset about the change in the formal communication channels. In the old inn, all of the employees were of equal status. Those who held the supervisory positions had almost no power. Therefore, in the new inn, it was difficult for the employees to accept the supervisors' power.

The grapevine was in a hyperactive state. The rumors being spread suggested more layoffs. The suggested layoffs were directed toward those positions that would require retraining to use the new equipment.

"Gagnon's coming was like a hurricane," said Levesque. "There was a lot of sudden damage, and then the climate at the Wayfarer was just different. People started grousing about Brendan and even became ornery with one another. Some of us even witnessed employees take it out on the customers. I left after a while."

identify with the organizational culture that has been internalized, be delighted to be considered "one of them," work for the organization without administrative directives, and become lifelong advocates for the institution.

Organizational assimilation theory reveals how communication affects the process of assimilating and the maintenance of organizational culture. Interviews, the establishment of formal and informal communication networks, signage, presentations, publications, and orienting conferences all affect organizational socialization and the extent of organizational identification.

The Seeds of Culture: Embedding and Transmitting Culture

In the Jamie at the Wayfarer case presented above, could Gagnon have employed communication more effectively to nourish the climate he desired? Can an organization and its leaders cultivate a culture that would be learned during an assimilation process? If so, what role does communication play in the creation of that climate?

Assimilation theory describes the process of learning about an organization and its culture. Edgar Schein has written about communicative mechanisms that serve to embed cultural values and assumptions. In an often-cited article published in *Organizational Dynamics* and then in his book *Organizational Culture and Leadership*, Schein itemizes several of these mechanisms:[26]

• **Formal statements of organizational philosophy:** This includes mission statements, codes of ethics, position papers, advertising policy, hiring policy, and other reports generated by the organization.

IBM was the leader in business computing after World War II, just as Silicon Valley is today, with firms such as Google. How have organization climate and culture changed?

- **Deliberate coaching and modeling by leaders:** What do leaders tell employees about how to behave? How do leaders behave intentionally or unintentionally that serves as a model of expected behaviors?
- **Promotion and salary increment criteria:** Communications that explain the rules that govern advancement in the organization. What determines who gets ahead?
- **Responses to crises:** What do leaders say when an organization is in the throes of crisis? Are they forthcoming? Do they suggest that when in crisis, stonewalling behavior is appropriate?
- **Organizational structure:** What are the policies in terms of reporting? Who reports to whom? Is the organization a very tall organization with many levels of authority, or is it flat with most persons having the same degree of responsibility and autonomy?
- **Design of physical spaces:** This refers to the look of the workplace, how it is furnished, where it is located, its external facade, how many buildings are part of the complex, and the arrangement of these buildings.
- **Focus of attention:** What do leaders actually pay attention to? Does it seem as if that attention is paid to human needs, the bottom line, comparative success, company landscaping? What do leaders suggest by their behavior is important?
- **Storytelling and legends:** As we discussed earlier in this chapter, the culture of an organization may be transmitted by storytellers who discuss heroes and incidents that reflect the values of the organization.

Manufacturing Culture

You may remember from Chapter 3 the comment made by Warren Bennis in the introduction to another of Edgar Schein's books entitled *The Corporate Culture Survival Guide*. Bennis's comment is worth repeating here: "The subtext of this terrific book is that you can't pop a culture in a microwave and out pops a McCulture." An organization that desires to instill a culture that encourages teamwork, for example, will have to do more than send out the memo. As Gagnon discovered, simply announcing that "the fun and games were over" does not guarantee that the employees will quickly abandon what had been valued routines.

Embedding cultural roots to whatever extent they can be embedded is a complex undertaking, even for the most perceptive and diligent individuals. Cultures and climates cannot be created prescriptively the same way in which a cake is baked or a building is constructed. As Miller has suggested, establishing culture and climate cannot "deemphasize the complex processes through which organization culture is created and sustained."[27] A supportive climate cannot be "made" by mixing a dollop of "modeling" with one-half pound of "storytelling." The human factors are too complex. Any attempt to cultivate supportive cultures must be founded on the implicit recognition that the elements needed for supportive climates are multifaceted, variable, and even capricious—to the extent that humans are multifaceted, variable, and sometimes capricious.

Illusory Cultures and Teams

In the novel *Cat's Cradle*, the late Kurt Vonnegut describes what he calls a "granfalloon." He writes: "If you wish to study a granfalloon, just remove the skin of a toy balloon."[28] A *granfalloon*, one of the many words Vonnegut donated to the lexicon, is an entity with no substance, a body that appears to be meaningful but after, closer scrutiny, is obviously meaningless. The word granfalloon has recently been used in conjunction with new social media networking. In Emily Yoffe's article subtitled, "Last week I had zero Facebook friends, now I have 775," she makes the case that social networks like LinkedIn and Facebook might be akin to granfalloons—bogus phenomena.[29] "I will be interested to see," she writes, "if Facebook and sites of its ilk end up being a granfalloon, or a revolution."[30]

One of the problems that occurs when managers attempt to engineer cultures is that the resulting constructions become—like some social network communities—nothing more than illusions. Root cultures and attendant organizational climates that are granfalloon composites not only aren't valuable but, like the punctured balloon, can make a disconcerting noise when they are exposed.

Family Values
A common example of granfalloon-type cultures is evidenced when managers make superficial claims about an organization's family atmosphere and team approach. Hare and Wyatt report that a majority of managers continue to practice autocratic, dictatorial behaviors in a world that talks teamwork.[31] The talking of teamwork, i.e., the attempt to communicate that there is, or henceforth will be, a family team atmosphere at Acme, will be undermined by antithetical behavior. This behavior will lather to form an evolving culture that is quite different from the one management expects to engineer. No one desires to be part of a "family" that is really a contrivance to motivate staff to work harder. No one desires to work together to create a "team" when that notion was fabricated as a ruse to dupe employees to sweat harder and longer to improve the lots of those who conceived of the ploy. This type of manipulative communication behavior is an example of what critical theorists are concerned with when they study organizational communication.

Often organizations claim to foster supportive environments but attempt to manufacture them unsuccessfully.

If an organization declares that it supports teamwork and asserts that it empowers employees and respects associates, it is making the type of claims that require "walking a walk" that is obstacle strewn—particularly if management glibly and myopically "talks the talk."

A March 2002 Dilbert cartoon makes this point rather well. The dullard boss is seen in the first panel of the cartoon handing buttons to two employees. The boss says: "Every employee will wear a button that says 'I'm empowered.'"

In the next panel there is an exchange between the boss and one of the employees, who has been told to wear the "I'm empowered" pin. The employee simply says, "I don't want to." The boss's response is also simple. "You have to," says the empowering supervisor.

In the third panel the two employees are depicted walking away. One employee says to the other, "That was everything you need to know about life in one package."

In addition to explaining much of "life," the cartoon also explains a good deal of what one needs to know about communication and the cultivation of organizational culture. There are at least two important points brought out: one, you cannot force-feed culture; two, you cannot nourish organizational culture by declaring x and modeling y.

Constitutive Communication and Emergent Cultures

Moreover, organizational culture should not be construed as a discrete entity that can be placed like a tarpaulin on top of an organization. As Pacanowsky and O'Donnell-Trujillo comment in their groundbreaking article, "Communication and Organizational Cultures," culture is the "residual" of the communication processes within the organization.[32] Communication behavior by all members of the organization—on formal and informal networks, related to task-specific activities or social activities, by executives and all others—actually *constitutes* what becomes the culture. These constituting communicative behaviors are affected by the culture, but the evolution of what becomes the culture is not independent of communication behavior; it is the vestigial amalgam of routine daily communication behavior. "How was your weekend" messages are quarks of this culture just like PowerPoint explanations of "flex time." Even e-mails that superficially declare that "henceforth we will have a team culture" contribute to the culture, although probably not in the way the authors desire them to. The vessel the organization becomes will be determined by how all members communicate.

In the movie *Joe*, a bigot—*Joe*—sits on a barstool and spews a beery venomous monologue disparaging the various ethnic groups who, he opines, are destroying "the culture." After wailing for several minutes, the barkeep in the nearly empty tavern says to Joe that he thinks it might be time for him to go home. Somewhat reluctantly, Joe slides off his perch, muttering about how the culture is going south because of everyone but him. What Joe does not realize is that the culture of which he speaks is not some substantive static entity that is parked by the mall waiting until morning to skew societal interactions. The culture is an evolving entity that is nourished as much by Joe's vituperations as by the behavior of the groups that he disdains. When Joe awakens the next day, the culture that he fears is being sullied is something that he, and everyone else, conspired to construct.

A Classroom Illustration

The following illustration may clarify this point about the constitutive nature of communication as it pertains to organizational culture. Consider your classes at college to be microcosms of organizations.

Your instructors will act as powerful contributors to the climate and culture of your classes. They will communicate, intentionally or otherwise, in ways that will affect the culture. All of the following are examples of their behaviors that may have effects: the extent to which they actively and genuinely solicit contributions from students, their responses to student inquiries, the tones of their voices, the rules they emphasize, the distribution of a syllabus on the first day, and the language they employ.

In addition to an instructor's communicative behavior, how the students in a class communicate will also affect the climate and culture. Are students regularly late? Do they raise their hands before speaking or simply say what they wish when they wish to? Are there students who use profanity? Perhaps your class is populated by two students who seem to usurp all the conversation time discussing their various accomplishments while others look at each other and roll their eyes. You may have a class in which students ask many intelligent questions reflecting their interest, and these inquiries stimulate enthusiastic participation in others. You may have another class that seems to be composed of highly apprehensive students, and if it were not for Nadine, every question posed by the instructor would be met with painful silence.

What will emerge as the culture in these classroom settings will be the residual of the communication behavior of the members of the class (including the instructor), and that evolving and emergent culture will, concurrently, affect how people interact in the class. Your instructors may arrive at the first session making claims that the class will be friendly, informal, interactive, and characterized by invigorating debate. Your instructors may do things that facilitate the emergence of such conditions. However, the environment that does, in fact, emerge will be the distillate of the communicative behaviors of the students and instructors in the class. Similarly, in organizations the evolving culture that influences communication behavior will be what has emerged *from* communication behavior.

The case has been made that climate and culture are important factors and that communication behavior affects and is affected by the culture. As we conclude this chapter, let us consider some key factors necessary for the evolution of supportive climates and culture.

Leadership

In large part, the book *Organizational Communication Imperatives* is a comparison of leadership styles. The leadership style of Dr. Wernher von Braun, who led NASA's Marshall Space Flight Center (MSFC) in the 1960s, is juxtaposed with that of Dr. William Lucas, who headed the center in the 1980s. Lucas was at the helm when *Challenger* exploded on January 28, 1986.

"The way they do business is laughable. Their corporate culture is cancerous. And all of this can be traced to one man and his never ending mission to show everyone who's boss. [He has a] destructive leadership approach, right down to his practice of dropping a towel and making a team employee wipe his shoes. How would you like to work in such an environment?"

—COLUMNIST MICHAEL SILVER DESCRIBING A COMPANY CEO

The book underscores the point that the leadership styles of the executives significantly affected the internal communication at the center. Whereas von Braun was encouraging, supportive, and engaging, Lucas was aloof and critical. Interviews with several of Lucas's subordinates were presented in the book. Below are some revealing descriptions of their leader:

"Lucas was a dead fish. Cold, vindictive, he would embarrass people publicly."

"I feel bad about saying this, but people were afraid to bring bad news to Dr. Lucas for fear that they would be treated harshly."

"I thought the world of Dr. Lucas even though he was so rigid and formal. [However,] people were afraid to raise problems with him. We started canning and preprogramming what went up to Dr. Lucas."

"Dr. Lucas's group expected us to be conversant about every technical detail. They made us apprehensive—reluctant to volunteer information."

"Communication with Lucas was more constrained than with von Braun, not as open, but you could get through if you wanted to. My opinion is that if somebody was forceful he could have been heard."

"Lucas wanted information filtered. His communicative style was intimidation."[34]

It is obvious that a leadership style like Lucas's would create a defensive climate and retard the flow of information in an organization. In similar ways, in every unit in every organization, the leaders are in a position to support or retard the flow of information. The individual departmental climates that affect communication within each unit will also influence interaction *between* departments and consequently will affect the overall quality of communication in an organization.

In order to illustrate how leadership affects the climate and how the climate affects communication, let's consider the MSFC communication tool known as *Monday Notes* was developed under von Braun to allow each unit at the center an opportunity to become familiar with other units' work. The Notes also served to keep von Braun aware of department activities.

Each Monday, departments would produce a one-page report related to their weekly business. The departments would send these reports to von Braun. Von Braun would read each submission and write feedback in the margins, "asking questions, making suggestions, and dishing out praise."[27] Then, all of the week's Monday Notes would be collated and distributed to each manager.

The Monday Notes system created upward, horizontal, and downward networks for the MSFC. Monday Notes was so successful that it spawned a related tool called Friday Notes. *Friday Notes* were reports generated on Friday by managerial subordinates. With their subordinates' Friday Notes in hand, the managers were able to do a better job constructing the following week's Monday Notes. Thus, with Friday Notes, another level of upward networks was established.

Turn the Beat Around: Leadership, Climate, and Communication

"Mr. Seviroli, how was the percussion?"

The issues surrounding this question are at the heart of quality communication in organizations. The inquiry was made by Stephen Hill, a sixth grade ne'er-do-well who banged the drums (indiscriminately, it sometimes seemed to me) directly behind my seat as second trumpeter for Mr. Joseph Seviroli's Fern Place Elementary School Band.

I was reminded of Hill's query recently when a colleague told me about a local organization that was going to test the quality of its internal communication. When I asked how they would undertake this task, my friend said that the company intended to collect all their "communications" and examine the effectiveness of each. This meant that the organization would examine their newspapers, bulletin boards, e-mail systems, etc., and then draw a conclusion about their overall communication quality. This company's test results will not be valid. They may discover some valuable information, but they will not find out about essential dimensions of their organization's communication.

Communication Quality and Human Needs

A key element in quality organizational communication relates to managerial sensitivity and effective superior–subordinate interaction. This comment may seem as if it's the stuff of airy philosophy, but there is nothing impractical about it. If you want to assess your organization's communication quality, you'll need to examine the quality of the humans who communicate in the organization. Moreover, you'll need to assess your leaders' will-

ingness (and ability) to meet the human needs of their subordinates, particularly when communications regarding these needs require perspicacity and diplomacy.

These communications are every bit as important to the overall communication quality of the organization as videotapes, house organs, and e-mail capabilities. In fact, they may be more significant. Interpersonal interaction that is gratuitously brusque, condescending, or otherwise insensitive can affect the entire climate of an organization—indirectly, if not directly—undermining communication and overall quality. And this brings me to Joseph Seviroli's Fern Place Band, Stephen Hill, and Mr. Hill's inquiry.

Controlled Authority

Joseph Seviroli was the leader of the Fern Place Band and the instrument teacher for the elementary school. He taught grade-school children how to play and then conducted the collective musicians. Seviroli was a kind and patient man. I clearly remember my first trumpet lesson with him. On that day, Seviroli sat with me and two other fledgling trumpeters in the tiny "lesson room"—a space that certainly had been a storage closet at some time in the past. The goal of this initial session was simply to get us to produce a sound from the end of the horn.

The others quickly blurted out something, were dismissed, and were told to return to the regular classroom. However, nothing came out of my trumpet. I couldn't get it. I was blowing ferociously, trying to make a peep, and Seviroli kept sitting there telling me not to panic. Suddenly I connected with a cacophonous blast that nearly rocketed the poor man into the wall. Without so much as blinking an eye, he told me that I'd done very well, and I marched back to my classroom feeling like I'd accomplished something, and eventually I became a member of the band.

Seviroli was no mollusk. For some reason the entire band, particularly the percussion section, seemed to be populated by wise guys, classmates who, like the aforementioned Hill, when not banging the drums, might otherwise be unleashing their energy in societally counterproductive ways. Yet Seviroli kept us in check. He seemed to have the right combination of control and support. We had become, the percussionists and others, truly a band of young kids following the lead of our respected director. The payoffs were internal more than anything else.

For weeks, if not months, the band was preparing for the big musical spectacular that annually was the event of events for the school. We were to accompany the Fern Place thespians in some original musical. While Seviroli led the band, a Mr. Mushnick directed the stage actors. Mushnick was no Seviroli. He may have been as musically talented, but the man was a screamer. Unlike Seviroli, Mushnick could lose control easily and go into tirades that were remarkable and, apparently, memorable. While bellowing admonishments, his face would contort as if he were holding his breath for some contest. After he began one such outburst, Stephen Hill leaned over to me and whispered, "Hey, watch this one now. Watch the veins pop out of his head."

So it was Seviroli and Mushnick leading our troops with different styles. Seviroli with strong controlled authority led the band below, and Mushnick, without the same control, but with more volume, led the actors above us.

Got to Have Percussion

Nerves became frayed as the day of the event approached. Each rehearsal had one form of crisis or another, and Mushnick, under what must have been considerable pressure, real or imagined, was spewing volcanically at least once an hour. One particular scene in the show had become a recurring problem. In it, a group of child actors emerged from audience level while singing to our music. They were to access the stage by climbing a short set of stairs that were near the percussion section of the band. We musicians were supposed to keep playing until the actors were all in place at their spots on the stage. Almost every time we rehearsed this scene something would go wrong. The actors wouldn't find their spots, the band would stop playing too soon, some of the kids would stop singing while they climbed the stairs—something would go wrong.

The day before opening night, during dress rehearsal, this scene from the Styx took a dive for the worse. It became clear that with costumes and various props, the actors would have a difficult time negotiating the walk around the percussion section to gain access to the stage. Mushnick became absolutely enraged by what must have seemed like a conspiracy and burst into a panicked screeching, during which he shouted that there were too many drummers and that we simply couldn't have that many. From his perch on the stage he pointed down to Hill, who was the last drummer in the line, and told him that he had to go.

This, to me, was unthinkable. I couldn't imagine how I would have felt if after all this time I would have been booted from the band. I turned around and saw that most of the members were stunned. Big, tough Stephen Hill was crying eleven-year-old tears. Seviroli waved to Hill as if to say not to worry. He hoisted himself on the stage and put his arm around Mushnick. Within minutes the matter seemed to be resolved. Seviroli moved the drums around a bit, and Stephen Hill could stay.

We went through the scene, and it worked just fine. We belted out the music, and the thespians accessed the stage. And then, during the temporary break that followed, Stephen Hill, this truculent young tough who went on to a career of petty theft and various scrapes with the law, asked both plaintively and genuinely,

"Mr. Seviroli. How was the percussion?"

Seviroli made the okay sign. I turned around and saw Hill positively beaming.

If an organization wants to test the effectiveness of its internal communication, it needs to begin by looking at personnel and the organizational climate and culture that is a function *of its personnel.* This, more than the internal newsletter, will determine the communication efficiency and quality.

We all need to do something meaningful in the band we call our work. And we need to have that work meaningfully acknowledged. As Vicki Sue Robinson once crooned in a popular song with an apt lyric, "Turn the beat around. Got to have percussion."

Had the climate under von Braun not been supportive, the Monday Notes would likely have been either valueless or not as valuable as they were. If departments had begun to wonder if the Notes would be critically evaluated, used as comparative indicators of one group's success as opposed to another's, or instruments that would justify financial rewards or demerits, the Notes would have lost their credibility and their value. In fact, Friday Notes gradually faded out of existence after the von Braun era. While Monday Notes survived (the name was changed to Weekly Notes), they became more sterile and less vital.

What made Monday Notes a vital communication tool had little to do with the writing skills of the employees. What made Monday Notes a success was the culture at the Marshall Space Flight Center. That culture was, in large part, a function of the kind of person who headed the operation.[35]

As it relates to the effects of leadership on organizational communication, consider the preceding boxed insert "Turn the Beat Around." Can you identify organizational leaders whom you've known who have had a significant positive or negative effect on internal communication because of their leadership styles?

Emotional Intelligence

In his book, *Emotional Intelligence*, Daniel Goleman discusses a type of wisdom that is typically not measured by conventional standardized tests.[36]

His argument—and that of others who have written on the subject—is that our efficiency at work is not only based on our abilities to solve complex problems, our dexterity with language, or our creative skill sets. A highly skilled computer expert, a multilingual communicator who is fluent in every language represented by an international company, a brilliant Web designer who can render a computer screen to be visually compelling—may all be of limited value if their emotional intelligence is low despite their high IQ.

The emotional intelligence of all those who work in an organization is an important factor that affects interpersonal interaction and the evolving culture in an organization.

What Is Emotional Intelligence?

Salovey and Mayer have defined emotional intelligence as "the ability to monitor one's own and others' feelings and emotions, to discriminate among them and to use this information to guide one's thinking and actions."[37] Goleman identifies five criteria reflecting emotional intelligence. He argues that people with high emotional intelligence know their emotions, can manage their emotions, are capable of motivating themselves, can recognize emotions in others, and can effectively handle relationships. What is implicit and important about the identification of these criteria is that none of them is about innate brilliance or dramatically superior skill sets.

> How would you rate yourself in terms of Goleman's criteria?
> In your last work group, how would you rate the emotional intelligence of your colleagues?
> Is this a significant factor in the culture that is developed in your group?
> Does emotional intelligence affect group productivity?

The Value of Emotional Intelligence

Testing emotional intelligence, like emotional intelligence itself, is in its infancy. A number of tools have been employed, but they largely are based on self-reports. Sometimes employers attempt to get a sense of the emotional intelligence of prospective employees during interviews and when reviewing letters of reference. Still, it is an elusive component to measure. Some people are adept at appearing emotionally intelligent during short intervals and only exhibit unhealthy behaviors in the long term. Interviewers, letters from former employers, and even phone conversations with colleagues may not provide reliable results.

It may be difficult to ascertain if someone is emotionally intelligent, but it is not difficult to realize how important emotional intelligence is as a factor that affects organizational cultures. It is interesting to note the following. In January 2009, Scott Pioli, a very successful National Football League player personnel director, was hired by the Kansas City Chiefs to be its player personnel director. On the day he officially took the job he commented that his task was not to find players who were extraordinarily skilled. His task was to find players who would make the team better.

The distinction is not insignificant. Any fan of sport knows how a personality who has trouble establishing relationships with teammates can damage the culture to the extent that communications are strained and performance negatively affected. Emotional intelligence can, in organizational contexts, trump skill sets. In some situations low emotionally intelligent people may not only damage an organizational culture and negatively affect productivity, but in the extreme can be menaces to the physical comfort level of employees.

Conclusion: Credibility and Human Values

In large part, organizational culture and climate fails or thrives on the basis of one of Redding's ideal criteria components: credibility, and whether an organization is value driven. Lardner comments that "what ruined Enron wasn't just accounting. It was a culture that valued appealing lies over inconvenient truths."[38]

Management consultant and communication expert Roger D'Aprix conducted a study at a company where management had positioned huge billboards on the outside of the plant building. The

Governor Michael Dukakis

Michael Dukakis served as governor of the state of Massachusetts from 1975–1979. He lost his reelection bid in 1978, but successfully regained the job by winning the 1982 gubernatorial race, and then, four years later, won reelection for a third term. In 1986, he was voted the most effective governor in the United States. In 1988, Governor Dukakis was the Democratic nominee for President of the United States. He has served as the Vice Chairman of the AMTRAK Reform Board and is a professor at both Northeastern University and UCLA.

As you read through this section please consider the following questions.

- Do most politicians appear to have attitudes that are similar to Governor Dukakis's attitudes?
- Do Pride and Performance events have an effect on the culture of an organization?
- Are the brown bag lunches described likely to create the culture that is desired?

Communication is very important, both externally and internally. Obviously, there is a huge job that has to be done in an external sense. It's largely through the media that you give the public a sense of what you're doing. I'm not sure I took the external factor as seriously during my first term as governor as I should have, which is one of the reasons I got thrown out of the place. I certainly took it a lot more seriously during my second and third terms. I had seen what happened when you don't communicate effectively.

We had a CEO at AMTRAK whose name was David Gunn, and he had an interesting technique when it came to communicating internally. He rode the trains. He talked to the engineers and conductors, and asked questions. He didn't come with an entourage. It was just him, talking to the employees. The buzz spread all over the company. "Geez," the employees said, "He's been on the trains." Gunn is a very good listener, which is an essential part of communication. Clinton was the best listener I ever knew. And it wasn't an act, he listened and he absorbed.

Now, what did I do as governor? Similarly, I tried to get out and talk to people. Of course, there were formal occasions when I would go out and visit agencies. Kind of say, "Hi, how are you? Nice to see ya; I'm the governor," this kind of thing. While I think that was helpful, it's not communication in any thoughtful two-way sense. You know the place has been scrubbed up for you, you know that people have been told to keep their mouths shut— that's just inevitable. I found riding the T [subway] to work and back was more effective than these planned visits. If you're at all open and invite communication, you'll have conversations on the train. In many cases, state employees would come up to me and talk. Another example: I would buy my groceries at the Stop and Shop. Kitty would say, "Why the hell does it take you an hour and a half to go shopping?" I'd tell her that people would come up to me to talk. And so, there's a lot to be said for sending the state limousine back to where it was leased, which is what I did, and doing the best you can to get out there. Now, I don't want to exaggerate the effectiveness of that only because you're talking about a state with 6,000,000 people and 65,000 employees, but I found it very important to have that kind of ongoing contact with state employees, with citizens, and to the extent that I could, try to get people to open up. Getting people to open up is difficult. I don't know how many meetings I've been to with people from the agencies where there'd be some polite questions and then the meeting would be over, right, but some-one would stop by the door and say, "I didn't want to bring this up at the meeting, but..." which was another way of saying, "I can't lev-el with you in that kind of atmosphere."

We had a Pride and Performance event. It was an awards ceremony held at the Park Plaza and it was a special night dedicated to honoring state employees who helped us reach our objectives toward state beau-tification. Three finalists from each of the several agencies that dealt with beautifica-tion attended the function. Somehow we got Sheraton to agree to a week or two in Florida and we got the airlines to provide seats on flights. Ten of the nominees would be identified as winners and receive a mon-etary award as well as the vacation. But all of the nominees were essentially winners who had been invited to this party because of their excellent contributions. This event was like the academy awards for these people. It was a great night and an opportunity for me to say "Thanks, you're doing a great job," and these folks—all of the nominees, not just the winners—could bask in the glow of being recognized for being outstanding public ser-vants. Again, is this the kind of rich, informal, two-way communication that is best for folks who are public managers? No, it is not two-way, but it was a way of saying that what you are doing is important to us, it's important for Massachusetts, and we appreciate what you've done.

When we started the Welfare to Work program in the 80s we had an extraordinary welfare commissioner who asked me to come down and be part of a meeting to be held with his welfare people on the Cape. The workers were given the time off. He was anxious to build a new kind of esprit within the depart-ment. Previously, the welfare employees were

essentially in a thankless position where they were cops having to chase people down. Now, we wanted to emphasize that their principal responsibility was to help people become independent and self-sufficient. So, the commissioner asked me to come down. We gave out a whole series of awards. And it was amazing. This was the Welfare depart-ment? I felt like I was at a pep rally and these folks subsequently did a fabulous job for us. Now, you would have to talk to the employ-ees to get a sense if they thought this was a dog and pony show or if they took it seri-ously, but my sense was that communicating this kind of appreciation and support was effective.

Bob Behn wrote a piece in the *Journal of Policy and Management* and talks about the value of rich, informal conversation. That's very important. Face-to-face communica-tion is so important. There needs to be lots of rich, informal communication. That's one of the reasons that I'm not a huge fan of e-mail. I don't mean the exclusion of it. But people are always e-mailing each other; that's not rich, informal communication. What's important is person-to-person stuff. It's spending time with people.

Tom Glynn, who used to be the general manager of the MBTA and is now the COO of Partners Health Care, had brown bag lunches every Friday at noontime with eight or ten working folks at the T. Glynn is a terrifically talented public manager. He had a set rou-tine. At about 11 o'clock on Friday, he would go over and meet with a supervisor. Then at noontime he would take his bag lunch and go over and meet with brown baggers with-out supervisors present. Very important—no supervisors were present. Glynn did this every Friday. Tom is not a "hail fellow well met" guy. He doesn't smile a lot, that sort of thing, but six months later I met with the head of the Carmens union—which is not an easy union. They represent most of the people at the T. And I asked how things are going. He told me, "This guy Glynn's terrific." I said, "Yeah, tell me about him." He said, "Well, he's talking to our people. These brown bag lunches. We never had anybody like this."

Pretty simple. [Boston Superintendent of Schools Thomas] Payzant has the teacher's union leadership in for coffee and doughnuts every Monday morning at 8 a.m. No set agendas. Just "what's happening, what do you hear?" Not too complicated. Not too difficult. Very important way to communicate. Now again, you've got to be a good listener. There's got to be some sense that this is not just some act, and that you will respond to what you hear if it makes sense to you. But brown bag lunches on Friday, coffee and doughnuts with union leadership, riding the trains. Very simple, but very effective communication techniques.

I used to say to my people, "Thank folks, will you!" When was the last time you complained because someone said thank you to you too much? People don't say thank you enough. Just say thanks. Call them up; tell them, "You did a terrific job." Very important. Did I always do this? No. Did I get better at it? I think so.

We had an employee of the month program at the MBTA. One year, we thought we'd invite the twelve employees of the month and their families to Fenway Park for a day game with the Red Sox. At the time, the Red Sox had a very good pitcher named Greg Harris. He lived in Chestnut Hill and would take the Green Line [a branch of the subway] to work. Work in his case was Fenway Park. So the twelve employees and their families all came down to the park at about noontime for a 1:30 game and they got to walk around on the field. Now, I've been on the field many times. We used to have a Democrat/Republican ball game there, but they stopped it because the Republicans didn't have enough legislators to field a team. Anyway, for the MBTA employees, being on the field at Fenway Park was an absolute thrill. Tony Peña talking to them. Dewey Evans around the batting cage. Because Harris rode the subway to work, we swore Harris into something we called the Green Line Hall of Fame. Just watching the employees and their families on the field was something. It didn't cost us anything, but it was a huge day in the lives of those employees. What was it? What did we communicate? Simple. It was, "Thanks, you're doing a great job."

billboards exhorted employees to strive for quality. When D'Aprix asked employees about the impact of the message, one burly man looked at him and said with disgust, "Look, there are two signs you can believe around here. One says, 'wet paint,' the other says 'pardon our appearance.' The rest is baloney." [39] Bartolome makes several suggestions regarding establishing credibility and trust. These are more easily listed than accomplished, but they do suggest a path to follow.

- Make communication two-way. Establish and utilize upward and downward communication networks.
- Respect employees implicitly by delegating authority.
- Relay appropriate human messages. That is, fairly attribute blame and give credit when credit is due.
- Be predictable, that is, react consistently to situations.[40]

Recognizing that employees are human—with all the needs, desires, fallibilities, and energy of people—is at the core of supportive culture and climates. When employees are managed as if they are chairs or inanimate cogs in a system, problems will inevitably arise. The classical theory notwithstanding, people can be made to enjoy work. People do identify with organizations and will work in concert under the right conditions.

Noel Coward wrote, "Work is much more fun than fun." It can be. American author Sydney Harris commented, "Few men [sic] ever drop dead from overwork, but many quietly curl up and die because of under satisfaction." But perhaps psychiatrist Theodor Reik was most to the point when he said, "Work and love—these are the basics. Without them there is neurosis."

Organizations that genuinely tap employees' human needs and desires to do something fulfilling and rewarding with their lives will be taking a giant step toward creating a supportive culture that facilitates effective organizational communication and productivity.

SUMMARY: A TOOLBOX

- Climate and culture are powerful forces affecting organizational communication, and daily routine communication behavior affects what emerges as the organizational culture and climate.
- The organization's culture can determine, or at least affect, the nature of the climate.
- Redding identifies five characteristics of an ideal supportive climate.
- Schein has identified several mechanisms that affect how culture is embedded in organizations.
- It is far easier to prescribe the ingredients for a supportive climate than it is to create the climate. Similarly, it is easy to identify desirable cultural traits of an organization and far more difficult to embed those traits in an organization.
- Assimilation theory explains how individuals within organizations are socialized and the role of communication in that socialization process.
- Credibility, leadership, and the extent of a human resource orientation are important planks in the floorboard of an organization's culture.

REVIEW AND DISCUSSION QUESTIONS

1. What is the distinction between *organizational climate* and *organizational culture*?
2. How can a Theory X orientation increase the chances of an organization having a defensive climate?
3. What is the relationship between climate and organizational communication?
4. How can leadership affect organizational communication?
5. How can the climate of an organization affect the credibility of human messages?
6. How would you describe the culture of any organizations where you have worked in terms of:
   a. Mottoes
   b. Values
   c. Heroes
   d. Rituals
7. What are the stages of socialization described in assimilation theory?
8. How do communication networks affect the socialization process?
9. How does an organization's culture affect the socialization process?

GROUP/ROLE-PLAY

In a group of four to six, review the issues surrounding the case that begins this chapter. Attempt to gain consensus regarding the questions at the end of the case.

- For the role-play:
  - One member of the group plays a worker who remains working with Elan.
  - Another assumes the role of top management, who knew of the VSP/QBS plan.
  - A third represents someone who took the VSP, assuming that QBS was inevitable and is no longer with the company.
  - A fourth plays the mid level manager who supervised both the worker who remains and the worker who took the VSP.

A face-to-face meeting of these four persons has been requested by the mid level manager. She feels as if her credibility has been compromised and wants to discuss the VSP/QBS and have her employees hear what happened from top management.

Chapter 8

Meetings and Teams: Conflicts and Interventions

Chapter in a Nutshell

Sir Barnett Cocks, a clerk in Britain's House of Commons, is credited with describing a meeting as a "cul-de-sac where ideas are lured and quietly strangled." Many within organizations would agree with him. Department members often meet to discuss common issues, analyze problems, and col-

> "I have witnessed so many staff meetings, so many conferences, and so many extended task forces, where intelligent and industrious people were getting into deeper and deeper confusion—getting more and more frustrated with each other—primarily because no one had thought to get an agreement on exactly what they were trying to do."
>
> —**DAVID EMERY,** *The Compleat Manager*

laboratively prepare reports for internal and external audiences. Interdepartmental teams also convene regularly to offer counsel to executives, generate policy for larger bodies, and share mutual concerns.

While many individuals describe meetings as difficult contexts for effective communication, meetings are nevertheless necessary in organizations. They are not only important for information dissemination and problem solving, but can provide opportunities for social interaction and cohesion. Collaboration in these contexts is also essential for seamless written and oral reports. These reports explain team decisions and affect the power, resources, and respect accorded the teams that generate the reports. This chapter examines the problems related to communication in teams and identifies strategies, or interventions, for improvement.

When you have completed this chapter, you should be able to:

- Identify common conflicts that surface during team interactions.
- Describe counterproductive tendencies of participants and groups.
- List and explain "interventions" (techniques) that can be used to reduce conflict and improve interaction.
- Identify and describe types of meeting leaders.
- Discuss methods that can facilitate creating and delivering effective team reports and presentations.

CASE 8.1:

Gerald Sweeney and the Regular Wednesday Meetings

Gerald Sweeney was a senior managing director who supervised several subordinate managers. One of Sweeney's obligations involved attending regular Wednesday meetings of all like managing directors. Subsequently, he was responsible for relaying information from these meetings to his subordinates at his own staff sessions.

Sweeney frequently complained to his staff about the Wednesday sessions. Among his complaints were that the meetings started late and took up time that could otherwise be more usefully served. One regular item on the agenda required each managing director to brief the others about what was "up" in his or her area. Sweeney felt that this was the biggest time waster.

"Nobody really cares what is happening over in another department. Everyone pretends to care. They nod their heads, say the strategic 'mmm' and 'ah ha' and 'interesting,' but nobody really listens. Ask someone to summarize what's been said during one of the sessions and they'd be silent or blabber nonsense. Some of these directors think they're on stage and make a big production about what their department is doing and how efficient they are. Number one, I don't believe what they are saying, and number two, worse, I don't care if they're telling the truth or not. It's about power and getting more of it. They're posturing or have hidden agendas. The guy from the budget office brings slides and graphs to justify his existence, and you really need an extra cup of coffee to stay awake."

Another problem identified by Sweeney was that sometimes managing directors don't attend or send ambassadors to the meetings in their stead. At the beginning of the session the chair might announce that one director or more had e-mailed, claiming that something had come up and that he or she was either not going to be there or was sending another to represent the department. When this occurred, some of the following session was spent familiarizing last week's absentees. The ambassadors, apparently, hadn't relayed information to the managing directors. There were minutes for each session, but they were distributed on the following Tuesday, a day prior to the Wednesday gathering. Attendees would bring these minutes to the meeting and would scan them during the early moments or while directors were chatting informally waiting for the session to begin.

Sweeney felt that any information that was relayed at the meetings could just as easily be communicated via e-mail or print. For this reason, because he saw the time as a period that could be more usefully spent, and because others were doing it as well, Gerald Sweeney began to attend these sessions only sporadically—e-mailing in his regrets now and again.

When presiding over his own staff, Sweeney had a clear agenda, followed it, allowed for little in the way of digressions, and made sure the session ended on time.

However, on one occasion he did not relay to his subordinates some information that had been disseminated at a Wednesday meeting that he'd missed. This was vital information about a new procedure. Because he hadn't attended the session and had not read the minutes, he could not and did not relay the message about the new policy to his subordinates. Subsequently, the subordinates were reprimanded by top management for not following the policy. They had to spend an extraordinary amount of time redoing the tasks. Somehow, Sweeney's reputation and power remained untarnished. His subordinates did not have easy access to top management, nor did anyone want to criticize the boss, perhaps for fear of reprisals. Sweeney himself did not want to communicate a message to his superiors indicating that he had been responsible for the errors. "It would hurt our department in the long run," he claimed.

Gerald Sweeney apologized to his staff, but they were not easily soothed. "Look, I'm sorry," he said. "But I couldn't stand going to those meetings."

- Can meetings like these Wednesday sessions affect organizational culture?
- Should Sweeney have attended the meetings?
- What, if anything, could Sweeney have done to change the way those meetings were run?
- Did Sweeney have an ethical responsibility to notify top management and explain that it was he who was responsible for the incorrectly completed tasks?

The Phenomenon of Meetings

Meetings, Bloody Meetings

People often have negative attitudes about meetings. John Cleese used the title *Meetings, Bloody Meetings* for his educational videotape on the subject.[3] DeWine writes that meetings are "usually thought of as time wasters."[4] A *Newsweek* commentary includes this commonly held sentiment: "Meetings . . . have become our national pastime, yet one is hard pressed to see any advantage to them."[5] Humorist Dave Barry commented, "If you had to identify, in one word, the reason why the human race has not achieved, and never will achieve, its full potential, that word would be 'meetings.'"[6]

"If Moses had been a committee, the Israelites would still be in Egypt."[2]

Meeting pessimism and frustration is also reflected in the following comments made by businesspersons:

1. I become annoyed during our regular—allegedly important—problem-solving meetings, when participants leave the room when they receive so-called "urgent" calls on their cell phones to which they "must" respond. If we need to meet, we should meet and take care of other business afterwards.

2. I am in a group with thirteen others. About seven of these persons come in five or ten minutes after the scheduled time of our meeting, and we don't begin until all persons are present. The next ten minutes are spent discussing the weather and social news. Therefore, we *begin* the session wasting twenty valuable minutes of my time. And this, of course, doesn't count the time we waste once we get started.

3. Our regional director schedules monthly meetings of the sales force. Regularly, the scheduled meeting time is changed on short notice, causing resentment from those of us who had planned our appointments around the scheduled meetings. In addition, the agenda for the meeting is disregarded within moments of the start. The meetings run 3 to 4½ hours and right through the lunch period.

4. Tuesday mornings we have a weekly staff meeting. Staff members have grown to dread Tuesday mornings and feel that the meetings are nothing more than perfunctory.

"I work in a small organization. Still, we need our weekly interdepartmental meetings. Sometimes I'm at a session and have to say, 'Whoa. I need the back story on this. What's this program about?' Also, I think it's good for empathy. Sometimes I am annoyed at someone, but when I hear what they're up against, I get it—and this happens I think to all of the department heads. So, the meetings are good for us as a whole."[8]

5. Our head manager calls regular staff meetings and spends valuable time discussing her personal life and passing around pictures of her children.[7]

Values of Meetings

Despite the common tensions, there are legitimate reasons for teams and departments to use meetings as venues for organizational communication. DeWine lists four such reasons:

- To announce organizational changes and keep employees up to date.
- To produce solutions and to increase the number of different solutions to organizational problems.
- To gain "buy-in" or acceptance of a decision through participation.
- To "cultivate members as individuals" and create group cohesion.[9]

John Cleese calls his training video *Meetings, Bloody Meetings.*

How can organizations obtain the potential benefits from meetings and not unintentionally encourage employees to mutter, "meetings, bloody, meetings?" An initial step is to analyze why communication problems in teams tend to surface.

Primary and Secondary Tension

Berko, Wolvin, and Wolvin define primary tension as the "normal jitters and feelings of uneasiness experienced when groups first congregate." Secondary tension is defined as "the stress and strain that occurs in a group later in its development."[10] Essentially, primary tensions refer to that anxiety that occurs before meetings begin, and secondary tension refers to that conflict that occurs once the session or sessions are underway.

Primary Tension

There are a number of reasons why people could feel tense even before a meeting begins. Participants may experience primary tension because:

- They fear that this group will be a team in name only and therefore they will have to carry a disproportionate burden of the team responsibilities.
- They're unaware of the topic for the meeting and are anxious because they imagine potential topics might make them uncomfortable.
- They *are* aware of the topic, but the topic itself creates anxiety. A department, for example, may be meeting to discuss criteria for individual evaluation, and people may be nervous about how their job performance will be rated.
- They're concerned that the culmination of the work will require a demonstration of written or oral communication competence and the participant has little confidence in one or the other or both.
- They have what is called high traitlike "communication apprehension." This means a participant is nervous about communicating regardless of the context. Therefore, people with high traitlike apprehension will be aware that they may be expected to speak during a meeting and become anxious about that prospect.

- They are concerned that the meeting will result in an assignment outside of their range of abilities.
- They are unprepared to participate.
- Their experience in teams, or with this particular team, has been negative.
- Their experience with an individual or individuals within the group has been negative. Similarly, they may not have a positive working relationship with the person who is chairing the session.
- They have other projects that are more urgent and don't have time for the meeting.
- There are personal issues that are pressing that make concentrated group work difficult.

Any one of these or any combination could result in primary tension and make it difficult for work in team meeting sessions to be successful from the beginning.

Take a moment to review this list. How many of these have affected your attitudes prior to attending a meeting?

Secondary Tension

Once any meeting begins, secondary tensions or conflicts are likely to surface. These can be categorized into four areas: procedural, equity, affective, and substantive.

Procedural

These tensions stem from feelings that the *process* of interacting in the group is unproductive. A member or members of the group may feel that the agenda is weak or they may be dispirited because the leader is not adhering to the agenda. There may be no agenda at all, which could cause procedural anxiety. Individuals who experience this type of conflict feel that if the session were to be conducted differently, it would be more effective and productive.

Equity

Equity tensions occur when there is a perception of inequality. Participants in the group feel as if something is not fair. Typically equity tensions fall into two subcategories. The first occurs when members feel as if they are assuming a disproportionate share of the responsibilities. In this instance, it may seem as if other participants are slackers or "social loafers"—a term used in the literature of group interaction to describe those who are derelict—and allow, if not compel, other group members to do their work.[11] If participants sense that they must carry the weight of noncontributing members, tension may surface because of the inequity.

A second type of equity tension occurs when participants want to be involved in the group but are ignored by more powerful or controlling members. In this situation a potential contributor feels bruised because what he or she says is not taken seriously. Members begin to wonder, "Why am I here?" Critical theorists discuss the marginalization of employees. Members can be invited, ostensibly, to participate with a team but be deprived of anything but nominal team membership. Equity conflict can upset associates who feel they have been asked to the table for little more than window dressing.

Affective

Affective tension surfaces when people in a team meeting begin to dislike one another. This may be the result of residual equity, procedural, or even primary tensions, but regardless of its source, when affective tension occurs, group interaction becomes very problematic. Participants will find it difficult to "hear" what adversaries are saying, let alone consider the wisdom of any suggestions. The personality tensions may make individuals contrary and the discussions gratuitously argumentative.

Applying the Principles—Test Yourself

Meeting Attitudes

Do the statements below describe your attitudes or your behavior in team meetings?

Directions: Please write a number 1–5 next to each statement using the following scale:

1. *The statement describes me and/or my attitudes very accurately.*
2. *This statement describes me "somewhat accurately."*
3. *The statement describes me neither well nor poorly.*
4. *This statement describes me "somewhat inaccurately."*
5. *This statement does not describe me at all.*

A. I'd prefer to work independently and not in teams.
B. I don't mind confronting people when they're wrong.
C. I'm a high communication apprehensive in meeting situations.
D. When two people are arguing in a team meeting, it bothers me.
E. I like doing things in a structured way.
F. When I'm in a problem-solving meeting, my objective is to get things done, period.
G. I make friends easily when I am on a committee.
H. It doesn't bother me when people come in late to meetings.
I. I'm often a pseudo-listener in meetings, that is, I tend to pretend to listen.
J. I have trouble respecting the values and communication norms of people from other countries and cultures when they are inconsistent with my own beliefs.
K. I'm reluctant to speak in groups because I think people won't understand me.

L. I can't understand why some people won't compromise.
M. I have sympathy for some people who "loaf" during meetings because I do that myself sometimes.
N. I cannot respect people who won't come to a meeting prepared.
O. I enjoy being a leader in a group.
P. I have a difficult time with people in authority, for example, people who are chairing meetings.
Q. When someone else is the leader of a meeting, I find myself thinking about how I might do things differently.
R. I think that women and minorities are disrespected during meetings.
S. When a leader doesn't follow an agenda, I become upset.
T. For me, primary conflict is great when I think someone with a big ego will be on my team.
U. Side talking during meetings is not such a bad thing. I think people in general should relax and not be so uptight.
V. I don't think it is appropriate for people to use profanity in a team meeting—even if we all know each other.
W. I have difficulty making eye contact with people when I speak about sensitive issues.
X. I'm reluctant to speak in meetings because I think people won't like what I say and therefore won't like me.
Y. When a subject is very sensitive to me, I just clam up.
Z. I don't think there's ever a reason to raise your voice and shout during a meeting.

Do you think your attitudes and tendencies help make teams effective? How would you want those with whom you interact in groups to respond to these statements?

A perceived foe may suggest a plan that is well grounded in logic, but the rival is unable to see through the personal tension to legitimately evaluate the proposal.

Substantive

A positive type of tension is called substantive conflict. This refers to conflict that surfaces because of legitimate disagreements regarding the subject being discussed. Most people typically think of conflict as something negative, but this is not necessarily the case. Conflict can:

- Promote creativity and therefore facilitate problem solving.
- Promote the sharing of different ideas and therefore increase the amount of relevant information available.
- Serve to test the strength of opposing ideas.

For example, assume an organization is considering building an indoor parking facility for employees. Further assume that a committee has been formed to discuss where the facility should be built. If one member of the committee suggests a lot on the west side of the property, another may disagree, point out the drawbacks of such a location, and offer another venue for parking. There's conflict between these two positions. But the conflict may well yield a better solution for the organization.

In short, substantive conflict is what you desire when you meet as a group. Leaders and all participants should actively try to create disagreement even when there seems to be total agreement on a particular subject. In the section of this chapter that deals with interventions. we will discuss methods of generating substantive conflict.

Counterproductive Group Tendencies

In the musical *Annie Get Your Gun*, Ethel Merman as Annie Oakley sang a song about how, despite her uneducated ways, she and others of her family knew how to behave by "doin' what comes natur'lly." While this may have worked for Annie and her brood, the fact is that doing what comes naturally causes problems for teams. Default tendencies of groups and group members are counterproductive and create tensions. Below are some of these counterproductive group behaviors.

Conformity: Groupthink, the Asch Effect, and Goal Lining

Groupthink, the Asch effect, and goal lining all refer to threats to team success. An assumption, when convening in groups, is that "two heads are better than one." However, if two or more "heads" actually act as one, then the value of collaborative interaction is diminished. When this occurs, meeting sessions will not do what they purport to do—provide a context for sharing multiple perspectives that can result in high-quality solutions.[12] As significantly, the meeting sessions will provide an illusion of group support. This illusion can have insidious consequences since a recommendation by many tends to be perceived as more persuasive than one endorsed by a single person. Decisions could consequently be made on the basis of majority or popular support when, in fact, only one or two persons were actually supportive.

Groupthink

Irving Janis popularized the word "groupthink" in a book about political decision making and a 1971 *Psychology Today* article.[13] Some authors have written that Janis actually "coined" the term, but the word was first used in 1952.[14] However, largely because of Janis, "groupthink" as a word has crept into the lexicon and has a home in a standard desk dictionary nestled securely between "group therapy" and "grouse."[15]

Groupthink refers to the tendency of groups to make decisions without considering alternatives. Janis described it as "a mode of thinking that people engage in when they are deeply involved in a cohesive in-group, when members' striving for unanimity overrides their motivation to realistically appraise alternative courses of action."[16]

Essentially, when groupthink occurs, one member puts forth an idea and others readily agree without considering the advantages and disadvantages of the proposition. The group might do this because the suggested idea was presented by a powerful member, or because individuals don't want to "rock the boat," or

When groupthink occurs, participants do not act as individuals, but rather think collectively—as if they were all one and the same person.

because the members have no great individual stake in the decision. The 1961 decision of the Kennedy administration to invade the Bay of Pigs is typically cited as an example of groupthink. Had groupthink not occurred, it would seem to be impossible that all members participating in the deliberation would have agreed to an undertaking so unlikely to succeed. As recently as October 2001, the U.S. Congress passed a controversial terrorism bill in the aftermath of the September 11 tragedy. Some people consider this quick collective response to be representative of groupthink.

Fear, inertia, or the desire to produce or conform reduces the potential for a group to be a dynamic unit where people think as individuals and pool their ideas. When groupthink occurs, there are few individual thoughts, just "group think." Because of groupthink, meetings sometimes result in unimaginative shortsighted solutions to organizational problems. In addition, participants can become frustrated since they might wonder why their presence was necessary at a meeting characterized by groupthink. Why should one spend valuable time at a meeting if the predisposition of the group is simply to support the positions articulated by a powerful member?

The Asch Effect

Solomon Asch designed an experiment to gauge how willing individuals would be to conform to clearly incorrect conclusions. The Asch effect, a name derived from the experiment, explains a good deal about conformity and how it can affect groups.

Asch's experiment involved graduate students who were asked to compare twelve pairs of cards. Each pair consisted of what was called a "standard line" card and a "comparison line" card. On the standard line card was a single line. On the comparison line card there were three lines of varying lengths. The procedure for each study was the same.

- Seven to nine graduate students were brought into a room.
- The students would view the first of the twelve pairs of standard line cards and comparison line cards.
- The first student would then state aloud which line from the "comparison line card" was the same length as the line on the "standard line card."
- Then the remaining students would, one by one, announce which line from the comparison line card was the same length as the standard line card.

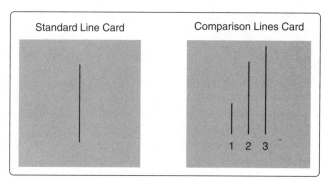

Figure 8.1 The Asch Experiment

- When all nine had announced the selection for the first pair, the students would view the second pair and follow the same procedure.
- The study would continue until each of the twelve pairs had been viewed and each of the subjects had orally declared their votes.

The correct answer in each case was obvious. For each of the twelve pairs of cards, only one line on the comparison card could possibly be construed as the correct match. However, among the seven to nine students involved in the experiment, *only one* was an actual subject. The others were conspirators helping to conduct the experiment. For each of the twelve comparisons, the helpers declared aloud that *another* line—clearly *not* the correct one—was indeed the one that matched the length of the line on the standard line card. After each of the conspirators would state that the *incorrect* line was the match, the lone actual subject (who was always the last to declare his or her vote) was put in the position of conforming, or disagreeing and identifying the correct and obvious answer.

Four out of five of the (real) subjects yielded to the pressures at least one time out of twelve. Nearly three out of the five subjects yielded to the pressure at least two times out of twelve. As Goldhaber points out, what may be the most stunning feature of this study is that these groups were not cohesive groups or any kind of standing committee.[17] What might have been the tendency to conform had these persons been part of a cohesive group? Asch's study has been replicated in countries and cultures beyond North America. Bond and Smith report Asch studies with similar results conducted in Portugal, Kuwait, Brazil, France, Zimbabwe, Fiji, and Ghana.[18]

If people are willing to succumb to peer pressure when to do so is to agree to an absurd conclusion, how likely are people to succumb to such pressure when the idea, however inappropriate, is not entirely beyond reason?

Goal Lining
Goal lining, while slightly different from groupthink and the Asch effect, also results in an absence of valuable substantive conflict. When goal lining occurs, participants see reaching the goal as the lone criterion determining quality team interaction. If a team is meeting to come up with a list of the advantages and disadvantages of building a health facility for employees, then the objective of the meeting is seen by goal liners as that and that alone.

At first, one might wonder what is wrong with that. Why should the team be concerned with anything other than the goal? The problem with goal lining is that it tends to encourage participants to seek a conclusion without necessarily seeking a *team* conclusion. In the rush to cross the goal line, the team loses the potential value of discussion, creativity, and interaction.

Applying the Principles—Test Yourself

Conforming Tendencies

In order to assess the effects of conformity on meetings, consider conducting this exercise with an organization with which you are affiliated.

Explain to your organization (e.g., sorority, club, class group members) that you're doing an exercise to strengthen the quality of future meetings. Randomly, break up your organization into subgroups of equal numbers. Ask each subgroup to rank the following in terms of the value of the terms/phrases for meeting success:

- Communication skills of individual members
- Commitment to goals of the group
- Leadership
- Individual preparation and responsibility
- Site/setting for meeting
- Creating and adhering to the group agenda

For example, if leadership is considered by the subgroup to be the most significant factor for meeting success, then the subgroup should rank it as 1. If site/setting for meeting is considered the second most significant, then the subgroup should rank it as 2, and so on.

What do you predict will occur in the subgroups?

- Will there be goal lining just to get the exercise done?
- Will the Asch effect be obvious? That is, will people conform regardless of the wisdom of ideas presented?
- Will groupthink prevail? That is, will the group agree quickly to one idea in order to "not rock the boat" or satisfy influential others?

Ethnocentrism: Cultural Elitism

Martin and Nakayama define ethnocentrism simply as the "tendency to think that our own culture is superior to other cultures."[19] (Ethnocentrism and intercultural communication will be discussed in Chapter 9.)

In an increasingly diverse workplace, ethnocentricity can create *affective* tension in groups, which will militate against successful communication. Ethnocentrism is also likely to create *equity* tensions as members of minority cultures may feel as if their opinions are discounted. Beebe, Beebe, and Ivy comment that "ethnocentrism and cultural snobbery is one of the quickest ways to create a barrier that inhibits rather than enhances communication."[20]

In your experience working in teams, has ethnocentrism been a factor? Do women and minorities, for example, tend to get the same "floor time" as other participants?

Inadequate Agendas and Hidden Agendas

Mosvick and Nelson asked 1600 managers what went wrong with meetings. Of the top six items cited as obstacles, five related to a poor agenda, no agenda, or not following an agenda.[21] An agenda is a list of topics to be addressed at a meeting session. Problems relating to agendas occur if (a) agendas are created to provide an illusion of structure and order as opposed to being designed to actually facilitate structure and order or (b) they are ignored. Some of the examples in the beginning of this chapter reflect *procedural*

"On the one hand, eliminating the middleman would result in lower costs, increased sales, and greater consumer satisfaction; on the other hand, we're the middleman."

Employees often bring hidden agendas to meetings. These hidden agendas can reduce the effectiveness of group decision making.

conflict that developed because agendas were illusory or disregarded.

Think of an agenda as a road map, as if it is the printout from a mapquest.com search you did online. If groups want to get from a starting point to a destination, they need to follow the directions. Otherwise they will spend hours traveling but will be terribly frustrated after the journey, because while they spent the hours "motoring" they didn't get where they wanted to go. As the Mosvick and Nelson study suggests, this occurs often in team meetings. Team members may or may not have the MapQuest directions, but unlike motorists, they often are not sufficiently disciplined to stay on course. An agenda is a road map that needs to be followed to allow groups to reach their meeting objectives.

Hidden agendas refer to personal and/or political meeting objectives that are "hidden" from the group. Let's assume that a department meets to discuss budget cutbacks. The alleged goal of the department is to determine what resources, programs, or personnel can and should be cut. The hidden agendas for each member are likely to be different from the alleged goal. Members may want to preserve resources that they require and may fight for their individual needs as opposed to the group objectives.

Consider another example. Assume you want a friend hired in your organization. Let's further assume that you are on the hiring committee and the committee decides that prior to interviewing anyone, they will identify those qualities necessary for any successful candidate.

If you were to attempt to engineer the discussion so that the "successful candidate qualifications" happened to coincide with your friend's credentials, you would be pursuing a hidden agenda. As is obvious, these hidden agendas can undermine the success of the group interaction. They can also create *affective* conflict, which may carry over to subsequent discussions on entirely other matters.

Competition vs. Cooperation

A spirit of cooperation, as opposed to a spirit of competition, facilitates effective communication in groups. What often happens in groups, however, is that participants tend to become ego-involved and competitive. Differences of opinion are good for groups, but fighting for your opinion *simply because it is yours* can create affective conflict.

As discussions develop in meetings, individuals may become more and more attached to their stated perspectives on an issue and be reluctant to consider opposing points of view. A discussant's position on an issue may become intertwined with that person's ego. Julie's position on the new hire may become *Julie's* position. If you disagree with the position, it may seem to Julie as a personal attack. What can occur is that participants cease discussing the merits of an issue and simply want to win. Very highly ego-involved individuals are a bane in groups, since the meeting may not develop beyond these persons' need to be victorious. Cooperation versus competition is a key to success in groups, yet cooperation should not be confused with conformity or "going along to get along." Cooperative participants seek substantive conflict. They do not, however, consider the meeting setting a battleground where the successful members are the ones whose ideas are adopted by the group.

ETHICAL PROBE

The Ethics of Hidden Agendas

Assume that the following were the actual objectives for individual meetings. Can you list the likely hidden agendas that participants might bring to the session?

- To decide on whether to use print or the Web for procedural manuals.

- To discuss the merits of flextime for middle managers.
- To examine criteria for annual bonus amounts.

Would there be anything unethical about pursuing any of the hidden agendas you have identified?

Tolerating High-Level Term Abstraction

Words have different levels of abstraction. A term with a high level of abstraction is more vague than a word with a low level of abstraction. For example, words like *benefits, success,* and *love* have relatively high levels of abstraction when compared to words like *cat, telephone,* and *stapler.* A group could be discussing the steps needed for a *successful* year, and members of the group could be defining *success* differently. Some people might think success means that individuals would get large pay raises. Others might think that the organization would add staff; still others might think that at year's end all employees would be *spiritually* enriched. Without clarifying the precise nature of the terms being discussed, meetings can be frustrating simply because individuals are not speaking about the same thing.

Consider this second illustration. Assume you were on a school committee and were being asked to decide which of the following subjects should be required of high school students.

- Health
- Religion
- Citizen responsibility
- Art appreciation
- Personal economics
- Sexual education
- Cultural diversity

Further assume that your group knew that only some topics could be taught, and you had to rank the items in terms of "value for an educated student in a great society." Would you think that "high-level term abstraction" would affect your discussions?

Interventions

An intervention is a tool or technique used to alter behavior that would likely not be altered had there been no intervention. In relation to organizational meetings, interventions can be used to reduce primary and secondary conflict. Some interventions can help create positive substantive conflict and reduce the harmful effects of ethnocentricity, conformity, high-level abstraction, and

even—in some cases—ego involvement. In short, in relation to team meetings, interventions can be employed to make these communication contexts less problematic and more successful.

Types of Interventions

Buzz Groups

Assume that you are working in a large group and it seems as if only some people are participating. You might want to employ the intervention technique called buzz groups to increase participation and decrease the potential for problems related to *equity* conflict. With buzz groups, larger groups are divided into smaller ones. A team of twelve persons discussing the merits of a particular plan would be broken into six groups of two.

Each group of two would discuss the same issue. After a period of time the six buzz groups of two would reconvene as a group of twelve. Each buzz group would express to the group as a whole what they had discussed within their particular dyad.

The main value associated with buzz groups is that it requires the participation of all and therefore tends to reduce equity tensions. A social loafer will have no place to hide in a buzz group, and a high communication apprehensive is likely to feel more comfortable speaking to just one other as opposed to speaking to a larger group. Large problem-solving teams often lose the value of potential contributors because, as the group evolves, some participants become especially vocal while others retreat. The retreating members may be able to contribute significantly, but the dynamics of the interactions when the team meets as a whole—and the emerging patterns of participation—can discourage contributions. Buzz groups can be used very effectively to reduce this counterproductive effect.

Brainstorming and Brainwriting

The commonly used term "brainstorming" is misused much of the time. It has a precise meaning as a team meeting intervention and can be used to generate desirable substantive conflict.

The following is not an example of brainstorming:

> A pan-Hellenic campus group gets together to discuss establishing a code of ethics for campus fraternities and sororities. The leader suggests that they "brainstorm" on the issue. One participant offers that it's probably a good idea to have a code of ethics because this way people will know what is morally appropriate and abide by the code. Another member responds and comments that the previous speaker is incorrect because people will not adhere to any code of ethics. A third person remarks that maybe a code of ethics will be recognized and adhered to because, after all, other pan-Hellenic codes are followed.

While this type of conversation might result in a valuable discussion, it is not an illustration of brainstorming, even though most people tend to think of brainstorming this way. Brainstorming is not an "advantages and disadvantages" discussion.

Brainstorming is an idea generating intervention that involves the identification and recording of any and all ideas germane to the topic being discussed. A key and essential feature of brainstorming is that at no point during the intervention is anyone permitted to criticize a "brainstormed" idea

Applying the Principles—Test Yourself

Meeting Criteria

Indicate how you feel about each of the following statements using this five-point scale:

1. **I strongly agree with the statement**
2. **I agree with the statement**
3. **I neither agree nor disagree**
4. **I disagree**
5. **I strongly disagree with the statement**

For each statement, explain why you feel as you do by providing an example from your experience to support your position.

1. Business meetings must have an agenda.
2. The key factor for successful meetings is responsible participants.
3. Meetings are a necessary time for social cohesion. They can help to create a team attitude.
4. The expression "two heads are better than one" makes sense as it applies to business sessions. You usually get a better result when you solve problems with others in a business meeting.
5. Leaders in groups should run the session but essentially stay out of the way. Otherwise meetings become little more than presentations.
6. Personality conflict can reduce meetings to battlegrounds, with people taking entrenched positions regardless of their true attitudes on a subject.
7. Brainstorming typically provides more drizzle than rain.
8. Information disseminated during meetings could as easily be communicated via e-mail or print.
9. A challenge for leadership is making sure each person in a group has a genuine chance to participate. Most of the time this doesn't happen.
10. Discussing ideas in meetings never works because people are too "sold" on their own suggestions to be objective when listening to criticisms, even when the criticisms are constructive.

that another has offered. Indeed, some people have argued that even outlandish ideas are welcome, because these ideas might be springboards for perhaps less bizarre but more creative ideas than others would consider and offer.[22]

The following describes how a brainstorming session might work using the illustration of the pan-Hellenic meeting. The leader would ask to hear the advantages of implementing a code of ethics. Group members would then identify, even shout out, any advantages they think to be appropriate. A member of the group would record, perhaps on a chalk board or on a flip chart, any comments made. A code of ethics would:

Increase the visibility of the Greeks
Increase the perception of Greeks
Help Greeks get funding
Reduce drugs on campus
Make my father happy
Encourage my mother to send me money
Improve race relations
Make it easy to recruit students

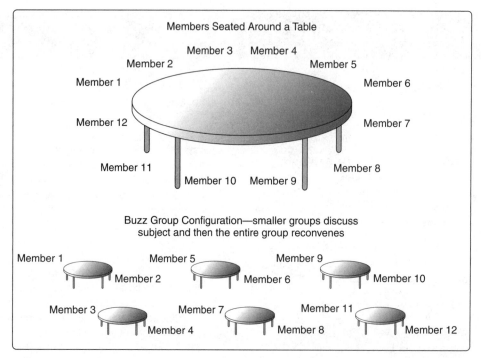

Figure 8.2 Buzz Groups

Result in the university supporting Greek activities
Cut down on profanity
Decrease communicable diseases

Even comments like "encourage my mother to send me money" are not to be derided. True brainstorming encourages any and all notions.

Subsequently, the ideas are discussed and evaluated. Adams and Galanes suggest that the group take a break after creating the brainstormed list before evaluation. Further, the authors comment that it might be wise to wait for a separate session for the evaluative discussion. "[I]ncubation is an important feature of creative thinking. After brainstorming has generated a lot of ideas and the group has had a chance to let the ideas sit for a while, critical thinking is used to evaluate each idea and to modify or combine ideas into workable solutions to the problem."[23]

A variation of traditional brainstorming is polling brainstorming. In polling brainstorming, the leader "polls" group members. Using the pan-Hellenic scenario, each participant in turn would be asked to identify an advantage of establishing a code of ethics. When their turn came, the members would offer an advantage until such time as all individuals had exhausted all ideas.

The advantage of polling brainstorming is that it encourages the participation of social loafers and high communication apprehensives. High communication apprehensives, particularly, may have valuable suggestions but may be unwilling to speak in a brainstorming session unless compelled to do so. A related advantage is that polling brainstorming makes it difficult for a dominating personality to overwhelm the session.

The polling approach can result, however, in a loss of spontaneity. Participants may just focus on having something to say when their turn comes, and the session may not lather in the way it otherwise could. A way to deal with this disadvantage is to use the alternative of *brainwriting*. With brainwriting, all individuals write down ideas and subsequently draw from their individual list during a brainstorming session. Brainwriting does not fully address the concerns of not being able to piggyback off of another person's ideas. However, with brainwriting a participant is not restricted to the prewritten list so she or he could react to another's idea.

Nominal Group Technique

Nominal group technique (NGT), developed by Delbecq and Van de Ven, attempts to avoid affective and procedural tensions.[24] This elaboration of brainwriting involves very little group interaction. The word nominal means "in name only," and this technique is, in fact, a "group" approach in name only.

In NGT participants are asked to write down their solutions to a particular problem as they would in brainwriting. Persons, in a polling format, then express their ideas for solving the problem. Subsequently, all of these ideas are written on a board or flip chart. The leader proceeds to review each item so that the authors can clarify what is meant by each suggestion. At this point in the process there is no defense or criticism of any of the presented ideas.

After the clarifications are made, each participant is asked to vote on the ideas advanced. On a sheet of paper, the participants rank the top five solutions that have been advanced. The leaders collect the papers with the rankings and tally up the votes. The ideas that receive the most votes are then discussed and evaluated.

Since there is relatively little discussion, this is considered a "nominal group technique"—a group in name only. NGT is designed to decrease the negative effects of affective conflict and, because of its rigid structure, reduce issues related to procedural conflict as well—assuming participants have bought into the wisdom of employing the NGT procedure.

An intervention that involves division of labor is a more common type of nominal group technique. This approach is used so frequently in task-related groups that it is unlikely that you have not employed this technique when working on group projects at your college.

When given a task, some groups will divide the task into subsections equal to the number of people in the group. A group of five assigned to describe the American presidency since Eisenhower might decide to count the number of presidents since Eisenhower, divide by five, and then assign each person two "presidencies" to research and describe. Subsequently, each member of the group returns with 20 percent of the assignment, and the group patches together the individual pieces.

The advantages of this approach are that it:

- Saves time.
- Allows individuals to go into greater depth on their individual subjects.
- Avoids affective tensions that might surface otherwise.
- Avoids equity conflict if the separation of responsibilities is indeed equitable.

The disadvantages are important to note as well. Dividing responsibilities:

- Reduces positive substantive conflict.
- Can create affective and equity conflicts if individuals do not or cannot do their work efficiently.
- Can result in a disjointed product as different sections may not seamlessly fit together.

This approach of dividing tasks in problem-solving groups is very risky. It can be used to avoid affective and equity tensions, but if participants are not willing to complete their share and work to seamlessly join individual sections, the solution to the problem may be incomplete and disjointed. The technique also circumvents and subverts the ostensible goal of problem-solving meetings, that is, to gain collective insights that would be lost if work was done individually. Highly responsible group members can overcome some of these risks by being diligent in regard to their own responsibilities, participating in the evaluation of other contributions as well as they are able, and working to seamlessly connect the various sections into a sensible whole.

Problem Census

In order to avoid problems related to high-level term abstraction or procedural conflict, problem-solving teams may wish to use the problem census. In this technique members are polled initially regarding their individual perspective and perceptions of the problem. This intervention is valuable because before teams begin to discuss a topic, the group can become relatively certain that participants are on the same page regarding the nature and dimensions of the topic.

Assume your group has been given the following charge: *"Assess the value and wisdom of implementing a companywide training program for dealing with multicultural sensitivity and diversity."* Prior to discussing ideas for the program, you might want to conduct a problem census. This polling process could reveal that individuals attending the workshop have a different sense of the meaning of:

- Multicultural
- Sensitivity
- Training
- Program
- Diversity

You may discover that when thinking of the *value and wisdom* of such a program, some members would be concerned with:

- Financial costs
- Long-term financial benefits
- Interpersonal social benefits
- Community service benefits
- Public relations value

You may discover that some people will consider the best way *to assess* the value and wisdom is by:

- Looking at how other organizations have done it
- Reviewing prior attempts
- Examining the ethnic diversity of the organization
- Polling other members of the organizational community

By using problem census you may derive, before you actually begin, a better sense of the task at hand and a clearer method of how your group intends to proceed to meet the group goals.

Risk Technique

To avoid issues that surface relating to the Asch effect or groupthink, meeting members might consider using risk technique. This approach requires each participant to play the role of "devil's advocate."

Devil's advocacy is a phrase used to mean arguing for a perspective that is contrary to whatever position has been advanced. For example, if your department meets and proposes making Fridays "casual dress days," you may want the department members to play the devil's advocate to that proposition. To assume the devil's advocate, members would take the stance that casual dress days were *inappropriate* and argue, regardless of their actual perspective on the matter, that Fridays should not be casual days. The value of devil's advocacy is that it forces groups to examine a proposal in depth by exploring opposite perspectives.

Risk technique works as a polling technique. After a team has decided on a solution, each member plays devil's advocate and identifies a risk associated with implementing that solution. These lists of risks are recorded. Subsequently the team reviews the list of risks and reevaluates the proposal. Most of the time the reevaluation does not result in the elimination of the proposal, but with the fine tuning of the resolution so that it addresses the concerns suggested by the risks.

For example, assume your team has decided to implement a new logo for your organization. When using risk technique you would ask each member of the team—*that had already decided to employ this new logo*—to play devil's advocate and identify problems with the utilization. For example, Donna might say that it would be too confusing to some customers to change the logo. Jermaine might suggest that it would be too costly to implement. Rita may argue that the new logo will be too similar to a competitor's.

On the basis of these risks, the team may fine-tune the proposal, adopting a revised version that accommodates these risks. It is possible that you might decide to retain what had been originally identified despite the risks because the value of that proposal exceeds the problems that were identified by the risks. In either case the risk technique has strengthened the quality of your team's solution.

It can be difficult for people to assume the role of devil's advocate particularly if moments earlier they presented the logic behind, and supported the plan, that's being considered. Yet, in order for the risk technique to work, each person, regardless of how involved she or he may have been in the composition of the plan, must play devil's advocate and assume a posture of someone who identifies proposed flaws. In this way the potential for groupthink and Asch effect conformity is reduced.

General Procedural Model

An intervention that combines many of the techniques described previously is called the general procedural model (GPM).[25] The GPM is an effective approach for problem-solving meetings and an excellent technique for those teams that are experiencing procedural conflict and, consequently, affective and equity conflict. It is a five-stage model:

1. *Identify the problem:* In this stage the team clarifies the objective for the meeting or the particular topic being discussed within the meeting. It is a good idea in this stage to use the problem census.
2. *Brainstorm:* In this stage the group uses brainstorming as it was designed to be used, i.e., without any evaluative component. Individuals brainstorm regarding solutions to the problem or dimensions of the problem. A team participant records the brainstormed ideas.
3. *Evaluation:* In this stage of GPM members assess the merit of the brainstormed ideas. With large groups it is a good idea to consider buzz groups for step 3 of GPM.
4. *Selection of best idea:* At this point, the group attempts to come up with a consensus of the best solution or, more likely, the best combination of solutions to the issue. At the conclusion of this stage, the team should consider using the risk technique to evaluate the merit of the proposal. After using the risk technique, fine-tune the solution so that it reflects the concerns identified during the risk technique intervention.
5. *Put the solution into effect:* Your team may need to generate a report, make a presentation, send a memorandum, contact officials, and/or even call another meeting to articulate the solution you've created. At this point in the process you decide how and when you shall put your solution into effect. Remaining portions of this chapter discuss the creation of team presentations and reports.

Making Interventions Work

Team Members as Participant-Observers

Any intervention technique is as good as the people who attempt to use the technique. Individuals need to be willing to employ interventions and not default to tendencies that are counterproductive. This is easier said than done. When I witness teams attempt to use, for example, brainstorming—regardless of the level or intelligence of the participants—it takes considerable effort for the members to avoid evaluating ideas as the brainstormed suggestions are made. When this occurs, steps 2 and 3 of the general procedural model are combined, rendering each step less valuable than it might otherwise be.

In order for interventions to work, members need to become "participant-observers." A participant-observer is someone *in* a group who concurrently participates and observes the process of participation.[26] A participant-observer, for example, comments on items on the agenda and also ensures that the agenda is followed.

This is work. Most people aren't accustomed to being participant-observers. Some individuals may be conscientiously active contributors, but few typically will concurrently evaluate the interaction process. However, in order for teams to function effectively in meeting contexts, members have to be vigilant. Interventions can work, but participants need to be committed to working at the interventions for them to be successful. *Intelligence, knowledge,* and *communication skill* do not guarantee effective team interaction. Members have to be both responsible participants and responsible observers of the process.

Leadership

An important dimension for effective meetings is group leadership. Leaders in groups have a number of specific responsibilities. They should:

- **Plan for the meeting**. Decide if a meeting is necessary. Define the meeting objectives. Solicit agenda topics, prepare, and distribute an agenda.
- **Get the meeting started**. Team participants often assemble slowly. Discussants will engage in pastimes until some member calls the meeting to order. The duration of the preliminary chitchat sometimes exceeds the appropriate few minutes for such orientation. A leader has the responsibility to ensure that not too much time is wasted at the beginning of a session.
- **Keep the discussion on track**. Meetings are notorious for lengthy digressions. Discussion that might begin with an analysis of departmental purchasing can result in commiserating about the cost of Amanda's home basement refinishing and the difficulties of finding a responsible contractor. A leader has the responsibility to keep the discussion on topic. Meetings typically have time limits, and lengthy digressions result in jamming the last few items on the agenda into an inappropriate time space.
- **Summarize periodically**. Because of different input and tangential commenting, it is wise to periodically summarize what has been brought out. After discussing one area on an agenda, a summary statement by the leader can provide closure for that area and allow the team to seamlessly segue to the next topic of the session.
- **Solicit comments from taciturn members**. Effective meetings require input from all participants. Often quiet members need prodding to voice their opinions. Quiet, here, is not synonymous with irresponsible. Taciturn members may be simply quiet and require

encouragement. Leaders, to the extent that they can, should ensure that reserved participants do contribute to the discussion.

• **Curtail verbose members**. The other side of the problem involves the loquacious discussant. Some people do not realize that they are monopolizing conversation. Others are aware and have no qualms about such inconsiderate behavior. A leader has the uncomfortable task of intervening when a member is hogging time to allow for others' comments and to facilitate progress toward the completion of the meeting's agenda.

• **Employ interventions**. A leader should consider and utilize approaches that can reduce negative group tensions.

• **Conclude the meeting**. Just as the leader has the responsibility to start the meeting, it is the leader's responsibility to end the session. At that time, the leader should summarize the progress of the session, indicate what remains to be done, and announce, if the information is available, when the next meeting will take place.

• **Plan for the next session**. Between meetings the leader has the job of planning for the next session. This includes sending out the minutes of the preceding session to committee members, taking care of the logistics for the next meeting (e.g., reserving meeting rooms, ensuring that the meeting time is appropriate for all parties and any guests who are to be invited to the next meeting), and soliciting additional agenda topics for the next session.

Being a leader is not an easy job. It is a complex task that requires tact and communication skill. As American author Caskie Stinnett once wrote about diplomats, a leader has to be "a person who can tell you to 'go to hell' in such a way that you actually look forward to the trip."

Examining Leadership Styles

There are three basic leadership styles. *Authoritarian* or *autocratic* leaders are, as the label suggests, dictatorial and nondemocratic. *Laissez-faire* leaders are the opposite of authoritarians. They believe that the best way to lead a team is by keeping your "hands off." A laissez-faire leader believes that a group can run itself, and, therefore, to guide it is to wield power that is not only unnecessary but counterproductive. A democratic leader seeks input and advice from group members. She or he may make the eventual decisions regarding directions for the group, but those decisions are not made without considering the concerns of other members of the group.

• An authoritarian leader would determine a meeting agenda.
• A laissez-faire leader would assume that if meeting members needed an agenda, the group would decide to create one.
• A democratic leader would ask for input on what should be in the agenda and when a meeting might be held. Then she or he would construct the agenda.

There are a few other related labels used to describe leadership types in teams. A *de facto* leader is someone who, essentially, is the leader despite the fact that there is a *designated* or *nominal* other leader. Someone may have been designated as the leader but acts as a leader in name only. When that is the case, someone else may begin to assume the natural leadership responsibilities. That person is, in reality, or de facto, the leader. Occasionally an autocratic leader may incur the wrath of a team such that another member becomes the de facto leader. In these instances the de facto leader emerges because the other members are not attending to the directives of the designated autocratic leader.

Leadership is important for most teams. If it were not, then there would be no such phenomenon as a de facto leader. The democratic leadership style is likely to be most effective in organizational contexts. There could be some very low-energy groups for which an authoritarian leader might be necessary and some very highly responsible groups for whom anything other than a laissez-faire leader would be counterproductive.

Team Reports

Often the final result of team interaction is a presentation or collaboratively constructed report. If your experience is typical, you have taken courses that required groups to research a subject and then present findings either in oral or written form. Team presentations, in organizations as well as in class, need to be seamless. However, sometimes team presentations appear disjointed, and reviewers are left thinking that they have heard or read several individual reports instead of one cohesive presentation.

Quality team reports require efficient communication well before actual delivery. It is important to remember that the quality of the collectively delivered reports not only explains team decisions, it also affects the subsequent power, resources, and respect attributed to the teams that generate the reports.

Consider the comments of John Arena, Vice President and Creative Director for Generation, a full-service advertising agency. I interviewed Arena about the importance of team interaction and presentations at his agency. He explained that his company is regularly required to make "capabilities presentations" to clients. On the same day that Generation makes its pitch, several agencies like Generation make competing presentations. If Generation's presentation is successful, Arena and his team will be invited back for a subsequent round in the competition. As Arena explains, quality team communication prior to presentation is crucial for his company's success:

> We have several meetings to prepare and rehearse the team presentation. It takes a lot of prep work. Our agency is busy, and the people that I select for the pitch team are not doing crossword puzzles waiting for me to identify them. They are all involved with other projects in their various stages. So when they are working on our pitch team, they are not doing what they typically would be doing in their own units. It is another team and another set of team dynamics. There is high energy in the preparatory meetings and high stakes with the presentations.
>
> The team presentation is crucial and has to be very tight. The time limits are finite, and each person on the team must adhere to his or her segment's restrictions or we will not get our message out. Getting this right takes run through after run through. We have to know what each of us individually is going to say and what everyone else is going to say.
>
> The capabilities presentations vary, depending on the individual client, but each one typically includes an introductory statement from the president, a comment about the distinctive nature of Generation, a review of successful case studies, a demonstration of past creative work, and remarks from the media representative regarding efficient advertisement placement. Everyone on the team participates in the presentation. No one warms a seat. It is imperative that we convince the client that we know them, their market, and their customers. We want them to know that we have a distinctive approach, that we have been successful in the past and that we anticipate being successful with them.
>
> Generation has an excellent success rate. We call ourselves Generation because we generate change for customers. We have been very successful at doing that. However, if it weren't for the team preparation and subsequent presentations, we would not have the opportunities to prove that we can generate change. There are many agencies that are brought in for capability presentations. Only a small percentage is invited back for second rounds. Generation makes the second round at least one out of every two times we make a presentation.

In organizational contexts, team presentations are common. In the case of Generation, the presentations are delivered to an external audience. However, teams present to an organization's internal audiences as well. Instead of a lone representative describing a fund-raising campaign or crisis communication strategy, the whole team that worked on the plan will participate in the description. Instead of a single person making a presentation about sexual harassment policy, the team that composed the policy makes the presentation and constructs the complementary written documents.

The next section examines how to overcome problems collaborating for team presentations. The emphasis is on oral team reports, but many of the same principles relate to collaboratively written documents as well.

Types of Collective Presentations

Collective presentations can be classified into three categories: panel discussions, symposia, and team presentations. The type that most involves actual collaboration is the last one. Consequently, this type is the most relevant to the discussion in this chapter. However, a brief description of each type is presented below.

Panel Discussions

In panel discussions, a group of individuals discuss a subject and are concurrently observed by an audience. These persons, one assumes, are knowledgeable about the subject that they are discussing. Each person may begin by making a statement that is prepared, but most subsequent comments are impromptu and are reactions to what others have said. Often panel discussions have moderators. These persons are required to keep the conversation moving, ensure that all participants have an opportunity to speak, disentangle contentious participants who may be making it difficult for audience members to hear *any* comments, and—if within the ground rules of the discussion—solicit comments and questions from the assembled. A panel discussion has been described as a group conversation, with an audience.[27] It is not a collaborative team presentation, even though there may be a team of individuals who are participating and there may have been some collaborating prior to the presentation.

Symposia

Assume that a group of six successful managers have been asked to speak at a companywide assembly. Each manager has been asked to prepare a talk entitled, "Motivation Communication and Leadership." The men and women who comprise this group enter a ballroom. A moderator introduces the six participants, and then each in turn delivers a speech on the topic. Subsequently, the moderator solicits questions from the audience for the speakers. These questions are directed to Jones or Smith or any of those who have spoken.

This scenario describes a symposium. Your university, no doubt, hosts student and faculty symposia. Successful alums may be invited to speak on "Co-Curricular Activities and Professional Advancement." Assuming that this was a symposium and not a panel discussion, each alumnus would be asked to deliver a talk about his or her experience. All talks would be germane to the symposium theme. Subsequently, speakers would be asked questions from participating audience members.

Symposia are essentially collections of individual presentations. They are not team presentations in the sense that there is no collaborative work performed by the symposium participants to ensure a cohesive unified message. In fact, symposium directors may deliberately solicit participants who are likely to present opposing perspectives on the same phenomena.

Team Presentations

Team presentations reflect collaborative effort and are, consequently, significantly different from symposia and panel discussions. Assume that the six managers described above were asked to form a task force. This task force was charged with studying the question "Motivation, Communication, and Leadership." Then, subsequently, the committee members were asked to present their conclusions. The requested report would be called a team presentation. The meaningful distinction between team presentations and other forms of collective presentations is the expectation that the speakers will have worked together prior to the event in order to present a cohesive message.

Desired Outcomes

Assume that a team has spent a good deal of time working to create an intelligent recommendation to an internal or external client. The team wants to ensure that the report reflects the quality of this recommendation. To do so the team would have to consider the following checklist. Prior to presentation, the team would have to be confident that it could make the following claims regarding the report it intended to deliver.

- The introduction is clear, descriptive, inclusive, and engaging.
- The presentation content comprehensively addresses the charge and describes the response.
- In an oral presentation, each person knows what others will be saying.
- Transitional statements have been considered and created that link one section of the report to another.
- The conclusion will summarize the entirety of the report and not simply the last segment.

Let's consider each of these items individually.

The introduction is clear, descriptive, inclusive, and engaging.

Team presentations should not be perceived as loose composites of peripherally related content. They should be seen as a cohesive whole. The introduction to the team presentation must identify the broad team objective as well as describe how all the pieces that will be discussed mesh with one another. As is the case with the introduction to any presentation, the introduction must seek to engage the receivers and explain why they should be concerned with the content.

The content comprehensively addresses the charge and describes the response.

When the team views all the pieces of the report, all members should feel as if the message that will be relayed responds comprehensively to the team's assignment. Your team should be able to respond affirmatively to the following questions: "Did we respond to the charge?" "Does the report comprehensively explain our solutions?"

Each person knows what all others will be saying.

It is shortsighted to assume that if all persons take care of their own individual areas, the team will be successful. Familiarity with all parts of the presentation will ensure that:

There will be no undesired content repetition. Awareness of all segments ensures that persons speaking third or fourth will not be startled to hear information that they intended to say uttered by previous speakers.

There will be no unexpected contradictory statements. Similarly, awareness will preclude the possibility that a point made early will be the antithesis of something to be claimed later on.

There will be no surprising omissions. The presentation will not conclude with one member saying to another, "I thought you were going to handle that information."

Members will be able to make intelligent references to other person's segments. If everyone know what the others will be saying, it becomes easier to prepare meaningful transitions and comments alluding to other portions of the talk.

There will be no sections that are clearly superficial when juxtaposed with others of significant depth. The presentation should be cohesive and consistent. If some segments are relatively detailed and others seem inappropriately thin, the presentation will lack the consistency desired.

Individual members and the group as a whole will adhere to time limits. Awareness of each person's segment allows the group to gauge how much time the presentation as a whole will take.

It will be relatively easy to answer questions during a Q and A. Knowing what others will say will help the moderator, and all group members, know who is best suited to respond to particular questions.

For all of these reasons, it is very wise to make sure that all group members know what all others will be saying during the team presentation.

Transitional statements have been created.

Transitional statements are not difficult to create, but they need to be considered before the time of the presentation. The transition need not be elaborate but has to be meaningful. For example, "The sexual harassment policy that has been described will protect both individuals within the organization and the organization as a whole from embarrassing litigation. However, as we all know, the existence of a policy is not sufficient. We need to do an effective job of communicating the policy to all of our employees. The next section will now examine how we intend to make all members of the organization familiar with our procedures."

The conclusion will summarize the entirety of the presentation.

Every report requires a synthetic recapitulation of main points. In collaborative reports the team has to prepare such a conclusion and be careful to make sure that the summary includes all aspects and not just the content presented by the final segment.

Getting There: A Step-by-Step Procedure

A process can be employed by teams to facilitate attaining the desired outcomes enumerated above while avoiding the common problems that teams face. As is the case with most procedures, the steps to this process are easy to enumerate. The key to success is the work necessary to complete each step.

Step One: Use a Modification of GPM

Previously we have discussed the general procedural model technique for solving problems in team contexts. Following is a modification of GPM applied to the challenges of a team report.

- Use the *problem census* procedure to identify required sections of your report. For example, assume that the group's mission has been to make recommendations regarding an organization's code of ethics. The problem census might identify the following dimensions to your problem, which will also serve as a series of subsections of the report.

- We need to define organizational ethics.
- We need to identify other organizations' codes of ethics.
- We need to explore how these other codes are enforced.
- We need to identify our objectives for our code of ethics.
- We need to identify components to such a code.
- We need to explain how to communicate the implementation of the code.

- Employ *brainstorming* appropriately. As has been discussed, brainstorming involves identifying, recording, but not evaluating possible solutions to problems. In this phase of GPM, members would brainstorm regarding which content to select as part of each part of the presentation and how the team should present this content for each step identified in the previous phase.
- Use the buzz group technique with any group larger than three to evaluate the merit of the various brainstormed ideas.
- Identify the best combination of recommendations from the evaluated list of brainstormed suggestions. At the successful completion of this stage, you will have addressed each of the bulleted topics identified in the problem census.

The team should then employ risk technique to fine-tune these solutions.

Step 2: Divide Responsibilities. Prepare Individual Outlines

At this point the team has to decide who is going to talk/write about what segment of the message. Then, each person is responsible for preparing a detailed outline of his or her segment and making copies for (or otherwise distributing copies to) the team members. Often groups decide to complete step 2 before doing step 1. That is, individuals will be assigned content areas identified in the problem census and then work on an individual area before collectively discussing the overarching issue. This is not a recommended approach. By addressing the problem collectively in step 1, all persons are familiar with content that will be part of the report.

Step 3: Review Outlines

Each team member is responsible for reviewing the other members' outlines. This review is necessary to ensure familiarity with all components of the message to be presented. It ensures that there will be no omissions or repetitions. It ensures that the same level of depth exists in each segment.

Step 4: Discuss Sequence and Transitions

Which section will be first? In an oral presentation, how will the first person "hand off" to the person speaking second so that segments of the presentation will seem related and seamless? In a written presentation, how will the sections be linked to facilitate a clear reading of the report?

Step 5: Identify Message Style

In an oral presentation, the team should all be using the same speaking style— for example, one person should not be reading a section while another uses an outline. Consistency is recommended if for no other reason than it increases the perception of a collective effort. Graphics used to support one section should be of the same variety as visual support in another section.

Step 6: Plan the Introduction and the Conclusion

As indicated previously, the introduction must be clear, descriptive, inclusive, and engaging. The conclusion must reflect the entirety of the report, not only the last person's segment.

Gail Hunter: Vice President of Events and Attractions, National Basketball Association

Gail Hunter has both an MBA and a law degree. Before working for the NBA she held positions with Major League Baseball, the NCAA, the Seattle Mariners, and the Seattle law firm of Scheweppe, Krug & Tausend.

As you read through this section please consider the following questions.

- How would systems theorists react to Hunter's comment about persuading internal audiences?
- Can the passion Hunter describes be manufactured?
- What are your reactions to the bolded comments in her narrative?

My group produces grassroots marketing events for the NBA. We execute programs that have been either created by the NBA solely or developed in conjunction with our league-marketing partners. For example, Gatorade might want to work with us. They'll suggest an idea based on their marketing strategies and overall marketing goals, and we work with them and try to develop a joint program. Or we conceive of a program and then seek out a marketing partner to determine if our objectives are similar. The Rhythm 'n Rims tour, the NBA All Star Jam Session, and the WNBA Summer Jam are examples of our programs.

Communication is vital for what we do. We have to present ideas, listen to suggestions, respond to reactions, and persuade internal audiences that proposals have merit. For examples, I (or someone from our staff) will need to make a presentation to sell a concept to other divisions. Communicating well during these presentations is essential. If we can't

effectively describe the project, it may never get off the ground. We need people from these internal audiences to help us produce and launch the program so we have to persuade them that we have an idea that's worth their buy-in.

I believe that a good speaker frames the talk for the audience, and becomes aware of the audience's needs and concerns well before the talk begins. It's not very prudent to arrogantly explain the advantages of a concept as if to say, "You would have to be crazy not to want to work with us on this project." **One has to listen to the audience. If a potential partner tells you that they're not attracted to some facet of your plan and that they'd like to see a revision, you don't come back the following week hammering home the advantages of precisely that facet that the audience has already rejected.** You're essentially being disrespectful if you do that, and one is not very successful in business contexts by dismissing the concepts that are important to your potential business partners.

It's also important that a speaker demonstrate that she or he really believes in the concept. I don't want people in my group delivering a talk on an idea if they are not sold on the idea. It's important to convey some passion and that cannot be easily manufactured, if it can be manufactured at all. We're fortunate. We, most of us, like what we do here. I mean this is fun. This is basketball. Programs like the WNBA Summer Jam are enjoyable for us as well as for the kids who participate. It's not that difficult to become passionate about what we do.

More important, our staff must know about all aspects and components of our product to effectively communicate with partners and co-workers. Each project is filled with multiple levels of execution, many of which are specialized and not applicable to all audiences, but critical to the overall program.

Step 7: Practice Individually

In an oral presentation, all persons need to rehearse their individual segments of the talk. Knowing what you know and knowing the sequence of what you intend to say does not necessarily translate into a quality presentation. Team members need to practice their parts.

Step 8: Practice the Team Presentation

In an oral presentation, the team needs to rehearse the presentation not only individually but as a team. This should be a "dress" rehearsal. That is, it should include all visuals, and, if possible, practice should be in the actual room where you will be presenting. You may not need to actually "dress" as you would for the talk, but your group would want to discuss how you expect people to be attired if the group desires a similar level of formality.

The rehearsal should include a simulation of the Q-and-A session if such a session will be part of the presentation.

Step 9: Evaluation

It is wise to conduct a self-evaluation of your team's interactions. This is recommended so that during your discussions you can rectify any problems. Also, an evaluation of the team and its presentation after the work has been completed can be helpful when you are next assigned a team project.

SUMMARY: A TOOLBOX

- Meetings are both problematic and necessary for effective organizational communication.
- Successful communication in groups requires:
  - Awareness of common conflicts that affect all groups.
  - Identification of conflicts and counterproductive tendencies that are typical of your group.
  - A willingness to work in order to overcome these problems.
- Intervention techniques can be used to:
  - Increase participation.
  - Reduce personality tension.
  - Increase the quality and quantity of ideas.
  - Reduce tensions associated with meeting procedure.
- Some intervention techniques include:
  - Buzz groups: to increase participation
  - Risk technique: to reduce "groupthink"
  - General procedural model: to decrease procedural conflict
  - Brainstorming/brainwriting: to increase creativity

REVIEW AND DISCUSSION QUESTIONS

1. What are the sources of primary tensions?
2. Why do secondary tensions surface in the organizations to which you belong?
3. Why do you find the results of the Asch studies surprising or not surprising?
4. Is it inevitable that groups will be burdened by social loafers? Explain.
5. Of the intervention techniques discussed in this chapter which are likely to:
   a. Involve communication apprehensives
   b. Avoid procedural tension

    c. Reduce equity tensions

    d. Increase substantive conflict

6. What are the benefits and drawbacks of problem-solving techniques that involve division of labor?

7. Describe the type of leader you find to be the most effective.

8. In your experience, what makes team presentations more challenging than simple team interactions? If your group was required to submit a paper and make a presentation, what additional sources of tension would the presentation requirement create?

GROUP/ROLE-PLAY

In a group of four to six, review the issues surrounding the case that begins this chapter. Attempt to gain consensus regarding the questions at the end of the case.

- For the role-playing exercise, one member of the group assumes the role of Sweeney. The others assume the role of Sweeney's department members.
- Role-play a face-to-face meeting between Sweeney and his employees. Assume he calls this separate meeting (different from the regular ones) specifically to discuss what occurred and to both apologize and explain why he did what he did.
- Make a presentation as a group that explains your assessment of the Sweeney case.

PART **3**

CONTEMPORARY ISSUES

Chapter **9**

Intercultural Communication and the Organization

Chapter in a Nutshell

Our world is shrinking. "Foreign" countries are increasingly less foreign. It can be cheaper to fly roundtrip from Boston to Ireland than it is to fly back and forth from Boston to New York. Because of

"*. . . too many American business people are not aware of the importance of understanding cultural differences. Business is Business they think. And they are wrong.*"[1]

the ease of travel, the pervasiveness of communication technology, and economic reliance on other countries, the societies of the twenty-first century are, and will continue to be, global and multicultural in a way that is more obvious than ever before. The effects of cultural diversity on organizations are significant. In this chapter we will examine intercultural communication in terms of why it is important for organizational success in this era of globalization and how persons who need to communicate interculturally can do so efficiently.

When you have completed this chapter, you should be able to:

• Explain why intercultural communication is essential for organizational success and organizational communication.
• Describe what we mean by culture and intercultural communication.
• Identify barriers to effective intercultural communication.
• Identify steps that can be used to overcome these barriers.
• Discuss the "Hofstede" dimensions as they apply to organizational contexts.

CASE 9.1
Rando Systems Expands Internationally

Rando Systems, Inc., based in an Atlanta sub-urb, is a developer and marketer of speech recognition software. The company was founded in 1984 and since 1990 has been actively developing and marketing products for foreign consumers—in particular consumers in Western Europe, Australia, New Zealand, South Africa, and Asia. Until recently, all international operations were managed by a small team based in the Atlanta office that worked closely with a network of trusted distributors and resellers.

In the late 1990s the company decided to open commercial offices in France, Germany, and the United Kingdom, staffed with all local employees. These new employees were to take over the sales and marketing activities for Europe and Africa. The company also hired a sales manager based in San Francisco for the developing markets in Asia. Research and development and training/technical support services are still based in the United States at the Atlanta office.

Until the opening of the European and California offices, most organizational communication involved face-to-face discussions, meetings, telephone conversations, and informal sessions such as lunches, after-work drinks, and weekend parties. These types of interactions resulted in a very tightly knit group and a constant flow of information about the market and the peculiarities of the technology. When the UK, French, German, and San Francisco offices were set up and new personnel hired, communication methods became less informal. The company began to use electronic mail extensively. Some people in the Atlanta office said that e-mail was used exclusively. Occasionally, but rarely, overseas managers would come to Atlanta for very brief visits to headquarters. No lengthy training period was set up by the home office to get international personnel acquainted with the teams in the United States.

Many communication inefficiencies occurred in the beginning of the expansion for a few obvious reasons: (1) new personnel had to learn a fairly sophisticated product and the peculiar market of speech recognition, (2) new personnel were unfamiliar with the organization, and (3) time differences. The first two problems would be overcome as time went by, and the time zone factors were easily adjusted to by adapting to different business hours.

However, communication breakdowns persisted. European offices were not on the same e-mail system as the rest of the organization, causing messages to get lost—especially companywide broadcasts. As the European personnel got more involved in the markets, they felt that they had less time available for communication with the San Francisco and Atlanta offices. As a consequence, there was very little information exchange between parallel departments in the United States and Europe. Sales and marketing missed many opportunities for joint sales and marketing efforts, especially with clients that had a global presence. That cost the company several accounts. Also, international service departments, such as training and technical support, found the European personnel unresponsive to solicitations about training needs and scheduling service events for clients. The European office only seemed to be responsive if the need was expressed as urgent. Those in the Atlanta office found the Europeans aloof and inaccessible. It was almost as if the European office envisioned itself as an autonomous entity. The European managers considered their Atlanta counterparts to be dictatorial and oppressive.

To improve communication, Rando Systems built a secure Web site for employees-only use and a parallel one for partners (distributors and resellers). Unfortunately, the site wasn't well maintained and the information was not updated regularly, so people stopped using it.

Expanding internationally continues to hurt the consistency of Rando's product and services. The problems related to communicating with the European offices have not been resolved and have made it difficult for Rando to maintain what had been an excellent reputation.

- What are the roots of Rando's communication problems?

- What could Rando Systems have done before the international expansion to reduce the communication problem?
- Given the present situation, what can Rando do to improve communication between the Atlanta and European offices?

Why Study Intercultural Communication?

Over forty years ago, media scholar Marshall McLuhan argued that we would soon be living in what he called a "global village."[3] McLuhan felt that media innovation would make our planet akin to the small villages of earlier centuries.

We are there.

"Columbus reported to his king and queen that the world was round, and he went down in history as the man who first made this discovery. I returned home and shared my discovery only with my wife and only in a whisper. 'Honey' I confided, 'I think the world is flat.'"[2]

—THOMAS FRIEDMAN, *The World Is Flat*

In 2009 we find out about events in Iraq more swiftly than our ancestors discovered what had taken place in the town square. We can e-mail colleagues on other continents as quickly as we can walk across the street and ask our neighbor to borrow a quart of milk. We can fly to other countries and meet members of other cultures as easily as we can drive to visit our relatives at holiday times.

On January 15, 2009, a commercial airplane crash-lands safely in the Hudson River in New York. Within minutes, information about the event and pilot is posted on Internet search engines. Depress a button on a television remote control device and viewers in any time zone can observe newscasters interviewing unnerved passengers who had miraculously escaped. Flip a switch on a radio on the banks of the Columbia River in Oregon and hear network talk radio hosts speak to eyewitnesses to the landing. People in Seattle, Japan, Singapore, Nigeria, and Atlanta can discover what is occurring at the crash site faster than employees working at the U.S. Tennis Association Center—located less than ten minutes from the emergency landing. The world is shrinking. We are a global village.

In Thomas Friedman's bestselling book, the author argued that now "the world is flat." It is. The ramifications of living in a global village where the world is flat extend to organizational contexts and organizational communication. Organizations are "going global," that is, expanding beyond their domestic borders, because it is easier to "go global" in the twenty-first century. However, expanding operations to other nations means that organizations have to concurrently expand their communication capabilities so that they can interact efficiently with their foreign offices and markets. Within domestic offices the shrinking world coupled with greater employment opportunities has created a work environment that is increasingly pluralistic. The demographics of the workforce in the twenty-first century reflect far more heterogeneity than those of your grandparents' and even your parents' generations.

The workforce diversity as well as the proliferation of multinational businesses compels organizations to expand their capabilities in terms of communication. You may recall the transmission model of communication discussed in Chapter 1. Using this model we know that there is communication interference in any interaction that can preclude the accurate receipt of information. The problems of communication are exacerbated in intercultural contexts. There is, simply, more

Organizations in the twenty-first century are far more culturally diverse than those fifty or even ten to fifteen years ago.

communication noise. We also discussed the constitutive model of communication in Chapter 1. Understanding the effects of multiethnic work populations is important from this perspective as well. The disparate values, priorities, and perspectives represented by diverse races, religions, and nationalities—reflected in communication behavior—will have an effect on an organization's evolving culture and formation, especially when that organization had been used to homogeneity.

If we are interested in studying organizational communication, we must acknowledge the mosaic that is the contemporary workforce, identify the challenges of diversity for efficient organizational communication, and examine how these intercultural challenges within organizational contexts can be addressed.

Effective Intercultural Communication Has Become Essential

DeVito has identified several reasons to explain why intercultural communication has become an imperative in contemporary society. Among these are mobility, economic and political interdependence, and communication technology.[4] Let's examine each of these three factors.

Mobility

Over the last twenty years my university has established an extensive study abroad program that allows qualified undergraduates to travel and study at any one of thirty-one colleges representing nineteen separate countries. This program was set up by college administrators who were able to easily travel to other universities, establish relationships, and discuss the mutual benefits of "study abroad." Our students can journey to these other countries because air travel has become relatively inexpensive and no longer foreign. An advertisement suggests that it is just as cost-effective to fly from Boston to Ireland as it is to take the Boston-to-New York airline shuttle.

Simply put, time and distance no longer restrict intercultural encounters as they once did. Individuals have tremendous mobility, and the direction and composition of organizations reflect that mobility.

Economic and Political Interdependence

To some extent the countries of the world have always been economically and politically interdependent. However, with the expansion of military capabilities, international safety is largely a function of economic and political cooperation.

Economic interdependence is apparent nearly any time you glance at the label of a garment and notice where the product was manufactured. On the morning news, North Americans are likely to hear how the Asian markets closed, and how the Asian markets closed is likely to affect what happens in the economies of the West. The Middle East countries, beset with historical tensions, are the focus of international concern in large part because of the political and economic significance of the region.[5] During President Obama's first day as chief executive, he phoned leaders of each political constituency in the Middle East as an indication of how significant it is for there be to peace in that region for reasons that reflect the world's interdependence.

Clearly, the countries and cultures of the world are interdependent. Therefore, we must be concerned with how we communicate to those persons, countries, and cultures with whom we are so interdependent.

Communication Technology

How many people do you know who do not have an e-mail address? The Maytag repairman used to be lonely. Soon, the loneliest folks are likely to be postal clerks. It is as simple to transmit a message overseas as it is to scrawl a note to your roommates reminding them to pay their share of the rent. Electronic mail and teleconferencing have reduced barriers to communicating that had restricted the frequency of intercultural communication. Costs associated with international telephoning have been reduced so that it no longer is prohibitive to phone persons in localities thousands of miles away from our homes. Satellite television transmissions make it as simple to witness demonstrators in Gaza as it is to observe the pedestrian traffic outside of your window.

If we needed a catalyst to improve intercultural communication capabilities, we now have such a catalyst. Friedman writes, ". . . the lever that is enabling individuals and groups to go global so easily and seamlessly is not horsepower, and not hardware, but software, all sorts of new applications—in conjunction with the creation of global fiber-optic network that has made us all next-door neighbors"[6] Technology has put us in easy contact with people from other worlds. We need to know how to communicate with them.

What Do We Mean by Culture?

We discussed the word culture as it pertains to organizational culture in Chapter 7. The word has a similar meaning in the analysis of intercultural communication. There are distinctions, however. Let's examine the word culture in the context of intercultural interaction.

As we stated earlier, Martin and Nakayama define culture as the "learned patterns of behavior and attitudes shared by a group of people."[7] Haviland writes that culture refers to the "abstract values, beliefs, and perceptions of the world that lie behind people's behavior, and which are reflected in their behavior."[8] Triandis and Albert, writing in the *Handbook of Organizational Communication*, use Herkovitz's definition that culture is the "human made part of the environment" and go on to clarify that by *the human made part of the environment*, they refer to the subjective culture of "norms, roles, belief systems, laws, and values" of a particular group.[9]

Essentially, culture *refers to the multiple perspectives a group has on the world and worldly phenomena.* The Triandis and Albert description is helpful as it breaks down cultural perspectives into categories of these "multiple perspectives."

- **Norms.** What does a group consider normal and abnormal? Is having a monogamous relationship "normal" in your culture? Is rearing children before the age of thirty normal? If your Uncle Willie is forty-five and unmarried, is he considered peculiar or normal in your culture?
- **Roles.** What are the responsibilities of certain persons in society? What is the role, for example, of the husband, or eldest son, or educators in a community?
- **Belief Systems.** Does the group believe in monotheism? Life after death? That the land belongs to the creator and therefore no human can really "own" land?
- **Values.** Does the group consider education more valuable than wealth? Is a high school athlete more respected than someone who excels in academic examinations?
- **Laws.** What are the laws of the group that, if violated, are punishable either by governments or the governance systems of the culture?

Culture is learned. It is not biologically transmitted.[10] *Enculturation* refers to the process of how one learns the perspectives of the culture. *Acculturation* refers to the ways your culture is modified by exposure to other cultures.

Elashmawi and Harris identify several ways in which cultural differences are manifested in people:

- Language
- Nonverbal messages
- Space and time orientation
- Patterns of thinking
- Self-images
- Aesthetics[11]

Take a moment to consider this list and complete the Applying the Principles exercise that follows.

Intercultural Communication in Organizational Contexts

Defining Intercultural Communication

Communication quality is affected by the abilities of communicators to overcome impediments, which collectively are called "noise." What makes intercultural communication especially problematic is that in intercultural contexts there is the possibility of additional noise that is a function of the disparate cultures of source and receiver. Samovar and Porter, in *Communication Between Cultures*, define intercultural communication as "communication between people whose cultural perceptions and symbol systems are distinct enough to alter the communication event."[12] Essentially, intercultural communication is a more complex form of interpersonal communication. It's more complex because there are more variables that can serve as impediments.

One step that can be taken to reduce intercultural noise involves becoming aware of how frequently we participate in intercultural interactions. This can be valuable because it may highlight how many of our interactions are, in fact, intercultural and how many are, consequently, affected by additional culture-related impediments.

Applying the Principles—Test Yourself

Do Cultures Really Differ?

1. Review Elashmawi's and Harris's list. Do you agree with the categories? Do cultures differ in these ways?

   • Do some cultural groups use language differently than others?
   • Are some nonverbal messages meaningful and/or appropriate in one culture and not another?
   • Do different groups of people have different perceptions of space needs or the importance of time?

• Do people in different cultures simply think differently?
• Can you identify cultural group members on the basis of how persons perceive themselves?
• Do members of cultures have diverse perspectives on what constitutes beauty?

2. Do any of these factors create problems for intercultural communication in organizations?

Types of Intercultural Exchanges and Problems

We engage in intercultural interactions regularly. We may be involved in communications with people from different countries, races, and religions. We may interact with those who are members of our own country but are representative of different regions of the country. We may communicate with those who share our own basic religious beliefs but are followers of different sects within the religion.

The list below identifies different types of intercultural interactions and suggests how pervasive intercultural communications are in our daily activities.

- An African American conversing with a Caucasian
- An African American speaking with a Kenyan
- An American speaking with a Brazilian
- A rural Arkansan speaking with an urban citizen of San Francisco
- A Hispanic corporate executive communicating with an Anglo executive
- A Canadian from Toronto communicating with a Canadian from the Gaspe
- An ardent red state Republican speaking with an ardent blue state Democrat
- A Jew speaking with a Christian
- A Hasidic Jew speaking with a Reform Jew

All of these are examples of intercultural communication because in each situation, cultural factors will likely create additional obstacles for the communicators. Because of the frequency of intercultural interactions in organizations (and elsewhere), organizational men and women are occasionally, if not regularly, faced with communication challenges related to cultural differences.

Take a moment to consider the three scenarios presented in the following exercise. How would you respond to each situation?

Applying the Principles—Test Yourself

How would you handle these situations?

1) Prior to Ramadan, Sophia, a practicing Moslem, approaches her manager with a request. During the holy month she wishes to be excused during portions of the day so that she may go to a local mosque to pray as, she claims, she is required to do during this period. Assume that Sophia is a vital member of the organizational team. If she is to leave the office, the manager will have to pay another person to assume Sophia's duties during her absence. Further assume that typically requests for personal time off during the day are not honored at this company except in cases of illness or family emergency.

   1. *How should the manager respond?*
   2. *How should the manager communicate the response?*

2) A bank manager is faced with a problem. She has hired several tellers whose primary language is Spanish. These persons are excellent employees. They are responsible, honest, and capable. When they speak to customers they demonstrate that their English is effective. However, when they speak among themselves they always speak in Spanish. If a customer has a question that one teller cannot answer, the teller will use Spanish to ask another one of her Spanish-speaking colleagues about the customer's inquiry.

   A few customers have approached the manager and have expressed concern. These customers feel uncomfortable not knowing what the tellers are saying about their accounts.

   In addition, some of the non–Spanish-speaking tellers have approached the manager about a similar concern. They fear that the Spanish-speaking tellers are talking about them. Both the non-Spanish tellers and the customers have asked the manager to forbid the Hispanic employees from using Spanish at work.

   1. *Should the manager request that Spanish not be spoken at work?*
   2. *How should the manager communicate her decision?*

3) A professor in a course entitled Contemporary Drama passes out a syllabus that contains the reading list for the semester. An African American student raises his hand and (politely) comments that all of the plays on the list have been written by authors of European descent. The student asks if there could be some representation of authors of African descent in the course. The professor (politely) comments that the semester is only so long and that all of the plays on the list are "must-reads." After class, the student approaches the chairperson of the department and restates his request.

   1. *Should the chairperson honor the student's request?*
   2. *How should the chairperson communicate her reaction to the student?*
   3. *How should the chairperson communicate her reaction to the professor?*

Barriers to Effective Intercultural Communication

There are a number of communication noises that are specific to, or become more prominent within, intercultural contexts. Let's consider a few of these intercultural barriers.

- Perceptual disparity
- Ethnocentrism
- Language dissimilarity
- Nonverbal dissimilarity

Perception

Singer defines perception as the process by which an individual selects, evaluates, and organizes stimuli from the external world.[13] In any interpersonal exchange the selectivity process inherent in perception can create or reduce communication noise. In intercultural contexts, selective perception and retention can be a function of disparate belief and value systems.

Assume that during your senior year in high school you met a young man from another country. Assume that one day you began to discuss your post–high school plans with this new acquaintance. Further, assume that you said to him that you "could not wait" until high school was over because you wanted to "get out of the house" and "away from your mother and father."

In many parts of the United States such an expression would not be particularly unusual. However, in other countries where family and respect for parents is an inviolable component of the belief system, your comment might have made you seem irresponsible as opposed to adventurous. In an intercultural context, your message may have become distorted because of the perceptual lens of your culturally different receiver. While it may have been clear that you wanted to leave your home and go off to college, you may also have unwittingly communicated that you were a ne'er-do-well and would soon be a community pariah. Of course, you would not have likely become a pariah, because your expressed desires would have been normal within your own culture, but your acquaintance might not have seen things that way, and his cultural vision may have affected (a) his notion of who you were and (b) the subsequent interactions you two may have had.

Consider some work-related examples.

(1) Assume that during a work break, you are having an informal conversation with a colleague who is new to this country. During the conversation you make a disparaging comment about your boss. If your colleague comes from a culture where employees consider it a duty to respect and honor one's employer, your colleague may attach more meaning than you intended to your casual remark.

(2) Assume that you insist on being clear and certain about facts and deadlines relating to a task assignment. This may be perplexing to another who perceives your insistence as peculiar, given his orientation that considers ambiguity to be normal and time relatively unimportant.

In short, cultural orientation can affect perception. "We experience everything in the world not as it is—but only as the world comes to us through our sensory receptors."[14] Our culture affects our sensory receptors.

Ethnocentrism

"The world teems with people who are sensitive to prejudice only when it is against them, not when they are inflicting it on others."[15]

The bane of intercultural communication and a barrier that is particularly problematic in businesses that expand globally is called "ethnocentrism." As we discussed in Chapter 8, ethnocentrism refers to the perspective that your worldview is superior to another's worldview. It is one thing to have beliefs and value systems that are different from others and quite another to assume that those who don't share your beliefs are misguided. If one consciously or subconsciously assumes that one's cultural group's worldview is superior to the perspectives of another's, any interaction with members of other groups will be ineluctably fraught with communication noise. An ethnocentric communicator implicitly considers alternative perspectives to be substandard. No person warms to the notion that his or her cultural orientations are inferior. Inevitably, then, ethnocentric perspectives create cacophonous interference.

Consider the following exercise. It may help you assess the extent of your own ethnocentrism. Think about a religious, national, racial, or ethnic group with which you identify.

- How would members of that group and you react to the following statements?
- More significantly, how would members of that group and you react to other cultural groups that, generally, take different positions regarding the statements?

1. Getting a college education is essential for individual success.
2. Men can engage in intimate relationships promiscuously.
3. Women should not engage in intimate relationships promiscuously.
4. A man should be a breadwinner for the family.
5. Organized religion is the "opiate of the masses," that is, religion is a drug for fools.
6. Gambling on sporting events reflects irresponsible behavior.
7. Business people should wear formal attire at the workplace.
8. Love is more important than money.
9. Athletic achievements are as valuable as academic achievements.
10. A female child should not move out of the parents' home until she is married. However, a male child may move out of the parents' home before he is married.
11. Cheating in business is acceptable if one can get away with it.
12. Adult men should not cry in public.
13. Some colors are appropriate for little boys, and other colors are appropriate for little girls.
14. Pornography is an abomination.
15. Heterosexual promiscuity is as good or bad as homosexual promiscuity.
16. A person who works hard, regardless of salary, should be respected.
17. Capitalism is a better economic system than any other.
18. Osama bin Laden is the Hitler of the twenty-first century.
19. Countries that win territory during wars should not have to return the land.
20. In the world of business, making a profit is the only real organizational consideration.

Assume that a few of the items in the above list generate some strong emotional reactions from members of a particular ethnic group. Further, assume that the same items generate either little reaction or the opposite reaction from members of a different group. Might it be difficult for the people in the former group to respect people in the latter group who held such disparate opinions? Might it be difficult to communicate with members of another group on *any matter* if one internalized the notion that people within this other group were generally misguided and, perhaps, intellectually or ethically inferior?

In any context, disparate attitudes between participants can undermine attempts to communicate effectively. However, if from the start of any intercultural encounter you assume that the person with whom you are conversing is intellectually or ethically inferior because of disparate worldviews, then nearly any communicative attempt will be drowned out by deafening noise. Even an innocent comment like, "How are you, Armindo?" is subject to distortion if Armindo believes that you perceive his cultural background to be inferior to your own.

Effects of Language

An obvious barrier to intercultural communication relates to the use of common language. Simply, a Spaniard may have difficulty speaking to a Finn if the two do not share the same language. Language issues need not only pertain to common languages, but also to the use of slang, regional expressions, and terms that have high levels of abstraction.

As it relates to intercultural communication, a more subtle language factor is related to a theory referred to as linguistic relativity.

Linguistic relativity assumes that words affect our ability to conceptualize, i.e., the way we think is dependent upon the language that we have. In the language of academics, "The lexicon of a given language shapes our thought processes by providing a specific repertory of cognitive schemata."[16] Simply, a cultural group may actually think in a way that is distinctive because their language is distinctive. If conceptualization is dependent on language, then language differences do not only make understanding what we *say* difficult, but language differences make it difficult for people to conceptualize phenomena similarly.

This can be a complicated idea to grasp. Some examples may be helpful for clarification.

In a family of several siblings, a Chinese family member doesn't simply refer to a sister as a sister, but rather older sister, or small older sister—the former meaning the sister who is the eldest and the latter meaning a sister who is older than the person with the sibling, but not as old as the eldest sister. Because of the specificity of language in regard to siblings and children, there is, it is argued, a clearer sense of the importance of family, and individual roles of family members, in Chinese culture than in cultures that simply refer to sisters, regardless of relative age, as sisters.[17] Is it possible that a conversation about filial responsibility that takes place between a Chinese employee and an American employee could become complicated because of conceptual variation based on language?

Another regularly cited example has to do with the numbers of words for snow that Eskimos are said to have. It has been argued that Eskimos, who have several words for snow, think of snow differently than persons from cultures with only one word for snow.[18] The Eskimo/snow example has been challenged,[19] but the point remains the same. If a group has multiple words for a concept, does that group conceptualize differently than a group that has fewer words for the same concept? Do multiple words with shades of conceptual differences create the possibility of greater and more sophisticated conceptualization?

Ludwig Wittgenstein is famous for commenting that "the limits of my language are the limits of my world." Is this true? Does language determine the scope and periphery of our vision?

Consider some organizational examples:

Could you understand the problems related to dealing with implacable employees if you did not have the word implacable in your vocabulary?
Could you settle disputes more effectively if you understood the word rapprochement?
Could you understand the dimensions of ethical communication without the word probity?

Is it true, as the theory of linguistic relativity suggests, that language affects our sense of the world, and therefore, groups of people who do not share the same language will inevitably have different perspectives?

These questions have no irrefutable answers, yet it can be valuable, or at least interesting, to consider the effects of language on thought and intercultural relationships.

Nonverbal Disparities

Nonverbal messages vary significantly on the basis of culture. Many research articles on intercultural communication are filled with examples of gestures that mean one thing in one culture but something quite different in others. For example, the "ok sign" commonly used in the United States is an example of a gesture that has various meanings depending on the country. "In France it means zero. In Japan it is

The meaning of nonverbal gestures and behavior can vary, depending on one's cultural background and orientation.

a symbol of money and in Brazil it carries a vulgar connotation."[20] There are "dos-and-don'ts" papers published for businesspeople who are traveling overseas, reminding them to be cognizant of nonverbal differences. "In Indonesia don't touch anyone on the head nor cross your feet at a business meeting. In India, an up and down nod can mean 'no' while a side to side toss of the head can mean 'yes.'"[21]

An *emblem* is a nonverbal motion or gesture for which there is a discrete one-to-one relationship between that motion/gesture and a unit of meaning. A gesture that is emblematic in one culture may well be emblematic in another culture. However, the meanings of the emblems could be different. Also, what is not emblematic in one culture may well be emblematic in another. In short, one cannot assume a universal nonverbal language.

In the following section we will look at some specific applications of intercultural communication to organizational contexts. We will discuss:

- Structural approaches to multinational expansion.
- Disparate perspectives of workers in various countries.
- Some suggestions for overcoming barriers to intercultural communication in organizational contexts.

Approaches to Multinational Expansion

Adler has identified five structural orientations of multinational organizations:

- Cultural dominance
- Cultural accommodation
- Cultural compromise
- Cultural avoidance
- Cultural synergy[22]

The cultural dominance model assumes a monocultural style and, as one might predict, encounters resistance. When this orientation is in evidence, the parent organization superimposes its culture on the subsidiary offices in other nations. Despite the clear problems with it, the cultural dominance model is the most common of the approaches.[23]

The cultural accommodation model is in contrast to the cultural dominance approach. This model assumes that a company should accept and assume the cultural values of the host country. Those who follow this model do "what the Romans do" while they are in Rome.

The cultural compromise orientation requires an attempt to identify the divergent cultural orientations among managers who represent the organization. However, only the similarities among the disparate managers are used in the formation of policies. The compromise model is more sensitive than the dominance model in that it is, at the very least, conscious of, and sensitive to, cultural diversity.

The cultural avoidance orientation is, indeed, an avoidance approach. Those who follow this model pretend as if there is no distinction between the cultures.

The cultural synergy model is, as the name implies, a synergistic approach to multinational operations. The policies and procedures of the organization are not superimposed by the parent organization or only a reflection of similar perspectives, but an amalgam of the various inputs of the evolving multifaceted organization.

What problems can the cultural dominance model create? What problems can the cultural accommodation approach create? Do you think that the preference of the dominance model is a function of ignorance? indifference? ethnocentrism? How would critical theorists react to the cultural dominance model?

The Hofstede Studies

Geert Hofstede conducted a study that is cited in many books and articles about intercultural differences in organizations. His study (a) suggests that there are perceptual differences based on culture and, moreover, (b) implies that these perceptual differences can account for misunderstanding and intercultural tensions in organizational contexts.[24]

Hofstede distributed surveys to over 117,000 employees in sixty-six different countries.[25] All of the respondents worked for the same multinational organization. The goal of the research was to see whether attitudes toward similar phenomena related to organizations and organizational work would vary depending on country and culture. Hofstede found that there were differences and he initially categorized the differences into four groupings: (1) uncertainty avoidance, (2) power distance, (3) individualism vs. collectivism, and (4) masculinity vs. femininity. Subsequently, Hofstede added a fifth category of perceptual difference. He called this fifth area long-term versus short-term orientation.

Uncertainty avoidance refers to the extent to which members of a cultural group require certainty and disdain ambiguity and uncertainty. A culture high in uncertainty avoidance would seek formal regulations and tolerate less in the way of aberrant behaviors and personalities. Low-uncertainty-avoidance cultures are less concerned with specificity. In a meeting, members of high-uncertainty-avoidance cultures might want to "nail down" all relevant information, whereas members from low-uncertainty-avoidance cultures might be content with greater degrees of abstraction.

Power distance refers to the acceptance of supervisor/subordinate authority distinctions in organizations. A high-power-distance culture would respect superiors and have disdain for those who challenge them. Low-power-distance societies would have little inherent respect for authority. If an organizational leader were to address a group from a high-power-distance society, that leader would be regarded more deferentially as a matter of course. However, if the same leader were to speak in a low-power-distance country, speaker authority would not be elevated solely on the basis of organizational role.

The category called *individualistic vs. collective* relates to whether persons in the group value free-spirited independence or community cooperation and compromise. Citizens of the United States who made popular the music of Sammy Davis Jr. singing "I Gotta Be Me" and Frank Sinatra crooning "My Way" are typically high on the individualistic side of the individualistic collective continuum. A mission statement created for an individualistic society might emphasize the respect for individual self-expression and creativity, whereas a collective society is likely to consider a "mission" emphasizing teamwork and cooperation more consistent with their cultural orientation.

The *masculine/feminine* scale pertains to whether the dominant values of the society emphasize assertiveness or nurturance. Adler and Rodman consider the labels of "masculine/feminine" inappropriate and counterproductive to a discussion of intercultural communication. They have changed the title of the masculine/feminine index label to task vs. social orientation.[26] A high masculine or task-oriented society would admire a committee leader who takes control of the session and is clearly the committee chief, whereas a feminine or social orientation society would identify with a committee leader who sought to make sure all participants were comfortable in their role as members of the group.

The *long-term vs. short-term orientation* category, as indicated above, was added after the initial four. The distinction between long-term and short-term orientation is likely to be what readers imagine it to be. A long-term orientation values thrift and persistence. A short-term orientation is concerned with issues and emphasis on immediacy.

Hofstede ranked the countries he explored in terms of those strongest in each of the categories. Table 9.1 shows the top four countries in each of the areas.

Triandis and Albert argue that the Hofstede dimensions have predictive value in that they can help multinational organizations anticipate how members of certain cultures "will respond to social situations."[27] This makes some sense and highlights the main value of Hofstede's study. At the very least, Hofstede has demonstrated that what some persons may assume are universal values and perspectives are not universal. For multinational organizations and for domestic organizations with a diverse workforce, it is important to consider that different perspectives are related to the same phenomena. Samovar and Porter suggest that these culturally different perspectives affect interactions dealing with business protocol, the use of time, and business negotiation.[28] Others comment that recognizing these cultural disparities affects greetings, telephone communication, cross-cultural meetings, presentations, and written communications.[29]

Suggestions for Overcoming Barriers

We have identified a number of obstacles to effective intercultural communication. A review of these follows:

(1) There are verbal and nonverbal differences among cultural groups. These language barriers range from the existence of separate language systems, to diverse meanings attributed to the same words, to varied interpretations of nonverbal behaviors. These language differences can make it difficult for managers to communicate with members of different cultural groups.

(2) There are perceptual disparities—people from different backgrounds tend to perceive the same phenomena in various ways. Cultural groups have different "worldviews," and these disparities

Table 9.1 Hofstede's Distinctions

High Power Distance	Low Power Distance
Philippines	Austria
Mexico	Israel
Venezuela	Denmark
India	New Zealand
High Masculinity (task orientation)	**High Femininity (social orientation)**
Japan	Sweden
Austria	Norway
Venezuela	Netherlands
Italy	Denmark
Individualism	**Collectivism**
United States	Venezuela
Australia	Colombia
Great Britain	Pakistan
Canada	Peru
High Uncertainty Avoidance	**Low Uncertainty Avoidance**
Greece	Singapore
Portugal	Denmark
Belgium	Sweden
Japan	Hong Kong
Long-Term Orientation	**Short-Term Orientation**
China	Sierra Leone
Hong Kong	Nigeria
Taiwan	Ghana
Japan	Philippines

can create confusion and/or disrespect. Disrespect or chauvinism can breed ethnocentrism—a perspective on ethnicity that assumes that your group and your way of perceiving phenomena is superior to another's. Ethnocentrism is toxic to intercultural communication as it immediately places the perceived other in a position of diminished credibility and legitimacy.

(3) Finally, there is ignorance. In addition to language, perception, and ethnocentrism, a barrier to effective intercultural communication is simply not knowing what you don't know. Asante argues, for example, that some persons have a "peculiar arrogance, the arrogance of not knowing that they do not know what it is that they do not know, yet they speak as if they know what all of us need to know."[30] This arrogance is the marriage of ignorance and ethnocentrism—a diabolical amalgam for intercultural communication in any context and certainly in organizational contexts.

The question becomes this: How can people overcome these obstacles?

Following Prescriptions

There is a distinction between having a prescription and following a prescription. It is easy to enumerate the steps for many tasks, yet sometimes difficult to follow the steps. Many people, and certainly any nutritionist, can explain how to lose weight. If you eat healthy foods and consume fewer calories than you expend, you will lose weight. Yet for many individuals the process is extraordinarily difficult. If you have ever tried to lose weight, you know that it can be painstaking and frustrating work. Weight loss businesses are lucrative *not* because the entrepreneurs who run them have a secret prescription, but because it is so very hard for so many people to follow the prescription. Indeed, if the formula was easy to follow, then these businesses would have a limited clientele.

Similarly, solving intercultural communication tension is difficult *not* because there is a secret regarding how to become effective in these contexts, but because the process of adhering to the "how-to" steps can be more difficult than it seems. Often people get off the track. One might know that it is important to adopt an egalitarian as opposed to an ethnocentric frame when engaging in intercultural interactions. Yet it may be difficult to shed your ethnocentric perspectives. You may know that communication noise is a function of perceptual differences, but you may become fatigued straining to view the world from another's perceptual lens when you feel as if the other is not making a similar effort.

Overcoming the barriers to intercultural communication is hard work. The formula is not difficult. The prescription, in fact, is remarkably basic, as will become apparent in the next few pages. The challenge relates to being willing to follow the steps.

Overcoming the Barriers: Learn About Other Cultures and Cultural Diversity

In their book, *Multicultural Management*, Elashmawi and Harris identify several characteristics of "multicultural managers"—people who can overcome cultural noises in order to communicate effectively in organizations. The essence of their argument is that multicultural management requires learning about diversity.[31] Specifically they suggest that multicultural managers:

- *Acquire multicultural competencies and skills, including foreign languages.*

The authors use a tree metaphor to explain their notion of cultural competence. A tree is a function of its roots. People, similarly, are a product of cultural roots. A culturally competent manager is someone who is aware of her or his own roots and is willing to learn about the foundations of others with whom they interact. This includes learning and respecting customs, norms, values, and, to some extent, language systems of the other cultural groups represented in the manager's organization.

DeWine comments that international business managers identify "showing respect" as a very important managerial skill for U.S. international business success.[32] Demonstrations of respect are reflected by learning about your employees' customs and respecting those customs. Ruben has indicated that respect can be demonstrated through nonverbal gestures, suggesting interest and awareness of cultural rules.[33]

To show appropriate respect, endeavor to learn the nonverbal language of others with whom you will be in contact when working in countries that are foreign to you. Try to learn the language, or about the language, of the countries where you will be working. Just because "everyone there

Ethical Probe

Cultural Artifacts

Organizations select paintings, furniture, and other furnishings to make their place of business look attractive both for clients as well as for those who work in the organization. Does the organization have an ethical responsibility to decorate their spaces with sensitivity to the culture of the employees? For example:

- Assume an organization, ACME, is composed of thousands of workers representing diverse ethnic groups and religions. Assume there is a sculpture of what appears to be a factory worker in the main hallway of the company building. At the base of the sculpture is a plaque that reads: the Spirit of ACME.

Should the sculpture be of a man if more women than men work at the company? Is there anything unethical about that sculpture being of a white male Caucasian if the only white male Caucasians in the company are the executives?

- Assume that a company is owned and administered by people from the United States, but its offices and factories are in Panama. Should the decorations in the offices and factories reflect the culture of those persons from Panama who are working in the factories? Is there anything unethical about the walls being covered with photos of the Statue of Liberty, the Golden Gate Bridge, the U.S. Capitol, and the president of the United States?

speaks English" doesn't eliminate the need to become familiar with the host language. Making no attempt to use the language of the host can, in and of itself, be a sign of disrespect.

- *Become students of worldwide human relations and values.*

This item is an extension of the previous one. A multicultural manager becomes a student, one who not only focuses on specific needs pertaining to managing a diverse workforce, but someone who continually attempts to broaden her or his knowledge base as it relates to diversity. The idea is that the more knowledgeable one becomes regarding global diversity, the more sensitive one will be when dealing with any one particular situation.

- *Think beyond local perceptions and transform stereotypes into positive views of people.*

This is certainly easy enough to write, and more difficult to accomplish. The idea is to work toward adopting a perspective that embraces diversity.

- *Become open and flexible in dealing with diversities in people.*

This is another item that is easy to write and difficult to accomplish. Yet the authors' point is important here. It is one thing to become knowledgeable and another to apply your knowledge appropriately when "dealing with diversity."

Rancer et al. discuss two types of training that can be used to assist those who seek to become more aware of other cultures. *Cultural specific training* educates motivated learners on the mores, attitudes, and worldview of a particular culture that individuals will be visiting or working in. *Cultural general training* refers to training where persons become more aware of cultural issues by learning about one's own culture and intercultural variables.[34]

Novinger, in *Intercultural Communication*, writes about the advantages of learning about other cultures. She argues that education can preempt default tendencies that are counterproductive in the intercultural context.

> The raising of one's culture consciousness through education . . . gives the intercultural communicator the freedom to consciously choose behavior and attitude in personal interaction, rather than submitting to the control of subconscious cultural norms and just reacting, usually negatively, to any deviation from these norms.[35]

Earlier in this chapter you were asked to consider the roots of cultural dominance in organizations. Novinger's remarks are worth considering particularly in this context.

If education provides the "freedom to consciously choose behavior," then ignorance coupled with the diverse perceptual perspectives described by Hofstede may deprive communicators of this "freedom." If people are inclined to "react, usually negatively, to any deviation" from their own cultural perspective, that may account for the tendency for persons to assume a culturally dominant posture when interacting with culturally different others.

"The raising of one's culture consciousness through education" is a key factor in the elimination of impediments in the intercultural communication context.

Overcoming the Barriers: Recognize Diversity within Cultural Groups

One problem with cultural specific training, or any attempt to learn about the culture of another group, is that a learner can fall into the trap of assuming that each individual from that culture adheres to the same monolithic value system. While it is important to be sensitive to cultural differences, it is also important to recognize that individuals can vary from the norm.

How would you feel if someone approached you and said, "Oh. You're Catholic. I understand Catholics go to mass regularly and are serious about religion. You, then, must be serious about religion."

It can be annoying to be categorized or generalized into one group. It can be exasperating to have people assume that everyone in that group, and therefore you, thinks and acts the same.

This renders the task of becoming sensitive to diversity a thorny challenge. On the one hand, you are encouraged to become aware of cultural mores, and on the other, you are discouraged from assuming that all members of a cultural group behave the same way. It is safe to wager that if you meet a Jewish employee who is wearing a skull cap, he's unlikely to be receptive to attending a welcoming celebration held on a Saturday afternoon, the Jewish Sabbath. However, on the basis of the skull cap one could not determine the employee's nonreligious interests, capabilities, or what his precise position is on contemporary Middle Eastern politics. To attribute prevailing cultural notions to all individuals is as insensitive as ignoring the possibility of cultural differences between you and another person. A component of successful intercultural organizational communication requires taking the time to acknowledge that within cultural groups there are individual differences.

Overcoming the Barriers: Assume an Egalitarian Frame

Understanding the language, mores, attitudes, and customs of another culture is a limited asset in the absence of an egalitarian perspective. The fundamental plank for effective intercultural communication requires that individuals assume, from the start, that all people are inherently equal and that culture in and of itself is not a factor that determines the quality of a person. One need not relinquish one's own cultural perspective in order to treat others as equals. Also, adopting an egalitarian frame does not mean that you must respect and honor a person whose behavior is reprehensible. It means that when you meet another person, from either your own culture or any other, you assume that

Please Visit My Great Aunt

A senior-level American businessperson was working for a three-week period in Italy, where his company had a satellite office. During his stay he was invited to attend the wedding of the daughter of his Italian counterpart. The late afternoon celebration included a sumptuous feast at which the American ate far more than he wished he had. It seemed as if the meal consisted of a series of never-ending courses.

Buoyed by the events of the day and delighted to share his happiness with his new American friend, the Italian asked his guest if he would do him the honor of joining him as he visited his great aunt who lived nearby but had been unable to attend the celebration. To be polite, the American agreed despite the fact that he was feeling very uncomfortable from all that he had consumed at the wedding. The host quickly scribbled the directions to his relative's home and promised to meet the American there shortly after the celebration ended—as soon as he was able to say a private goodbye to his daughter.

The American arrived at the great aunt's home an hour after the wedding concluded. He was welcomed in and was told that the bride's father had yet to arrive. Almost as soon as he sat down in the great aunt's home, the American was asked if he wanted some pasta. The American declined, quickly commenting on how he was stuffed from the plentiful meals served at the wedding. The elderly woman smiled and then a moment later again offered some pasta. Again, the American politely declined, pointing to his burgeoning stomach. The woman asked a third time, and when this third offer was respectfully declined, the great aunt stood up and ordered the American out of her house, saying that anyone who would not eat pasta in her house did not deserve to visit. Hastily, the American apologized and urged the woman to provide some pasta, which he, painfully, consumed.

PRACTITIONER PERSPECTIVE

Steve MacLeod, Senior Vice President

Steve MacLeod worked for the Fluor Corporation for thirty-five years. During this period he spent time serving as the company's president of its Middle East office and also president of the South American office. Mr. MacLeod has lived and worked in Saudi Arabia, Chile, Puerto Rico, and Mexico City as well as several states in the United States. He has traveled extensively throughout the world as a businessperson. The Fluor Corporation, based in California, is one of the world's largest publicly owned engineering and construction organizations. Fluor maintains a network of offices in more than twenty-five countries across six continents. It is consistently rated as one of the world's safest contractors.

As you read through this section, consider the following questions:

- Are people typically ethnocentric in the way that MacLeod describes?
- What do you think about the comments that are bolded in the narrative?
- Do any of the cultural differences he experienced and comments about them surprise you? Have you experienced similar surprises when working with people from other cultures?

Communicating is difficult enough for people who are from the same region, but when you are interacting with business partners who represent different cultures, the task of communicating effectively becomes particularly complicated. When you find yourself in a conference room and each person around the table has a different native tongue—even if all attendees can, and in fact do, speak the same language at the conference session—you are faced with a real challenge. In order to be a successful businessperson in an organization that has a global presence, it's important to be able to meet such challenges.

I think that the first step toward success in these contexts is to acknowledge that there are intercultural differences and to respect the diversity. Too many persons travel to another land and assume that any variation from their orientation renders the people from these lands somehow inferior. "How come these folks don't have a McDonald's in town?" "There are so few people here who speak English." "Gee, these people are not sophisticated." It seems to me that many American businesspeople are egotistical and view the world from their own cultural perspective. It's counterproductive to think and act this way. Also, you miss out on the chance to truly learn about other people.

My attitude when I went to a new country was to consider it a great opportunity. It was a wonderful chance for my family and me to learn about other cultures. You don't want to superimpose your attitudes on the people from another group. That kind of thing is disrespectful, and it creates impediments from the start that can make intercultural communication more difficult than it needs to be. It seems to me that the wisest tack to take was to learn about the group and attempt to meld in. It's a cliché, but "when in Rome. . . ."

Some intercultural issues are difficult to predict. Even the most sensitive and intelligent businessperson may not know the nuances of every cultural group. For example, in America it is quite common for business acquaintances to ask about the spouse and children of a business partner. In Saudi Arabia, such inquiries are considered inappropriate, and it would be offensive to your colleague to pose such a question. While living in Saudi Arabia, I became personal friends with several Arab businessmen, and if I were to meet privately with them I would always ask about their children. However, I would never insult them by asking such a question in the presence of others.

Notions of time vary significantly from region to region. Suppose you and I had an appointment to speak at 11 A.M. today. I could pretty much count on talking with you at 11. In Saudi Arabia, 11 A.M. could mean 10:45, 11:15, or tomorrow. Should one think that there's something inferior about the Saudis because their custom frowns on business partners asking about their family, or because their sense of time is different than it is here? I don't think one should, and, as significantly, it would be counterproductive for businesspeople to make such assumptions.

I don't know how you can function in today's contemporary business arena without being sensitive to intercultural differences. **Actually, I don't know how you can function without being bilingual or trilingual in this global environment.** It's true that the new technology can allow for some greater ease in terms of international communication. For example, I have some software that allows me to translate documents relatively easily. E-mail and teleconferencing also eliminate some problems that distance creates. Yet it's difficult to have a heart-to-heart business negotiation with someone who is a relative stranger unless you can be with that person face to face and demonstrate that you respect that person and his or her culture.

neither you nor your culture is superior. It means that you do not attribute to a member of a group all characteristics associated with particular individuals of that group. The roots of cultural dominance may be ignorance and perceptual disparities, but the fuel that propels cultural dominance is a composite of ignorance and entrenched assumptions about the innate superiority of individual cultures.

Most people assume that they are, indeed, egalitarians. Are you? Do you adopt an egalitarian frame when you meet people:

- From different regions of the country?
- From different countries?
- Of the opposite sex?
- Who have different sexual orientations?
- Who have a different religion?
- Whose race is not the same as yours?
- Who seem to come from a different economic bracket?
- Who have different careers or different career aspirations?

An egalitarian predisposition coupled with a willingness to learn about the customs, language, and mores of another culture are the ingredients for successful intercultural communication in the twenty-first century.

We are a global village. It's easy to write "abandon ethnocentrism" on your workplace "to do" list. It's far more difficult to put in the time, effort, and introspection that will allow you to legitimately check the item off.

SUMMARY: A TOOLBOX

- The world is becoming smaller. Organizational men and women, sooner or later, will need to be adept at communicating interculturally.
- Intercultural communication contexts have additional communication noises. Among these noises are:
  - Perceptual and world view disparities
  - Disparate language systems
  - Disparate nonverbal systems
  - Ethnocentrism
- Overcoming these barriers requires:
  - A willingness to become knowledgeable about others
  - Respect for differences
  - Familiarity with other language systems, nonverbal behaviors, and customs
  - Awareness that cultures are not monolithic entities
  - Adopting an egalitarian frame and abandoning ethnocentric perspectives

REVIEW AND DISCUSSION QUESTIONS

1. Why is effective intercultural communication essential for contemporary organizations?
2. How has ethnocentrism affected interactions you've observed between people at work?
3. Is intercultural communication noise inevitable, regardless of egalitarian perspectives of the communicators?
4. What types of intercultural encounters do you typically experience:

- At the university?
- At work?

5. Do you think that linguistic relativity (the Sapir-Whorf hypothesis) can affect the extent of communication noise in intercultural contexts? Explain.
6. As the world continues to become more and more of a global village, will results from Hofstede-type studies reflect fewer cultural distinctions?
7. Do the events of September 11, 2001, create or reduce intercultural communication noise? Explain.

GROUP/ROLE-PLAY

In a group of four to six, review the issues surrounding the case that begins this chapter. Attempt to gain consensus regarding the questions at the end of the case.

- For the role-play, group members assume the role of a representative from Atlanta, the United Kingdom, Germany, France, and San Francisco. Assume that one of the infrequent meetings referred to in the case is taking place. Assume that the salesperson from San Francisco has called the meeting and all five persons are in the Atlanta office.
- Role-play the face-to-face interaction. The goal is to agree to a policy for communicating internationally that will be in the best interests of Rando.

Chapter 10

Crisis Communication

Chapter in a Nutshell

Crises in organizations are inevitable. Regardless of the nature of the enterprise, whether it is profit or nonprofit, global or local, product or service related, an organization is susceptible to crises. By definition, crises are un-

"We learn from history that we learn nothing from history."

—GEORGE BERNARD SHAW

"There is one thing to be sure of mate; there's nothing to be sure of."

—LYRIC from the musical *Pippin*

foreseen events. Nevertheless, organizations can be prepared to communicate when confronted with these unforeseen events. The quality of communication during crises can have enduring effects. The Schwan Food Company, for example, will be remembered for years because of its efficient and honorable communication during the food contamination crisis it faced. Other companies are burdened with tarnished reputations not primarily because of a crisis incident, but because of how these organizations communicated during and after the incident. This chapter discusses how to communicate in times of organizational crisis.

When you have completed this chapter, you should be able to:

- Describe what is meant by proactive crisis communication.
- Explain what is meant by stakeholder theory and image restoration theory.
- Identify, evaluate, and apply image restoration approaches.
- List the steps of a crisis communication plan.
- Construct a plan that can be used for communicating during crises in an organization to which you belong.

CASE 10.1

The Nuance Group

Background

A successful management consulting company, The Nuance Group, boasts that its consultants are all highly educated with significant consulting experience in the areas of marketing, economics, and finance. Nuance has created a glossy brochure that includes a description of its services, its contact information, and brief biographical statements about each consultant. Next to each biographical blurb is a photo of the consultant. Over 50,000 of the brochures have been mailed to people in organizations all over the world who have been identified as potential clients. The brochure is also displayed on the Nuance Group Web site. Visitors to the Web site are encouraged to download the PDF file and read the brochure. The site can be accessed without any password simply by visiting nuanceconsulting.com.

The Potential Client—Dorfman Associates

A potential client, Charlene Dorfman, the founder and director of Dorfman Associates, phoned the Nuance Group and requested some information about the services that the Nuance Group could offer. Dorfman had visited the Web site but had additional questions. She told the people at Nuance that she was considering several consulting firms and wanted hard copy and any related literature that she could distribute to her senior associates. The associates would be meeting shortly to decide which consultant to hire. The Nuance Group sent Dorfman several dozen brochures.

The senior associates at Dorfman met the following week to discuss which consulting group to hire. During the discussion, Randy, one of the associates, was scanning the Nuance Group brochure and was taken aback by a picture of one of the consultants. There was no doubt that the photo was a picture of one of Randy's college classmates, Jack Patten.

However, as Randy read Jack's corresponding bio, he knew for certain that the biographical profile was a grand fabrication. The bio read that Patten had studied in New Haven, attending Yale as an undergraduate. Patten had indeed studied in New Haven, having graduated from another college in the area. He may have visited Yale to use its library now and then, but he did not enroll at or graduate from the Ivy League school. Randy stopped the discussion and explained the misrepresentation. Charlene Dorfman immediately eliminated the Nuance Group from consideration.

Dorfman Contacts the Nuance Group; The Nuance Group Confronts Patten

After the meeting, Dorfman phoned the Nuance Group and described Randy's observation. When Jack Patten was confronted by his superior about the allegation, Jack did not deny the charge. He did, however, claim that all of the consultants had embellished their bios. Jack commented that he was told informally to "put his best foot forward." "Apparently," his boss retorted, "You put someone else's foot forward."

However, as the boss continued to investigate the situation, he discovered that several of the biographical blurbs were factually inaccurate and contained self-congratulatory embellishments.

- Does the Nuance Group have a crisis?
- Do most readers of such publications expect embellishments?
- Must the Nuance Group communicate to various audiences about the misrepresentations?
- If the answer to the prior question is yes, who must be contacted? How should they be contacted? Changes on the Web? New brochures? When should they be contacted?
- What must be communicated to each of these audiences?

Organizations and Crisis Communication

What Is a Crisis?

"There is no good arguing with the inevitable. The only argument available with an east wind is to put on your overcoat."[1]

Bob Roemer, the author of *When the Balloon Goes Up: The Communicator's Guide to Crisis Response*, defines a crisis as "any unanticipated event, incident, situation, or development that has the potential to damage or destroy your organization's reputation."[2] Coombs offers a slightly different definition. He writes that a crisis is "the perception of an unpredictable event that threatens important expectancies of stakeholders and can seriously impact an organization's performance and generate negative outcomes."[3] Fishman adds a meaningful dimension with his definition. He writes that a crisis is an "unpredictable event which threatens important organizational values and which creates pressure for a timely response requiring effective communication."[4]

As is apparent, these definitions all have similarities. By culling them we can conclude that a crisis is an incident that:

- Occurs unexpectedly.
- Could damage an organization's reputation, values, and/or performance.
- Requires effective communication.

For example, a crisis for your university might involve:

- An epidemic illness spreading in the dormitories
- A fraternity hazing episode resulting in student injury
- A campus officer found to be embezzling tuition dollars
- A professor's speech that's exposed as plagiarism
- A student cheating scandal

A crisis for the airline industry might involve:

- The revelation that some pilots have consumed alcohol before flying
- Apparent conspiratorial fare fixing among carriers on common routes
- Skyjacking depicted as a reflection of poor security
- A strike called by pilots
- A crash landing

What Is Crisis Communication?

Crisis communicators conceive, create, and disseminate messages to internal and external audiences during times of organizational crisis. Crisis communication has proactive and reactive dimensions. Crisis communicators plan how they will communicate during times of crisis and also react/respond to the unique situations presented by crises when such events take place.

Sometimes the phrase crisis communication is used interchangeably with crisis management. The two are not synonymous. Crisis management involves communication but is not only about communicating.

Similarly, crisis communication is not synonymous with image management. Crises may require image restoration, and communicators may be able to repair damaged reputations. However, crisis communication involves more than controlling or shaping how a company is, and will be, perceived by others.

Finally, crisis communication is sometimes equated with "spinning." Spinning is a pejorative term for altering a reality to make some phenomenon—which otherwise would be unattractive—more attractive. Some crisis communicators do "spin." However, as we will discuss in this chapter, altering reality is not a long-term remedy. Spinning is a superficial approach to crisis communication and certainly not synonymous with crisis communication.

Why Study Crisis Communication?

Crisis communication is a very real problem for contemporary organizations. Not reacting well to a crisis can result in the generation of employee rumors, plummeting stock values, a lack of employee confidence, and a reduction in consumer trust. The effect of not communicating well during a crisis can be an intensification of the crisis. To make this point more clear, consider two of the examples presented earlier in this chapter. What would be the effects of poor communication during such crises?

- Assume an epidemic of meningitis swept through your college or university. If such an event took place, would your school be compelled to communicate to various audiences? If so,
  - Who, specifically, would have to be contacted?
  - What information would these persons need to receive?
  - What methods of communicating should be utilized to get this information to these receivers?
  - What would be the (specific) repercussions of your university not communicating effectively if there were such an epidemic?
- Assume an airline was accused of not studying the substance abuse history of prospective pilots. Assume further that some of the airline's pilots were accused of attempting to fly a plane when under the influence. Would the airline be compelled to communicate to various audiences? If so,
  - Who within the company would need to receive information immediately?
  - Who outside of the company would need to receive information immediately?
  - What information would these audiences need?
  - What would be the repercussions if the airline did *not* communicate efficiently to its internal and external audiences when faced with such a charge?

Theory and Practice

As we will see, successful crisis communication has theoretical underpinnings. That is, in order to be effective, crisis communicators would be wise to understand, for example, stakeholder theory and image restoration theory. We will discuss these theories in upcoming sections of this chapter. However, it is important to emphasize here that there is nothing abstract or hypothetical about the practical need to communicate efficiently during crises. Firestone, Archer Daniels Midland, Union Carbide, Coca-Cola, Ford Motor Company, Enron, The Catholic Church, and WorldCom comprise a short list of major organizations that have had public crises in recent years to which they needed to respond. All companies—regardless of size and regardless of how fortunate they have been in the past—are susceptible to devastating crises.

On Valentine's Day 2008, a snowstorm trapped JetBlue passengers on the runway for hours. What should JetBlue executives have said to customers after excruciating delays?

Consider a few recent examples of organizational crises and the clear need to communicate during them.

- The governor of Illinois, Rod R. Blagojevich, faced an enormous crisis when he was accused in December 2008 of trying to, in effect, *sell* the open Illinois senate seat vacated by then President-Elect Barack Obama. The charge could be (and proved to be) devastating to the Illinois governor and embarrassing to the president-elect. What should Blagojevich have said to his constituents? What should the then president-elect have communicated, if anything, to the citizens of the state of Illinois, the citizens of the country, and leaders in the world community?

- It was more than embarrassing to the city of Boston in 2008 when a firefighter on paid leave because of an alleged physical disability was discovered to be a finalist in a body sculpting competition. The competition, obviously, required strenuous physical exercise and grueling hours in a gymnasium. Throughout the city and state, people were losing their jobs, and yet a malingerer was on the government payroll? How was it possible that taxpayer dollars were being used to support a firefighter with a backache when the city employee had, apparently, spent time in a health club pumping iron? What should the city communicate? To whom should they communicate messages? How should these messages be relayed?

- During the weekend of Saturday, September 13, and Sunday, September 14, 2008, rumors proliferated in the financial community that a Wall Street giant, Lehman Brothers, would soon declare bankruptcy. When on Monday, September 15, this fear was realized and related concerns rocked Wall Street, the stock marketed plummeted 500 points. On Tuesday, September 16, the market went down another 400 points. On September 29, the market went down a record 777 points. Companies like Lehman—Fidelity Investments, for example—were faced with the enormous task of communicating to its clients that their money was safe so that these customers would not immediately withdraw investments and place funds elsewhere. The result of not communicating effectively to current and even prospective clients could be devastating. What should companies like Fidelity communicate to clients? What should Fidelity say to its employees who interact with clients on a daily basis?

- On March 31, 2009, the University of California at San Diego e-mailed 46,377 prospective students and congratulated them for gaining acceptance to the institution. Unfortunately, only 17,000 students were supposed to receive this electronic letter. The letter was inadvertently sent to all who had applied, and consequently nearly 29,000 students who had been rejected were incorrectly informed that they had been accepted. The university realized its error and sent out a follow-up e-mail. Nevertheless, the school faced the prospect that many students who had been rejected would not receive the second e-mail or would contend that they had been accepted because of the initial mailing.

Applying the Principles—Test Yourself

Crisis Experiences

- What was the last job you held?
- What types of crises could have affected that organization?
- What crises, if any, did affect that organization?

- How did your company communicate during the crises?
- How should the company have communicated during the crises?

- On Valentine's Day, 2008, JetBlue experienced disaster when a snowstorm forced excruciating delays. As planes sat on the runway for several hours, passengers awaiting takeoff were trapped, unable to use toilet facilities as they stewed on board, essentially imprisoned on the stuck vessel. The national press that reported the incident was excoriating in its criticism. What should JetBlue executives say to customers? How should they communicate to them?[5]

Crisis Communication Planning

Proactive Crisis Communication

Proactive crisis planning is something done in anticipation or in preparation for the crisis. A crisis may be an unanticipated event, nevertheless, an organization can create a plan well before any unanticipated event surfaces. Of course, some components of crisis communication activity must, inevitably, be reactions. Once a crisis occurs, an organization will and should respond to the unique characteristics of the individual crisis. However, there is much that can be done in anticipation of a crisis so that in the event of calamity (or perceived calamity) the organization can begin to communicate as efficiently and rapidly as possible. Ed Klotzbier is the former Vice President for Communication at Northeastern University. Currently he is the Vice President for Student Affairs at the school and a member of the universitywide crisis communication team. Klotzbier is also a lawyer and, prior to his work at the university, served on presidential campaign committees. He has had close to twenty years of experience communicating in crisis situations. His perspective on the importance of proactive planning is unequivocal. "The time to fix your roof," he asserts "is when the sun is shining."

Steps to Crisis Communication Planning

Leaper identifies several stages of crisis communication planning. The following list is an edited version of these steps.[6]

1. Securing commitment from top management to be open and honest during crises
2. Establishing a crisis communication team
3. Brainstorming regarding crises

4. Stakeholder identification and message preparation
5. Choosing methods for communicating messages
6. Message sequencing
7. Identification of spokespersons and establishing a communication center
8. Recording the plan
9. Simulating and coaching
10. Periodic updating

Let's consider each of these stages.

Commitment from Top Management to Be Honest during Crises

In *Public Relations Quarterly*, James Lukaszweski lists what he calls categories of "trustbusting" behavior during crises:

- **Stonewalling**: e.g., issuing "no comments," stating "to the best of our knowledge, we have done nothing wrong in this matter"
- **Arrogance**: e.g., no expressions of apology or concern, telling media representatives or employees to keep out of "our" matters
- **Defensive threatening**: e.g., "Should you continue to insinuate . . . then we will have to . . ."
- **Delaying**: e.g., "We are hiring a consultant to investigate . . ."
- **Disdain**: e.g., "Only a fool would think that a company of our stature . . ."[7]

In order to plan meaningfully for crisis communication activities, an organization has to be committed to open, transparent communication and not trustbusting. We all have an ethical obligation to be honest in our communications. This moral responsibility complements the pragmatic value of open communication during crises.

Nearly all of the advice for crisis communication stresses the importance of honesty. Dishonesty and evasion might appear to be attractive when faced with the alternative of admitting to embarrassing activities. However, deceptive communication typically adds to the organization's crisis. Watson Wyatt consultant Linda Grosso comments that "the most critical challenge [in crisis communicating] is establishing a sense of trust. To that end, it's vital for management not to blow its credibility by putting out incorrect or confusing information."[8] Benoit writes that an "organization that falsely denies responsibility for offensive actions risks substantially damaged credibility if the truth emerges."[9]

If avoiding trustbusting and communicating honesty is a crisis communication imperative, an initial step in crisis planning requires obtaining a commitment from top management to be forthcoming when faced with crisis situations. Marra argues that the culture of an organization can dilute the effectiveness of crisis communication planning. "Many practitioners devote significant resources to produce a communication plan that is destined to fail because [it contradicts] the dominant and accepted communication plans used by their organizations."[10] If an organization typically is evasive, deceptive, or misleading in its communication, a plan based on forthcoming admissions is unlikely to succeed.

In short, the presence of a plan does not guarantee implementation. It requires a commitment from leaders to work the plan.[11] A first step is to obtain that commitment.

How would a cultural theorist react to this imperative? Can an organization's formation, its constitution, be affected by executive decisions to be transparent during crises?

How would a critical theorist react to this imperative? Can perceptions of power and empowerment be affected by executive decisions related to ethical communication during crisis?

Establishing a Crisis Communication Team

A crisis communication team is a committee composed of highly trusted members from various departments throughout the organization. Persons on this committee could be representatives from corporate communication departments and senior administration. It would be wise, however, to include persons on this team who represent various units of the organization and different organizational strata. By having a diverse membership in terms of experience, expertise, and culture, the crisis communication team can be better suited to deal with its mission as an anticipatory planning agent of the organization. Remsik recommends that the team have approximately six members and include persons who would fulfill identifiable roles. (The persons fulfilling the roles would not need to be members of designated departments.)

- Team chairperson
- Representatives for:
  - Government relations
  - Employee or internal relations
  - Operations/Facilities
  - Community relations
  - Media relations[12]

Brainstorming Regarding Crises

Regardless of the nature of your organization, crises can occur because of factors that have both everything to do with your organization and nothing to do with your organization. A bank might lose its records because of a natural disaster like a hurricane or because of the actions of an outside thief or arsonist. The bank may also suffer a crisis because of the unethical behavior of an internal thief, for example, a manager who is embezzling client funds.

At this stage of the process, the crisis communication team must attempt to predict all possible crises that could surface in the organization. Subsequently, the team can place like types of crises into related groups. For example, the team could brainstorm and identify potential crises related to charges of racial, gender, sexual orientation, or age discrimination. While there are differences in the nature of each discriminatory type, the team could group all potential crises related to such charges into a single class.

Mitroff suggests that crises can be categorized as follows:

- **Economic**: The stock market unexpectedly drops nearly 10 percent and financial giants topple.
- **Informational**: Because of a computer glitch, a major university loses the names and related data of all students who have applied to the institution in a given year.
- **Physical**: Nuclear equipment appears to malfunction, threatening the security of employees and all the citizens in the region.
- **Human resources**: A highly successful mutual fund manager in one of the largest investment firms in the world suddenly leaves his position to begin his own investment company.
- **Reputational**: A company is faced with dismissing thousands of rumors suggesting that their logo indicates that the company is involved with the devil's work.
- **Psychopathic acts**: A deranged employee enters a workplace and systematically shoots seven of his fellow employees.
- **Natural disasters**: An earthquake hobbles the infrastructure of a city.[13]

Applying the Principles—Test Yourself

Brainstorming for Crises

Assume you are on a crisis communication planning team for the organizations listed below. What potential crises might occur?

- The Islamic Student Association
- Your former high school
- A soft drink company
- *The Washington Post*

- The tobacco industry
- The National Guard
- A country club
- A theater company
- A furniture manufacturer
- A Wall Street investment firm
- The American Red Cross
- NATO
- A construction company
- The St. Louis city council

Stakeholder Identification and Message Preparation

What Is a Stakeholder? The word "stakeholders" is used in the language of crisis communication almost synonymously with what we have called "receivers" throughout the text. More specifically, a "stakeholder" is someone who has a "stake" in the information that an organization needs to communicate during a crisis *or* someone whom the organization wants to receive information, or have a stake, in receiving and reviewing information related to a crisis. An internal stakeholder is someone who is such a receiver *within* the organization. An external stakeholder is a receiver who is external to the organization.

Stakeholder theory refers to the assumption that during crises there are multiple stakeholders, and each discrete group is likely to need to receive different messages. Ice, in his "Corporate Publics and Rhetorical Strategy" article about the Union Carbide tragedy, makes this point explicitly.[14] His contention is hardly an isolated one. A 2007 article in the *Journal of Applied Communication Research*, for example, discusses marginalized publics who were excluded from consideration in the events surrounding Hurricane Katrina.[15] When identifying stakeholders, all internal and external audiences need to be considered, and the appropriate messages for these audiences need to be created and disseminated.

For example, if there is a measles epidemic in your college dormitories, students who live in the same dorm as the infected persons would be considered one of several groups of internal stakeholders. The residence hall directors would be another group of internal stakeholders. The instructors who had been working with the afflicted students would be a third group of internal stakeholders. The editor of the campus newspaper would be an internal stakeholder. The editor of the town or city newspaper would be considered an *external* stakeholder. Parents of all students in the affected dormitory would be a group of external stakeholders. All parents of residential students (other than those in the affected dormitory) would be another group of external stakeholders. The news managers for the local radio stations would constitute a group of external stakeholders.

Discrete Populations It's important for the committee to separate stakeholders into the smallest possible groupings to whom unique messages will need to be communicated. For example, in the case of a campus epidemic, it is not sufficient to identify "students" as internal stakeholders. The crisis communication team would have to break down the student population into discrete student populations that would receive unique messages from the university. For instance, students who live on the same floor as the infected persons would get a different message or messages than those students who lived in another dormitory or off campus. Parents of the infected students would be sent messages that are different from the messages that would be sent to other dormitory student parents or the parents of prospective university students.

Identification of Message Content In the event of crisis, each discrete stakeholder population will receive a series of messages. The committee would list all types of messages that the identified populations would need to receive.

For example, in the event of a campus epidemic, your committee might decide that all parents of prospective students receive:

- An updated account of the situation and how it has been addressed
- A history of the health records at the university
- A list of various medical services available for students
- A comparison of health records at your university as compared to national institutions
- A list of contact numbers for questions related to health services
- A message from the university president
- A message from the head of residential life
- Testimonials from the governor's office about health standards
- Clippings from media sources indicating the arrest of the illness

You will note that many of the items above can be prepared for in advance of any crisis. For example, the list of contact numbers, the various medical services for customers, the comparative health records of your university—these as well as other items on the list can be constructed and ready to disseminate well before any crisis develops. If you intend to release a report published by the Food and Drug Administration as part of your plan, then having this report ready for print or electronic dissemination is a component of your preparation. If an area is highly technical, prepare written "background" literature that will clarify the information for the lay receivers. Leaper suggests creating a glossary for terms that are likely to be unfamiliar to a stakeholder population.[16]

In the best situation your organization will have paid for the production of materials that your team will never need to utilize.

Choose Methods for Sending Messages

As we discussed in Chapter 5, all communicators have options when they send information to receivers. In this phase of crisis communication planning, the team needs to consider the most effective ways to send the various messages to the particular group of stakeholders. For example, would:

- The list of medical services be *e-mailed* to each prospective student?
- All parents receive a letter that identified *a Web site* that, when accessed, reveals all on-campus health service contacts?
- The "message from the president" be on *a DVD* that would be sent Priority Mail to each prospective student's home?
- A campus representative personally *phone* each prospective student, updating the parents and student about the state of the epidemic?

The planning committee would decide what would be the best approach for each of the messages that needed to be communicated. Some decisions might be dependent on the specific nature of the actual, as opposed to anticipated, crisis. However, as you can see, some of the decisions could be made ahead of time and, therefore, reduce the chaos and increase the efficiency of communicating during crisis periods.

Sequence for Communicating Messages

The committee might decide to send out all messages to all stakeholders at once. It's unlikely, however, for that to be the wisest way to sequence the communications. For each crisis that has been anticipated, and each set of messages that need to go the stakeholders, the committee would want to consider who should get what messages when.

For example, if toxins were found in a cafeteria housed in an office building that served twenty independent businesses:

- Would you want external stakeholders to get messages before your internal stakeholders? Would you want media representatives to receive statements about corrective steps that will be taken *before* you've explained these steps to your kitchen staff?
- Do you need to send messages to wholesalers who provide you with product before you contact the local newspaper? Before you contact each of the businesses within your facility?

The sequencing, of course, will be dependent on the particular crisis identified. In terms of whom to contact first, Lukaszweski makes the following general recommendations:

First: Those most directly affected, for example, crisis victims
Second: Employee (i.e., internal) stakeholders
Third: Those indirectly affected, for example, neighbors of victims, friends, suppliers
Fourth: The news media[17]

Anticipate the Need for Follow-Up Messages As indicated above, the committee might need to send out a series of messages to some stakeholders. The initial communications would be followed by a second group of messages that would depend on reactions to the initially communicated ones. These subsequent messages would be determined by the evolving nature of the crisis and/or reactions to the initial communications. It is impossible to predict every permutation in the evolution of a crisis, but the committee might want to anticipate what messages might need to be sent on the basis of potential developments.

For example, let's assume that a company research and design facility has been inadvertently discharging noxious chemicals into nearby lakes. Your initial series of messages may precede any news of persons who became ill after swimming in these areas. In the initial messages you may comment that you are taking measures to ensure that people who did swim in the lakes can receive free medical attention so that the contact with the toxins will not result in illness. If persons, despite your company's efforts, do become ill, then your team would have to communicate the *reactive messages* you *proactively* determined to issue given such an eventuality.

In short, the committee should make an attempt to anticipate likely reactions and eventualities and prepare for follow-up messages to meet the evolving communication needs of the crisis.

Identifying Spokespersons and Establishing a Center for Communicating

For each crisis, and perhaps for all crises, your committee should identify a spokesperson who will be the focal point for communications during the crisis period. An organization does not want to have several persons making comments to stakeholders. If that were to occur, it is possible that conflicting messages emanating from the same alleged source (your organization) could confuse the stakeholders and dilute the value of your overall communication plan. An organization doesn't want one person commenting that the procedure you are following is the official plan (i.e., steps a, b, and c) and another musing about whether in this instance your company will be following protocol.

The organization also needs to establish a place that will serve as the headquarters for communicating during crisis. This location needs to be equipped with phones, computers, fax machines, and any other equipment required for the "nervous system" of your operation. If print documents are part of any plan, then these materials should be located in or near this center. Monitoring media reaction is part of the crisis communication plan. The center therefore should be equipped with televisions and radios and personnel to permit such monitoring. A place should be set aside for examining print and computer/electronic media content. An organization may decide to employ a "clipping service" like Bacon's to assess media reaction during crises. A "clipping service" is an organization that is hired to "clip" all relevant media messages related to a client's needs. "Clip," given contemporary media, is no longer a descriptive or inclusive word for what these clipping services do. However, the term "clipping" is still often used. Should you wish to discover how the three local television stations have responded to a measles epidemic, you could employ the clipping service to assess media reaction as opposed to monitoring the stations yourself.

Record the Plan

After creating the crisis communication plan for any anticipated event, the committee needs to prepare written versions of the plan. The committee should ensure that all persons who will be required to participate in the implementation of the plan have a copy and are familiar with their roles. As appropriate, the committee or committee representatives should meet with key organizational members and explain that a plan for crisis is in place. For example, all internal medical services staff at your university should be made aware that a crisis communication plan is in place in the case of a student epidemic—regardless of whether the informed persons will have an active role in the implementation of the communication plan.

Coaching and Simulating

It is one thing to plan for a crisis and another to be able to implement the plan.

- If part of your approach to a particular crisis involves subjecting a spokesperson to a press conference, then it is wise to simulate the press conference for that spokesperson.
- If you intend for the head of campus public safety to meet with parents after an unfortunate incident on campus, you want to give the head of public safety an opportunity to practice, in a relatively safe environment, the presentation she or he would give to the parents. Your group would be wise to simulate the tense and confrontational Q-and-A session that would likely follow that presentation.
- If, in an attempt to reach your employees following an anthrax-type scare, you intend to hold an immediate video teleconference to be "broadcast" internally, you would want to see how quickly you could set up that teleconference in terms of notifying audiences, setting up the studio, and "broadcasting" the message.

Practitioners who have written books on crisis communication—Rene Henry in *You Better Have a Hose If You Want to Put Out a Fire* and Steve Wilson in *Real People, Real Crises,* for example—emphasize the significance of simulation.[18] Laurence Barton, an academic as well as a consultant to industry, in his book, *Crisis in Organizations*, devotes an entire chapter to simulations.[19]

Updating Periodically

The best scenario that can develop for the crisis communication team is that its plans are never implemented. However, the absence of crisis does not eliminate the necessity for the committee. Every three months the committee should reconvene to:

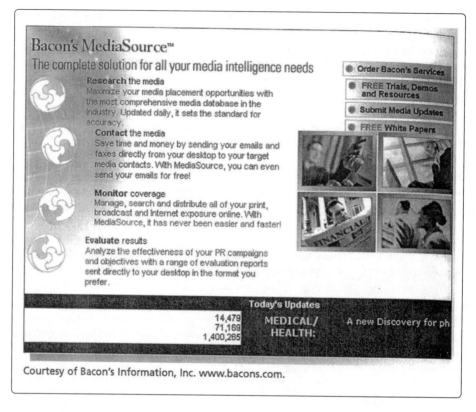

Figure 10. 1 Media Monitoring
Courtesy of Bacon's Information, Inc. www.bacons.com

- Review the crisis communication plans that are presently in place
- Ensure that all contact information for key persons remains the same
- Consider any other potential crises
- Plan for any other potential crises

Image Restoration Theory

Legitimacy and Stability

In the crisis communication literature, "legitimacy" is a term used to describe stakeholder perception of appropriate organizational behavior. When an organization is perceived as acting appropriately, it has earned legitimacy. For example, if an organization is honest when it deals with stakeholders, is law abiding, takes safety precautions, prices fairly, and has a reputation for treating its employees well, the organization will likely have earned stakeholder perceptions of legitimacy.

If, however, an organization operates bait-and-switch operations, produces materials that are health hazards, and/or advertises deceptively, they are likely to lose legitimacy. Legitimacy is not something an organization has; it is something that is attributed to it by stakeholders.

The word stability is another term used in crisis communication studies. Its meaning is counterintuitive. Stability refers to the frequency of crises in an organization. If crises are a "stable" phenomenon, then an organization can lose legitimacy. NASA, for example, is an organization that has had many crises. Of course, the business of NASA is such that any malfunction can result in catastrophe. Nevertheless, issues with *Apollo,* the *Challenger,* the Hubble telescope, and, most recently, the *Columbia* contributed to the perception that NASA is an organization that is crisis prone. Stable companies, predictably, have more difficulty attaining stakeholder perception of legitimacy.

Organizational behavior and crisis stability are not the only factors that affect legitimacy. How one communicates in response to crisis affects legitimacy. NASA's problems, for example, were compounded because in each of their crisis cases there were issues with how the organization responded in the wake of the crisis. As significantly, investigations into *Challenger and Columbia,* for example, indicated that recurring communication issues might have been sources of the crisis.

NASA is by no means the only organization that has lost legitimacy because of how it communicated during crisis. Dow Chemical, Union Carbide, Exxon, and Intel are just a few other organizations who probably wished they had responded differently in the face of their crises. Dow Chemical initially denied that they were aware that their breast implants were defective. Eventually they had to acknowledge that this was inaccurate. Union Carbide, despite what may have been humanitarian intentions, has been criticized for not communicating speedily in regard to their tragedy in Bhopal. Exxon has been challenged because it attempted, initially, to displace responsibility for the *Valdez* oil spill on the ship captain. Intel suffered because of the proliferation of communication on the Web. Intel's communications attempting to downplay the flaws in their processors were the subject of ridicule by Internet chat groups.

The Schwan Food Company, on the other hand, has enjoyed perceptions of legitimacy because of how it communicated during a crisis they experienced with their products. In the Schwan case, consumers of foodstuffs became ill, and the cause of their sickness was traced to Schwan foods. Ice cream mix that had been transported on trucks Schwan leased had been tainted. The ice cream made from the mix was consequently foul and consumers became ill. Schwan could have ducked responsibility for the crisis. Instead, all their communications accepted responsibility despite the fact that the true source of the problem was the leased trucking company, not Schwan. Nevertheless, Schwan's communications of apology were sincere, and they used the richest medium possible to deliver the message. Schwan, a company that typically delivered products door to door, delivered their messages of apology and corrective action the same way, door to door. In addition to how they communicated, what they communicated was also honorable. They offered to pay any medical costs associated with illness and also pay any medical costs of any person who wished to check to see if they had become infected but were not yet ill. Schwan also announced that they would discontinue the practice of leasing trucks and would buy their own fleet.

Four Rs

Image restoration theory asserts that when an organization loses legitimacy, it can restore its image by the use of symbols. In other words, how an organization communicates in response to a crisis can affect perceptions of legitimacy or, more broadly, company image.

Typically, four Rs are identified as variables that affect appropriate communication choice. That is, on the basis of four factors, a company may choose to communicate one way or another. The four variables are the *reputation* of the company in terms of stability, *relationships* organizations have previously developed with stakeholders, perceived *responsibility* the organization has for the evolution of the particular crisis, and the quality of the *response* in terms of content and appropriate delivery. A company might be coached to communicate in one way if it was stable and if relationships between particular groups of stakeholders were tense or another way if the opposite was true. If a company is likely to be perceived, or be, responsible for a crisis, then some methods will work better than others that might have been successful if the company was not perceived as responsible for the crisis.

As discussed earlier, image restoration theory is not a euphemism for spin control. Nearly all research suggests that such a ploy will, in the long run at least, reduce an organization's legitimacy. An analysis of the Hubble telescope case, in fact, suggests that it was spinning prior to the crisis that exacerbated the crisis. NASA had embellished what the Hubble could do, and when the telescope did not deliver (in part because of technical problems), this further eroded the perceptions of the organization's legitimacy.

Image Restoration Approaches

Image restoration theory identifies several different types of messages that can be employed toward the objective of restoring images.

Attack

This approach attempts to restore legitimacy by attacking those who are accusing the organization of wrongdoing. Instead of accepting responsibility, a spokesperson can attack:

- The media for creating a "media circus"
- Adversaries who are "smearing" the organization
- Employees who are delinquent

Bolstering

Bolstering occurs when spokespersons identify the achievements of an organization in an attempt to deflect attention from the specific crisis and highlight the organizational attributes. If a fire has destroyed a company's records, an organization might identify its history of safety, lack of any prior fires, its community efforts, quality product line, awards for civic responsibility, or any other related or nonrelated positive attribute about the organization.

Compassion

Compassion approaches attempt to restore legitimacy by expressing consideration and compassion for those affected by the crisis. If an insane employee barges into the workplace and indiscriminately slaughters co-workers, the organization of course would be wise to express compassion for the victims.

Compensation

A method for restoring legitimacy involves compensation: compensating people who have lost something because of the crisis. Compensation may be in the form of replacing a defective item, paying for medical expenses, or otherwise providing injured stakeholders with something to compensate for what has been lost.

Corrective Action

Organizations employ the restoration strategy called corrective action when they explain to stakeholders what they are doing or will do to ensure that such a crisis never occurs again. This can be a very effective form of image restoration. Corrective action could, for example, involve a new policy for evaluating prospective employees, replacing defective equipment, hiring new management, or creating an independent review board to assess company procedures.

Defeasibility

Sometimes organizations argue that blame should not be attributed to them because it does not make sense that they should be held responsible for actions that created a crisis. A company may argue that given certain facts in the case, assertions that the company was responsible are not feasible. A company may suggest that an applicant lied when interviewing for a position and consequently they could not possibly be accused of being derelict when they inadvertently hired a person with a substance abuse problem.

Denial

A common, but often counterproductive approach to image restoration is to deny allegations that your company is responsible for the crisis—or to deny that there is a crisis at all.

Differentiation

Differentiation is a technique used to explain why what has occurred in your situation is different from a similar event that involved another organization. If, for example, an organization has lost legitimacy because of behavior that is inappropriate, the company may claim that what had been done was an inadvertent offense, differentiating the behavior from that of someone who deliberately acted inappropriately.

Displacement

Displacement is a very common image restoration technique in which an organization or person attempts to place the blame on someone else. A construction company may face charges that it did an unprofessional job if an elevator in a building fails and workers are fatally injured. The company might use displacement to claim that the elevator construction had been contracted out to another company who was to blame for the accident.

Ingratiation

Organizations may attempt to eliminate, reduce, or preempt negative media reactions by ingratiating themselves with those who have lost or may lose respect for the company. Ingratiation involves identifying values that the organization and stakeholder share, citing attributes of the company that are consistent with these values, and praising the stakeholder for believing and acting in accordance with these similar values.

Intimidation

As the label suggests, an organization may employ intimidation to reduce charges that it has been delinquent. An organization that has been accused of polluting the air might attack the accusers, deny the allegations, and intimate that if attacks persist they will relocate, pulling jobs away from an area that needs them.

Minimization

Minimization is an image restoration strategy used to downplay the significance and damage of the crisis. An organization may claim that the problem may seem to have powerful repercussions but, in fact, is not as major as originally thought.

Mortification

When an organization expresses its embarrassment or humiliation because of what has occurred it is, wittingly or otherwise, using the technique called mortification. Often this technique is accompanied by an apology—all too often only when the person has been caught.

Penitential and Causal Apologies

A causal apology expresses remorse but explains why there is a need for an apology. A penitential apology includes no causal explanation. It is simply a statement of remorse. A penitential apology would be, "We are sorry for what occurred and apologize to anyone who consumed our product." A causal apology would be, "We are sorry that the result of our contractor not adequately cleaning its trucks, not adequately doing the job for which they were paid, resulted in injury to our loyal customers."

Suffering

When an organization suggests that it too has been victimized by a crisis, they are using the technique referred to as suffering. A spokesperson might say that while the tragedy affected the victims most significantly, all company employees have been victimized by the emotional duress, financial impact, and psychological damage related to an event.

Transcendence

When an organization juxtaposes the crisis with something more significant, the communication strategy is referred to as transcendence. Essentially, this response suggests that other issues transcend the one that is current and render this event insignificant.

Below you will see brief descriptions of ten crisis cases. Take a moment to read through these. For each case, identify:

- Which image restoration technique was used by the organization
- What other techniques you believe should have been used

(1) (a) Major League Baseball faced a crisis when it was revealed that baseball players were using illegal drugs to enhance performance. One accused player issued a statement to this effect, "Look, there is a war in Iraq, people are being flooded out of their homes in New Orleans, should we really care a lot about what products that might have been illegal that I might have inadvertently consumed?"

(b) Another player admitted usage, but claimed he had taken the drug not to enhance performance but to speed up recovery from an injury.

(2) In the wake of a horrific school shooting tragedy, a spokesperson offered condolences to those who had lost their precious family members and friends. He also made a statement to this effect: "This is a painful time for all of us. We have all, whether or not we have been directly victimized, been violated, and we all are reeling from the void left when trust in the inherent decency of our neighbors was breached."

(3) When former New York State governor Elliot Spitzer was exposed as someone who frequented brothels, he expressed his embarrassment and humiliation.

(4) It was discovered that there was a flaw with Intel computer processors. The company acknowledged the flaw but said that this error would only affect the average person every 27,000 years. Therefore, they claimed, this was a minor problem.

(5) After a Super Bowl victory, a wild celebration resulted in many injuries, damaged property, and two deaths. The city was accused of not having enough police personnel on the scene. The city's mayor commented that local university students were irresponsible, school officials were responsible, and local colleges should not tolerate delinquent student behavior.

(6) President Obama's secretary of the treasury appointee was confronted with the allegation that he had not paid $34,000 in taxes during a prior year. The appointee acknowledged the transgression, but claimed it was an oversight and not a deliberate act. It would have

been different, he intimated, had he intentionally tried to swindle the government.

(7) In the face of charges that their breast implants were defective, a company spokesperson issued a statement that contained this sentence: "The devices were safe and the data proved it."[20]

(8) When a hamburger chain was accused of serving tainted products, one of the company's initial arguments in defense was to argue that new guidelines regarding the cooking of meat had not been distributed to the affected franchises.

"Look, Let's just say I haven't seen anything, Charlie hasn't heard anything, and Tom hasn't said anything."

In times of crisis, organizational communicators are urged not to stonewall, be silent, or be deceptive.

(9) When a publicly owned company was criticized on *60 Minutes* for allegedly wasting taxpayer dollars because of managerial inefficiency, the organization responded by producing its own *60 Minutes*-style video. In it they used a *60 Minutes* knock-off set replete with a ticking clock. They called the production, *60 Minutes—Our Reply*. In the rebuttal tape, the power company, among other things, challenged the credibility of two employees who had alleged company misconduct in the original *60 Minutes* segment. The rebuttal claimed that one of the employees was a malingerer and the other an inveterate liar. Any person who wished to receive a copy of the rebuttal tape only needed to request one and the company mailed its video response free of charge.

(10) A municipality lost legitimacy when it was revealed that a citizen had committed a horrific race-related homicide. In response to the act, the town spokesperson apologized to those offended and also listed the history of racial tolerance in the community, the diverse ethnic composition of the city council, and the aggressive policies of local prosecutors addressing hate crimes.

Recurring Counsel for Crisis Communicators

When one reviews what has been written about crisis communication, a number of suggestions recur about how to act and respond in times of crisis. Below is a list of the recurring advice.

Respond quickly: All recommendations for crisis communicators emphasize the need for speedy reactions. The first twenty-four hours after a crisis is the most critical period.[21] Marra argues that excellent crisis communication "requires the ability to provide information to an organization's publics almost immediately."[22]

Use your plan: One of the problems with crisis communication is that in the throes of the crisis, organizations sometimes do not use the plan they have in place. The organization must be committed to using the plan that you have painstakingly established. The simulation step discussed earlier can be helpful in that your team will gain experience executing the plan prior to any incident.

Be accessible: Do not risk the wrath of internal or external stakeholders. Employees and media representatives will need information and will become frustrated if your plan doesn't include some way for these stakeholders to reach you.

Applying the Principles—Test Yourself

The Bayside Inn

This case describes what The Bayside Inn did in the face of crisis. What would you have done differently? Which approaches would you have employed?

A prestigious East Coast inn located in a resort community had enjoyed a fine reputation for decades. Sitting aloft a gorgeous bay, the inn had seventy rooms, a four-star restaurant, an outdoor bar with magnificent views of the water, and several function rooms. The Bayside Inn was open year round and attracted affluent customers. Men and women were required to dress formally for dining, and there was never a shortage of persons willing and eager—if one were to judge by the long waiting lists—to pay large sums and wear whatever was prescribed in order to dine (and be seen) at the Bayside Inn. In the worst of times—during the recession years of the mid-1970s and late 1980s—the Bayside was filled to capacity regardless of season.

In the summer of 2001 the Bayside Inn nearly went out of business. In July 1999 several persons who had eaten at the Bayside were hospitalized with food poisoning. Subsequently, articles in the *Gazette*, a local newspaper, suggested that the illnesses were likely the result of a problem with meat served at the Bayside.

When contacted by the *Gazette*, the general manager of the Bayside indignantly refuted the charges. He characterized the rumors and newspaper articles as "absurd." His entire statement was printed in the newspaper: "The Bayside Inn, as all who have dined here for years are well aware, has impeccable standards for quality and cleanliness. These rumors are absurd and slanderous. Anyone who assumes that these lies are truths is simply mistaken."

However, within a week of having made the remarks, several employees of the Bayside became ill and were bedridden. Matters became worse when a subsequent issue of the *Gazette* included a feature about seven persons who had become violently sick after attending a wedding that had been held at, and catered by, the Bayside.

Management attempted to thwart the negative publicity by quickly issuing statements reiteratively denying that any foodstuffs from the Bayside were responsible for the epidemic. The owner, the executive chef, and then again the general manager claimed that it was a matter of coincidence that these diners became ill after visiting the inn.

Nevertheless, the community grapevine continued to be active and the *Gazette* continued to pursue the story. At one point, a *Gazette* reporter interviewed a disgruntled former Bayside sous chef who commented that he had witnessed "iffy cleanliness" in the kitchen. The executive chef immediately denied the charge. However, a day after the "iffy cleanliness" comment appeared in the *Gazette*, a waiter was approached by a college student intern from a local radio station. The intern, prepared with a tape recorder and microphone, stopped the waiter and asked him what he thought of the conditions at the Bayside. The young man flippantly commented, "I've seen cleaner places." The waiter later said that he hadn't been thinking when he made the remark and had been "kind of in a hurry to get home." Nevertheless, the radio station played the "I've seen cleaner places" sound bite every hour on the hour during their local news segments.

The Bayside Inn management fired the waiter immediately. They then attempted to portray the sous chef's comments as the whinings of a bitter ex-employee.

"What do you expect Harold to say? We fired him because he was irresponsible. Of course he would speak disparagingly about the Inn."

The local radio station made the waiter's firing a cause celebre. The *Gazette* printed an interview with Harold the former sous chef.

When the public outcry over the young waiter's treatment for being "honest" became too much for the inn, the general manager rehired the waiter and promised a "thorough investigation."

The thorough investigation never culminated with any conclusions. To date, there has never been any definitive evidence that customer or employee illness was related to food served at the Bayside. There has never been any acknowledgment by the inn that the community and staff illnesses were related to the Bayside.

Occupancy at the Bayside Inn has dropped dramatically. Despite offering several "specials," dropping the dress code requirements, and reducing room rates, the Bayside is struggling to stay in business.

Remember your internal stakeholders: The tendency is for crisis communicators to focus on the media and other external populations. Crisis communication is much more than external image management. Crisis communicators are compelled to consider internal stakeholders as central to the process as external stakeholders.

Avoid silence and "no comment": Messages are sometimes communicated regardless of speaker intent. We know that what has been communicated is not what we say, but how receivers perceive what we say. We also know that people can say nothing at all and yet will still be communicating.

When spokespersons say, "no comment," they are sending messages that are probably perceived negatively. A "no comment" is likely to imply that the company has something to hide. Kearns suggests that "silence in a crisis is never golden."[23] Olcott comments that one never should "hide behind a no comment. . . . If there's information you can't disclose, give a reason why."[24] Pirozzolo writes, "Never, never appear on camera with a lawyer, and remember saying 'No Comment' is about as positive as taking the Fifth.'"[25]

Be truthful: Without question, the most often written recommendation pertaining to crisis communication relates to the requirement that communicators be open and "transparent" with their messages. Whether the suggestion is to be "credible,"[26] "obviously open,"[27] "candid,"[28] or "scrupulously honest,"[29] the idea is the same: shoot straight. Clients are advised by one consultant to "be as forthcoming as they can be, and then be a little more forthcoming."[30] Wilson writes, "If you can't live with the idea of seeing your prized crisis plan in the local newspaper, then you probably don't have such a good plan after all."[31]

Crisis communication is an important element of effective organizational communication. There is a cliché that suggests that the only things one can be sure of are "death and taxes." An organization might be wise to add *crises* to that list of inevitable eventualities.

Would you be able to create a crisis communication plan for an organization to which you belong? Could you develop a plan for your former high school? For your college?

SUMMARY: A TOOLBOX

• Crisis communication is an essential component of organizational communication.
• Crisis communication is a component of crisis management; it is not the same as crisis

PRACTITIONER PERSPECTIVE

Jason Vines, Vice President for Communication

Jason Vines has worked for the Chrysler and Ford Motor Companies and was also a principal in the Midwest Office of Strat@comm, a Washington, D.C.–based firm dedicated to strategic communication counseling. In the role of Vice President for Communication for Ford, Vines was at the helm during the tempestuous crisis related to damaged Firestone tires that were on Ford vehicles. Prior to his stint at Ford, Vines worked for Nissan North America. For his efforts in rebuilding Nissan's image worldwide, Automotive News named Vines the 1999 "All Star" in public relations.

As you read through this section, please consider the following questions:

- What is Vines's support for his perspective that honesty is always the best policy in terms of crisis communication?
- What is Vines's perspective of the value of informal networks?
- What is your perspective on the bolded section in this narrative?

The key to crisis communication comes down very simply to this: openness, honesty, and credibility. Eventually the truth catches up. And it catches up a lot faster in the twenty-first century than it ever did before. Twenty years ago something that occurred in the Far East might take some time before people in the West would hear about it. Now the information is spread in twenty seconds.

You don't have to go much beyond the front pages of your newspaper to see why honesty is the key to effective crisis communication. Look at Enron and Arthur Andersen. They both were involved in deception.

Citizens do not like companies and persons who are deceptive. Remember Nixon. When it became clear that he was covering up, the people went for the jugular. It's wise, in a very practical sense, to be sincere and apologize when you are wrong. If you remember, in the mid-1980s Chrysler was faced with a crisis. Some assembly plant officials were rolling back the odometers on so-called new cars and shipping these driven cars to dealers as new. What did Iacocca do? He came right out, apologized, acknowledged that some company people had engaged in that activity, said it was stupid, and promised that it would not happen again. People respect that kind of corporate behavior.

With all the communication tools we have, it all comes down to being frank. **And a lie by omission is still a lie. Any notion that ambiguity is somehow strategic or justifiable I categorically state is nonsense.** Deception, whether explicit or implicit, is strategic—a strategic lie that will catch up to you sooner rather than later. When it does, your credibility is kaput.

The Ford-Firestone situation was a gut-wrenching time. Firestone was either constantly getting the facts wrong or not being forthright, and it was extraordinarily difficult to keep reacting to their bogus communications. We were getting "Scud missile" attacks from them daily that we had to address. Eventually, the media caught on to them. When you lose your credibility in crisis communication, you are a "dead man walking."

You can plan for crises, but the best way to do this is get your team on board. You want to have a very solid communication system in place ahead of time. Some of the most powerful external communication is word of mouth. Your associates meet neighbors at soccer games, weddings, and various community activities. The neighbors may ask them about the situation at the company. If your organization has created a solid communication system and has communicated credibly to its own employees, the messages the employees relay to their neighbors, friends, and relatives can very much enhance the quality of your overall crisis communication effort.

management. Crisis communication is fundamentally different from image management because not all messages that are communicated during a crisis are related to building or restoring the company image. Also, crisis communication must involve communicating to internal as well as external receivers.

- Effective crisis communication requires:
  - Support from top management
  - Comprehensive brainstorming regarding potential crises
  - Identification of internal and external stakeholders
  - Designated spokepersons
  - A commitment to implement the plan
- Crisis communicators are advised to:
  - Quickly respond to crisis situations
  - Be scrupulously honest when communicating with your internal and external stakeholders
- Image restoration is largely a function of four Rs: relationship, reputation, responsibility, and response.

REVIEW AND DISCUSSION QUESTIONS

1. Why would cultural theorists examine how organizations communicate during crises?
2. Why is the word *stakeholder* used in the language of crisis communication instead of *receiver*?
3. Why would a presidential aspirant be wise to have a crisis communication plan? What types of crises have presidential candidates faced? For those crises, who were the internal stakeholders?
4. At your university, who should comprise the crisis communication team?
5. How can poor communication during a crisis intensify a crisis?
6. Why do stakeholders have to be separated into discrete populations?
7. Which of the image restoration approaches are likely to be seen as appropriate by critical theorists? Explain.

GROUP/ROLE-PLAY

In a group of four to six, review the issues surrounding the case that begins this chapter. Attempt to gain consensus regarding the questions at the end of the case.

- For the role-play, one member of the group assumes the role of Jack Patten. Another plays Jack's boss. The remaining members are other consultants in the Nuance Group.
- Role-play a face-to-face meeting called by the head of Nuance. The goal is to discuss the practice of elaborating on résumés, new policies on representation, and how to address the current crisis caused by the Patten revelation.

Chapter **11**

Assessing Organizational Communication Quality

Chapter in a Nutshell

"If you're not being critical about your business and yourself, you should be."

—ROBERT HELLER, *Business author*

In the preceding chapters we have made the case that communication is central to organizational activity and have discussed the various components of healthy organizational communication. If communication quality is an essential component of organizational success, then an organization must be willing to assess how well or how poorly it is communicating. Methods of measuring communication quality in organizations are called communication audits. Successful audits require understanding audit objectives, selecting appropriate testing methods, and reporting results meaningfully. This chapter explains how you can examine the extent to which your organization is meeting its communication-related responsibilities.

When you have completed this chapter, you should be able to:

• Define the phrase communication audit.
• List what an audit must test in order for it to be valid.
• Describe the strengths and weaknesses of various audits.
• Describe the components of what is called the ICA audit.
• Identify the challenges related to reporting audit results.

CASE 11.1
STIG: Perspectives of a Staffer

Background

The Sales Technology and Information Group (STIG) of a large metropolitan HMO provides data analysis reports for the sales and services department of the HMO. The STIG is comprised of a manager, four analysts, one senior analyst, and two data coordinators. The nature of the work requires employees to have a strong technical background as well as business knowledge. Also critical to the position is the ability to communicate effectively with team members and other departments within the company.

Problem Description

The major communication problem in the department—according to one of the four analysts—is between the manager of STIG and her staff. The same staffer reports that a secondary problem relates to the communication between the manager and other departments, particularly the sales and services department.

The analyst summarizes the nature of communication within STIG as follows:

- **One on one meetings:** On a biweekly basis, the manager is scheduled to meet with each staff member to review projects and issues. The major problem with this forum is that the manager regularly cancels these meetings. Often staff members will "save" information that they need to discuss with the manager, only to find out that the manager is not available to meet as scheduled. This is particularly frustrating for staff members who spend time preparing for this meeting, only to arrive at the manager's office and be told that the manager had to cancel. Because these sessions are regularly called off, information that the manager should be receiving is not communicated on time, and in other cases

information the manager should receive is not communicated at all.
- **Staff meetings:** On a biweekly basis (alternative week of the one-on-one meetings), the manager holds staff meetings. The meetings are two hours in length and dreaded by most staff members. The manager sets the agenda for the meeting, but the staff does not receive the agenda until the time of the meeting. Therefore, staff often find themselves unprepared to speak about specific topics on the agenda. In addition, the meetings often run over the allotted two-hour time frame. Furthermore, certain items on the agenda are not particularly relevant to the group (for example, information about sales presentations), and some team members feel that the manager "just likes to hear herself talk."
- **Written communications:** The majority of the written communication between team members and the manager is via e-mail. In fact, e-mail is often used instead of face-to-face interaction. The manager is very timely when responding to e-mail inquiries and often forwards work requests and policy information via e-mail. In some cases, e-mail has been effective, but in other cases, a face-to-face meeting may be more appropriate because of the nature of the topic being discussed or the need for immediate verbal and nonverbal feedback on the issue.

As it relates to communication with other departments, the analyst contends that the sales and services department repeatedly complains that information from STIG is not timely or clear. Occasionally, there are complaints about the accuracy of information. It is the STIG manager who is responsible for communicating information to sales and services.

- Is there definitely a communication problem in this department?
- Can you assume that the assessments of this one staff member are accurate?

- Assume that a number of staffers speak to the manager about problems with communication in the department. Further assume that the manager decides that it would be best to get an assessment of communication quality from a professional. Consequently, she hires you to examine the quality

of organizational communication. How would you proceed?
- Assume that you conduct the test and find that the manager is indeed deficient in terms of organizational communication. How would you tactfully communicate these conclusions to her?

What Is a Communication Audit?

"We need very strong ears to hear ourselves judged frankly and because there are few who can endure frank criticism without being stung by it, those who venture to criticize us perform a remarkable act of friendship."[1]

Most people are familiar with the word "audit" but associate the term with an accounting procedure or an action of the Internal Revenue Service. A financial audit is an assessment of the financial condition of a particular organization or person. The word "audit" has a similar meaning in organizational communication study. In the same way a financial audit tests the financial conditions of an organization, a communication audit is an examination of the quality of communication within an organization. In simple terms, an audit is a test.

Sometimes the phrase communication audit is perceived to mean a particular type of audit called the ICA communication audit. We'll discuss the ICA audit technique later in this chapter. However, at this point, keep in mind that a communication audit is any test that is designed to examine communication quality within an organization.

Gordon identifies several values of conducting communication audits. Communication audits can:

- Portray the overall nature of communication in a particular organization
- Describe the value and relevance of specific communication tools
- Assess whether employees have received key messages
- Help organizations develop a strategic plan for overall communication quality
- Develop an ongoing process for measuring effectiveness of communication in an organization.[2]

A key to effectively realizing these potential benefits is using an auditing technique that will provide meaningful results.

Audit Qualities and Components

Validity and Reliability

Two terms used in testing are *validity* and *reliability*. Regardless of what is being examined, your test needs to be both valid and reliable.

A *valid* test is one that tests what it is designed to test. A *reliable* test is one that could be replicated; i.e., if you were to employ a reliable test a second or third time, you would get similar results on the subsequent occasions as you did on the initial, or any other, occasion.

These qualities are very important to auditors or anyone who is conducting any research study. In order to clarify the terms, consider some examples related first to validity and then to reliability.

Validity

Assume you took a course called *The History of Advertising*. If your two-hour final exam for the course required that you analyze nine contemporary advertising campaigns, then that test would not be valid. It would not be considered valid for at least two reasons. The first reason is that your course covered the *history* of advertising. The final exam appears to be based on specific current advertisements. Therefore, the final exam did not test what it was allegedly designed to test. Also, since you needed to analyze nine cases, you would be tested on how quickly you could read and write, because you only had two hours for the exam. The test wouldn't be testing your knowledge of the history of advertising; it would be testing how quickly you could analyze specific current cases. Therefore, it would be an invalid test.

Consider another example. Assume that you were being tested to see if you could *deliver* a business presentation. An exam that only asked you to provide definitions of extemporaneous and manuscript speaking would *not* be valid. The test would have to include some behavioral component that evaluated how well you could deliver a speech, not simply if you knew the names of different presentation styles. Otherwise it would be invalid since it would not assess if you could *deliver* a business presentation.

Similarly, any comprehensive communication audit should test what it was designed to test in order for it to be valid.

Validity and Communication Skill Testing

If an auditor decided to assess the communication skills of all employees in terms of their written, oral, listening, and reading capabilities, then that auditor could—if the testing mechanism was a good one—derive some meaningful information about employees' communication skill sets. However, as we have seen in previous chapters, organizational communication consists of much more than just employee writing and speaking skills. Therefore, in order to conduct a valid audit, we need to assess much more than individual communication skill sets. Were we only to assess skill proficiency and assume that what we discovered reflected the core communication problems in the organization, we would be making a serious testing error. Our results would be both invalid and illusory.

Consider the bulleted paragraphs below. Each paragraph reviews a principle that has been discussed in the book. Also, each example suggests why parochial skill set testing will provide incomplete, invalid, and illusory audit results.

- Contemporary organizational communication requires understanding the relative values of alternative approaches to communicating information. We know, for example, that indiscriminate and overabundant e-mail usage can swamp diligent employees and undermine the overall communication system. Excellent writers or speakers may be skilled and gifted, but if they do not make wise choices when selecting media for communicating, their writing and speaking skills will be a limited asset.
- Source credibility is a key factor in effective organizational communication. Communication skill sets are irrelevant if receivers do not perceive a source's communications, however eloquently articulated, to be credible.
- Organizational culture can affect communication, and, concurrently, communication can affect organizational culture. Organizational culture is an important factor that affects

productivity. Communication skill set capabilities do not necessarily correlate with a supportive communication climate and culture. Some persons who are skilled writers or speakers may actually employ their skills to create an uncomfortable culture and climate.

• Since most organizations are made up of interdependent units or departments, it is important to establish channels for communication between these related units. Regardless of communication set skill levels, these networks must exist in order for employees to exercise their inherent skills.

In sum, we know that organizational communication is multidimensional. Therefore, if all a company did when conducting (what was intended to be) a comprehensive organizational communication audit was test how efficiently people could read, write, speak, and listen, it would obtain test results that were incomplete. The analysis of these incomplete data would be worse than meaningless. The organization would be under the illusion that it had assessed its internal communication when it had simply examined an aspect of it.

Consider this analogy: assume that you sensed that you needed a complete physical check-up. You wanted to be very sure that you were in good health and that no insidious infections were coursing through your system. Would you be content to visit a dermatologist, and then be relieved when an unattractive blemish was removed? It is not likely that you would feel relieved. You would want the physical examination to be comprehensive.

Similarly, an organization communication audit must be comprehensive. Otherwise the test would not be valid. It would not be testing what it was designed to test.

Reliability

If you are the type of person who gets on the scale in the morning, you are no doubt interested in finding out how much you weigh. If you stand on the scale once and check your weight and then get on the scale a second time and see that you weigh forty pounds more than you had only seconds earlier, you would assume that there was something wrong with your scale. The results you were getting from standing on the scale were, apparently, not reliable. If the device was providing reliable results, the test of standing on the scale would yield about the same result each time you got on it. Similarly, when you conduct any test, you want to make sure that the testing mechanism is such that the results you obtain one time will be similar to the results you would obtain on a second or third or any other occasion.

Let's look at an organizational communication example. Assume that you were going to audit the communication quality at your university. In order to accomplish your goal, you decide to interview four separate groups of six persons. Each group would include a randomly selected population composed of two students, a faculty member, a chairperson, an academic dean, and a student affairs dean. Assume that during the group interview you plan to ask a comprehensive set of questions pertaining to organizational communication and you intend to meticulously record the responses. Subsequently, you and your team of analysts would review the records from each of the four groups and then draw conclusions about the quality of communication in the organization. Would this test be reliable? It could be but only would be if you could conduct this test again and reproduce the results.

There are a number of reasons why your test might not be reliable. Let's assume you, personally, were not conducting all of the focus groups, but that you had four associates who were helpers. It would be essential that each associate asked questions and perceived responses similarly. If Miranda and Jesse were researchers who drew different conclusions from the same observation, then your test does not have reliability. Depending on who is conducting the focus group, the results will vary.

Consider another example: let's assume you were doing all of the interviewing. After you completed interviewing the first group, you went on to conduct the second, third, and fourth focus groups. It is possible that your recording during the fourth session might not be as meticulous as it was during the first. By the time you interviewed the fourth group, you might have stopped asking follow-up questions or may have even altered the original questions you were to pose to the group. The test would not be reliable. Depending on fatigue and focus level, the test results will vary.

Relationship between Reliability and Validity

The following two related points may be helpful for clarifying reliability and validity as well as the relationship between the terms.

1. Reliability does not determine validity: This means that a test is not valid by virtue of its reliability. For example, assume that you desired to test how efficiently a particular work team communicated during their regular department meetings. If you tested the speaking abilities of each person in the team several times, and your results each time were consistent, then the test would be reliable. However, that reliability would not render the test valid. In this instance, for example, the test would be invalid—despite the reliability. Individual speaking skills are not the sole or primary criterion that determines effective team interaction. Your objective was to assess group interaction. Therefore, your test of members' speaking skills is not valid despite the fact that it happens to be reliable. A key point to remember then is that if a test is not valid, the reliability of the test is irrelevant.

2. Although reliability doesn't determine validity, it is a precondition for validity: If the results of a test cannot be replicated, then that test could not possibly be testing accurately what it is designed to test. If each time you stand on the scale on a given morning the results are wildly different, by definition you are not obtaining reliable results from the testing procedure. You also could not possibly be testing what you desired to test—your weight. If you were a wrestler and needed to "make weight" to compete in a match, you would need a scale that you could stand on repeatedly and provide reliable results. Otherwise you would never know if that test was valid—testing what you needed to test in order to see if you would "make weight." In order for researchers to have any chance at validity, they must use a test that is reliable.

Audit Components

As we have discussed, a communication audit must be multidimensional in order to be valid. Two questions naturally surface: (1) What are those dimensions that need to be tested? (2) What does each dimension entail?

Dean suggests that an audit must examine information management, organizational networks, the communication climate, and individual communication skill sets.[3] Let's examine each of these areas.

Information Management

Organizations must intelligently communicate information to employees. A valid audit will test whether information is getting to employees and whether vehicles used for communicating information are effective. Specifically an audit will address the following questions:

- Are messages communicated that describe job tasks, organizational policies, and performance evaluation?
- Are these messages communicated in a timely manner?

- Do recipients consider these messages credible and pertinent?
- Are messages communicated clearly and accurately?
- Does the organization use appropriate methods for communicating information? For example,
  - Are e-mail, social networks, and teleconferencing used appropriately?
  - Are printed manuals/the company newsletter/internal magazines effective?
  - Does the Web site represent the organization appropriately?
  - Are briefings efficiently delivered and conducted?
  - Are messages disseminated at the annual meeting effective?
- What "noises" typically create "message distortion?"

Communication Networks

In order for an audit to be valid, it must test the quality of the various networks within the organizations. Specifically:

- Regarding upward networks:
  - Do workers trust the networks?
  - Can employees comfortably communicate:
    - Problems?
    - Suggestions?
    - Feedback related to messages sent downward?
  - Is there a mechanism for providing feedback to upwardly sent messages?
- Regarding downward networks:
  - Are there channels that allow management to communicate to subordinates?
  - Do serial transmissions create:
    - Serial distortions?
    - Untimely communications?
- Regarding horizontal networks:
  - Do networks exist that allow for interaction between interrelated departments?
  - Are there "redundancies" ensuring interdepartmental "penetration"? (See Chapter 6.)
  - Does interdepartmental communication reflect cooperation or competition?
- Regarding external networks:
  - Are there navigable channels that permit prospective clients, or current clients, an opportunity to communicate with the organization?
  - Are there channels that allow organizational representatives easy access to clients and potential customers?
- Regarding formal network systems:
  - To what extent does information travel on the informal network or grapevine, as opposed to the formal network?
  - Is the informal network overwhelming the formal network?
  - Who are the isolates, bridges, and liaisons within the organization?
  - How would employees describe the grapevine in the organization?

Communication Climate

As we saw in Chapter 7, Redding and others argue that organizational climate and culture is a significant factor. Auditors, therefore, would need to test to see if the culture facilitated or retarded quality communication. Specifically,

- Is the organization's culture supportive or defensive?
- Do communications reflect indifference, manipulation, dogmatism, a sense of superiority?
- Do employees consider the organization's communications credible?
- Would employees characterize the organization as open or "transparent" in terms of willingness to share information?
- Do communications reflect a credible desire to emphasize excellence?
- Are employees encouraged to voice their opinions and participate in the decision making of the organization?
- Do employees feel as if management communicates messages of support when supportiveness is warranted?

Communication Skill Sets

If, as we have seen, a large percentage of an employee's daily activities deal with some form of communication, then employees must possess basic communication competencies. Daly lists seven skill sets that need to be tested.[4]

- *Predisposition to Communicate.* Specifically, are employees inclined to communicate or do they have a predisposition toward avoiding interaction? Shyness or communication apprehension is not an insignificant factor to examine. It is possible that when compelled to speak, someone may reflect oral communication competencies. However, they may rarely exercise these skills if not compelled to do so.[5]
- *Knowledge of Communication Principles.* Are individuals aware of basic tenets of communication, for example, the need for audience analysis, the concept of communication noise, transmission, as well as constitutive definitions of communication? The assumption is that understanding principles will affect communication competence.
- *Public Speaking Capabilities.* Can individuals deliver messages clearly, use appropriate language, select appropriate speaking styles, use extemporaneous as well as manuscript formats, organize a message, handle questions, adapt to audiences, and use visual aids?
- *Interviewing Skills.* Can individuals interview prospective employees? Can they interview for internal positions?
- *Listening Skills.* Can employees comprehend information, evaluate what they hear, nonverbally display they are listening to messages, and successfully make use of what they have heard?[6]
- *Conversational Performance.* Conversational performance includes abilities to express thoughts clearly; encourage and generate information from others; understand what others are saying; adapt to particular situations, persons, and topics; and cope with deception, persuasion, and difficult people.[7]
- *Communicate in Small Groups.* An assessment of one's ability to communicate in small groups would examine the ability to participate, focus on team goals, assess the process of team interaction while contributing (notion of participant-observation discussed in Chapter 8), and help make intelligent team decisions.[8]

Methods for Conducting Audits

Once you have clarified what it is you need to test, you are ready to begin to conduct the audit. Your primary consideration involves selecting an appropriate research method for collecting and analyzing the data.

A communication log is difficult to keep. Employees may not always capture how they have reacted to the messages they receive, and this information can be relevant to the overall assessment of communication in the organization.

There are several methods that can be used for conducting communication audits. Below you will find a brief description of a number of approaches. As will likely become apparent, each approach need not be used in isolation, but can be used in combination with some of the other methods. As will also become apparent, some of these techniques, when not used in combination with other methods, will present problems related to validity and reliability.

Focus Groups

"Focus group" is a term used to describe a group of individuals who convene to respond to questions about a particular issue. Marketing companies, for example, utilize focus groups to discover how customers react to certain types of products. Communication auditors can use focus groups as well. A group of organizational women and men are invited to meet and are asked questions pertaining to communication in the organization. The groups can be heterogeneous or homogeneous. Sometimes a facilitator will sit in a room and another researcher will be seated behind a one-way window. (The participants would be made aware that there is an external observer.) After concluding several focus groups, researchers compile information gleaned from the group interviews and draw conclusions based on that pooled information.

Communication Logs

A communication log is a diary completed by individuals who are asked to document their communication-related activities. Participants might record their meetings, whom they phoned, when they responded to e-mail, reactions to briefing sessions, memoranda they received, and other communication-related information. Subsequently, researchers would collect the diaries, review them, and draw conclusions based on the information contained therein.

Observation

Sometimes this technique is called *shadowing*. Observers or shadowers simply follow a participant during a specific period of time. The observers record information regarding the person's communication activities. It is, in part, an objective assessment of what is taking place and a subjective assessment of the quality of interaction. An observer may record that a manager met with four employees individually to discuss performance and also that the manager spoke and listened effectively during the period. The subjective assessments could be based on objective criteria. That is, an observer might have a checklist of things to look for while observing, but still needs to make qualitative assessments of how well or how poorly the subject was meeting these communication objectives.

Executive One-on-One Interviews

Instead of a focus group composed of executives, this approach is dyadic. An auditor meets individually with several executives and asks questions pertaining to the executives' perspectives on organizational communication issues. The interview questions could be similar to those used for focus groups. For example, questions might include: What is your feeling about the value of your company's Web site? Do you prefer printed methods for communicating information? Are you comfortable using electronic media when you need to relay information to your subordinates? Do you feel as if you receive adequate information from related departments? Do you find that people communicate efficiently during your various meeting sessions?

Surveys

A survey used in this context is synonymous with what is typically called a "questionnaire." Employees are asked to write responses to questions pertaining to organizational communication issues. Respondents will complete a questionnaire and leave the completed forms with an auditor, and subsequently these results will be recorded and analyzed. This approach offers the advantage of anonymity. Also, surveys provide quantitative data that can be attractive to people who respond positively to results presented statistically. Finally, this approach allows for easy demographic comparisons. Let's assume that an audit is being conducted at an organization that has multiple sites. Further assume that one demographic question asks respondents to indicate the particular site where they are located. Survey analysis will allow auditors to make distinctions between work sites in terms of communication quality.

Communication Experience or Critical Incident Interviews

Critical incidents refer to a particular type of interview where the respondent is asked, essentially, only two questions. They are asked to describe an excellent communication experience and to describe a poor communication experience. The incident must indeed be an experience. If a respondent were to say, "our meetings are terrible," the auditor would ask for more specific information and ask the interviewee to describe a particular incident when a meeting was problematic because of some communication-related issue. Auditors would subsequently review these experiences and determine if certain types of problems and successes recur.

Publication Content Analysis

Content analysis is a very specific method of examining communication content. Some people use the phrase "content analysis" to mean any subjective assessment of communication content. However, originally the phrase was meant to describe a quantitative procedure that is used for examining such matters as sexist language in elementary school readers, national perspectives on international issues, language usage in novels, etc.[9] For communication audits, content analysis would be used to examine publications, such as a company's rules and regulation manuals, newsletters, Web sites, or any other text-based communications. Content analysis has also been used to evaluate nontext material as well, for example, photographs in publications.

ECCO Analysis

ECCO analysis was developed by Keith Davis, whom we met in Chapter 6 when we discussed communication networks and the grapevine. ECCO is an acronym for episodic communication channels in organizations. The ECCO analysis procedure required that participants complete a short survey referring to a particular unit of information they had received.

For example, a question might read: "Do you know that Joan Podkowsy has been appointed to be the head of marketing?" If the respondent writes "no," the survey is over. Respondents who write

Gender: ☐ Female ☐ Male

Age: ☐ Under 20 years ☐ 21–30 ☐ 31–40 ☐ 41–50 ☐ Over 50 years

Post: ☐ Full-time ☐ Part-time ☐ Temporary full-time
☐ Temporary part-time

How long employed: ☐ Under 1 year ☐ 1–5 yrs ☐ 6–10 yrs
☐ 11–15 yrs ☐ Over 15 yrs

Present position: ☐ I don't supervise anyone ☐ Middle manager
☐ Senior manager

Other (please specify) _____

What is your job? _____

Please check the box beside each of the statements below if you knew this information before you completed this questionnaire. If you did not know it, please leave the box blank. If you leave all boxes blank do not complete any more of the questionnaire.

☐ Willie Meyers is leaving.
☐ Willie Meyers is going to Head Office.
☐ Willie Meyers was Head of Customer Services.
☐ The post of Head of Customer Services will not be re-advertised.
☐ The new Head of Communications is Jose Ortiz.
☐ Jose Ortiz will now be responsible for customer services.

From what source did you first hear or read about this information (please check only one box)?

Written medium

☐ Posting on Web site
☐ Notice on staff board
☐ Formal memo
☐ E-mail

Talking medium

☐ Colleague
☐ Line manager
☐ Senior manager
☐ Overheard someone

Other (please specify) _____

Through which channel did you learn about this information?

☐ Staff meeting
☐ Company video
☐ Written communication

☐ Informal conversation
☐ Telephone call
☐ Intranet

Other (please specify) _____

When did you first learn about this information (please circle only one)?

| *Days ago* | Today | 1 | 2 | 3 | 4 | 5 | 6 |
| *Weeks ago* | 1 | 2 | 3 | 4 | | | |

Where were you when you first learned about this information?

☐ Cafeteria
☐ While visiting another department
☐ Outside of the company

☐ At my normal working location
☐ At a formal staff meeting

Other (please specify) _____

Figure 11.1 ECCO Analysis Survey Sheet

Source: Adapted from Hargie, Owen, and Dennis Tourish, "Data Collection Log-Sheet Methods," in *Handbook of Communication Audits for Organizations,* edited by Owen Hargie and Dennis Tourish, Routledge, 2000: pp. 109–110.

"yes" would be asked from whom they had first heard the information and where they were when they heard it. If a respondent has the general idea that Joan Podkowsky has been hired but is not sure what she was hired to do, that information would be recorded on the form as well. With ECCO analysis, an auditor hopes to acquire a sense of message flow and use of organizational networks, both formal and informal.

Skill Testing

Previously, we discussed the need for employees to have basic communication skill competencies. Some communication audits do not involve testing employee skill competence but do contain questions that ask employees if they perceive other employees to have such competence. Instead of testing to see if all those who give daily briefings can deliver these presentations well, the audit would assess whether those who listened to the briefings were satisfied with the qualities of the presenter and the presentations.

A Blended Approach

In the early 1970s, the International Communication Association (ICA) developed an audit tool in an attempt to address problems associated with the relatively weak communication audits that had been previously utilized.[10] The instrument the association designed blended several different testing formats. Auditing is sufficiently misunderstood such that some people are under the assumption that all communication audits are ICA audits. This is incorrect from two vantage points. First, as we have discussed, there are several types of communication audits. Second, the ICA audit has been in the public domain since 1979.[11] It no longer exists as it once did. Any person can adapt, and many have adapted, what was this audit, but none of these adaptations are or could be an ICA audit.[12]

What is important to remember about this approach is that (a) it was designed because other techniques were weak and (b) it used a blended format that incorporated various complementary tools. Let's consider five components of this type of blended approach.

A Questionnaire The questionnaire is a standard survey that is administered to all members of an organization. Persons respond to the survey anonymously, and all respondents are told that they will receive a "short report" of the audit results. This short report is, essentially, a synopsis of the more detailed analysis provided to the client. Questions on the survey pertain to several communication areas, including networks, information management, culture, and perception of skill sets. The survey includes a series of demographic questions that are developed on the basis of discussions with a client. A client, for example, may wish to see if men typically are more satisfied with communication in teams than women and analyze data on the basis of this and other demographic categories.

Interview Procedure Subsequent to the analysis of the survey data, auditors ask a series of questions of a percentage of the population that has been either randomly or purposefully selected. There are two objectives for these interviews. The first is to obtain corroboration of the data gleaned from the survey. The second objective is to encourage respondents to elaborate.

Let's assume that data gleaned from the survey suggested that workers were very satisfied with information they had received regarding safety procedures in the organization. During the interview respondents would be asked how they felt about information they received regarding safety procedures. The hope would be that the respondents would comment that they indeed were satisfied with that information. If only two or three respondents said they were unhappy, that would not be an issue. However, if dozens indicated that they were not satisfied, then

Receiving Information from Others

Topic Area	This is the amount of information I receive now					This is the amount of information I need to receive				
	Very Little	Little	Some	Great	Very Great	Very Little	Little	Some	Great	Very Great
How well I am doing in my job	1. 1	2	3	4	5	2. 1	2	3	4	5
My job duties	3. 1	2	3	4	5	4. 1	2	3	4	5
Organizational policies	5. 1	2	3	4	5	6. 1	2	3	4	5
Play and benefits	7. 1	2	3	4	5	8. 1	2	3	4	5
How technological changes affect my job	9. 1	2	3	4	5	10. 1	2	3	4	5
Mistakes and failures of my organization	11. 1	2	3	4	5	12. 1	2	3	4	5
How I am being judged	13. 1	2	3	4	5	14. 1	2	3	4	5
How my job-related problems are being handled	15. 1	2	3	4	5	16. 1	2	3	4	5
How organization decisions are made that affect my job	17. 1	2	3	4	5	18. 1	2	3	4	5
Promotion and advancement opportunities in my organization	19. 1	2	3	4	5	20. 1	2	3	4	5

Figure 11.2 Sample Format of ICA Communication Audit Survey
Source: Adapted from Goldhaber, Gerald, and Donald Rigers, *Auditing Organizational Communication*, Kendall Hunt Publishing Co., 1979: p. 6.

something would be wrong with the survey results. Therefore, an objective of the interview is to corroborate survey results.

After corroborating the information, an interviewer might present the following question: What is there about the way the safety information was communicated that you liked? The respondent might comment that it was timely or that it was presented both orally and in writing. Whatever the response, the auditor would have additional explanatory information about the item in question.

Communication Experience This technique often called Critical Incidents, was described earlier in this chapter. The communication experience approach is a complementary strategy in this blended format. By reviewing communication incidents and culling them, an auditor may find several examples of outstanding communication about, for example, a particular innovative safety procedure. Communication experiences can help auditors explain why the reaction to safety-related communication is positive. The procedure can also be used to determine modeling approaches. If a particular method for communicating safety information proved efficient, then perhaps the same method can be used when relaying other information in the organization.

During a typical workday, I usually communicate about work-related matters with the following people through the following channels:

	Identifi-cation	Formal Organizational Structure	informal (Grapevine) Organizational Structure
Executive		How Important Is the Communication?	
Stenographer-secretary	0001	_____ A B C D E	_____ A B C D E
Senior Stenographer	0002	_____ A B C D E	_____ A B C D E
Executive secretary	0003	_____ A B C D E	_____ A B C D E
Assistant executive director	0004	_____ A B C D E	_____ A B C D E
Assistant manager	0005	_____ A B C D E	_____ A B C D E
Telephone operator	0006	_____ A B C D E	_____ A B C D E
Executive director	0007	_____ A B C D E	_____ A B C D E
Administration and Finance			
Assistant director for administration	0008	_____ A B C D E	_____ A B C D E
Typist	0009	_____ A B C D E	_____ A B C D E
Accounting clerk	0010	_____ A B C D E	_____ A B C D E
Accounting clerk-typist	0011	_____ A B C D E	_____ A B C D E
Assistant accountant	0012	_____ A B C D E	_____ A B C D E
Senior accountant	0013	_____ A B C D E	_____ A B C D E
Typist	0014	_____ A B C D E	_____ A B C D E
Stenographer	0015	_____ A B C D E	_____ A B C D E

Key: A = not at all important
B = somewhat important
C = fairly important
D = very important
E = extremely important

Figure 11.3 ICA Communication Audit Network Analysis Instrument
Source: Goldhaber, Gerald, *Organizational Communication,* 6th ed., Brown/Benchmark, 1993: p. 363.

Similarly, the communication experience approach can be valuable for negative incidents. If interview and survey data suggest that upward networks are illusory, the communication experience sheets can identify specific incidents that contributed to this perception.

Network Analysis This component involves employing a brief questionnaire, as shown in Figure 11.3.

Members of a particular department are asked to complete the survey in order to gauge who in the group interacts with whom and to assess who is an isolate, a liaison, or a bridge.[13] The goal of network analyses is to compare the formal network with the actual organizational network, which includes both formal and informal channels.

Communication Diary The communication diary component is similar to the communication log explained previously in this chapter. The goal is to obtain "indications of actual communication behavior among individuals, groups, and the entire organization."[14] The value of the diary depends on the approach taken by the persons completing it. In isolation, the diary can lack validity if respondents enter items that reflect positively on behavior regardless of whether the actual behavior occurred. As a complementary strategy in a blended format, recurring items in several diaries can support results gleaned from other parts of the testing instrument.

External or Internal Auditing?

An audit can be conducted by external consultants or by internal agents. Some communication consulting companies will actually sell their products to clients. The clients can then administer the audit procedures themselves.[15] An organization would not have to buy any particular audit, however. An organization could—by studying information that is available to the public—construct, administer, and then analyze its own communication audit.

The value of hiring an external agent is that an organization runs less of a risk of the audit's credibility being questioned by employees who might speculate that the results have been laundered to portray the administration in a positive light. Another advantage of hiring external consultants is that they are allegedly experts in the area. Organizational women and men have other work to do. It may demand more time for internal agents to conduct the audit because of their lack of familiarity with the process.

Certainly it can't be ignored that an advantage of conducting the audit internally is financial. Audit expenses are not insignificant. An external communication audit can cost from $25,000 to several hundred thousand dollars.[16]

Another consideration that can affect cost is time frame and sequencing. How much time an organization can dedicate to conducting the audit can affect not only the expense but the decision to undergo the process altogether. It requires a relatively short amount of time to distribute questionnaires. Even the analysis of the survey data need not require a lengthy period. However, the interviews, network analyses, and communication experience evaluations can involve months of investigation. An external auditor needs to explain time issues to the client, and if a client undertakes the process as an internal project, time considerations must be a factor when deciding whether to proceed with the audit.

Reporting Results

When the audit is complete, whether conducted internally or externally, the data and recommendations must be presented to the client. This can be done by presenting a written report that is complemented by an oral presentation, or simply by submitting a written report and inviting questions subsequently. The written report should include:

- Detailed explanations of the findings
- A set of specific recommendations that could be implemented by the client
- A schedule for implementation and follow-up assessment

Reporting results to clients can be a sensitive and difficult matter. Conclusions from a study conducted by DeWine, James, and Walence are important to note. These researchers examined the value of the ICA audit specifically, but one comment they made is likely applicable to all audits and all audit reporting. They found that: "Managers maintain their own form of

Reporting Results

Assume that you have conducted an extensive audit of an organization. Your findings indicate the following. Subordinates believe that:

- Communication from upper management is not timely and not credible.
- Administrators actively discourage upward communication.
- They are not told whether they are performing well or poorly and, in general, feel that they are underappreciated.
- Administrators have very weak public speaking skills as demonstrated in large organizational meetings.

Further, assume that you had met with representatives of upper management before you began the audit. On the basis of what they told

you then, you know that they will be stunned to hear the results of the audit. Management had essentially claimed that the company's communication problems were due to employees not paying attention to communications from management.

Finally, assume that you fear that the clients will reject your findings, even though you are certain that your test was both valid and reliable. You are concerned that the clients might be suspicious of your diagnostic abilities since your results vary from what the clients were certain would be the results. You wonder if perhaps they will not recommend you to other potential clients.

When you report your results to your clients, do you "soften" the nature of the information to make the results seem more palatable and less critical of management?

organizational reality. The administrators select and accept issue analysis and recommendations from an audit according to their own perceptions of organizational reality and what is most appropriate for their organizations *regardless of the nature of the recommendations*"[17] (emphasis added).

This conclusion is remarkable, yet not surprising. The value of any audit is a function of how willing administrators are to accept the conclusions of the auditors. It is easy for people to dismiss information that is inconsistent with what they want to hear. As an auditor I have confronted this phenomenon firsthand. Administrators who very genuinely sought a communication analysis were nonplussed when some conclusions were different from those that they had expected. It requires diplomacy and skill to inform administrators that a problem with communication may relate to their own habits, which undermine efficiency. Such diplomacy may be as significant a factor for auditing as any measurement technique an auditor employs. And even the most diplomatic communicator will be unsuccessful if information is antithetical to what a recipient is willing to process. This is the essence of the DeWine et al. excerpt. Communication auditing is only valuable if individuals in an organization are willing to accept criticism and the culture of the organization genuinely supports acknowledging deficiencies in order to excel.

PRACTITIONER PERSPECTIVE

Angela Sinickas: Founder and President

Angela Sinickas is the founder and president of Sinickas Communications She is a pioneer in the field of organizational communication measurement and the author of *How to Measure Your Communication Programs*. Her company's recent clients include Merck, Nordstrom, 3M, Raytheon, ExxonMobil, and Lockheed Martin. Ms. Sinickas's work assessing communication quality has been cited in *Harvard Business Review* and *Investor's Business Daily* as well as several other publications.

As you read through this section, consider the following questions:

- How do Sinickas's comments relate to the importance of validity?
- Why does Sinickas favor quantitative approaches over qualitative approaches like focus groups?
- What is your reaction to the bolded statement in her narrative?

The biggest challenge for auditors is to make sure that they're measuring the right things. All too often communicators measure only their outputs—the messages and channels they're producing—without connecting them to the outcomes of using these outputs.

For valid and reliable information, you need to use a quantitative auditing approach. In many cases that means using a survey, but only if you're careful in selecting a large enough, and truly random, sample and being sure that the completed surveys are returned in the same proportions. Many other quantitative techniques can be used in an audit. For example, a content analysis can quantify to what extent the communications you send out are aligned with the goals of your organization. You can also quantitatively track changes in your audience's behaviors due to your communications—either over time or using a pilot/control group study to isolate the impact of communication versus other possible change agents.

I have had situations where clients did not want to "hear" what our research had uncovered. Executives are all too often sheltered from the reality of their organizations by middle managers who don't want to be the bearers of bad news. Even when executives conduct meetings with employees, the employees won't always be candid if their supervisors are also in the meeting. Focus group findings are more often challenged than survey results, and with good reason. There are too many variables in how the focus group participants are selected and how the facilitators conduct the sessions. Plus, few organizations involve enough participants to constitute a valid sample for projecting findings to the entire group. I did have one executive who refused to believe some negative results from a survey administered to all employees, in spite of having a very large response rate. And I've known executives who give more credence to lots of direct quotes from focus groups than to survey results.

There's no reason an organization can't do an audit without outside help, as long as they have appropriate resources available inside. For example, if they're doing a survey, they should find someone in HR, finance, or marketing who can help them in determining sample sizes. They should use the experience of someone in organizational development or market research to ensure the questions they're asking and the response scales they're using will provide usable data. **Most important, for any type of qualitative research, the facilitators must not be the individuals who are responsible for creating the communications that are being audited, for a number of reasons that affect the quality of the interaction in the sessions.** However, if the communication department has recently hired someone who has no vested interest in the existing communication program, that person could conduct the qualitative research pretty well, assuming he or she had some training in the process. Otherwise, I'd recommend using someone from HR or market research to conduct interviews and focus groups more objectively.

The downside of doing it all yourself is that you will make mistakes and it will take longer because you're inventing everything yourself. The halfway solution is to do as much as you can in-house but use outside resources judiciously, perhaps for peer review.

If you choose to hire someone from the outside, choose an auditor who has had lots of experience. Talk to his or her previous clients. Ask to look at samples of the types of reports he or she has presented to other clients. Determine if the reports would be useful to you or if they are organized and written in a way that only a researcher would find useful. Try to find an auditor who not only knows research but has also worked in communication. Preferably, find one who has spent some time working within organizations, not just in consulting firms. You'll find that the recommendations the auditor comes up with will be more practical and usable.

SUMMARY: A TOOLBOX

- If communication is important, then testing communication becomes a priority.
- Any method of auditing must examine organizational communication comprehensively.
- There are several methods available. Consultants and techniques have proliferated over the last decade.
- A manager can pick and choose from the available methods to suit the needs of the organization.
- Audit findings should include a detailed explanation of findings, a set of recommendations for solution, and a sequence for implementation.
- Audit results may vary from client expectations. Auditors, therefore, must be diplomatic when relaying information that may be inconsistent with client expectations.

REVIEW AND DISCUSSION QUESTIONS

1. How would you describe the phrase *communication audit* to someone who was not familiar with the study of organizational communication?
2. What would make a test on this chapter material valid?
3. Why would a communication audit that only examined printed communications not be valid?
4. What must be tested in order for a communication audit to be valid?
5. What are the advantages of having a "communication experience" or "critical incident" component to an audit?
6. How can reporting audit data to clients provide an ethical challenge?

GROUP/ROLE-PLAY

In a group of four to six, review the issues surrounding the case that begins this chapter. Attempt to gain consensus regarding the questions at the end of the case.

For the role-play, one member of the group assumes a representative form STIG. Another assumes the role of the manager. A third represents someone from the sales and services department

- Role-play a face-to-face meeting between these three persons that has been called by the STIG employee who wishes to discuss the communication problems that employees and other departments are having.

Chapter **12**

Careers in Organizational Communication

Chapter in a Nutshell

As you've read the Practitioner Perspectives throughout this book, you may have found yourself wondering how you could join them. If so, you are not alone. Students who become interested in organizational communication are often curious about career options. As has been discussed throughout the text, organizational communication principles are applicable to nearly any work-related activity. Graduates find jobs in sales, marketing, fund raising, advertising, and other varied occupations. In addition, an increasing number of positions focus specifically on issues pertaining to organizational communication. This chapter discusses jobs available to those who study organizational communication and how you can prepare to compete successfully.

When you have completed this chapter, you should be able to:

- Describe the range of work opportunities available to those who have studied organizational communication.
- Identify job titles for people who work in this field.
- Describe the responsibilities of some organizational communication practitioners.
- Discuss the educational preparation necessary for those seeking work in organizational communication.
- List recommended co-curricular activities for those interested in this field.
- Identify two professional associations for organizational communication practitioners.

CASE 12.1
What Can I Do with This?

Thirty students enrolled in an introductory course in organizational communication. Many of these students would not have registered for the class had it not been required. In fact, several were under the impression that the class was not about communication in organizations, but rather about how to organize speeches and other forms of communication. Few, if any, of the students intended to pursue a career in organizational communication. A survey on the first day of class revealed that 80 percent anticipated seeking careers in marketing, finance, and the media, with 10 percent considering other career paths and the other 10 percent undecided.

Eight weeks into the term, several students began considering work in organizational communication but were unsure: Would there be any jobs in this field to pursue? One sophomore told his parents that he wanted to switch his major. His father sounded perplexed: "What

are you going to do with that, open a communication store?"

A number of students approached the instructor with variations of the same question: "What can someone do with a degree in organizational communication?" The instructor responded with a series of questions of her own:

- How does someone go about discovering the job opportunities available in any field?
- What careers do you think might be available to people knowledgeable about the topics you have now studied, including communication networks, knowledge and information management, crisis communication, group interaction, intercultural communication, external organizational communication, and interpersonal conflict and communication?
- How should you prepare to compete for these positions?

What are your answers to the instructor's questions?

Communication as Critical to Success

As we saw in Chapter 1, communication within organizations is both pervasive and critical to success. All women and men—regardless of whether their job title includes the word *communication,*

and regardless of whether their job description identifies communication as a responsibility—must be effective communicators. Managers, engineers, actors, librarians, instructors, physicians, and politicians—all of these function more effectively if they are aware of organizational communication principles *and* are able to apply what they know in order to communicate skillfully and responsibly.

"Communication majors often struggle with this [career] problem because unlike their fellow students in more applied fields such as accounting ... [they find that] the job possibilities [in communication] are vast as are the kinds of organizations that hire for such positions."[1]

The study of organizational communication thus prepares students for nearly every career that involves collaboration.

However, students often, and understandably, want to know how a degree in organizational communication can lead directly to related employment. Accounting majors become accountants. Marketing majors get positions in marketing firms. Education majors often become teachers. Since the phrase *organizational communication* is unfamiliar to many and relatively nebulous compared to other areas of study, you and your parents may be concerned that organizational communication is not as practical as other majors.

There *are* careers for persons who study in organizational communication. Graduates with a corporate communication major find employment in a wide variety of fields.[2]

What Jobs Are Available?

Tables 12.1 and 12.2 list career areas for communication practitioners and the industry sectors that employ them. As you can see, the particular career areas listed are not dedicated communication positions, but do require communication skills. Students who have graduated from programs in organizational communication have gone into advertising, customer relations, and fund raising, to name just three areas. Human resources, investor relations, and management are among the industry sectors.[3]

In addition, many jobs have organizational communication responsibilities as their primary focus, as seen in Table 12.3. There is no guarantee that individuals in these positions will have had training in organizational communication. However, students with credentials in organizational communication often do secure these jobs. Table 12.4 identifies positions that have been secured by graduates in organizational communication at one university. Several college and university Web sites include links to similar lists.

Table 12.1 Organizational Communication Career Areas

Advertising	Management
Crisis management	Marketing
Customer relations	Public information
Fund raising	Public relations
Human resources	Publishing
Investor relations	Sales
Labor relations	Special events planning

Table 12.2 Industry Sectors

Automotive	Health care
Banking and finance	Insurance
Chemical	Manufacturing
Computer industry	Medical/health
Construction	Military
Education	Nonprofit associations
Engineering	Pharmaceuticals
Food and beverage	Retailing
Government	Transportation

Table 12.3 Job Titles: Organizational Communication

Communication campaign director	Employee orientation coordinator
Communication consultant	Employee publication editor/assistant
Corporate communication research analyst	Employee training director
Corporate speech writer	Governmental press secretary
Corporate television/producer/scriptwriter	Labor relations consultant
Director/manager/coordinator of:	Legal communication consultant
corporate communication	Marketing communication specialist
crisis management and communication	Media manager
employee communication	Ombudsman or corporate mediator
employee communication and training	Press secretary
employee information	Product promotion writer
employee involvement systems	Publications editor
employee publications	Script writer
external communication	Speech writer
internal communication	Spokesperson
investor relations	Sports information director
media relations	Technical writer
photo/audio/visual services	Trainer
public affairs	Upward communication coordinator
public information	Web coordinator
special events	Writer/editor corporate publications

Table 12.4 Positions Secured by Organizational Communication Students from One University

Community outreach coordinator	Managing director
Conference coordinator	Media buyer
Consumer hotline manager	Media coordinator
Customer service representative	National advertising manager
Director of client services	Promotions associate
Director of marketing	Public information officer
Events coordinator	Public relations director
Information management officer	Sales representative
Management trainer	Special events counselor
Manager of corporate communication	Supervisor human resources
Manager of marketing communication	Vice president of operations
Manager of public relations	Web project manager

Table 12.5 Advertised Openings in Organizational Communication, December 16, 2008, to January 27, 2009

Associate manager, communications	Internal communication consultant
Business proposal writer	Internal communications manager
Change communication consultant	Manager, customer communications
Communications advisor	Manager, external communications
Communications analyst	Manager of communications
Communications and marketing director	Manager, communications, and public affairs
Communications assistant	Manager, executive, and employee communications
Communications business partner	Managing director, collaborative communications group
Communications director	Marketing and communications coordinator
Communications manager	
Communications resource coordinator	Media relations manager
Communications specialist	Media relations representative
Content consultant	Public information officer
Contract writer	Public relations officer
Corporate communications manager	Senior business communicator
Corporate communications specialist	Senior communications advisor
Corporate communications, director	Senior communications specialist
Deputy director—global health communications	Senior corporate communications specialist
Digital communications specialist	Senior director, corporate media relations, public relations, and financial communications
Digital communications supervisor	Senior manager, internal communications
Director, communications	Senior manager, recognition programs
Director, marketing and communications	Senior marketing communications consultant
Director, media relations	Senior specialist, public involvement
Director of alumni affairs	Stakeholder engagement specialist
Director of communications, Brookings	Vice president, communications
Director of marketing and strategic communications	Vice president, internal communications
Director of outreach and communications	Vice president, public affairs and publishing
Director of public affairs	Web and CRM coordinator
Diversity communications manager	Web communications coordinator
E-marketing coordinator	Web manager
Employee communications manager	Writer/editor
Human resources communication analyst	
Human resources communication manager	

Are There Sufficient Openings?

Are there enough positions available, however? Table 12.5 lists over sixty job notices on just one Web site (www.iabc.com) for professional communicators. All appeared during a five-week period from December 16, 2008, through January 27, 2009. The number of openings is especially noteworthy since the interval included a major holiday time, and it occurred during one of the worst economic declines in U.S. history.[4] Often there were multiple postings for the same title.

What Do These Jobs Entail?

Many students wonder about specific responsibilities for people working in organizational communication. "What exactly will I be doing as manager of employee communication?" "What are the responsibilities of an internal communication consultant?" The responsibilities for these positions vary greatly. Consider some actual job descriptions.

Tables 12.6 and 12.7 give two examples—one for a former student who is now employed as a business communication specialist, the other for a manager of employee communication. Camenson, in *Great Jobs*, provides a more general description for another actual position, this one for a senior employee and communications specialist.

Table 12.6 Job Description: Business Communication Specialist

Duties and Responsibilities

- Overall development of communications plans
- Message development for publications and broadcasts
- Evaluation and data tracking of feedback on communications vehicles and products
- Development of video segments and broadcast communications
- Development and oversight of daily electronic communications on intranet
- Research and article writing on a variety of business topics
- Development, coordination, and production for companywide and business unit publications
- Meeting facilitation for editorial boards, focus groups, and usability groups
- Advise content submitters on proper positioning of their message in a way that reaches target audiences with maximum impact

Key Responsibilities

- Help enhance the employee experience by developing employee communication and engagement strategies to address multiple audiences, brands, and geographical regions.
- Develop and manage various companywide communication channels and vehicles, including in-person (e.g., CEO town halls), online (e.g., corporate intranet, social media), and written (global e-newsletter).
- Design and support employee forums and programs (e.g., senior leader efforts, guest speakers) and work across the business to provide input or assistance in business unit efforts.
- Help develop employee communication, branding, and engagement strategies for our 6,000+ employees across different brands and regions.
- Design and implement communication tools and vehicles that support a brand-infused culture.
- Create and drive a variety of employee communications and collaterals, such as change management planning, announcement timelines, Q and As, etc.

Table 12.7 Job Description: Business Communication Specialist

Sample Job Description: Employee Publications

• Lead a writing team

• Supervise the publication of internal magazines and newsletters

• Work with department heads to explore areas of interest for internal readers

• Supervise writers responsible for publishing in-house publications

• Write and edit news releases, publications, special projects, recruiting brochures

Sample Job Description: Corporate Training

• Identify training and development needs

• Plan, organize, and coordinate training and development activities

• Hire external resources to provide needed training for employees

• Seek out internal resources to assist in employee training

• Conduct management development workshops

• Evaluate training efforts

The qualified applicant will be able to plan communication strategies, lead a writing team, edit/write for nationally recognized publications, and serve internal clients.[5]

As you can see, in each case the responsibilities are both detailed and wide ranging.

Preparing for the Job Market

Once you become aware of the opportunities in the field, the next step is to consider how to prepare for these opportunities. That preparation includes educational foundations, in both theory and skill sets, and valuable co-curricular activities. It also includes the hard work of job hunting, including portfolio construction and networking.

Education: Theory and Principles

Preparation for a career in organizational communication requires continued study of the principles that were presented in this foundations course. As we discussed in Chapters 2 and 3, there can and should be symbiotic relationships between theory and practice. An understanding of principles and theories puts you in a more informed position when it comes to quality decision making. An awareness of systems theory, for example, enables you to recognize the need for links between interdependent units. An understanding of critical theory makes you more sensitive to the potential for destructive communication practices that can marginalize employees.

Beyond the principles and practices you have learned in earlier chapters, students who aspire to work involving organizational communication should consider advanced courses. Some typical course topics are:

- Information management
- Group dynamics and interaction
- Innovative communication technology

Applying the Principles—Test Yourself

Precareer Training

Select an area of organizational communication that you are most interested in. Assume that you have an opportunity to select your dream job in this area.

- What would your job responsibilities be?
- Why would you be qualified to meet these responsibilities?
- Why would it be necessary for an organization to have a person who handled these responsibilities?
- What have you done at school, at work, or while pursuing hobbies that could serve as evidence of your ability to excel in this capacity?
- What might you do to prepare yourself to be a strong candidate for the position you have described?

- Communication networks and networking
- Ethics and organizational communication
- Organizational culture and communication
- Interpersonal communication and conflict resolution
- Crisis communication
- Intercultural and international communication
- Business presentations and organizational training
- Consultation skills
- Communication assessment

Education: Communication Skill Sets

Career preparation also requires courses that focus on performance. These classes develop individual skill sets in listening, writing, reading, and speaking. There are four reasons for taking such classes.

First, knowledge of theory is not enough. There is absolutely no guarantee that familiarity with principles of communication will translate into communication skill. For example, knowing that orally communicated messages *should* be well organized does not guarantee that speakers will organize their presentations and communicate appropriately. Some communication majors—and even some faculty members with advanced degrees in communication—are inept communicators. Rigorous classes that force students to write, speak, read, and evaluate messages in simulated organizational contexts are particularly valuable.

A second reason for completing skills-based courses pertains to the application process itself. Your communication skills will affect the letters of application you write, your interviewing behavior, and the presentations you may be asked to make during an interview. Courses that develop communication skills make you a more competitive job applicant.

Third, in order to initiate, integrate, and administer communication programs, organizational communicators must be adept at informing and persuading internal audiences of the value of their innovations. For example, assume that in your role as business communication specialist you propose an employee suggestion program. This program necessitates conducting focus groups that you would conduct. After the focus group discussions, you must present your ideas to top management and other internal stakeholders. In forming your plan, you had to consider basic theories and communicate well during and after the focus groups. Making the case for its implementation, however, depends most on your ability to persuade employees and management of its merit.

Finally, it is wise to hone communication skills—advancement within organizations often depends on them. That is true throughout the workplace, but particularly in communication-related positions.

Co-curricular Activities

In pursuing careers in organizational communication, you may wish to supplement your work with relevant co-curricular activities. Wendy Ford, now dean at Western Carolina University and previously a professor of communication at Western Michigan University, suggests several activities that may render a candidate attractive to potential employers:[6]

- **Develop and present a communication skills workshop**. Your club may have trouble conducting its regular meetings. If so, you might offer to run a workshop on how to make sessions more effective. Communication practitioners often direct communication workshops. Organizing and delivering such a session would be good practice and would force you to organize what you know about this aspect of organizational communication.
- **Get involved in recruiting efforts for an organization**. Your department might be hiring a new faculty member and may seek student participation on the hiring committee. Participation may require (a) helping to construct a job description, (b) advertising, (c) interviewing, (d) group discussion to assess the relative merits of candidates, and (e) articulating to students and faculty why your group has selected the persons recommended. All of these activities would result in valuable experience.
- **Lead an orientation program for newcomers.** Your university may be interested in students who will serve as ambassadors and orientation counselors. Participation may require drafting relevant materials and making presentations to the new students.
- **Organize a guest speaker series.** A club to which you belong may decide to hold monthly sessions at which guests are invited to speak. Your participation would involve contacting the speakers, communicating the event to the public, and perhaps facilitating the Q-and-A session that is held after the speakers deliver their presentations.
- **Conduct a survey and prepare a formal report of findings.** Research on an assignment may be supplemented with the results of a survey that you conduct pertaining to the assigned topic. You would be responsible for creating the survey and articulating its results in writing. Many communication professionals regularly distribute surveys and then report the results to top management.
- **Create a Web site.** The ability to construct a Web site may soon become as necessary as securing an e-mail address. For yourself, your club, a class, or a group within a class, a Web site can inform others about yourself and the group.
- **Produce a video.** Many contemporary universities have instructional or production television studios. Consider taking a course in video production or participating in the production of an instructional video. Create a video, for example, explaining why undergraduates should engage in co-curricular activities relevant to their major.
- **Prepare a handbook for organizational members.** If your club benefits from the workshop you conduct on group interaction, perhaps you can develop a handbook for future

generations of club members. The handbook would explain the principles dicussed at the
workshop.

- **Develop a newsletter to circulate to organizational members or alumni.** Many units
within organizations distribute a newsletter, sometimes electronically. Volunteering to
work on one—or even initiating one—is a good way to gain experience that can enhance
your candidacy for positions in organizational communication.

The Communication Portfolio

As you prepare for job applications, consider creating a portfolio of your various curricular and
co-curricular activities. Jacqui Sweeney, a faculty member in cooperative education at Northeastern
University, notes that portfolios help students demonstrate their experience. "Many students complete a portfolio project, look at the result, and often say aloud, 'Did I do all that?'"[7]

In addition to reminding you of your work, creating a portfolio may help you realize how various activities are interrelated. It can also help you organize what you know so that you can better
articulate it during interviews.

Finally, a portfolio can be taken to interviews and may favorably impress those evaluating candidacies. Sweeney recommends that a portfolio include:

- A table of contents
- A current résumé
- An actual or model cover letter
- At least two letters of recommendation
- A writing sample from class
- Any newsletters, brochures, handbooks, Web sites, workshop agendas, advertising, art
  work, and other communications you have produced.
- Sample of any work conducted by a team of which you were a participating member,
  along with an explanation of your role on the team.

Networking

Networking is a valuable activity for anyone regardless of major field of study and career aspirations. Informal relationships are often crucial in determining life's successes. For those considering
organizational communication careers, it would be wise to join organizations that are comprised of
people in those fields. Two such organizations are the International Association of Business Communicators (IABC) and the Public Relations Society of America.

The IABC publishes the magazine *Communication World*, an easy-to-read magazine for corporate communicators. In addition, the IABC holds an annual convention, has regional chapters that
have monthly meetings, is a resource for people in the field, and publishes materials for those in
the field. The Public Relations Society of America, despite its name, also deals with issues in *both*
internal and external organizational communication. A visit to iabc.com and prsa.com will reveal
the wealth of information available to members.

In addition to organizations like these, there may be clubs on your campus for students interested in marketing communication, crisis communication, international business, corporate television, intercultural communication, or competitive forensics. Participating in such clubs can nourish
your network. Your university may also have an alumni association whose members would be eager
to discuss career paths with you. Contact the university members who administer this association to
see if alums are willing to help.

ETHICAL PROBE

A year ago you were a member of a team on a class project related to ethics and business communication. Although the group's final report was outstanding, your own participation on the project was minimal. It had to be limited: the team leader was tyrannical, usurping authority from others. "I can't deal with these idiots," he seemed to think. "I'll do it myself." Nevertheless, you reluctantly have to acknowledge that his contribution to the final report was as good as his behavior was bad.

As you are putting together your portfolio, you come across a copy of the report. You are reminded that it is aesthetically and substantively impressive. However, you are also reminded that, while it has your name on it, it has very little of you in it. Should you include it in your portfolio?

(A)

Jane Smith			
100 Jacob St. #6	Brooksdabe, MA 04224	(617) 264-000	jsmith@frontier.net

Education

Northeastern University	**Boston, Massachusetts**
QPA: 385	September 1998 June 2003

Major: Communication Studies

Concentration: Organizational Communication

Minor: Business Administration/Management

Honors: Golden Key National Honor Society, The Academy of the College of Arts and Sciences Society, Dean's List

Professional Membership: International Association of Business Communications (IABC)

Experience

General Electrical	**Elmsford, New York**
Sales Assistant, Northeast Region Lighting Division	June 2001–January 2002

- Audited business lighting systems, customized recommendations based on end-user lighting needs
- Made account solicitations; signed a 165,000 sq. ft. relamping deal after one cold call
- Performed training pitches to employees of key accounts
- Organized trade shows for General Electrical customers
- Worked with and learned from 16 account managers at GE Lighting's four Metro New York offices in Manhattan, Long Island, New Jersey, and Elmsford

Davis Paper	**Boise, Idaho**
Wrupshect Editior	June 2000–January 2001
	June 1999–January 2000

- Wrote the company's daily newsletter to an audience of over 1,600 people reading both printed copies and an online version

- Contributed articles to the corporate newsletter, and wrote the Fall 1999 edition of the division quarterly

Figure 12.1 The portfolio should include a résumé, letters of support from employers, and evidence of accomplishment in organizational communication related work. **(a)** Résumé, **(b)** Letter of Support from Employer.

- Submitted industry-related press releases to local and national newspapers/trade journals
- Directed facility tour program and created subsequent ad campaign
- Assisted Government and Community Affairs Managers

Walt Disney World   **Orlando, Florida**

College Program   September 1999–January 2000

- Lived, learned, and worked at Disney World
- Attended weekly business seminars and workshops taught by Disney professionals
- Served as Lifeguard Hostess at Disney's Yacht & Beach Club Resort, a 3-acre pool, CPR, Water Rescue, and Basic First Aid Certified

Computer Skills

Microsoft Windows, Word, PowerPoint, Excel, Access, and Photo Editors; Lotus Notes, MS400; Recode Photo Paint; Photo Shop 5.0

Volunteer Work

United Way campaign coordinator, Big Brother/Big Sister Corporate Mentor Program coordinator, Can Do! Mentor for adolescent girls, Project S.H.I.N.E. tutor (Students Helping in the Naturalization of Elders)

(B)

Paper Division

November 7, 2002

To whom it may concern:

It is my pleasure to describe to you Jane Smith's performance and what I observed during her internship.

I will begin by stating the Jane is a credit to herself, her family and to Northeastern University. It is rare that someone can be introduced to a new environment and immediately add value to an organization. Far rarer is the case wherein a students can perform in this manner. Jane did this while accomplishing her tasks with a maturity, a poise, a tenacity, and a commitment to excellence that exceeded all expectations.

Jane's internship began with a brief orientation to the Communications Department and a trial assignment. To find out where her abilities stood, she was given the task of writing an article, with instructions to make a first pass attempt. The piece was returned less than three hours later, four wording changes were made, and the article ran. When asked how she had accomplished this, she answered that she was applying what she had learned the previous trimester.

The remainder of the summer repeated this pattern. Jane successfully ran the public mill and forest tour program, wrote articles for internal and external publication, assisted in video production and photography, and managed the summer advertising campaign.

Jane derives great pleasure in stretching herself professionally. She is well-rounded, she is well-spoken, she possesses a professional demeanor, and she is always eager to learn. As an illustration of this, Jane took the initiative during the school year to call our office on a number of occasions to discuss real-world examples of material she was studying to help her better apply what she was learning. This speaks to Jane being a very dedicated student.

Please feel free to contract me if you have any questions.

Sincerely,

angelo Napolitano

Angelo Napolitano

Figure 12.1 (Continued).

(C)

(D)

(E)

Figure 12.1 (Continued) Samples of work completed for academic assignments can be placed in the portfolio to reflect the student's capabilities and industry. (c) ACS Group (d) The Elan Informer, (e) The Elan Corporation.

Figure 12.2 Berrier Associates. Many consulting companies have divisions that specialize in employee communications and other related organizational communication activities.

PRACTITIONER PERSPECTIVE

Marcia Meislin: Owner

Marcia Meislin is the owner of MCM Management Consultants. MCM is a management development firm that works with corporations and nonprofits. She and her associates provide consulting services to address the needs of leaders and to develop organizational "bench strength." Meislin is the author of *The Internal Consultant*.

As you read through this section, consider the following questions:

> Do you agree that persons tend to sugarcoat criticism to the detriment of communication quality?
>
> Do you agree with Meislin's Ping-Pong and bowling ball metaphor?
>
> Is the highlighted statement accurate? That is, is communication imperative for all of these things?

Everything I do is about communication. When I run a training program or facilitate workshops, communication is central to my success. I must employ language efficiently and present information with enthusiasm. In addition, I must be an effective listener. For example, in one-on-one coaching sessions I must listen carefully to what participants say—and what they do not say—in order to offer meaningful advice.

I also must be an efficient communicator when developing business. I have to ask intelligent questions to determine whether I can meet a client's individual needs. If I do not make appropriate inquiries, I cannot create solutions that are appropriate for individual clients. My success at MCM is not based on boilerplate programs doled out indiscriminately to whoever phones up. MCM has done well by establishing relationships with clients and acknowledging that each client has a unique set of concerns. **Communication is essential for establishing relationships, acknowledging the individual problems, articulating a solution for the problems, and then delivering the solution.**

Clients often have communication-related issues. One recurring problem relates to confronting underperforming employees. Many leaders are unable to give feedback, particularly negative feedback. Many who claim to be able to deliver these critical messages tend to sugarcoat the criticism. Another recurring and related problem pertains to resolving ongoing conflict. The following metaphor is not original, but I tell clients that often they are communicating as if they are playing Ping-Pong on top of the table when there are bowling balls hurling underneath the table that need to be addressed. We have to be willing to, and capable of, placing bowling balls on top of the table so that we can talk about them.

Deception is counter to everything I teach and everything I believe in. I coach employees to own their messages, and I cannot condone communications that deliberately attempt to confuse listeners. I cannot look myself in the mirror when I am deceptive and certainly could not do so if I suggested to others that such behavior would be appropriate.

SUMMARY: A TOOLBOX

- All jobs require an understanding of organizational communication.
- Jobs exist in a broad array of industries and organizations.
- Many students obtain jobs in sales, marketing, and public relations.
- Dedicated careers in organizational communication are proliferating.

Job Search Results

Listed below are all the jobs available on this site. Check back to this page often to see the new opportunities posted, or create a Job Alert to notify you when jobs are posted.

1–50 of 120 Jobs	View Detailed Results	Next ▷

Position	Location	▽ Posted
Communicaions Consultant-Alcoa Automotive ⊘ Alcoa Inc.	Detroit, MI, US	11/03/04
Director, Media Relations ⊘ Maytag Corporation	Newton, IA, US	11/03/04
HR Communicator ⊘ Hewitt Associates	Lincolnshire, IL, US	11/02/04
Communications Manager ⊘ The Coca-Cola Company	Atlanta, GA, US	11/02/04
Communications Director ⊘ Confidential	TX, US	11/02/04
Dept. Communications Leader ⊘ The City of Calgary	Calgary, AB, CA	11/02/04
MEDIA RELATIONS SPECIALIST ⊘ Sonnenschein Nath & Rosenthal	New York, NY, US	11/02/04

Figure 12.3 There are many varied jobs for people pursuing carrers in organizational communication. This is only a partial listing. Go to http://jobs.iabc.com/c/search_results.cfm?site_id=65 to see the entire list.

- Preparation for careers in organizational communication involves:
  - Understanding principles and theories
  - Honing communication skill sets
  - Obtaining co-curricular experience
  - Creating a portfolio
  - Networking
  - Joining related organizations

REVIEW AND DISCUSSION QUESTIONS

1. On what basis could you make the case that all careers are organizational communication careers?
2. Why would understanding principles related to systems theory, communication networks, and information management be valuable to someone who was employed as an employee communication specialist?
3. What educational preparation is important for those seeking careers in organizational communication?

4. What co-curricular activities might be advantageous for those who seek careers in this field?
5. What Web sites might you visit if you were interested in seeing what jobs were available in organizational communication?
6. How would you construct a job description for the type of organizational communication you envision as ideal?

GROUP/ROLE-PLAY

In a group of four to six, review the issues surrounding the case that begins this chapter. Attempt to gain consensus regarding the questions at the end of the case.

- For the role-play, one member of the group assumes the role of a parent who is visiting the university. Another represents the son or daughter of the parent who aspires to be a communication studies major. The remaining group members represent students who have completed this course.
- Assume that the parent and prospective student have called this meeting to discuss opportunities postgraduation in the field and how to prepare for these opportunities.

NOTES

CHAPTER 1

1. *Daniel Webster cited in* James McCroskey, *An Introduction to Rhetorical Communication*, Allyn and Bacon, 2001: p. 19.
2. Barnard, Chester, "The Functions of the Executive," Harvard University Press, 1960: p. 175.
3. Foltz, Roy, "Communication in Contemporary Organizations," in *Inside Organizational Communication*, Longman, 1985: p. 3.
4. Some may quibble with this designation and cite Goldhaber's 1974 book, *Organizational Communication*, as the first true textbook. Also, Redding with George Sanborn actually published a book called *Business and Industrial Communication* in 1964 that could be called the first organizational communication text. The Redding and Sanborn publication, however, is a reader and, as an anthology, is not quite the same as Redding's 1972 publication or Goldhaber's 1974 book. (*Business and Industrial Communication* is, however, comprehensive and twenty to thirty years ahead of its time in terms of its description of the breadth of organizational communication issues.) Goldhaber, a student of Redding, published his book with W.C. Brown in 1974. Redding's publisher, the Industrial Communication Council, is not a textbook publisher. The book itself reflects this and has more of a self-published workbook look and feel than a conventional text. The argument has been made, however, that in terms of content this Redding publication is the first true textbook in organizational communication. Jablin, Putnam, Roberts, and Porter comment in *The Handbook of Organizational Communication* (Sage, 1987: p. 7) that Redding's 1972 book is the first "comprehensive review and interpretation of the literature."
5. DeWine, Sue, *The Consultant's Craft*, 2d ed., St. Martins, 2001: p. vii. Redding's stature as a pioneer is further evidenced by the piece he was invited to author in *Readings in Organizational Communication* (1992) that exhaustively traced the evolution of the field. *Readings* is edited by Kevin Hutchinson. Redding's article appears on pages 11–44 and is called, "Stumbling Towards Identity: The Emergence of Organizational Communication as a Field of Study."
6. Ibid., DeWine, Sue, *Consultant's Craft*, p. xxiii.
7. The sequel was entitled *Apollo, Challenger, Columbia: The Decline of the Space Program: A Study in Organizational Communication*, Roxbury Press, 2005.
8. This is a theme throughout Philip Tompkins's entire book, *Organizational Communication Imperatives*. Roxbury Press, 1993. However, comments that focus on this point in particular are found on pages 166–167 and 195. In the 2005 sequel *Apollo, Challenger, Columbia*, the central problem of poor organizational communication is also identified throughout. Chapters 3, 4, and 7 in particular focus on communication-related problems.
9. Pace, R. Wayne, and Don F. Faules, *Organizational Communication, 3d ed.*, Prentice Hall, 1994: p. 23.
10. Quote attributed to Paul Strassmann in Richman, Tom, "Face to Face: Information Strategist Paul Strassman," *INC*, March 1988: p. 40.
11. From a paper presented by Dr. Raymond Beaty, at the Speech Communication Association annual convention in Louisville, November 1982. The paper was entitled "A Consultant's Perception of Speech Communication." The following quotation appears on page 3 of the paper: "Either through direct observation within a corporation or looking at a variety of studies which have been published, a good percentage of a manager's total behavior is some form of communication—most indicate 70–80%." The variation of course is based on varying notions of what constitutes communication behavior.
12. Mintzberg, Henry, *The Nature of Managerial Work*, Prentice Hall, 1973: pp. 58–94.
13. Penley, Larry, Elmore Alexander, I. Edward Jernigan, and Catherine Henwood, "Communication Abilities of Managers: The Relation to Performance," *Journal of Management*, Vol. 17, No. 1, March 1991: p. 57.
14. Gellerman, Saul, *The Management of Human Relations*, Holt Rinehart and Winston, 1966: p. 59.
15. The following list reflects topics discussed at recent IABC meetings:

    Building Employee Relationships through Communication
    Communicating Your Organization's Ethics Program
    Communication Auditing
    Creating Speeches with Impact

Crisis Communication: Ford's Perspective on the Tire Crisis

Integrating Print and on Line Communication

Integrity and the Ethics of "Spin"

Intranet and Internet Use

Linking Communication to Business Performance and Organizational Behavior

Motivating Employees Using Visual Media

Persuasive Communication and Leadership

Upward Communication

Using Communication to Transform Culture

16. Zaremba, Alan, "Communication in Its Entirety," *Journal of Employee Communication Management*, March 1999: pp. 24–32.

17. I conducted a similar study in March 2004. In it thirty-one MBA students were asked to identify the two greatest strengths and two most glaring communication weaknesses at their place of work. Approximately 80 percent of the weaknesses were in areas not traditionally identified as the communication skills of reading, writing, speaking, and listening. Approximately two-thirds of the communication strengths were in non–skill-set-related areas.

18. Several books make this claim. Originally, Frederick Taylor in his book the *Principles of Scientific Management* suggests that while his principles are designed for businesses they can be applicable to other areas. As we will see in Chapter 2, Taylor's principles relate directly and indirectly to organizational communication. Taylor writes: "It is hoped, however, that it will be clear to other readers that the same principles can be applied with equal force to all social activities, to the management of our homes, the management of our farms, the management of the business of our tradesmen, large and small; of our churches, our philanthropic institutions, our universities, and our governmental departments." This appears on page 8 of his book: Taylor, Frederick, *The Principles of Scientific Management*, Harper and Brothers, New York and London, 1923 (originally copyrighted by Frederick Winslow Taylor in 1911). Katherine Miller in her 2009 text *Organizational Communication* (p. 41) uses a family metaphor to describe applications of human relations theory to organizational communication.

19. This quote appeared in the *Wall Street Journal* on July 2, 1985 (page 1, column 5) in a section entitled "Worker Communication Programs Take Many Forms to Keep Talk Flowing." In the article there are references to how Quaker Oats, TRW, and other corporations "keep talk flowing." The specific quote cited in the chapter was made by a Mead corporation representative.

20. Iacocca, Lee, with William Novak, *Iacocca: An Autobiography*, Bantam Books, 1984: p. 54.

21. Again, as indicated in the previous note about Tompkins, this point is thematic throughout the book *Organizational Communication Imperatives*. On page 128 there is a specific reference to rocket scientists' failure to communicate based on not understanding the essence or importance of organizational communication.

22. Tompkins, *Organizational Communication Imperatives*, pp. 144–146.

23. The book was called *Transracial Communication*, written by Arthur Lee Smith (Prentice Hall, 1973). I have paraphrased the quotation for contextual readability without changing the essence of the author's sentiments. The precise quote is, "All analyses end in definition. This book is no different" (p. 9). In the mid-1970s, Arthur Lee Smith changed his name to Molefi Kete Asante. Smith/Asante was the Chair of the Department of Communication at the University of Buffalo from 1973 to 1979.

24. Op. cit., Tompkins, p. 24.

25. Shockley-Zalabak, Pamela, *Fundamentals of Organizational Communication*, 7th ed., Allyn and Bacon, 2009: p. 15.

26. Haney, William, *Communication and Organizational Behavior*, Richard D. Irwin, 1973.

27. Pamphlet: Communication the Ultimate Science, Project Communication Inc.

28. Modaff, Dan, Sue DeWine, and Jennifer Butler, *Organizational Communication: Foundations, Challenges, and Misunderstandings*, Allyn and Bacon, 2008: p. 3.

29. You may have seen other textbooks entitled Managerial, Business, or Corporate Communication. There is a distinction among these areas based on how scholars, departments, and universities have defined the subjects' domains. Annette Shelby's 1993 article "Organizational, Business, Management and Corporate Communication: An Analysis of Boundaries and Relationships," makes a good attempt to explain the domains of each area. Yet she comments right from the start about the accuracy of S. I. Hayakawa's notion that the true meaning of a term is to be found by observing what a [person] does with it, not by what the person says about it (*Journal of Business Communication*, July 1993: p. 241). To be sure, the domains are blurry at times and will continue to overlap as the fields evolve.

There isn't anything terrible about the overlap. Writing in *The Journal of Business Communication*, Reinsch tried to make a distinction between business communication, managerial communication, and organizational communication. He began by comparing the topics to "three candles on a small table, providing overlapping spheres of illumination" (Reinsch, "Editorial. What Is

Business Communication," *Journal of Business Communication*, Vol. 26, Fall 1991: p. 306). However appropriate the comparison, there are real problems when attempting to identify which discrete sphere is which. These problems are compounded by finding articles in *The Journal of Business Communication* about what many typically call managerial communication and finding articles in *Managerial Communication Quarterly* that many would claim to be on business communication topics.

Therefore, with the qualifier that these fields are complementary, evolving, and overlapping, below are some traditional areas of distinction for each label.

Business communication courses typically deal with the essential "how to" areas of communication, for example, how to write business materials and make presentations. Employee skill deficiencies can retard an organization's success. The focus in business communication is on developing and improving these communication skill sets. **Managerial communication** has more of a theoretical component than business communication. The focus in managerial communication is on the communication concepts and skills managers must understand and possess to successfully meet their managerial responsibilities. **Corporate communication** is a more slippery label. In some books, corporate communication refers to the creation of informational media, and in others the emphasis is on external organizational communication. The *Corporate Communicator's Quick Reference* by Peter Lichtgarn is an example of the former. The Paul Argenti text *Corporate Communication* is an example of the latter. **Organizational communication** is the broadest of the labels. Organizational communication is a theoretically based, comprehensive approach to studying the sending and receiving of messages in a complex systemic environment. It includes an analysis of employee communication skill set needs and the discussion of how to improve these skill sets. Similarly, organizational communication involves understanding why and how managers must communicate to meet their responsibilities as well as why and how organizations need to interact with their internal and external audiences. In essence, organizational communication is a more research-based inclusive area of study. The perspective and focus of organizational communication is on the organization as opposed to individual employees or managers.

30. Stevens, S. S., "Introduction: A Definition of Communication," *Journal of the Acoustical Society of America*, Vol. 22, 1950: p. 689.

31. http://spot.colorado.edu/~craigr/Communication.htm. At this site Craig also formulates a slightly different metaphor with the transmission model. In it he uses bananas being shipped in a crate from A to B instead of water in a bucket.

32. Op. cit., Pace and Faules, p. 23.

33. Lasswell, Harold D., "The Structure and Function of Communication in Society," in *The Communication of Ideas*, edited by Lyman Bryson, Harper and Brothers, 1948: pp. 37–51.

34. *That Was the Year that Was*, Tom Lehrer, 1964.

35. That researcher was Albert Mehrabian, who is the author of *Silent Messages* (2d ed, Wadsworth, 1981) and other books. He made the claim in a 1968 *Psychology Today* article entitled "Communication Without Words" (Vol. 2, No. 2: p. 53). Other authors have indicated that the figure is somewhat lower, but still sufficiently high to recognize the importance and pervasiveness of nonverbal messages. See Leathers, Dale, *Successful Nonverbal Communication*, 3d ed., Allyn and Bacon, 1997: pp. 5–6.

36. Manusov, Valerie, and Julie Billingsley, "Nonverbal Communication in Organizations," in *Organizational Communication: Theory and Behavior*, edited by Peggy Yuhas Byers, Allyn and Bacon, 1997: p. 66.

37. Hopper, Robert, *Human Message Systems*, Harper & Row, 1976: p. 8

38. Timm, Paul, and Kristen Bell DeTienne, *Managerial Communication: A Finger on the Pulse*, Prentice Hall, 1995: pp. 15–17.

39. Arnold "Red" Auerbach is the author of a number of books relating to coaching and general ideas about management, including *MBA* Management by Auerbach*. This quote is from another book he co-authored with Joe Fitzgerald entitled *On and Off the Court* (Macmillan, 1985: p. 59).

CHAPTER 2

1. Corman, Steven, "That Works Fine in Theory But," in *Foundations of Organizational Communication*, edited by Steven Corman, Stephen Banks, Charles Bantz, and Michael Mayer, Longman Publishing, 1995: p. 3.

2. Infante, Dominic, Andrew Rancer, and Deanna Womack, *Building Communication Theory*, Waveland Press, 2003: p. 356.

3. West, Richard, and Lynn Turner, *Introducing Communication Theory Analysis and Application*, 3d ed., McGraw-Hill, 2007: p. 48.

4. K. Lewin quoted in Corman, p. 9.

5. Corman, Steven, "The Need for Common Ground," in *Perspectives on Organizational Communication*, edited by Steven Corman and Marshall Scott Poole, The Guilford Press, 2000: p. 3.

6. Miller has stated "an examination of the vast majority of present day organizations reveals the prevalence of classical management thought." Miller, Katherine, *Organizational Communication: Approaches and Processes*, 5th ed., Thomson Wadsworth, 2009: p. 31.

7. The book was copyrighted by Taylor in 1911. It was not published by Harper and Brothers until 1923 (see footnote 8 for complete citation).

8. Taylor. Frederick, *The Principles of Scientific Management*, Harper and Brothers, 1923: p. 5 (originally copyrighted by Frederick Winslow Taylor in 1911).

9. Ibid., p. 7. Scientific management's explicit, precise, and unequivocal nature is reflected in the numerous sections of Taylor's book that are written with *"First, Second, and Third"* reasons why *"First, Second, and Third"* steps need to be taken.

10. Ibid., p. 19. Taylor writes that he is quoting extensively from a paper that he previously presented to The American Society of Mechanical Engineers in June 1903, eight years prior to the copyright of the book. The paper presented to this engineering society was called "Shop Management."

11. Ibid., pp. 19–20.

12. Ibid., pp. 20–21.

13. This self-deprecating assessment appears on page 88 of the *Principles of Scientific Management*. Taylor identifies himself often in this book as *The Writer*. In this section he comments, "The writer had not been especially noted for his tact so he decided that it would be wise for him to display a little more of this quality by having the girls [sic] vote on the new proposition."

14. Op cit., Taylor, pp. 43–46.

15. Fayol, Henri (translation from the original French by Constance Storrs), *General and Industrial Management*, Pitman Publishing Corporation, 1949.

16. Ibid., p. 34.

17. Ibid., p. 35.

18. Ibid., p. 104.

19. Ibid.

20. Ibid., p. 107.

21. Shenon, Phillip, and Kevin Flynn, "Panel Criticizes New York Action in September 11 Attack," *New York Times*, May 19, 2004: p. 1.

22. Fayol, pp. 41–42.

23. Ibid., p. 100.

24. Ibid., p. 104.

25. Weber, Max, *The Theory of Social and Economic Organization*, translated by A. M. Henderson and Talcott Parsons and edited by Talcott Parsons, Oxford University Press, 1947.

26. Taylor, Frederick, "The Principles of Scientific Management," article adapted in Corman et al., p. 65. Article in Corman is an adaptation of an article from the same title by Taylor published in 1916.

27. Byers, Peggy Yuhas, ed., "The Process and Perspectives of Organizational Communication," in *Organizational Communication Theory and Behavior*, Allyn and Bacon, 1997: p. 24.

28. Ibid., p. 21.

29. The second, third, and fourth phases of the studies were conducted by Elton Mayo of Harvard University. The first phase, called the "Illumination Phase" did not involve Mayo or Harvard. It was conducted by the Western Electric Company in conjunction with the National Academy of Sciences. Roethlisberger, F. J., and William Dickson, *Management and The Worker*, Harvard University Press, 1939: p. 14.

30. Roethlisberger and Dickson, p. 17.

31. See Gillespie, R., *Manufacturing Knowledge: A History of the Hawthorne Experiments*, Cambridge University Press, 1991. Also see Carey "The Hawthorne Studies: A Radical Criticism," in the *American Sociological Review*, No. 3, 1967: pp. 403–416.

32. "Limited Praise Tops Reasons to Quit Job," *Laconia Citizen*, September 29, 1994.

33. *Fortune*, December 4, 1989: p. 57.

34. Electronic interview with John [Anonymous] at [xyz] corporation September 2001.

35. Magarrell, Jack, "Decline in Faculty Morale Laid to Governance Role, Not Salary," *Chronicle of Higher Education*, November 10, 1982: pp. 1, 28.

36. Radio advertisements encourage those interested to "check out our Web site." If you visit the Southwest Web site and click on "Careers" you read the words "our people are our single greatest strength and our most enduring long term competitive advantage," March 2009.

37. Goldhaber, Gerald, "Cold Flesh Beats Warm Plastic," *Vital Speeches of the Day*, September 1, 1979: p. 686.

38. Falvey, Jack, "Manager's Journal: To Raise Productivity Try Saying Thank You," *Wall Street Journal*, December 6, 1982.

39. Op. cit., Byers, p. 26.

40. Miles, Raymond, "Keeping Informed, Human Relations or Human Resources," *Harvard Business Review*, July-August 1965: pp. 148–163. The specific use of the words "feel" and "lubricant" is on page 149. The quote including "accrue as long as managers cling to human relations view" is on page 158. The title of the article is identified here (and elsewhere) as "Keeping Informed, Human Relations or Human Resources." Readers

will note that the title is written in the text as just "Human Relations or Human Resources" without the first two prefatory words. In some citations the title of the article is written one way and in other places, the other. The reason for this discrepancy is because at the time *Harvard Business Review* had a periodic feature called *Keeping Informed*. The Miles piece was an article in that series.

41. That footnote begins as follows: "It may fairly be argued that what I call the human relations model is actually the product of popularization and misunderstanding of the work of pioneers in the field. Moreover, it is true that some of the early research and writings of the human relationists contain concepts which seem to fall within the framework of what I call the human resources model." Miles goes on in the note to write that he believes that the lack of emphasis of certain components of human relations led to the misunderstandings that developed. Ibid., p. 151.

42. The Kreps quote appears in his *Organizational Communication*, Longman, 1990: p. 85. Also, Pace and Faules (*Organizational Communication*, Prentice Hall, 1994: p. 41) and Byers (op. cit., pp. 26–27) make similar claims in their books. Miles himself supports this claim, as evidenced in comments quoted from and described in footnote 42.

43. Likert, Rensis, *New Patterns of Management*, McGraw-Hill, 1961; *The Human Organization*, McGraw-Hill, 1967.

44. This list is an extrapolation from the extensive chart that appears in op. cit., Likert, Rensis, *The Human Organization*, pp. 4–10. Table 2.2 on pages 47–49 of this textbook reflects a portion of this chart.

45. McGregor, Douglas, *The Human Side of the Enterprise*, McGraw-Hill, 1960.

46. Goldhaber, Gerald, *Organizational Communication*, William C. Brown, 1993: p. 87.

47. Op. cit., Byers, p. 27.

48. Op. cit., Miller, p. 21.

49. Levinson, Harold, "Asinine Attitudes Towards Motivation," *Harvard Business Review*, January 1973: pp. 72–76.

50. Ibid., p. 74.

51. Barlett, Christopher, and Sumantra Ghoshal, "Building Competitive Advantage through People," *MIT Sloan Management Review*, Winter 2002: p. 34.

CHAPTER 3

1. Senge, Peter, *The Fifth Discipline: The Art and Practice of the Learning Organization*, Doubleday Currency, 2006: pp. 6–7.

2. Goldhaber, Gerald, *Organizational Communication*, 6th ed., Wm. C. Brown and Benchmark, 1993: p. 47.

3. Op cit., Senge, p. 14.

4. See, for example, Couilllard, Denis, "Why Creating a Learning Organization Leads the High Tech Firm to Succeed," *Ivey Business Journal Online* (July–August 2007).

5. Bator, Melissa, "Failures Within the Intelligence Community," *Meniscus*, Autumn 2004. http://www.meniscusmagazine.com/5_issue_ site/5pages/elements017.htm

6. Fox News report, September 21, 2001, approximately 5:50 P.M.

7. Quote from Edgar Schein, *The Corporate Culture Survival Guide: Sense and Nonsense About Cultural Change*, Jossey Bass, 1999: p. xiv. See, for example, Lee, Siew Kim Jean, and Kelvin Yu, "Corporate Culture and Organizational Performance," *Journal of Managerial Psychology*, Vol. 19.4, April 2004: pp. 340–359.

8. The web metaphor is typically attributed to Clifford Geertz in *The Interpretation of Cultures*, 1973.

9. Pacanowsky, Michael, and Nick O'Donnell-Trujillo, "Communication and Organizational Culture," in *Foundations of Organizational Communication: A Reader*, edited by Steven Corman, Stephen Banks, Charles Bantz, and Michael Mayer, Longman, 1995: p. 165.

10. Tretheway, Angela, "Organizational Culture," in *Organizational Communication: Theory and Behavior*, Allyn and Bacon, 1997: p. 211.

11. Exactly what "interpretivist" means in this context and what "interpretivist research" is has unfortunately been vaguely and, I would argue, conveniently left ambiguous. Interested readers might review George Cheney's article "Interpreting Interpretive Research" in *Perspectives on Organizational Communication* (Guilford Press, 2000), particularly pages 24–25.

12. Deal, Terrence, and Allan Kennedy, *Corporate Cultures: The Rites and Rituals of Corporate Life*, Addison Wesley, 1982: pp. 13–15.

13. Ibid., pp. 15, 98.

14. Peters, Thomas, and Robert Waterman, *In Search of Excellence*, Harper & Row, 1982.

15. Bennis, Warren, "Foreward," in *The Corporate Culture Survival Guide: Sense and Nonsense About Cultural Change*, Jossey Bass, 1999: p. xii.

16. Critical theory is a derivative of Marxism. Marx advocated "relentless criticism of all existing conditions, relentless in the sense that the criticism is not afraid of its findings and just as little afraid of the conflict with the powers that be." *Writings on the Young Marx on Philosophy and Society*, Anchor Books, 1967: p. 212.

17. Miller, Katherine, *Organizational Communication*, 5th ed., Cengage Wadsworth, 2009: p. 100.

18. Op. cit., Trethewey, "Organizational Culture," p. 228.

19. In a well-balanced article about emancipation, Alvesson and Willmott describe emancipation in the following way: ". . . the goal is to liberate people from unnecessarily restrictive traditions, ideologies . . . that inhibit or distort opportunities for autonomy. . . ." Alvesson, M., and Willmott, "On the Idea of Emancipation in Management and Organizational Studies," *Academy of Management Review*, 1992: p. 435.

20. Lutgen-Sandvik, Pamela, "Take This Job and . . .: Quitting and Other Forms of Resistance to Workplace Bullying," *Communication Monographs*, Vol. 73, No. 4, 2006: pp. 406–433.

21. Op. cit., Miller, p. 124: the "job of the critical theorist . . . is to lay bare hegemonic structures and processes and to help people realize that they have 'the key' for self emancipation."

22. Cheney, George, "Democracy in the Workplace: Theory and Practice from the Perspective of Communication," *Journal of Applied Communications Research*, August 1995: pp. 167–200.

23. Marta Calas and Linda Smircich have identified seven categories of feminist theory: liberal, radical cultural, psychoanalytical, Marxist, socialist, poststructuralist, and Third World–postcolonial. Calas, M. B., and L. Smircich, "From the Woman's Point of View: Feminist Approaches to Organization Studies," in *Handbook of Organization Studies*, edited by S. Clegg, C. Hardy, and W. R. Nord, Sage, 1996: pp. 218–257.

24. Shockley-Zalabak, Pamela, *Organizational Communication*, 7th ed., Pearson, 2009: p. 52.

25. Op. cit., Trethewey, p. 228.

26. Buzzanell, P. M., "Gaining a Voice: Feminist Organizational Communication Theorizing," *Management Communication Quarterly*, Vol. 7, No. 4, 1994: pp. 339–382.

27. Roth, Philip, *The Counterlife*, Farrar Straus and Giroux, 1987: p. 306.

CHAPTER 4

1. *Business 2.0*, March 2002, Cover.

2. Eichenwald, Kurt "Warning to Executives: Honesty Is the Best Policy," *New York Times*, July 10, 2004: p. B1.

3. The article was entitled, "The Emperor Is as Naked as a Jaybird" and was published in the June 1987 edition of *Educational Horizons*, pp. 71–74. The article argued that the emphasis placed on learning in colleges and universities was insufficient despite claims to the contrary made by colleges and universities.

4. Redding, Charles, *Communication Within the Organization*, Industrial Communication Council, 1972.

5. Vaughan, Diane, *The Challenger Launch Decision*, University of Chicago Press, 1996: p. 119.

6. Cooper, Cynthia, *The Journey of a Corporate Whistleblower*, John Wiley and Sons, 2008: p. 1.

7. Saltzman, Joe, "Lying as America's Pastime," *USA Today Magazine*, Vol. 135, July 2006.

8. Op. cit., p. x

9. Callahan, David, *The Cheating Culture*, Harcourt, 2004: p. viii.

10. Graham, Ginger, "If You Want Honesty, Break Some Rules," *Harvard Business Review*, April 2002.

11. Pearce, W. Barnett, and Stephen W. Littlejohn, *Moral Conflict*, Sage Publications, 1997: pp. 49–50.

12. Ibid., p. 68.

13. Ibid., p. 212.

14. Eisenberg, Eric, "Ambiguity as Strategy in Organizational Communication," *Communication Monographs*, Vol. 51, 1984: pp. 227–242.

15. Tompkins, Phillip, *Organizational Communication Imperatives*, Roxbury Press, 1993: p. 137. Interestingly, graduate students and undergraduate students who have read Eisenberg's 1984 article and who have been asked to either support or reject his perspective have almost uniformly supported the idea that strategic ambiguity can be valuable.

16. Eisenberg, Eric, and Marsha Witten, "Reconsidering Openness in Organizational Communication," in *Readings in Organizational Communication*, edited by Kevin Hutchinson, William C. Brown, 1992: p. 127 (originally published in *Academy of Management Review*, Vol. 12, No. 3, 1987: pp. 418–426). Eisenberg and Witten reference the 1984 Eisenberg article as support for the excerpted claim.

17. Paul, Jim, and Christy Strbiak, "The Ethics of Strategic Ambiguity," *Journal of Business Communication*, Vol. 34, 1997: pp. 149–159.

18. Corman, Steven, Stephen Banks, Charles Bantz, and Michael Mayer have the seminal article by Eisenberg in their reader *Foundations of Organizational Communication*, Longman, 1995: p. 246; also *Readings in Organizational Communication*, edited by Kevin Hutchinson, includes the similar article entitled "Reconsidering Openness in Organizational Communication," Eric Eisenberg and Marsha Witten, p. 122. Texts by Eisenberg, Eric, and H. Goodall Jr., *Organizational Communication Balancing Creativity and Constraint*, 3d ed.,

Bedford/St. Martins, 2001: p. 24 and Trenholm, Sarah, *Thinking Through Communication*, Allyn and Bacon, 2001: p. 95 are two that refer to the benefits of strategic ambiguity.

19. Adler, Ronald, and Jeanne Marquardt Elmhorst, *Communicating at Work: Principles and Practices for Business and the Professions*, 7th ed., McGraw-Hill, 2002: p. 82.

20. Taussig, Suzanne, "Strategic Ambiguity in Sales Communication," Master's thesis, University of Houston, May 1999: pp. 2–3.

21. Eisenberg, Eric, and H. Goodall Jr., *Organizational Communication: Balancing Creativity and Constraint*, 3d ed., Bedford/St. Martins, 2001: p. 24.

22. Ibid.

23. Op. cit., Eisenberg, "Ambiguity as Strategy," pp. 230–232.

24. Ibid., p. 233.

25. Op. cit., Eisenberg and Witten, p. 127.

26. Op. cit., "Ambiguity as Strategy," p. 236

27. Ibid.

28. Ibid., p. 235

29. Op. cit., Eisenberg and Goodall Jr., p. 25.

30. Ibid.

31. Op. cit., Eisenberg and Goodall Jr., p. 25; Eisenberg, p. 239.

32. Frank, Mary, and Thomas Feeley, "To Catch a Liar: Challenges for Research in Lie Detection Training," *Journal of Applied Communication Research*, Vol. 31, No. 1, February 2003: p. 60.

33. Op. cit., Tompkins, p. 137.

34. Bok, Sissela, *Lying: Moral Choice in Public and Private Life*, Vintage Books, 1999: p. 23.

35. Ibid., p. 20.

36. Ibid., p. 23.

37. Covey, Stephen, *The Speed of Trust. The One Thing that Changes Everything*, Free Press, 2006.

38. Dalla Costa, John, *The Ethical Imperative: Why Moral Leadership Is Good Business*, Addison Wesley, 1998: p. 11.

39. Merrill, John *Existential Journalism*, Hastings House Publishers, 1977: p. 132.

40. Zaremba, Alan, "Is Honesty Overrated?", *Journal Communication Management*, May/June 2000: pp. 42–43.

41. For the purposes of the survey, unethical behaviors were defined as those that were perceived by the respondents as "not right regardless of the legal aspects" of the action. The survey items themselves were "real world" as opposed to hypothetical. Over several years I collected descriptions of issues reported as work-related communication concerns. In order to create the survey, I reviewed the collected descriptions, selected communica-tion problems that had ethical dimensions, and then digested the problem into a statement of behavior to which someone could react.

42. Ciancutti, Arky, and Thomas Steding, *Built on Trust: Gaining Competitive Advantage in Any Organization*, Contemporary Books, 2001: p. ix.

43. Op. cit., Dalla Costa, p. 204.

CHAPTER 5

1. *Mike and Mike in the Morning*, ESPN2, July 8, 2008.

2. Daft, R. L., and R. H. Lengel, "Organizational Information Requirements, Media Richness, and Structural Design," *Management Science*, Vol. 32, No. 5, 1986: pp. 554–569.

3. Ibid., p. 567.

4. The idea that uncertainty is deleterious to organizational health is presented in several sources, including the previously cited Daft and Lengel article. The clean air metaphor is adapted from Zaremba, *Management in a New Key: Communication in the Modern Organization*, 2d ed., Industrial Engineering and Management Press. 1993, Norcross, Georgia pp. 6–7.

5. Tompkins, Phillip, *Organizational Communication Imperatives*, Roxbury Press, 1993: pp. 18, 21. Tompkins refers to this phenomenon while discussing the "mushroom anecdote." In this section of the book, the author explores four anecdotes germane to organizational communication. The mushroom anecdote pertains to a conversation Tompkins had with a laboratory director who was discussing organizational communication problems. The director comments that the way mushrooms are grown reflects a common problem with organizational communication. "You put them down in the basement and keep them completely in the dark. Every once in a while you open the door and throw some horse manure on them." Neither the director nor Tompkins supports this approach to organizational communication. Tompkins writes that "too often top management keeps employees in the dark" in ways akin to how one cultivates mushrooms.

6. The task, maintenance, and human taxonomy was first introduced by Charles Redding. See Goldhaber, Gerald, *Organizational Communication*, 6th ed., 1993: p. 146. Goldhaber discusses human messages on pages 148–149.

7. Ibid., pp. 148–149.

8. Op. cit., Daft and Lengel, p. 560. The appropriate attribution for this statement is difficult to identify with certainty. Daft and Lengel in the cited piece define information richness as "the ability of information to change understanding within

a time interval." They go on to discuss media richness in terms of a medium's capacity to generate information that would be rich because the information that would be sent using the medium would result in changed understanding. It is on this basis that the authors rank the media in terms of richness. However, it is in Huber and Daft's article (cited in references 9 and 11) where the authors, referring to the Daft and Lengel piece, define richness as a "medium's capacity to change understanding." Huber and Daft also rank media in terms of richness.

9. Huber, George, and R. L. Daft, "The Information Environments of Organizations," in Jablin, Frederic M., Linda L. Putnam, Karlene H. Roberts, and Lyman W. Porter, *Handbook of Organizational Communication*, Sage Publications, 1987: p.152; Christopher Sullivan, *Journal of Business Communication*, Vol. 32, No. 1, January 1995: p. 49. The lists from the two sources are not exactly the same. Huber and Daft include "language variety," whereas Sullivan does not. Huber and Daft refer to "timely" feedback, whereas Sullivan refers to immediate feedback.

10. Mark Knapp and Judith Hall present the position in the early pages of their book, *Nonverbal Communication in Human Interaction*, 4th ed. (Harcourt Brace College Publishing, 1997: p. 11), that messages can be seen as *always* being both nonverbal and verbal. They write that while messages may be nonverbally sent, words are used intrapersonally to decode the message. Therefore, since communication requires receipt of messages, no message, however nonverbally uttered, could be purely nonverbally communicated.

11. Op. cit., Huber and Daft, p. 152.

12. Utz, Sonja, *Information, Communication & Society*, Vol. 10, Issue 5, 2007: pp. 694–713.

13. Dehkordi, Majid A., Behrouz Zarei, and Shabnam A. Dehkordi, "The Effect of Gender and Age Differences on Media Selection in Small and Medium Tourism Enterprises," *CyberPsychology & Behavior*, Vol. 11, Issue 6, 2008: pp. 683–686.

14. Mark Rosenkar, quoted in Tetzeli, Rick, "Surviving Information Overload," *Fortune*, July 11, 1994: p. 60.

15. Milana, Paolina, "Search Engine Optimization and Social Media," Presentation at the International Association of Business Communicators Meetings. New York, New York. June 23, 2008.

16. J.W. Marriott, Jr. "Marriott on the Move," Presentation delivered at the International Association of Business Communicators Meetings. New York, New York. June 23, 2008.

17. http://www.facebook.com/apps/application.php?id=5525167977&_fb_noscript=1 site accessed August 5, 2009.

18. *Boston Globe*, March 30, 2009, Sports Log: p. 2.

19. Sinickas, Angela, "Measuring Your Social Tools," presentation at 2008 International Association of Business Communicators Meetings, New York, June 24, 2008.

20. Kiesler, Sara, and Lee Sproull, *Connections: New Ways of Working in the Networked Organization* MIT Press, 1991.

21. Ibid., p. 49.

22. Zaremba, Alan, "Effects of E-Mail Availability on the Informal Network," *International Journal of Technology Management*, January 1996: pp. 151–161.

23. Krebs, Valdis, "Planning for Information Effectiveness: A New Opportunity for Human Resources and Organizational Effectiveness," unpublished paper copyrighted by Vladis Krebs, 1988: p. 1.

24. Kiesler, S., and L. Sproull, *Computing and Change on Campus*, Cambridge University Press, 1987: p. 34.

25. Itzoe, Donna, and Angela Peluso, "Unified Messaging Across the Enterprise: Clearing the Clutter" presentation at International Association of Business Communicators Meetings, New York, New York, June 23, 2008.

26. There are several similar job titles. Chief knowledge management officer is another. Some authors and organizations even refer to employees with knowledge as "knowledge workers." The three job titles used in our text are identified in Probst, Gilbert, Steffen Raub, and Kai Romhardt, *Managing Knowledge: Building Blocks for Success*, John Wiley & Sons, 1998. Interested readers will find this book well edited and concise. Other recent titles include *Knowledge Management Foundations* by Steve Fuller, published in 2002 by Butterworth-Heinemann, and *Knowledge Management: Best Practices in Europe*, edited by Kai Mertins, Peter Heisig, and Jens Vorbeck, published in 2001 by Springer.

27. www.functionalknowledge.com/glossary.html

28. www.vnulearning.com/kmwp/glossary.html

29. www.sirsi.com/glossary.html

30. www.convergemag.com/specialPubs/Portal/glossary.shtm

31. The distinction between information and knowledge is subtle, and the terms are often used interchangeably. Consequently, it is a chore to differentiate meaningfully between the two terms. Information has been described as a "component of knowledge" and as "knowledge on the move." We can think of it, then, as a building block of knowledge or, equally, as what

knowledge becomes when it is available to others. For example, in order to decide whether to hire Sam or Shirley, members of a committee need information. When compiled and analyzed, this information provides members with knowledge that helps them make that decision. When they relay the rationale for the decision to colleagues, this knowledge becomes information that may be helpful to others in making similar decisions. Despite whatever clarifying value this illustration may have, the demarcation line between knowledge and information is blurry. The task of clearly making any distinction is particularly onerous, since the terms are used nearly interchangeably in articles and job descriptions pertaining to knowledge management.

32. Senge, Peter, *The Fifth Discipline: The Art and Practice of the Learning Organization*, Doubleday, 2006: p. 14.

33. Hutchens, David, *Outlearning the Wolves: Surviving and Thriving in a Learning Organization*, Pegasus Communications, 2000.

34. Hallowell, Edward, "The Human Moment at Work," *Harvard Business Review*, January-February 1999: pp. 58–64.

35. Ibid., p. 59.

36. Ibid. "high tech without high touch" quote appears on page 64. Reference to requirements of "human moments" appears on page 59. Reference to mental acuity appears on page 61.

37. Paul Argenti, "Strategic Employee Communications," *Human Resource Management*, Volume 37, Issue 3–4, Fall-Winter 1998: p. 205.

38. Op. cit., Schonfeld.

CHAPTER 6

1. Quote attributed to Paul Strassmann in Richman, Tom, "Face to Face: Information Strategist Paul Strassman," *INC*, March 1988: p. 40.

2. Keith Davis's groundbreaking article was "Management Communication and the Grapevine," *Harvard Business Review*, September–October 1953: pp. 43–49.

3. Spangler, W. Scott, Jeffrey T. Kreulen, and James F. Newswanger, "Machines in the Conversation: Detecting Themes and Trends in Informal Communication Streams," *IBM Systems Journal*, 45.4, October-December 2006: **pp. 785–799.**

4. Hellweg, Susan, "Formal and Informal Communication Networks," in Byers, *Organizational Communication: Theory and Behavior*, 1997: p. 43.

5. Rowan, Roy, "Where Did that Rumor Come From," *Fortune*, August 13, 1979: p. 130.

6. Op. cit., Hellweg, p. 51.

7. Kreps, Gary, *Organizational Communication*, Longman, 1990: p. 208.

8. Pace, R. Wayne, and Don Faules, *Organizational Communication*, Prentice Hall, 1989: p. 116.

9. Op. cit., Davis, p. 43.

10. Davis, Keith, *Human Behavior at Work*, 4th ed., McGraw-Hill, 1972: p. 263.

11. Ibid., p. 271.

12. Daniels, Tom, and Barry Spiker, *Perspectives on Organizational Communication*, William C. Brown, 1997: p. 98.

13. Beslin, Ralph, "Developing and Using Employee Feedback Mechanisms," paper presented at IABC meetings, New Orleans, Louisiana, June 1998.

14. Love, John, *McDonald's Behind the Arches*, Bantam, 1986: p. 149a. The franchisees were Herb Peterson (Egg McMuffin), Lou Groen (Filet-O-Fish), and Jim Delligatti (Big Mac).

15. With minor editing, this is a precise message received by a senior manager via an upward network system.

16. Tompkins, Philip, *Apollo, Challenger, Columbia: The Decline of the Space Program: A Study in Organizational Communication*, Roxbury Publishing Company, 2005: p. 78.

17. Ibid.

18. Feynman, Richard, as told to Ralph Leighton, *What Do You Care What Other People Think?*, Norton, 1988; Feynman, Richard, as told to Ralph Leighton, *Surely You're Joking, Mr. Feynman!*, Norton, 1985.

19. Feynman, Richard, "An Outsider's Inside View of the Challenger Inquiry," *Physics Today*, February 1988: p. 33.

20. Ibid., p. 34.

21. Op. cit., Tompkins 2005, p. 120.

22. Op. cit., Feynman, "An Outsider's Inside View . . . ," p. 37.

23. Edmondson, Vickie Cox, "Organizational Surveys: A System for Employee Voice," *Journal of Applied Communication Research*, Vol. 34, Issue 4, 2006: pp. 307–310.

24. Adapted from Kraut, Allen, and Frank Freeman, *Upward Communication in American Industry*, Center for Creative Leadership, 1992. The authors included these items on a list of networks that (a) were used as indicated by the literature or their experience with the network, (b) were formal, and (c) could be used or not used by employees.

25. Katz, Daniel., and Robert L. Kahn, *The Social Psychology of Organizations*, John Wiley and Sons, 1978: p. 444.

26. Tompkins, Philip, *Organizational Communication Imperatives*, Roxbury Press, 1993: p. 211.

27. Op. cit., Tompkins 2005, pp. 119–120.

28. Leary, Warren, "Poor Management by NASA Is Blamed for Mars Failure," *The New York Times*, March 29, 2000: p. A-21.

29. Ibid., p. A-1.
30. This point is made throughout Tompkins 2005, which examined these incidents specifically. See particularly pages 129–161.

CHAPTER 7

1. Weiner, Eric, *The Geography of Bliss*, Twelve, 2008: p. 3.
2. Weinzimmer, Laurence, Jennifer Franczak, and Eric Michel, "Culture-Performance Research: Challenges and Future Directions," *Journal of Academy of Business and Economics*, April 2008.
3. Brown, Andrew, and Ken Starkey, "Effects of Organizational Culture on Communication and Information," *Journal of Management Studies*, Vol. 31, No. 6, November 1994: p. 808.
4. Redding, W. Charles, *Communication Within the Organization*, Industrial Communication Council, 1972: p. 111.
5. Taguiri, R., "The Concepts of Organizational Climate," in *Organizational Climate: Exploration of a Concept*, edited by R. Taguiri and G. H. Litwin, Harvard University Press, 1968: p. 27.
6. Kreps, Gary, *Organizational Communication*, Longman, 1990: p. 193.
7. Op. cit., Weinzimmer et al.
8. Kreps, for example, uses this metaphor in the above citation, as does Tompkins in "The Functions of Human Communication in Organization," in *Handbook of Rhetorical and Communication Theory*, edited by C. C. Arnold and J. W. Bowers, Allyn and Bacon, 1984: pp. 659–719.
9. Guion, R., "A Note on Organizational Climate," *Organizational Behavior and Human Performance*, Vol. 9, 1973: pp. 120–125.
10. Gibb, Jack, "Defensive Communication," in *Communication Theory*, edited by C. David Mortensen, Transaction Publishers, 2008: pp. 201–208.
11. This list of components is found in op. cit., Redding.
12. Pace, R. Wayne, and Don Faules, *Organizational Communication*, Prentice Hall, 1990: pp. 121–122.
13. Daft, R. L., *The Leadership Experience*, 4th ed., Thomson Learning, 2008: p. 444.
14. Schein, E. H., *Organizational Culture and Leadership*, Jossey Bass, 2004: p. 17.
15. http://www.businessdictionary.com/definition/organizational-culture.html
16. Denison, Daniel, "What IS the Difference Between Organizational Culture and Organizational Climate? A Native's Point of View on a Decade of Paradigm Wars," *Academy of Management Review*, July 1996: pp. 619–654.
17. Ibid., p. 625.
18. Jablin, Fred, "Organizational Entry, Assimilation, and Disengagement/Exit," in *The New Handbook of Organizational Communication*, edited by Fred Jablin and Linda Putnum, Sage, 2001: pp. 732–818. His article "Superior-Subordinate Communication: The State of the Art" can be found in *Readings in Organizational Communication*, edited by Kevin Hutchinson, Wm C. Brown, 1992: pp. 285–309.
19. Jablin, Fred, and K. J. Krone, "Organizational Assimilation," in *Handbook of Communication Science*, edited by C. R. Berger and S. H. Chaffee, Sage, 1987: p. 712.
20. Van Maanen, J., "Breaking in: Socialization to Work," in *Handbook of Work, Organization and Society*, edited by R. Dubin, Rand McNally, 1975. **pp. 67–130.**
21. Modaff, Daniel, Sue DeWine, and Jennifer Butler, *Organizational Communication*, Allyn and Bacon, 2008: p. 19.
22. Bullis, C., and Phillip Tompkins, "The Forest Ranger Revisited: A Study of Control Practices and Identification," *Communication Monographs*, Vol. 56, 1989: p. 289.
23. Tompkins, Phillip, *Apollo, Challenger, Columbia. The Decline of the Space Program: A Study in Organizational Communication*, Roxbury, 2005: p. 62.
24. Attributed by Phillip Tompkins to Elaine Tompkins in *Apollo, Challenger, Columbia The Decline of the Space Program: A Study in Organizational Communication*, Roxbury, 2005: p. 193.
25. Gossett, Loril, "Falling Between the Cracks. Control and Communication Challenges of a Temporary Workforce," *Management Communication Quarterly*, Fall 2006: pp. 376–415.
26. Schein, Edgar, "The Role of the Founder in Creating Organizational Culture," *Organizational Dynamics*, Summer 1983: p. 22. Schein, Edgar, *Organizational Culture and Leadership*, 3rd ed., San Francisco: JosseyBass, 2004: p. 246. The lists in the article and the book are slightly different. The embedding mechanisms identified in the text above are selections from both lists.
27. Miller, Katherine, *Organizational Communication*, Cengage Wadsworth, 2009: p. 83.
28. Kurt, Vonnegut, *Cat's Cradle*, Delacorte Press, 1963 (reference to granfalloon is on page 82).
29. Yoffe, Emily, "Fifty Something; Facebooking and Fabulous: Last week I had zero friends on Facebook. Now I have 775," *Slate*, March 16, 2007: http://www.slate.com/id/2161920/ accessed August 5, 2009.
30. Ibid.
31. Cole, Larry, and Michael Cole, "Why Is the Teamwork Buzz Word Not Working?" *Communication*

World, February-March 1999: p. 29; referring to Hare, Chauncey, and Judith Wyatt, "Work Abuse: How to Recognize and Survie It," Schenkman Books, 1997.

32. Pacanowsky, Michael, and Nick O'Donnell-Trujillo, "Communication and Organizational Cultures," in *Foundations of Organizational Communication,* 2d ed., edited by Steven Corman, Stephen Banks, Charles Bantz, and Michael Mayer. Longman: White Plains, New York. **1995** Page 162 contains the reference to communication constituting culture. Page 165 includes the residue quote.

33. Silver, Michael, "Davis Wants to Win . . . Just Not on the Field," Yahoo Sports Exclusive, September 19, 2008.

34. Tompkins, Phillip, *Organizational Communication Imperatives,*" Roxbury Press, 1993: pp. 164–165.

35. Interested readers might look at two articles that support this contention. See Salah, Eldin, and Adam Hamza, "Capturing Tacit Knowledge from Transient Workers: Improving the Organizational Competitiveness," *International Journal of Knowledge Management,* April-June 2009; p. 87; also Sarros, James, Brian Cooper, and Joseph Santora, "Building a Climate for Innovation Through Transformational Leadership and Organizational Culture," *Journal of Leadership and Organizational Studies,* November 2008: p. 145.

36. Goleman, Daniel, *Emotional Inteligence,* Bantam Books, 2005.

37. Salovey, Peter, and Mayer, John. "Emotional Intelligence." *Imagination, Cognition, and Personality* vol. 9 no. 3, 1989–1990: p. 189.

38. Lardner, James, "Why Should Anyone Believe You?" *Business 2.0,* March 2002: p. 41.

39. Roger D'Aprix is a pioneer in organizational communication who has worked as a consultant to organizations for decades. In 1998 the International Association of Business Communicators referred to him as "one of the most influential thinkers in the communication profession in the last 25 years." This particular quote appeared in an interview with D'Aprix published in a Towers Perrin Forster and Crosby regular publication entitled *Communication and Management.* The interview was called "A Strategy for Success" and was published in January/February 1985.

40. Bartolome, Fernando, "Nobody Trusts the Boss, Now What?" *Harvard Business Review,* 1999: p 80.

CHAPTER 8

1. Emery, David, *The Compleat Manager,* McGraw-Hill, 1970: pp. 27–28.

2. Attributed to J. B. Hughes in many sources. http://www.famousquotesandauthors.com/authors/ j__b__hughes_quotes.html found on August 8, 2009.

3. Antony, Jay, and John Cleese, *Meetings, Bloody Meetings,* directed by Peter Robinson, Video Arts Limited, Chicago, 1993.

4. In Sue DeWine's *The Consultant's Craft: Improving Organizational Communication,* the author actually entitles her chapter on meetings: "Why Are Meetings So Boring and Unproductive?" Bedford/St. Martin's, 2001: p. 206.

5. Barash, Isadore, "A New Economic Indicator," *Newsweek,* September 9, 1985: pp. 11–12.

6. Barry, Dave, "Twenty-Five Things I Have Learned in Fifty Years," in *Dave Barry Turns 50,* Crown, 1998: p. 183.

7. Zaremba, Alan, "Meetings: Why We Need Them, Why We Hate Them. How to Fix Them," *Journal of Employee Communication Management,* May/June 2001: p. 25.

8. Interview with department head from small nonprofit arts organization, January 2009.

9. DeWine, Sue, *The Consultant's Craft: Improving Organizational Communication,* Bedford/St. Martins, 2001: pp. 208–211.

10. Berko, Roy, Andrew Wolvin, and Darlyn Wolvin, *Communicating: A Social and Career Focus,* 7th ed., Houghton Mifflin, 1998: pp. 427, 429.

11. "Social loafing" as a term was first used in an article by B. K. Latane and S. Harkins in, "Many Hands Make Light the Work: The Causes and Consequences of Social Loafing," *Journal of Personality and Social Psychology,* Vol. 37, 1979: pp. 822–832. The concept has been studied extensively since then. See, for example, Lin, Tung-Ching, and Chien-Chih Huang, "Understanding Social Loafing in Knowledge Contribution from the Perspectives of Justice and Trust." *Expert Systems with Applications,* 36.3, April 2009: p. 6156. Also Blaskovich, Jennifer L., "Exploring the Effect of Distance: An Experimental Investigation of Virtual Collaboration, Social Loafing, and Group Decisions.(Report)," *Journal of Information Systems,* 22.1, Spring 2008: p. 27.

12. The technical term for this phenomenon is "nonsummativity." This literally means that the result of team interaction will be unequal to the sum of its parts. The hope is that the interaction of all persons in a team will result in a discussion that is positively nonsummative. However, because of various issues, including conformity, the primary and secondary tensions discussed earlier in the chapter, and the other counterproductive factors discussed in this chapter, it is not impossible that the result of group interaction could be *negatively* nonsummative. "Two heads" can be "worse than one."

13. Janis, Irving L., *Groupthink: Psychological Studies of Policy Decisions and Fiascoes*, Houghton Mifflin, 1982. The *Psychology Today* article was entitled simply "Groupthink," Vol. 5, No. 6, November 1971: pp. 43–36, 74–76.

14. The date of origin of "groupthink" varies depending on the dictionary one uses. *The Third Barnhart Dictionary of New English*, published in 1990, lists the date of origin as 1959. *The Random House Unabridged*, 2d ed. published in 1987, lists the origin between 1950 and 1955. It is the *Merriam Webster Collegiate*, 11th ed. 2004, which lists the origin as 1952. John Brilhart and Gloria Galanes. Irving Janis "coined" the term on page 269 of *Effective Group Discussion*, 9th ed., McGraw Hill, 1998. Brilhart and Galanes are essentially correct in that the meaning prior to Janis's publications referred to the thoughts that came out of group work as opposed to the counterproductive qualities of what is contemporarily considered as groupthink.

15. *Merriam Webster's Collegiate Dictionary*, 10th ed., 1993: p. 515. Interestingly, the 1964 *American College Dictionary* that omits "groupthink" also omits "group therapy." Grouse remains. Some might argue that "grouse" and "group therapy" do indeed belong together.

16. Janis, Irving L., *Groupthink: Psychological Studies of Policy Decisions and Fiascoes*, Houghton Mifflin, 1982: p. 9.

17. Goldhaber, Gerald, *Organizational Communication*, 6th ed., Wm C. Brown/Benchmark, 1993: p. 249.

18. Bond, Rod, and Peter Smith, "Culture and Conformity: A Meta Analysis of Studies Using Asch's (1952b, 1956) Line Judgment Task," *Psychological Bulletin*, January 1996: p. 112.

19. Martin, Judith, and Tom Nakayama, *Intercultural Communication in Contexts*, McGraw-Hill, 2010: p. 5.

20. Beebe, Steven, Susan Beebe, and Diana Ivy, *Communication Principles for a Lifetime*, Allyn and Bacon, 2001: p.161.

21. Mosvick, Roger, and Robert Nelson, *We've Got to Start Meeting Like This*, Park Avenue, 1996: p. 31. The sixth item, ranked number two on the list, was "Inconclusive: No results, decisions, assignments or follow up."

22. Sunwolf, and David Seibold, "The Impact of Formal Procedures on Group Processes Members and Task Outcomes," in *The Handbook of Group Communication Theory and Research*, edited by Lawrence R. Frey, Sage, 1999: p. 400.

23. Adams, Katherine, and Gloria Galanes, *Communicating in Groups*, 7th ed., McGraw–Hill, 2009: pp. 184–185.

24. Delbecq, Andre, Andrew H. Van de Ven, and David H. Gustafson, *Group Techniques for Program Planning: A Guide to Nominal Group and Delphi Processes*, Scott Foresman, 1975: pp. 7–10.

25. Brilhart, John, and Gloria Galanes, *Effective Group Discussion*, 7th ed., Wm C. Brown, 1992: p. 238.

26. Op. cit., Adams and Galanes, p. 24.

27. Lucas, Stephen E., *The Art of Public Speaking*, 8th ed., McGraw-Hill, 2007: p. 503.

CHAPTER 9

1. Reeder, John, "When West Meets East: Cultural Aspects of Doing Business in Asia," *Business Horizons*, January/February 1987: p. 69.

2. Thomas, Friedman, *The World Is Flat*, Farrar, Straus and Giroux, 2005: p. 5.

3. McLuhan, Marshall, with Quentin Fiore and Jerome Agel, *The Medium Is the Message: An Inventory of Effects*, Bantam, 1967. Also referenced in McLuhan, Marshall, and Quentin Fiore, *War and Peace in the Global Village*, Bantam, 1968.

4. DeVito, Joseph, *Human Communication: The Basic Course*, 6th ed., Harper Collins, 2006: pp. 39–40. The effects of new technology in particular on the creation of a shrinking world and the implicit need for intercultural communication is described in Cairncross, Francis, *The Death of Distance: How the Communications Revolution Will Change Our Lives*, Harvard Business School Press, 1997: pp. 1–26.

5. A study I conducted reflected this economic interdependence and demonstrated that mass communicated messages regarding perspectives on the conflict were a function of political and economic self-interest: Zaremba, Alan, *Mass Communication and International Politics: A Case Study of Press Perceptions of the 1973 Arab-Israeli War*, Sheffield Press, 1988. This study examined newspaper reactions after the Yom Kippur War that began in October of 1973 and juxtaposed reactions prior to the oil embargoes and after the oil embargoes. Also, the results of the study indicated clearly that political orientation had an effect on expressed attitudes regarding the conflict.

6. Op. cit., Friedman, p. 10.

7. Martin, Judith, and Tom Nakayama, *Intercultural Communication in Contexts*, McGraw-Hill, 2010: p. 84.

8. Haviland, William, *Cultural Anthropology*, Holt, Rinehart, and Winston, 1993: p. 29.

9. Triandis, Harry, and Rosita Albert, "Cross Cultural Perspectives," in *Handbook of Organizational Communication*, 1987: p. 266. The Herkovitz definition is from *Cultural Anthropology*, Knopf, 1955. Triandis and Albert make a distinction between

objective culture and subjective culture. The objective culture would be apparent by examining, for example, the "tools, roads, and gardens" of the group, and the subjective culture would be concerned with the "norms, roles, belief systems, laws, values." "Cross Cultural Perspectives," p. 266.

10. Op. cit., DeVito, 2006, discussing the same principle, writes, "Culture is passed on from one generation to the next through communication, not through genes," p. 37.

11. Elashmawi, Farid, and Phillip Harris, *Multicultural Management. New Skills for Global Success*, Gulf Publishing, 1993: p. 50.

12. Samovar, Larry, and Richard Porter, *Communications Between Cultures*, 5th ed., Wadsworth, 2004: p. 15.

13. Marshall, Singer, *Intercultural Communication. A Perceptual Approach*, Prentice Hall, 1987: p. 9.

14. Ibid.

15. Marannis, David, *When Pride Still Mattered*, Simon & Schuster, 1999: p. 242.

16. Maas, Anne, and Luciano Arcuri, "Language and Stereotyping," in *Stereotypes and Stereotyping*, edited by C. Neil MacRae, Charles Stangor, and Miles Hewstone, The Guilford Press, 1996: p. 197. See also "Sapir-Whorf-Hypothesis Redux," *ETC.: A Review of General Semantics*, Vol. 59, Winter 2002: p. 456.

17. Infante, Dominic, Andrew Rancer, and Deanna Womack, *Building Communication Theory*, Waveland Press, 1997: p. 403.

18. See discussion in Barfield, Thomas, ed., *The Dictionary of Anthropology*, Blackwell Publishers, 1997: p. 492. Also, for example, Lustig, Myron, and Jolene Koester, *Intercultural Competence*, Addison Wesley, 1999: pp. 186-187.

19. Pullum, Geoffrey K., "The Great Eskimo Vocabulary Hoax," in *The Great Eskimo Vocabulary Hoax and Other Irreverent Essays on the Study of Language*, University of Chicago Press, 1991: pp. 159-171.

20. "Understand and Heed Cultural Differences," *Business America*, U.S. Department of Commerce, January 1991: p. 26.

21. Baraban, Regina, "Cultural Protocol Tips," in *Cultural to Dos and Taboos in the Global Marketplace: References and Resources*, edited by Karen Tucker, Meeting Services Connection. New England Meeting Industry Conference 2000.

22. Adler, Nancy, *International Dimensions of Organizational Behavior*, 3d ed., South-western, 1997: pp. 115-117.

23. Op cit., Triandis and Albert, p. 273.

24. Hofstede, Geert, *Culture and Organizations: Software of the Mind*, McGraw-Hill, 2005. The original Hofstede book that reported the studies was

Culture's Consequences: International Differences in Work Related Values, Sage, 1980.

25. Several accounts of the Hofstede studies indicate that the respondents to the surveys were managers. Hofstede, in the preface to the 1991 edition of his book *Culture and Organizations: Software of the Mind*, seems to be appalled by the misrepresentation. He affirms in the preface that the respondents in the original studies were employees, not managers.

26. Adler, Ronald, and George Rodman, *Understanding Human Communication*, 8th ed., Harcourt College Publishers, 2003: p. 279.

27. Op. cit., Triandis and Albert, p. 277.

28. Op cit., Samovar and Porter, pp. 215-222.

29. Op. cit., Elashmawi and Harris, pp. 98-123.

30. Molefi, Asante, *The Afrocentric Idea*, Temple University Press, 1987: p. 4.

31. Op. cit., Elashmawi and Harris, p. 6.

32. DeWine, Sue, *The Consultant's Craft*, St. Martin's, 2001: p. 374.

33. Ruben, Brent, "Assessing Communication Competency for Intercultural Adaptation," *Group and Organization Studies: The International Journal for Group Facilitators*, Vol. 1, No. 3, September 1976: p. 339. See also ibid., p. 374.

34. Op. cit., Infante et al., p. 410.

35. Novinger, Tracy, *Intercultural Communication*, University of Texas Press, 2001: p. 158.

CHAPTER 10

1. James Russell Lowell. From a speech delivered by Russell called "Democracy." From a book *Democracy and Other Addresses*, Boston: Houghton Mifflin, 1887.

2. Roemer, Bob, *When the Balloon Goes Up: The Communicator's Guide to Crisis Response*, Trafford Publishing, 2007: p. 19.

3. Coombs, W. Timothy, *Ongoing Crisis Communication: Planning, Managing and Responding*, 2d ed., Sage 2007: pp. 2-3.

4. Attributed in Glascock, Jack, "The Jasper Dragging Death: Crisis Communication and the Community Newspaper," *Communication Studies*, Spring 2004: pp. 29-45.

5. Maynard, Micheline, "At Jetblue Growing Up Is Hard to to Do," *New York Times*, Sunday October 6, 2008: Business Section: pp. 1, 12.

6. Leaper, Rae, "Important Single Purpose Programs," in *Inside Organizational Communication*, edited by Carol Reuss and Donn Silvis, Longman, 1985: pp. 259-261. The list in the text is an edited version of her suggestions. The discussion that follows the list is not from the Leaper article.

7. Lukaszweski, James, "Establishing Individual and Corporate Crisis Communication

Standards: The Principles and Protocols," *Public Relations Quarterly*, Vol. 42, No. 3, Fall 1997: pp. 13–14. The list that appears in the text comes from Lukaszweski; the examples do not, but they are similar to examples that the author provides. There are several other items on the author's list of trustbusting behaviors, including aloofness, no commitment, and irritation.

8. Kiger, Patrick, "Lessons from a Crisis: How Communication Kept a Company Together," *Workforce*, November 2001: p. 34.

9. Benoit, William, "Image Repair Discourse and Crisis Communication," *Public Relations Review*, Vol. 23, No. 2, Summer 1997: p. 184.

10. Marra, Francis J., "Crisis Communication Plans: Poor Predictors of Excellent Crisis Public Relations," *Public Relations Review*, Winter 1998: p. 465.

11. See Cohn, Robin, *The PR Crisis Bible: How to Take Charge of the Media When All Hell Breaks Loose*, Truman Talley Books, St. Martin's Press, 2000: p. xii.

12. Remsik, Jeffrey, "A Crisis Communication Plan—A Vital Element in Y2K Readiness," *Direct Marketing*, July 1999: p. 34.

13. The categories come from Mitroff, Ian, *Managing Crises Before They Happen*, Amacom, 2001: pp. 34–35. The examples are not from his book.

14. Ice, Richard, "Corporate Publics and Rhetorical Strategies: The Case of Union Carbide's Bhopal Crisis," *Management Communication Quarterly*, Vol. 4, No. 3, February 1991: pp. 341–362.

15. Waymer, Damion, and Robert Heath, "Emergent Agendas: The Forgotten Publics in Crisis Communication and Issues Management Research," *Journal of Applied Communication Research*, Vol. 35, No. 1, February 2007: pp. 88–108.

16. Op. cit., Leaper, p. 161

17. Op. cit., Lukaszweski, p. 8.

18. Henry, Rene, *You'd Better Have a Hose If You Want to Put Out a Fire*, Gollywobbler Productions, 2000: p. 38. Wilson, Steve, *Real People, Real Crises: An Inside Look at Corporate Crisis Communications* Oak Hill Press, **2002**: pp. 119–127.

19. Barton, Laurence, *Crisis in Organizations II*, Thomson South-Western, 2001: pp. 206–224.

20. Brinson, Susan L., and Benoit, William L., "Attempting to Restore a Public Image: Dow Corning and the Breast Implant Crisis," *Communication Quarterly*, Vol. 44, No. 1, 1996: p. 32.

21. Op. cit., Remsik, p. 37. See also op. cit., Cohn, p. xi.

22. Op. cit., Marra, p. 469.

23. Kearns, I. M. "Protect Your Company's Image," *Communication World*, Vol. 15, No. 7, August/September 1998: p. 42.

24. Olcott, William, "Communicating in a Crisis," *Fund Raising Management*, October 1992: p. 6.

25. Pirozzolo, Dick, "Crisis Communication Tips Are Food for Thought," *Nation's Restaurant News*, May 26, 1997: p. 22.

26. Hoffman, Judith, "Stakeholder Focus, Effective Crisis Communication," *Chemical Market Reporter*, October 1, 2001: p. 27.

27. Op. cit., Kearns, p. **42**.

28. Op. cit., Lukaszweski, pp. 10–11.

29. Op. cit., Olcott, p. 6.

30. Ian, Mitroff, *Managing Crises Before They Happen*, Amacom, 2001: p. 78.

31. Op. cit., Wilson, p. 61.

CHAPTER 11

1. Michel Eyquem de Montaigne. sixteenth-century French author from *Complete Essays of Montaigne*, translated by Donald M. Frame, Stanford, California: Stanford University Press, 1976.

2. Gordon, Greg, "A Buyer's Guide to Communication Audits," *Journal of Employee Communication Management*, March 2001: p. 51.

3. John Dean's list actually includes a fifth item, "communication systems controls." By this he means a person, persons, or mechanism for regulation or ensuring effective communication. This fifth feature is either implicit in the cases of networks, climate, and information management or a feature to be recommended as it relates to communication skill sets. Dean's article, "Internal Communication Management," appears in the edited volume by Howard Greenbaum entitled *Management Auditing as a Regulatory Tool*. The reference to the basic elements of internal communication appears on page 297. The description of the items continues from pages 297 to 303. The language Dean uses is somewhat different. He does use communication climate, but instead of individual communication skill sets he uses interpersonal communication skills. He uses "design of the formal communication subsystem" and "information systems" for communication networks and information management respectively.

4. Daly, John, "Assessing Speaking and Listening: Preliminary Considerations for a National Assessment," *National Assessment of College Students Learning: Identification of Skills to be Taught, Learned, and Assessed: A Report on the Proceedings of the Second Study Design Workshop*, U.S. Department of Education, November 1992. NCES94-286.

5. Daly comments further in the piece cited in the preceding note that communication apprehension has been comprehensively examined over

the last twenty years and that more than 2,000 studies have been conducted related to communication apprehension. For more information see the book Daly and James McCroskey edited on the subject: *Avoiding Communication: Shyness, Reticence, and Communication Apprehension*, Sage, 1984.

6. Persons unfamiliar with communication study might wonder if these skills can, in fact, be measured. Such tests do exist. See Bostrom, Robert, *Listening Behavior: Measurement and Application*, Guilford, 1990.

7. See Brian Spitzberg's *Handbook of Interpersonal Competence Research*, Springer-Verlag, 1989, for testing techniques.

8. There are several measurement devices for evaluating individuals' communication in small groups: Bales's SYMLOG is one. See Bales, Robert, *Symlog: Case Study Kit*, Free Press, 1980.

9. See Holsti, Ole, *Content Analysis for the Social Sciences and Humanities*, Addison-Wesley, 1969, pp. 5–6. My first book, *Mass Communication and International Politics: A Case Study of Press Reactions to the 1973 Arab-Israeli War*, Sheffield, 1988, is an example of how the procedure can be used to examine communication content.

10. Goldhaber, Gerald, *Organizational Communication*, 6th ed., Brown/Benchmark, 1993, p. 358.

11. Ibid., p. 359.

12. As someone who worked as an analyst on audits as early as 1975, I am aware that there is considerable confusion regarding the original tool and the various blended approaches that are employed currently.

13. As reported in op. cit., *Organizational Communication*, p. 362. There were occasions, however, when this component was not utilized as part of the ICA audit procedure.

14. Ibid., p. 366.

15. Sinickas Communication is one such company. At the 2001 IABC annual meetings I spoke with a Sinickas representative and was impressed with the comprehensive approach Sinickas had developed for audits. Sinickas will conduct audits for clients or sell the materials to the clients to allow clients to do the work themselves. Among Sinckas's

materials are a Focus Group Discussion Guide, an Employee Communication Survey, and a Communication Vehicle Survey (which assesses whether clients are using the correct type of media when communicating internally).

16. Op cit., Gordon, p. 51.

17. The quote is from DeWine, Sue, *The Consultant's Craft*, Bedford/St. Martins, 2001: p. 149. The referred-to study was conducted by DeWine, A. James, and W. Walence and presented in the paper, "Validation of Organizational Communication Audit Instruments" at the International Communication Association May 1983 meetings in Hawaii.

CHAPTER 12

1. Camenson, Blythe, *Great Jobs for Communications Majors*, Chicago: VGM Career Books 2001: p. 48.

2. This claim is made by many. On Drexel University's Communication Study's Web site the claim is made that: "Graduates with a corporate communication major find employment in a wide variety of fields." A Google search for Careers in Organizational Communication yields several university Web sites that make similar claims. Readers may wish to visit www.scils.rutgers.edu, www.drexel. edu, www.uwm.edu, for examples.

3. Ibid., pp. 123–124.

4. The Web site of the International Association of Business Communicators is iabc.com. As indicated, there were more than these fifty-plus notices on this site during this period (December 16, 2008, to January 27, 2009). The list in Table 12-3 reflects a selection and does not indicate if a position was listed several times.

5. Op. cit., Camenson, p. 120.

6. See "Preparation for Careers in Organizational Communication: Personal Advice from Dr. Wendy Ford," at homepages.wmich.edu/~rspeller/ Careers1.htm The items referred to appear under a heading "Gaining Marketable Experiences" on that Web site.

7. Interview with Jacqui Sweeney, Cooperative Education Adviser for Communication Studies Students, Northeastern University.

CREDITS

CARTOONS

page 55, © The New Yorker Collection 1992 Robert Mankoff from cartoonbank.com. All Rights Reserved.; page 114, © 2009 William Hamilton from cartoonbank.com. All Rights Reserved.; page 137, © The New Yorker Collection 1993 Donald Reilly from cartoonbank.com. All Rights Reserved.; page 141, © The New Yorker Collection 1991 Gahan Wilson from cartoonbank.com. All Rights Reserved.; page 168, DILBERT: © Scott Adams/Dist. By United Feature Syndicate, Inc.; page 190, © The New Yorker Collection 1997 Robert Mankoff from cartoonbank.com. All Rights Reserved.; page 192, Arlo & Janis: © Newspaper Enterprise Association, Inc.; page 249, © The New Yorker Collection 1977 William Hamilton from cartoonbank.com. All rights reserved.

PHOTOS

page 2, LWA/Getty Images; page 5, © Bettmann/Corbis; page 6, © Bettmann/Corbis; page 21, © Tetra Images/Corbis; page 30, Comstock Images/JupiterImages; page 34, © Tim Pannell/Corbis; page 36 (left), © Louie Psihoyos/Corbis; page 36 (right), © John Springer Collection/Corbis; page 60, © Premium Stock/Corbis; page 74, © Mark Peterson/Corbis; page 78, © Martin H. Simon/Corbis; page 82 (left), © Sue Ogrocki/Reuters/Corbis; page 82 (right), © Peter Andrews/Corbis; page 104, Comstock Images/JupiterImages; page 128, Image Source/Getty Images; page 152, PNC/Getty Images; page 157, Image Source/Getty Images; page 166 (left), © H. Armstrong Roberts/ClassicStock/Corbis; page 166 (right), © Kim Kulish/Corbis; page 180, © Anderson Ross/Blend Images/Corbis; page 183, Sahm Soherty/Getty Images; page 187, © Michael Prince/Corbis; page 210, Comstock Images/Getty Images; page 213 (left), George Marks/Getty Images; page 213 (right), Stockbyte/Getty Images; page 221, Ronald Martinez/Getty Images; page 232, Chris Hondros/Getty Images; page 236, © Ted Horowitz/Corbis; page 254, Comstock Images/JupiterImages; page 262, BananaStock/JupiterImages; page 272, © Michael Stuckey/Comstock/Corbis

INDEX

Note: Page numbers followed by *f* refer to figures and those followed by *t* refer to tables.